Italian
Wine

TEN SPEED PRESS
California | New York

Italian Wine

The History, Regions, and Grapes of an Iconic Wine Country

Shelley Lindgren and Kate Leahy

Photography by Valentin Hennequin

Contents

Part I

Under- standing Italian Wine

Introduction

An overhead lamp lit the cellar like a poker den, illuminating a table surrounded by a dozen men. One wore a motorcycle jacket, others had just come from the farm, and a few looked dressed for the office. They passed around a box of red cherries as they talked, collecting pits into neat piles in front of them. One man mentioned that his son had returned home after studying winemaking in France; another brought up the weather, which was too hot for June. The cellar was cool, its stone walls lined with glass jars of soil taken from vineyards around the world: some light, some rocky, some nearly black. Upstairs, the ground floor baked under the afternoon sun as temperatures soared past 100°F (37.7°C). Climate change was playing its hand.

"Benvenuti, benvenuti!" Massimo Alois stood at the head of the table among fellow members of Vitica, the consortium for Caserta winemakers. As talk died down, he introduced us, two road-weary Americans who had arrived a couple of hours late after taking a wrong turn somewhere between Campobasso and Caserta. More *benvenuti*s filled the air. A few gruff faces softened. One winemaker handed us olive oil from his farm; another passed us the box of cherries. In the spirit of introductions, Massimo popped open a bottle of Prima Gioia, a sparkling wine from Masseria Piccirillo made with the same technique employed in Champagne. Carmine Piccirillo, who brought the bottle, grinned. The idea to make it came from his son, Giovanni, the one who had studied in France, Carmine explained. The pale wine's delicate bubbles revived our flagging energy. "*Saluti*," we said, raising our glasses above the cherry pits.

Pallagrello Bianco, the grape used in the wine, once grew in the vineyards of the Caserta Royal Palace. By the twentieth century, the grape was nearly ancient history until a handful of enthusiasts rehabilitated the few remaining vines, along with a local grape called Casavecchia. Today, Pallagrello Bianco, Pallagrello Nero, and Casavecchia are common around Caserta, though it would be tough to find the grapes growing anywhere else in the world. Cesare Avenia, the president of Vitica, started his winery, Il Verro, in the early 2000s to work with local vines. He grows both Pallagrellos and Casavecchia as well as Coda di Pecora, a grape that remains obscure—even by Italian standards. To unlock the potential of these varieties, the members of Vitica are working together to lift the reputation of their winemaking corner of Italy—a high tide raising all boats.

North of Naples, the province of Caserta is only one pocket of winemaking in a country loaded with them. After the Second World War, most grape farmers around Caserta grew the crop for bulk production, keeping some of the harvest to make wine for themselves. Volume was more important than quality, so they chose grapes that were easier to grow and sell. Native grapes that weren't well known outside their local areas or proved finicky in the vineyard were pulled out or abandoned. Yet in many cases, the vines survived, either through neglect or because a family became attached to the local vine and kept it around to make wine for themselves. The same thing happened all over Italy, and many of the country's most renowned winemakers came from families that grew such grapes and made wine simply to have something to drink throughout the year.

While wine has been made and traded in Italy since before the time of the Greeks and Romans, Italian wine as we know it today is a relatively new idea. In his seminal 1980 book *Vino*, Burton Anderson described his first trip to Italy in the 1950s, where he drank local wines poured from reusable bottles in nearly every region. What he tasted was simple but good, and when he came across a bad bottle, it was so inexpensive that he couldn't get upset about it. Starting around the 1960s, Italian wine began to change rapidly, and in some places, it became part of large-scale businesses aided by technological advancements in bottling and temperature control. Cheap Chianti, Verdicchio in fish- and amphora-shaped bottles, and sweet Lambrusco poured into the United States.

At the same time, Italian winemakers started to think through ways to bring attention to the country's best bottles, formalizing a quality scale modeled after the system used in France. Italian wines made in a certain place with approved grapes and techniques were granted a quality designation, setting them apart from mass-produced wines. What came to be called the DOC system (page 24) soon became recognized for all its faults. Why was this wine elevated to a higher status over that one? Why was this grape allowed in this wine but not in that one? Some of the most famous Italian wines of the twentieth century, like Sassicaia from Tuscany, skirted DOC regulations by labeling their premium product *vino da tavola* (table wine). Yet in between cheap wine and rarified bottles, most Italians were drinking whatever was made around their town. Even today, Italian wine is local wine, with each region making it in their own way.

The biggest shift in the past three decades has been the focus on native grapes. While wine grapes likely originated in Western Asia, vines spread and mutated across Italy. There are more than 590 official grapes in the Italian government database, but the true number could easily be double the official

count. It's Italy's grape biodiversity that makes it possible to make wines like the sparkling Pallagrello Bianco we tasted with the members of Vitica.

In 2007, on our first research trip together, we arrived in Naples with flip phones and driving directions printed out from MapQuest. While the trip focused on a handful of regions in southern Italy—we were researching the wine chapters of our cookbook *A16: Food + Wine*—it was long enough to visit an experimental vineyard in Cirò, meet families in Avellino transitioning from being farmers who sold grapes to winemakers, and encounter professionals who left careers in Milan and returned home to make wine with the grapes their grandparents grew. Along the way, we bought bags of blood oranges and sampled fresh ricotta and mozzarella in nearly every town we visited.

Early in the trip, we met Bruno De Conciliis, a winemaker from Cilento in the southern part of Campania, the region surrounding Naples. We told Bruno that we would drive from Naples to his winery, but the idea of two Americans driving through the city worried him. To Bruno, driving in Naples requires staying liquid: a driver shifts to the left or right and everyone else shifts, too, without tapping the brakes. The same isn't so for Americans, he said. We drive like a solid mass, and if we don't stay between the lines, we cause a collision. To prevent disaster, he took the train into Naples and met us at the rental agency, where we gladly handed him the keys to our beat-up silver Opel. As he drove, he told us how he pumped jazz into the cellar to help his wines relax. The jazz may have been more for his benefit, but it fit with Bruno's goal to create wine in a personal way, not like wineries that made their wine taste the same, no matter the year. "If you force a wine in a particular direction, it will become angry with you," he said. "You lose its life if you control it too much. I don't want to make Coca-Cola."

The reality is that Italy makes about a sixth of the wine in the world, and there are not enough Italians to drink it all. Fortunately, Italy has America—30 percent of all imported wine in the United States is Italian. A lot of Italian wine also goes to the United Kingdom and Germany. In fact,

Italian wine reaches nearly every continent (we're not sure about Antarctica, but maybe it's there, too). If gaining a foothold in the export market is essential for survival for many wineries, making "Coca-Cola" won't cut it. The breakthroughs today aren't with cellar technology, like they were in the 1960s, '70s, and '80s. Instead, it's about returning to the old ways of making wine while learning how best to showcase the grapes and land in a glass.

When Shelley's southern Italian restaurant, A16, opened in 2004, she sought out wines from that part of the country. But few importers had bottles to choose from, and the ones who did gratefully unloaded inventory that no one else in San Francisco seemed to want. To sell these wines, the A16 staff explained each one. If you liked white Burgundy, you may like Fiano di Avellino, they'd advise. Syrah lover? How about a glass of Taurasi? Fan of Sauvignon Blanc? Try Falanghina made just outside Naples. As more people came to the restaurant to taste wines they had never tried, importers and Italian winemakers also came to the restaurant, sharing wines that were new to us. Some were amazed to see a wine list across the world filled with their friends' and neighbors' bottles. But we still had a lot to learn. There was so little information about grapes like Coda di Volpe and Piedirosso back then; to get familiar, we went to Italy and literally knocked on doors, shared meals with winemakers in our limited Italian, and spent the night in their towns—and sometimes their homes—once taking over the twin beds in a pink bedroom of two daughters, who stayed the night with friends to make room for us.

Today, as A16 has built up a deep collection of regional Italian wines, we no longer need to compare them to French wines to get someone to try them. More often, the request is "Surprise me" or "Pour me what you're into." And out comes a glass of Gragnano, an easy-going sparkling wine from the Sorrentine Peninsula. Or Valtellina, a Nebbiolo made from grapes grown on ancient stone terraces. Or Trebbiano Spoletino, a wine that comes from vines that grow up trees in Umbria.

Massimo Alois was one of the first winemakers to visit A16, and we've been friends ever since.

After the Vitica meeting, he walked us through his vineyard of Casavecchia at the foothills of the Trebulani Mountains. In the distance, his son, Gianfrancesco, shot hoops behind the winery, a Stephen Curry Warriors jersey dwarfing his frame. The Alois family's roots in Caserta date to the fifteenth century. For centuries, the family made silk. Then, in the 1990s, Michele Alois, Massimo's father, began planting local grapes. Pointing at the vines, Massimo explained that he collected soil samples from vineyards around the world as a way of documenting quality, helping him understand why one place yielded better wine than another. What could he learn from other winemakers? Could there be a better way to grow Casavecchia vines? What heights could Casavecchia realistically achieve? A few decades of data aren't a lot to work off compared to grapes like Pinot Nero (Pinot Noir) and Chardonnay, which have much longer track records. "We need to do more to understand our land and the grapes," he said, picking up his pace as we walked back to the cellar to cool off.

Unfamiliar grapes can be harder to grow and their wines are harder to sell. Yet Italy's sheer diversity makes it impossible to get bored. These wines can be the palest white, ruby red, inky purple, deep orange, and nearly every shade of pink. When A16 opened, we were still in the days when the best reds had to be big, and the best whites needed to be light and crisp. Now reds are being made with a lighter hand, more like whites, and whites are being treated more like reds, coming in deeper hues and richer textures. We also now recognize that great Italian white wines, such as Benanti's "Pietra Marina," from Mount Etna, and Tiberio's "Fonte Canale," from Abruzzo, can age gracefully for years, just like their red counterparts.

Yet with so many grapes and styles of wine—and opinions on what and who makes the best—this wine country will never be straightforward. What's the best way to understand Italian wine? Embrace the chaos and stay liquid, as Bruno De Conciliis would say. As Italian wines evolve, no one will have all the answers, but we can go along for the ride.

About This Book

In *Italian Wine*, we travel through each region of Italy alphabetically, from Abruzzo in central Italy to Veneto in northeast Italy. If you pick up a bottle of wine from a region and want to learn more about it, you can flip to that section and read about its history, land, wines, and grapes. Since some grapes grow in multiple regions, we include page numbers on where to find a grape description if it is not in the specific region. Whenever you want to consult a map of all the regions, please see pages 17–21.

When it comes to designations within each region, such as DOP, IGP, DOCG, DOC, or IGT zones (see Wine Laws, page 23), we mention them when they are historic or important in some way, but we don't list all zones in Italy because some are inconsequential, and many of our favorite winemakers work outside DOP regulations.

Each region has a list of producers, though this is only one way to get started in exploring the wines of the area, since we find new winemakers all the time. We also include a summary of the types of food found in the region to give a sense of what people traditionally eat with the wines. It's the adage "What grows together, goes together," the idea that local wines and local foods have evolved together over the years.

A final note on language and capitalization: For simplicity, we have used the English spellings of most Italian names and places (Lombardy instead of Lombardia, Piedmont instead of Piemonte), but in some places, we have retained the Italian. For instance, we opt for "Le Marche" instead of "The Marches" to indicate the central Italian region along the Adriatic coast, use "Valle d'Aosta" instead of "Aosta Valley" to talk about the tiny alpine region bordering Switzerland and France, and say "Alto Adige" instead of "South Tyrol" for the subregion bordering Austria. All grape names are capitalized. Designated wine areas, like Barolo and Chianti Classico, are also capitalized, while specific wine names, like "Le Pergole Torte," are in quotations to set them apart from grape or place names.

Becoming Italy: A History

Even though its shape—a heeled boot cutting through the Mediterranean—is one of the world's most iconic, the country of Italy is relatively young. Throughout history, the map of Italy's peninsula and islands has resembled a quilt of ever-changing patches. Some sections were part of kingdoms (the Kingdom of Naples, the Kingdom of the Two Sicilies, the Kingdom of Sardinia, the Kingdom of Lombardy-Venetia), while others were republics and city-states (Venice, Genoa, Amalfi, Florence, Siena, and others). Arabs, popes, royal European houses, and Napoleon all had a turn controlling parts of Italy, impacting local customs, languages, and food and wine traditions. When the peninsula and islands were unified in 1861 under King Victor Emmanuel II of the House of Savoy, to say that everyone in nineteenth-century Italy felt "Italian" was a stretch. Italian wine reflects this evolution.

Italy's history took a few dramatic turns from 1861 onward. An economic depression in the late nineteenth century prompted thousands to leave for the Americas. From the late nineteenth century to the early twentieth century, farmers grappled with phylloxera, an insect that killed grapevines across Europe. The first part of the twentieth century brought two brutal World Wars as well as Mussolini and fascism. Toward the end of World War II, King Victor Emmanuel III declared war against Germany, and Italians waged a guerrilla war against the Nazis. After World War II, Italy rebranded itself as a republic in 1946, abolishing its monarchy, but borders remained in flux until 1954, when Italy officially annexed the city of Trieste and the land around it.

Within the Italian wine world, there has always been a tension between old and new. Some wineries preserve the labor-intensive tradition of making *passito*, a honeyed dessert wine once fashionable with royals, while others embrace the modern ease of making *spumante* in pressurized tanks, which is how most Prosecco is made. But the majority of Italy's wines evolved out of everyday life, something to drink with a meal and share with family and friends.

Italy's First Winemakers

While *Vitis vinifera*, the vine species from which all fine wine is made, is indigenous to Western Asia, it made Italy its spiritual home, a place so perfect for vines that hundreds—maybe thousands—of grapes evolved here.

Winemaking started in southern Italy and then moved up the coast. The early Italian tribes, such as the Ligurians, Enotrians, and Etruscans, cultivated grapes for wine, training unruly vines up trees or on man-made structures. In the present-day commune of Aversa in northern Campania and in Montefalco in Umbria, some growers continue to "marry" vines to trees. When the ancient Greeks started colonizing southern Italy and Sicily, they introduced a new way to grow grapes, training vines to stand alone without stakes in the ground or any other support. Today, while the wine world refers to this way of growing vines as "head training," Italians call the system *alberello*, meaning "little tree." The Greeks also brought their own favorite grapes, and as a result, there are a lot of Italian grapes called "Greco," even though not all Greco grapes are related, or even originated in Greece. In southern Italy, the Greeks set the foundation for fine wine that the Romans built upon.

The Romans transformed Europe in ways that lasted far beyond their rule. One of their lasting legacies was its network of ancient highways. The Via Appia, or the Appian Way, connected Campania and Puglia to Rome; Via Salaria brought salt from the Tiber River to Le Marche; and Via Postumia connected Genoa in the west with Aquileia to the east by land. There were other notable highways as well. Via Aemilia gave rise to Emilia-Romagna's most important cities, including its regional capital, Bologna, and Via Claudia Augusta became an important trade route between Italy and northern Europe until the Brenner Pass took its place. Tracing the western coastline from Lazio all the way to France, the ancient Via Aurelia is now Strada Statale 1 (State Road 1), and the coastal grape Vermentino grows along its path. Roman infrastructure helped spread favorite wines and winemaking practices through trading networks. Certain wines were recognized for greatness. Pliny the Elder praised Falernian (*Falernum* in Latin), which may have come from northern Campania. After the Romans, political turmoil ensued, and epicurean pursuits fell by the wayside.

Dark Times and the Rise of the Republics

The fall of Rome in 476 put a pause on progress (wine or otherwise) for centuries. During the Middle Ages, Northern European tribes took over parts of the Italian peninsula while the Papacy built up influence from its base in Rome, controlling a chain of territories called the Papal States. Frederick II reigned in the south, while city-states in Tuscany and a few other areas ruled themselves. Yet stability and security were hard to find, the Roman roads became dangerous, and inhabitants withdrew to fortified towns in the hills for safety. Today in Le Marche, walled medieval towns define the production area for Verdicchio dei Castelli di Jesi wines. During this time, most wine was made by monks for sacramental uses or by farmers for home, and vines continued to evolve and mutate. Plagues caused population shifts, and as people moved around Italy to escape illness, they brought their favorite vines with them.

Starting in the fourteenth century, during the Renaissance, the wine trade picked up steam thanks to Venice and Genoa, two maritime republics that controlled trade in the Mediterranean. Every city along the Adriatic Sea was awash with wine from the Venetians, such as Ragusa (present-day Dubrovnik in Croatia). In his book *A Mediterranean Feast*, historian Clifford A. Wright shares the story of sixteenth-century Serafino Razzi, an Italian Dominican monk living in Ragusa. In his writings, the monk described markets filled with imported fruit and Malvasia wine. Exactly what "Malvasia" meant to Razzi isn't clear—today there are several wines called Malvasia—but the monk's enthusiasm for it may explain why so many vines carry the name today. On the other side of the Italian peninsula, the Genoese dominated the coastline, building ships designed to carry heavy loads of wine and setting up trading posts as far as the Black Sea. At home, wealthy Genoese traders drank a white wine from Cinque Terre called Vernaccia, though, like Malvasia, it's unclear how much the wine has to do with the many wines called Vernaccia today.

The maritime dominance of Venice and Genoa gave way to the British and Dutch, who engineered superior ships. Soon, British merchants were buying up Italian wine and growing a robust business for Marsala from Sicily. From the Renaissance to the nineteenth century, the rest of the peninsula and islands had varying levels of prosperity under foreign rulers, from the Spanish to the Austrians and French. The Bourbons ran Parma, Naples, and Sicily, while the Habsburgs controlled Milan, Tuscany, Friuli Venezia Giulia, and many places in between. The House of Savoy, the dynasty of King Victor Emmanuel II's family, aligned itself culturally with the French and controlled Liguria, Sardinia, and Piedmont, as well as the French Riviera. And the Papal States included Rome and most of central Italy. Vineyards were owned by landed gentry and—in the case of Tuscany, Umbria, Le Marche, and Emilia-Romagna—worked by *mezzadri* (sharecroppers). These farmers grew as many grapes as they could, saving any extra for their families. In some places, the *mezzadria* system stayed in place until after World War II.

Around the turn of the nineteenth century, the Napoleonic Wars disrupted life across Europe, drawing part of the Italian peninsula under French control for a handful of years. With French influence came deeper interest in French grapes, such as Cabernet Sauvignon and Merlot, as well as French winemaking techniques, but bigger changes were on the horizon, starting with the movement to unify Italy known as the Risorgimento.

The Risorgimento

Today Giuseppe Garibaldi's name blazes across street signs and *piazze* across Italy. Inspired by unification activist Giuseppe Mazzini, Garibaldi became an icon of the Risorgimento, Italy's unification movement. By most accounts, he was a valiant leader who fought for his fellow Italians, guiding an army from Sicily and working his way north to liberate Italians from foreign rule. But revisionist history suggests he may have been a pawn in Camillo Benso's power play. Benso, better known as the Count of Cavour, used political maneuvering to unify Italy and benefit the Turin-based House of Savoy, making its head, Victor Emmanuel II, Italy's first king and Benso its first prime minister.

For a southern Italian, becoming part of the Kingdom of Italy felt less like a moment of Italian solidarity and more like trading one foreign ruler for another. As such, when Italy declared itself unified, revolts broke out in Basilicata, Abruzzo, Calabria, and Puglia, ushering in a civil war, and strife between the north and the south carried over into the twentieth century. Even during the post–World War II economic boom, the north became wealthy while the south struggled. Poverty had a silver lining: lack of money to invest in new vines or pesticides preserved biodiversity in parts of the deep south, like Calabria and Basilicata. Farmers worked with what they had, or they moved away, letting vineyards go wild.

The new Kingdom of Italy faced challenges in uniting its people, but it made progress in modernizing agriculture. In the nineteenth century, most vineyards had other crops growing in the same field. In Veneto, vines were trained up mulberry trees, whose leaves were used to feed silkworms. With all the shade from the trees, it was hard for grapes to ripen. Plus, harvests often began well before the fruit was ripe so farmers wouldn't lose their crop to fall hailstorms. To improve the country's wine, in 1863 the Kingdom of Italy started the Royal Oenological Commission. A decade later, the king granted a royal decree to start the country's first enology school in Conegliano, a city in the region of Veneto. The need for better agricultural education continued to grow with the arrival of new vine pests and diseases, namely downy and powdery mildews and phylloxera.

Phylloxera, Depression, and War

Discovered in Europe in 1863, phylloxera was a major cause of grape biodiversity loss across Europe. Arriving on the roots of American grapevines (which tolerated the insect), phylloxera spread quickly through Europe, killing vines at the root and hobbling the European wine industry. In Italy, the insect was discovered in 1879 in Lombardy and spread to the rest of the country. Within two decades, around 247,105 acres (100,000 hectares) had been destroyed. Some regions had it worse than others. Sardinia, Tuscany, Liguria, Piedmont, Lombardy, and Sicily were all hit badly. To rebuild, grape growers across Europe began grafting *Vitis vinifera* cuttings onto the rootstocks of resistant American vines, embarking on a slow process of rebuilding their vineyards. Native vines that didn't take to grafting were lost for good.

Some areas were spared. The phylloxera insect couldn't travel as easily through sandy volcanic soils, and it didn't tolerate high altitudes, leaving pockets of the country where vines could grow ungrafted. Today, Prié Blanc, a white grape from the western side of Valle d'Aosta near Mont Blanc, grows on its original rootstock at more than 3,000 feet (915 meters) above sea level. And in Campania, century-plus old ungrafted Aglianico vines survived phylloxera thanks to the region's volcanic soil, giving a glimpse of what viticulture looked like before the twentieth century.

Meanwhile, from the late nineteenth century, Italians left the countryside in droves. Some moved to cities for jobs in factories, but even more left the country. Between 1880 and 1980, around fifteen million Italians emigrated, many resettling in the United States or Argentina. The Great Depression, the rise of fascism, and two world wars also suppressed progress in wine and nearly everything else. After World War II, nationalistic sentiments were frayed, and some regions—especially those that spoke German, French, or Slovene as their first language—lobbied for autonomy. To assuage resentment toward the government, in 1948, Italy allowed Sicily, Sardinia, Trentino–Alto Adige, and Valle d'Aosta to become autonomous regions. Friuli Venezia Giulia followed in 1963.

In postwar Italy, loans were easy to get, labor was cheap, and regulations were loose, all of which resulted in a boom in development. New factories sprang up making everything from cars to textiles to home appliances. During what came to be called Italy's "economic miracle," some wine areas lost their footing due to lack of attention. In the present-day towns of Alto Piemonte, prime Nebbiolo vineyard land is covered with forest after families abandoned their vines to take jobs in textile factories. Seeing it today, it's hard to imagine that wines from this area were once some of the most famous in Italy.

The Next Italian Winemakers

As the economy grew in the second part of the twentieth century, Italians had more money to explore their country. Guided by articles written by food and wine writer Luigi Veronelli, they bought cars and drove on the new *autostrade*, or highways. At the same time, the 1960s brought student protests challenging traditional sources of power; workers went on strike demanding improved working conditions in factories. In this era, a new generation of winemakers learned to question the old way of doing things. Veronelli also inspired young winemakers to champion their regions and local grapes and rebel against industrial wine production. Giusto Occhipinti, who studied architecture at university, started making wine with friends Giambattista Cilia and Cirino Strano in Sicily under the name COS, an acronym created from the initials of their last names. By focusing on making a small amount of wine in low-tech ways, the friends helped revitalize the sleepy Cerasuolo di Vittoria winemaking area in the southeastern corner of the island.

This was also the era when ambitious winemakers began to explore wines outside of Italy, visiting France and California for new ideas and technology, and tasting everything from Burgundy to the wines from the Jura and the Napa Valley. Some began planting international grapes instead of native Italian varieties and choosing French barrique, the small barrels made of French oak, over *botti*, the large casks traditionally used for aging wine. Elio Altare, who left a career in finance to go back to his family's vineyards, famously took a chainsaw to his father's old prized *botti* to make firewood, declaring it was time for a new era in Barolo. The combination of French oak and shorter skin macerations (the time the grape skins and seeds stay in contact with the juices after the grapes are crushed) made smoother red wines that were easier to sell abroad. Traditional winemakers were horrified by the new wines and stuck to using *botti*, slowly fermenting and aging the wines to showcase the complexity of Nebbiolo. Altare's chainsaw statement defined these so-called Barolo Wars, the fight over what Barolo should be: whether it was something you had to age for at least a decade before drinking or something you could enjoy a few years after harvest. Today winemakers in the Langhe and elsewhere look at winemaking in more nuanced ways—some use barrique in their cellar, and many still use *botti*, but almost no one brags about either to prove a point about quality.

For Italian winemakers, protecting heritage is more important, whether it's by making wine with native grapes or recreating winemaking methods from their grandparents' and great-grandparents' era, such as making white wines like red wines. If Italians look abroad for inspiration today, it's most likely to be for philosophy, not technique or style. This is especially the case when it comes to making low-intervention wines, which are wines made with fewer technical guardrails. In general, these wines are made from organic grapes and their juices are fermented with the yeasts naturally occurring on the grapes and in the vineyard and cellar. As the wine is made, little to no sulfur is added to stabilize it, and the wines are never filtered or fined (processes that make wine clear). At La Distesa in Le Marche, Corrado Dottori gradually let go of control to express something deeper in his wines, and then never looked back. Some have been working this way for a few decades. Elena Pantaleoni of La Stoppa in Emilia-Romagna has long made white wines like reds, with extended skin contact with the grape juices. The time spent on the skins allows the wine to absorb some of the skins' tannins, naturally preserving the wine for years. Elena's low-tech methods became a source of inspiration for Arianna Occhipinti, Giusto's niece, who not only makes wines and grows grapes in Sicily but also raises livestock and grows vegetables, a nod to the old Italy, where wine was one of many products from the farm.

Land and Grapes

With the Alps to the north and the Apennines forming a chain down its spine, Italy is a place where mountains are never very far from the sea. This topography defines the country, creating microclimates galore for an astounding number of grapes to flourish.

Italy is made up of twenty regions, and each has its own unique cultural heritage, grapes, and land. It's easy to assume that the south is hotter than the north, but factor in sea breezes, altitude, sun exposure, and wind, and the logic no longer holds. Italy is also not as far south as it may seem. Sicily has the same latitude as central California, while Tuscany is aligned with Oregon. In a very general sense, northern Italy (from the Po River to the Alps) and inland areas, such as Umbria, have continental climates, with warm summers and cold winters. The islands and the coasts are Mediterranean, where summers are long and dry, days are warm, and winters are mild. In the center of the peninsula, the Apennines, which run from Liguria down to the tip of the boot, create an east-west barrier that walls off weather patterns. And in inland areas, lakes and rivers create their own microclimates. What you end up with is climate variety in a compact area. In Italy, it's not unheard of to drive from a sandy beach to a snow-capped mountain in an hour.

Climate affects what grapes grow well in each part of Italy. In the northeast, from Friuli Venezia Giulia down to Le Marche, more of the wine made is white than red. This is Italy's rainiest corner, and the grapes that grow there handle rain well, or at least better than grapes do in Sicily, which is nearly always dry. Weather patterns along the Adriatic coast become warmer farther south, especially in Puglia. This region, the heel of Italy's boot, is warm, flat, and more suited to red wines. Its neighbor, Basilicata, also specializes in red wine, though its high-altitude climate is cooler. On the west side of Italy, Piedmont and Tuscany are more known for red wines, and Campania and Lazio are known for whites. Campania has one of the richest collections of white grape varieties in the country, rivaled only by Friuli in the northeast. In Calabria, the toe of Italy's boot, the grapes and wines are split between white and red, though the region is best known for red. And on Sicily and Sardinia, certain areas focus on either reds or whites depending on the climate, soils, and tradition. As a result, no single vintage description paints a picture for all of Italy. What might be an outstanding year for Tuscan wines could be dismal for Le Marche on the east side of the Apennines. The reverse is true as well, and a challenging harvest for Chianti Classico could be ideal for Le Marche's Verdicchio dei Castelli di Jesi.

Rocks and Soils

Italy's geology ranges from really old to really young. Parts of Sardinia date back billions of years, while Mount Etna, the active volcano on Sicily, creates new layers of igneous rock (see Rock Types: Sedimentary, Igneous, and Metamorphic, below) with each eruption. In Friuli Venezia Giulia, unique *ponca* and karst soils are essential to the character of the region's white wines, and the same is true in Tuscany regarding Chianti Classico's *galestro* soils. From the peninsula to the islands, you can find basalt and tuff as well as tufa, marl (a mix of clay and limestone), and so much more.

In a general sense, clay soils produce denser, more powerful wines; sandy and stony soils yield lighter wines with fruity or floral notes; limestone-rich soils offer structure and acidity; and chalky soils (chalk being a soft, white limestone) yield lighter wines with elegance. But soil isn't the only factor in determining the best vineyard. The interplay between climate, geology, grape variety, and the actual human beings who tend the vines and make the wine is just as important. Over time, winemakers have learned that the best vineyards in rainy places, like Friuli Venezia Giulia, are vineyards that drain well, while the best vineyards in dry regions, like Cirò in Calabria, have soils that hold on to precious water. Areas that are cold at night, like Valtellina in northern Lombardy, benefit from rocky soil that absorbs heat throughout the day. And to top it off, the specific grape that has adapted to the soil and climate also contributes to a sense of place.

Rock Types

Sedimentary, Igneous, and Metamorphic

There are three main kinds of rock: rocks that came from sediment compressing for centuries (sedimentary), rocks that were once molten and created during a volcanic eruption (igneous), and rocks that have changed from one kind to another with the help of heat and pressure (metamorphic). Sedimentary rock includes sandstone, limestone, and marl. Limestone and marl, as well as limestone-based chalk and dolomite, are also calcareous, a term that means the rock is based on calcite, a carbonate mineral. Calcareous soil is also called *tufa*, and it is not the same as tuff—*tufo* in Italian—which is igneous. Granite and basalt are also forms of igneous rock. Meanwhile, marble, slate, schist, and gneiss are all metamorphic rock. Some metamorphic rocks are quite strong and resistant, and others crumble easily. The composition of soil and rock will affect the root system and vine development—clay soils give resistance to vine growth compared to light, sandy soils, which allow vines to grow faster and easier. Calcareous soils are often prized because they allow for better water flow and nutrient uptake. Still, any combination of rock and soil needs to be paired with air, water, and a human hand for a vine to reach its potential.

Switzerland

VAL D'AOSTA

Alps

LOMBARDY

TRENTINO-ALTO ADIGE

Austria

France

Aosta

Trento

Julian Alps
Carnic Alps

PIEDMONT

Turin

Milan

FRIULI VENEZIA GIULIA

Venice

Trieste

Slovenia

VENETO

Genoa

Bologna

LIGURIA

Croatia

Gulf of Genoa

EMILIA-ROMAGNA

Ligurian Sea

Florence

Apennines

LE MARCHE

TUSCANY

Ancona

Perugia

Adriatic Sea

UMBRIA

ABRUZZO

LAZIO

L'Aquila

Rome

MOLISE

SARDINIA

Tyrrhenian Sea

Campobasso

Naples

Mt Vulture

Cagliari

Bari

PUGLIA

Gulf of Naples

Mt Vesuvius

Potenza

CAMPANIA

BASILICATA

Catanzaro

Palermo

CALABRIA

N

W

E

Mt Etna

Ionian Sea

S

SICILY

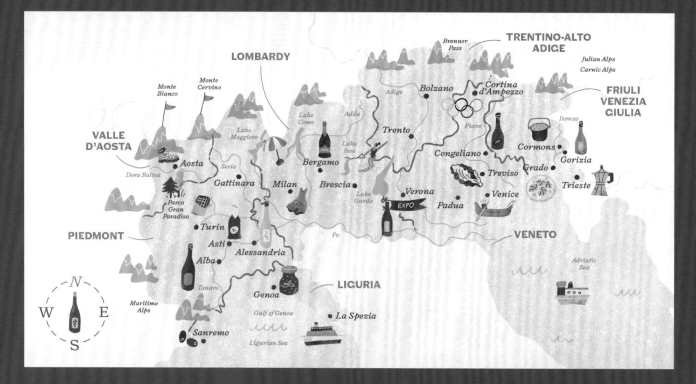

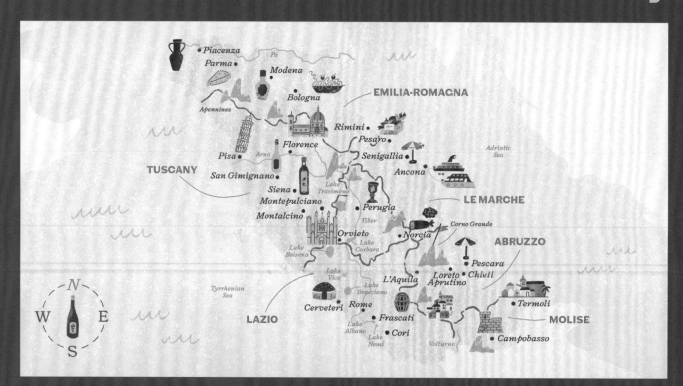

Climate Change and Farming Practices

In the past, Italian grape growers had challenges getting grapes to ripen every year. As late as the 1950s and '60s, vines were frequently grown side by side with other crops. In Maynard Amerine and Vernon Singleton's 1965 book *Wine*, the authors disparaged this system because it was more challenging to prune and spray vines for disease.

By the 1980s, that had changed, and growers were doing all that they could to expose grapes to the sun. Some began green harvesting, a process that involves removing some of the unripe grapes earlier in the year to encourage the fruit that remains to become more concentrated when ripe. Today's warmer climate means grapes ripen easier than before, with more sugar, which leads to more alcohol in wine. According to the Italian agricultural lobby Coldiretti, the alcohol level of the average Italian wine has increased by 1 percent since the 1990s. The problem is getting grapes to reach physiological ripeness—the point at which the skins and tannins have matured—before they lose acidity. In 2018, on episode 440 of the podcast *I'll Drink to That! Wine Talk*, Aldo Vacca, managing director of Produttori del Barbaresco, spoke with host Levi Dalton about the changing nature of harvest. From 1958 to 1998, the Barbaresco wine co-op measured only the sugar level of the grapes of its growers—the higher the sugar, the more growers were paid. Since 1998, Vacca explained, the co-op assesses the maturity of skins and tannins as well, since sugar alone doesn't guarantee the best grapes.

Another challenge for wineries is finding labor for harvest and year-round vine maintenance. As estate owners age and foreign investments increase, smaller wineries are getting swallowed up by larger ones, and larger wineries can't manage the harvest by asking favors from family and neighbors, like they did in the old days. The Italian agricultural federation Confagricoltura estimates that around 180,000 people are employed at the peak of the harvest, and 40 percent are foreign, mostly from Macedonia, Albania, Romania, and Morocco.

To make vineyards easier to manage and reduce pesticide use, a handful of Italian winemakers are experimenting with growing hybrids. Created to be more resistant to common diseases, these vines combine resilient traits from different vine species—taking a European *Vitis vinifera* vine and crossing it with an American *Vitis labrusca* or *Vitis riparia*, for instance—to make a new, stronger vine. (To be clear, *Vitis vinifera* vines grafted onto American rootstock are not hybrids; the vines retain the characteristics of the *vinifera* variety.) For most of their history, hybrid vines were planted in cold climates in North America where *Vitis vinifera* vines struggled to grow. In Europe, it's taken much longer for hybrids to be accepted. In 2021, this changed when the European Union began allowing hybrid grapes in wines of Protected Designation of Origin to give winemakers another tool to combat climate change. Even so, hybrids are rare in Italy. Among the pioneers, the Pizzolato winery in Veneto and the Dornach estate in Alto Adige make table wine with Pilzwiderstandsfähige, a disease-resistant hybrid nicknamed PIWI.

For now, Italy's adaptation to climate change focuses on native grapes and traditional farming methods. When grown in the areas where they've evolved for centuries, these vines tend to be naturally resilient. Some growers are returning to pergolas to protect grapes from sunburn while others are phasing out green harvesting. Most important, the way people farm is gentler. Only a couple of decades ago, orange burn stripes often ran under the vines, the result of herbicide use. Today, more vineyards are being worked in healthier ways. There's greater understanding about the microbiological systems in the vineyard, which include native grasses, plants, and insects. When in balance, they can help vines (and the environment around them) stay healthy without much intervention.

Native Grapes

The official list of Italian grape varieties is around 590, but there are likely hundreds more that haven't been recognized. There are also international grapes, like Pinot Grigio, Pinot Bianco (Pinot Blanc), Merlot, Cabernet Sauvignon, and Pinot Nero (Pinot Noir), that have also grown in Italy for centuries, especially in northern regions like Friuli Venezia Giulia, Trentino–Alto Adige, and Lombardy. No other country in the world comes close to Italy's grape biodiversity.

Even though Italy has had wild and domestic grapevines for thousands of years, it's amazing that so much biodiversity survived the phylloxera outbreak of the nineteenth and twentieth centuries, the world wars, and Italy's postwar economic boom. Some vines were protected simply because they were neglected, left behind as families moved to cities. For the past couple of decades, there have been so many stories of a grape being discovered that it's become a clichéd marketing strategy. But we welcome all the grapes—the wine world is better with them.

Grape diversity in Italy also comes from variations within the same grape type. In his book *Italy's Native Wine Grape Terroirs*, Italian wine expert Ian D'Agata notes that when you find a lot of grape biotypes, it's an indication that a vine has grown in an area long enough to mutate and adapt. Biotypes are technically the same grape, just with a genetic mutation that makes it look, act, or taste slightly different from the original. These biotypes are not the same as clones, which have identical DNA to the original plant. D'Agata explains that finding a variety with a lot of mutations is a sign that it was popular enough to be grown by many.

There's an effort in the Italian wine industry to preserve genetic diversity within the same grape variety. Dr. Anna Schneider, the head researcher at the National Research Council of Italy, Institute for Sustainable Plant Protection in Turin, stresses the importance of preserving biodiversity by protecting old vineyards. A mutation of Nebbiolo or Sangiovese in an old vineyard may stand up better to changing weather patterns. By contrast, if everyone plants the same vine clones and one disease affects a cloned vine, the rest will be affected.

Old vines are valuable for other reasons. They are more resilient, capable of enduring extreme heat and drought because their roots are more developed and capable of reaching deeper into the earth to access water while limiting the amount of energy needed to grow new vine shoots. (The root systems of young vines sit at the surface, making them more vulnerable to extreme weather.) Plus, in any given year, old vines deliver fruit with more character and concentration than young vines.

All these aspects—the land and the grapes, the farming methods, and climate change—help us to better understand what's in a bottle of Italian wine.

Southern Italy

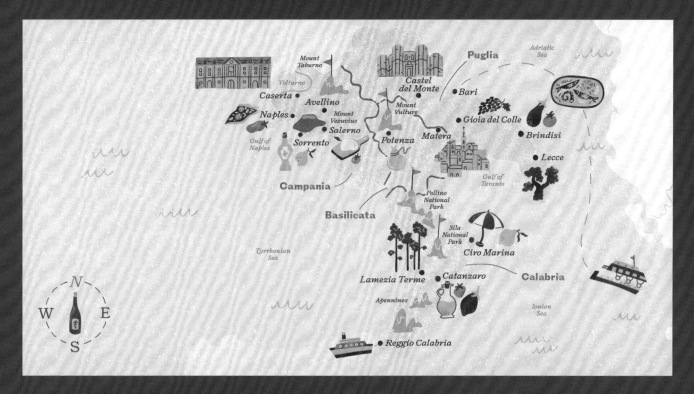

Adriatic Sea

Puglia

Mount Taburno

Castel del Monte

Bari

Caserta

Volturno

Avellino

Mount Vesuvius

Naples

Salerno

Mount Vulture

Gioia del Colle

Brindisi

Sorrento

Gulf of Naples

Potenza

Matera

Lecce

Campania

Basilicata

Pollino National Park

Gulf of Taranto

Sila National Park

Tyrrhenian Sea

Ciro Marina

Lamezia Terme

Catanzaro

Calabria

Apennines

Ionian Sea

N
W   E
S

Reggio Calabria

Sardinia

Sicily

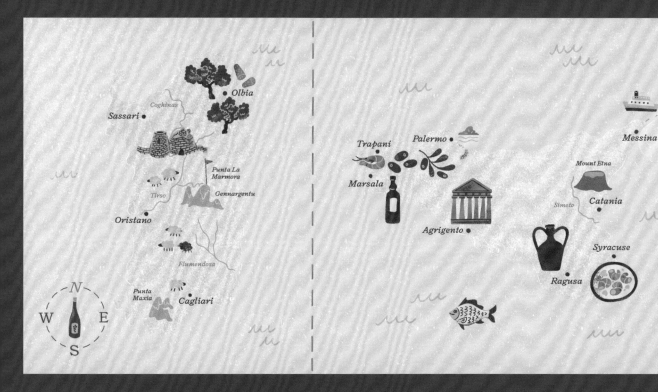

Olbia

Sassari

Coghinas

Trapani

Palermo

Messina

Marsala

Mount Etna

Punta La Marmora

Tirso

Gennargentu

Simeto

Catania

Oristano

Agrigento

Syracuse

Flumendosa

Ragusa

Punta Maxia

Cagliari

N
W   E
S

What's in the Bottle: Italian Wine Names and Laws

Most of the time, American wines are identified by grape, like Cabernet Sauvignon from the Napa Valley. In Italy, this isn't often the case, which can make reading Italian wine labels confusing. While many of the wines from Liguria, Trentino–Alto Adige, and Friuli Venezia Giulia are named after the grape, making it easy to decipher what's in the bottle, regions such as Piedmont, Tuscany, and Sicily rely on the drinker to know about the wine in more detail. With Chianti Classico, you need to know that Sangiovese is the main grape and that Chianti Classico is the area in Tuscany where the wine is made. Another example of a wine that requires further knowledge: Vino Nobile di Montepulciano is a wine named for its location, the Tuscan town of Montepulciano. Its wine is mostly Sangiovese. Montepulciano *the town* has no link to Montepulciano *the grape* from the region of Abruzzo. There are also plenty of wines made from blends, such as Cerasuolo di Vittoria in Sicily, which combines the grapes Frappato and Nero d'Avola. With those wines, a little more research is needed to know what's in the bottle.

It's easier when wines are named after both the grape and the place, like Fiano di Avellino: Fiano is the name of the grape; Avellino is the province in Campania where it's from. There are other wines made with Fiano, but only Fiano di Avellino comes from Avellino. There are also names that sound confusing on the surface but are easy to sort out when broken down. The red wine Lacrima di Morro d'Alba doesn't have anything to do with the Lacryma Christi wines of Mount Vesuvius in Campania, and it is not related to the town of Alba in Piedmont. But once you know that Lacrima is a local grape that nearly only grows around the coastal village of Morro d'Alba in Le Marche, it all makes sense. Finally, there are wines given so-called fantasy names, such as "Sassicaia" and "Le Pergole Torte." When these premium wines were first made, they surpassed the government's quality standards of the time, yet because they didn't follow DOC requirements, they could not be labeled as DOC wines. These wines became famous years ago and still go by name alone.

Wine Laws

In 1963, the Italian government launched a national wine classification system modeled after the *appellation d'origine contrôlée* (AOC) system in France. This system was the government's way of raising the prestige of Italian wine around the world, creating standards for wines to meet to be granted a designation of quality. Essentially, Italians wanted everyone to know that only certain wines met the qualifications to be called Chianti Classico or Brunello or Barolo. The first designation was *denominazione di origine controllata* (DOC); wines that weren't DOC were simply *vino da tavola*, or table wine. In 1966, the Tuscan white wine Vernaccia di San Gimignano became

Italian Wine Quality Rankings

When the European Union introduced its wine guidelines for member countries, Italy was allowed to keep its old system. Today, the EU's terms–DOP, IGP, and Vino–are used interchangeably with the Italian terms DOCG, DOC, IGT, and Vino da Tavola. (See full definitions in the text below.) The categories are arranged like a pyramid. DOP wines are at the top and have to follow the most regulations. They are usually made in the smallest quantities while the wines at the bottom of the pyramid have the fewest restrictions and are made in bulk. Yet the quality at the top of the pyramid is not always better than what you find in the middle, and many winemakers prefer to use IGP (IGT) on their labels instead of DOP (DOCG or DOC) so they have more flexibility to call the shots.

DOP/PDO: Protected designation of origin

- **DOCG:** Requires annual analysis at bottling. Quality regulations can include the quantity of grapes allowed, vineyard location, growing and harvesting techniques, winemaking methods, and aging requirements before wines are released.

- **DOC:** Adheres to some of the same production regulations as DOCG but is less restrictive.

IGP/PGI: Protected geographical indication

- **IGT:** Indicates the area where the grapes grow and can include any of the grapes permitted in the area.

Vino: Wine

- **Vino da Tavola:** Wine being made outside of the requirements for DOP and IGP wines.

the first DOC, and more soon followed. In 1980, the government introduced *denominazione di origine controllata e garantita* (DOCG), upping the ante on quality. Some DOCs quickly achieved the new DOCG status, including Barolo and Barbaresco in Piedmont and Brunello di Montalcino and Vino Nobile di Montepulciano in Tuscany. There were plenty of head-scratchers, too, and some complained about political favors. Even so, there were more standards to come. In 1992, the government introduced a level between DOC and table wine called *indicazione geografica tipica* (IGT), indicating that a wine was made in a specific area. This designation offered more flexibility for winemakers who wanted to experiment beyond what was allowed in the DOC and DOCG wines.

In 2008, a lot changed and a lot stayed the same. That year, the European Union put forth a wine law that overrode existing laws for member countries. The EU's quality pyramid is slightly different from Italy's old DOC system. At the top are wines with protected designation of origin (PDO), followed by wines with protected geographical indication (PGI), and those classified simply as "wine" at the bottom. In Italian, this translates to *denominazione d'origine protetta* (DOP), *indicazione geografica protetta* (IGP), and *vino*. The EU allows countries to continue using their old quality standards on labels. So, you'll still see "DOC" and "DOCG" bands around bottle necks and "IGT" and "Vino da Tavola" on the label. But the Ministry of Agriculture, Food, and Forestry, which oversees Italy's wine regulations, officially uses DOP and IGP on its website. Today, a DOC or DOCG wine is also a DOP wine, an IGT wine is an IGP wine, and *vino da tavola* and *vino* both mean table wine.

Politics being what it is, the quality standards for many of the wines are too broad in some places and too limiting in others. Many Italian wines historically were made from blends, so most DOCs allow other grapes in the mix in addition to the grape named on the bottle. Other DOCs cover too much land to be able to "guarantee" any kind of style. For instance, the Abruzzo DOC covers the entire wine-producing part of the region. In other words, DOC/G and IGT markers are helpful when figuring out where a wine is coming from. But don't base your shopping strictly on assuming the best wines in Italy carry a DOCG band around the bottle neck.

What Grows Together, Goes Together: Italian Wine at the Table

Wine in Italy has always been treated as part of a meal, and the best way to appreciate its nuances is at the table. But what to serve? Sommeliers often use the "what grows together, goes together" adage, which is the idea that food and wines that evolved together also complement each other at the table. On the island of Pantelleria, that could be swordfish and capers paired with a glass of dry Zibibbo; while in Umbria, it's earthy lentils, porcini, and truffles with Montefalco Rosso. Here's a summary of Italy's regional foods:

On the Italian mainland, the northern regions have the richest food. Pasta is made with eggs. The north also specializes in cows' milk cheeses. Rice (as in risotto) and polenta are common starches. Butter is a main cooking fat, though olive oil is also used, especially around Lake Garda, where olive trees grow. Cured meats, such as lardo, prosciutto, and other kinds of salumi, are eaten nearly everywhere. Emilia-Romagna is especially famous for its rich cuisine, and it's the birthplace of Parmigiano-Reggiano and prosciutto di Parma. Milan, a wealthy city, specializes in risotto and ossobuco, while Piedmont and Valle d'Aosta have fonduta, the northern Italian version of fondue, and white truffles. Friuli Venezia Giulia and Trentino–Alto Adige both share similarities with Austrian cuisine, with dumplings on the menu and poppy seeds, rye, and speck in the pantry. In the Veneto, meals lean toward fish for protein and polenta and rice for starch. Liguria is an outlier in the north; with olives, olive oil, basil, and anchovies, its main flavors have more in common with central and southern Italy.

Compared to the riches of the north, the cooking of Italy's central and southern areas is more aligned with *la cucina povera* (peasant cooking). Instead of butter, olive oil is the main cooking fat, and pastas are made without eggs and dried before cooking. Tomatoes are abundant. The piece of meat cooked with the tomato-rich ragù is removed and served as a separate course, while the remaining tomato sauce is used to lightly coat pasta. Umbria and Tuscany are known for their beans, but beans are eaten throughout the south as well. Tuscany is the most austere about food, famous for its bread without salt. There, leftover bread becomes panzanella, bread salad.

In place of Parmigiano-Reggiano, pecorino, a sheep's milk cheese, is the main grating cheese in the south. In Campania and Puglia, you'll also find fresh mozzarella made with cows' or buffalo milk and burrata, which is mozzarella filled with cream and torn bits of curd. Caciocavallo is a semifirm cows' milk cheese made throughout southern Italy and served with slices of salumi. Spicy peppers are served fresh and dried, and tomatoes, potatoes, and eggplant are just as common. As in southern Italy, beans, pecorino, olive oil, and vegetables are essential parts of Sardinian and Sicilian meals. Sicily has its caponata made with eggplant, and some of the best capers in the world. There, pastas are filled with seafood, from sardines to tuna to swordfish. Sardinia also has seafood, but much of the island's cooking stems from shepherd communities, who eat more lamb than fish. Both islands grate bottarga,

cured mullet roe, on top of pasta for a salty accent. Yet no one area is a monolith, and there are differences in the foods favored by different provinces in the same region.

Nearly everywhere in the country, people eat simply and seasonally. This means if you visit Veneto in November and December when radicchio is in season, you'll see radicchio at every meal. And if you visit Rome in the spring, you'll be eating a lot of artichokes (which can be a tricky wine pairing, but not if you pick a good Frascati). In general, wines from coastal areas with Mediterranean climates complement simple meals filled with vegetables and seafood, while wines from cooler inland areas pair better with heartier food, though there is plenty of wiggle room to experiment.

Italian wines also complement food from other parts of the world, and you can find thrilling pairings such as sushi and orange wine from Friuli, or a classic American burger with Montepulciano d'Abruzzo. Rather than be restrictive, the "What grows together, goes together" strategy is simply a starting point.

Serving Italian Wine

There's no need to buy a lot of new glassware or get fussy about precise temperatures to enjoy Italian wine, but here are some best practices:

- **Sparkling wines:** At A16, we serve bubbles in a modern Champagne glass, which is closer to a white wine glass than a champagne flute. This allows you to breathe in the wine's aromas and appreciate its nuances. Serve sparkling wines chilled. To chill a bottle quickly, use an ice bucket with 75 percent ice, 25 percent water. When opening any wine with a wire cage, first loosen the cage, then tilt the bottle slightly so it's not straight up and down. Rock the cork gently side to side, using the cage to help grasp it, while rotating the bottle. Or remove the cage completely, drape a napkin over the cork, and then follow the same steps. Some gently sparkling wines have regular corks and can be opened with a corkscrew, but make sure the bottle is chilled before opening. Chill sparkling wine with crown caps and open them like you would a bottle of beer. (For more on sparkling wine styles, see page 262.)

- **White wine:** Use a traditional white wine glass, which brings out the acidity and minerality that Italian white wines are known for. Serve lighter white wines, like Vermentino from Liguria, Falanghina from Campania, and Müller-Thurgau from Alto Adige, chilled and straight from the fridge. For more complex wines, such as Fiano di Avellino or aged Carricante, let these sit at room temperature after pulling them out of the refrigerator so it is easier to taste their nuances. We serve white wines somewhere between 44° to 48°F on average.

- **Orange wine:** Some orange wines we serve like white wines, while others we serve like reds, and it requires a bit of experimentation to find the right fit. At A16, we serve Cantina Giardino's "Paski," a lighter orange Coda di Volpe wine, like a white wine but Paolo Bea's "Arboreus" and Radikon's "Oslavje" are more savory, so we serve them in larger glasses with less of a chill to best savor them. (For more on orange wines, see page 84.)

- **Rosato (rosé):** Serve rosato like white wine—chilled, especially those from Puglia and Calabria, which are ideal for beating the heat on hot summer days. The exception is Cerasuolo d'Abruzzo and some of the rosato from Mount Etna, which can be served like a lightly chilled red wine (55° to 58°F) to better appreciate their nuances. (For more on *rosati*, see page 39.)

- **Red wine:** The ideal red wine glass is all about controlling how the wine hits your palate. For lighter-bodied reds, like Schiava, Pelaverga, or Piedirosso, use Burgundy glasses, which have a rounder base and help emphasize the tannins, acidity, and aromas in the wines. For reds like Chianti Classico, Brunello, Barolo, Barbaresco, and Sagrantino, opt for Bordeaux glasses, which are taller and direct the tannins to the back of your palate. And if we're not sure, we get a couple of glasses and experiment, seeing whether the shape of the glass makes an impact on how we experience the aromas, taste, and finish of the wine. Serve these wines at a cool room temperature, about 60° to 64°F.

- **Passito/Vendemmia Tardiva/Marsala:** These special sweet wines should be savored, served in smaller pours with a slight chill to mellow their higher alcohol content. A port or cordial glass does the trick. (For more on dessert wines, see page 190.)

Part II

The Regions

Abruzzo

"Quarmari! Quar-mar-ee-ee!" At the sound of his name, the 150-pound Abruzzese sheepdog lumbered under the pergola, looking for the shade. A late-afternoon breeze had started to cool the hills around Cugnoli, but with white fur at least twice as thick as a golden retriever's, the dog needed all the natural air-conditioning he could get. Cristiana Tiberio put Quarmari's enormous head between her hands and scratched his cheeks. When a local shepherd had more dogs than he needed, he asked Cristiana to foster Quarmari for a few months. That was several years ago, and he's been with the winemaker ever since.

For most Americans, Abruzzo is not a well-known place; there isn't any famous city here, no Florence or Venice or Rome. Every few decades, a devastating earthquake draws attention to the region (its capital city, L'Aquila, is still recovering from a fatal 2009 tremor), but otherwise, things stay quiet. For most of the region's history, the Apennines, whose highest peak is in Abruzzo, walled off the region from the busier, western side of the country. With his thick coat, Quarmari is perfectly comfortable in cold winters, and so is the Montepulciano grape, which originated in Abruzzo's mountains. Even with the mountains

ever present, Abruzzo is often characterized by the outside wine world as a hot place that makes cheap and cheerful Montepulciano wine along a warm, flat coast. But it was only after World War II that Abruzzo's coast became the region's main vineyard area. Grow Montepulciano—or nearly any grape—in a warm climate, encourage high yields, pick it early, and you'll get cheap table wine. Grow it in the mountains and foothills, where the seasons are longer and the day–night temperature swings more dramatic, and Montepulciano wine can stand up to Italy's best.

Rather than coexisting with cities and highways, Abruzzo's vineyard land shares space with a mix of agriculture and parkland. In the foothills, almond, olive, and fig trees divide up hills growing sunflowers, beans, or grains before giving way to nature. More than 30 percent of the region is parkland, including three national parks, one regional park, and a handful of nature reserves. Ginestra, a yellow wildflower, fills the hillsides in the summer, and its faint honeysuckle scent finds its way into tasting notes for Abruzzo's white wines. The foothills are also home to purple saffron crocus flowers, which are harvested for their red stigmas and sold to saffron lovers around the world.

Thanks to its coastal vineyards, Abruzzo makes a lot of wine. Compared with the rest of Italy, the region ranks fifth in production, yielding more than 76 million gallons (2.887 million hectoliters) in 2020. But the best bottles stand apart. Take the wine made from the Tiberio family's Fonte Canale vineyard. Here, more than sixty-year-old Trebbiano Abruzzese vines are trained in a double pergola, an arrangement in which two vines grow twisted together. Between each double vine, there is plenty of room to walk around. A few decades ago, it would have been tempting to rip out the vineyard and replant the vines closer together; viticulture and enology schools teach that densely planted vines yield more concentrated grapes. That didn't happen here. While the vine's canopy of leaves grows thicker than most vineyards', a disadvantage for many grapes, it's an asset to Trebbiano Abruzzese since the grapes sunburn easily. The space between the vines also turned out to be an advantage. In 2013, a snowstorm hit in November, before the vines had lost their leaves. Nearby pergola-trained vineyards collapsed because the weight of the snow on the leaf canopy crushed the vines. But at Fonte Canale, the extra space allowed the snow to pile up on the ground, easing the load. Grapes from the vineyard make Tiberio's Trebbiano d'Abruzzo "Fonte Canale," one of Italy's most interesting, age-worthy white wines. It's filled with verve, with notes of green apple, lemon peel, and apricot that come together in vibrant fashion.

For Tiberio and other acclaimed producers, including the legendary Emidio Pepe and the late Edoardo Valentini, making the best wine in Abruzzo means surpassing the establishment's DOP regulations (see Italian Wine Quality Rankings, page 24). Instead, they study the local grapes and land and grow conscientiously, learning more every year about the best ways to showcase native Montepulciano, Trebbiano Abruzzese, and Pecorino grapes. They also knew of the importance of *rosato*—here called Cerasuolo—well before pink wines became summer clichés. Taken together—winemaking talent, natural land, and popular grapes—Abruzzo has all the makings of a region on the brink of being recognized as a special place for Italian wine.

History

On a map, Abruzzo looks like part of central Italy. But culturally and historically, it has more in common with the south. Prior to Italy's unification, it was part of the Kingdom of Naples and then part of the Kingdom of the Two Sicilies, just like Campania, Calabria, and the rest of southern Italy. The food of Abruzzo also echoes the foods found farther south on the peninsula: *arrosticini* (skewers of lamb grilled like shish kebabs), pecorino cheeses, and a preference for dried pasta over fresh.

Abruzzo was part of Abruzzi e Molise until Molise (page 133) became its own region in 1963. The two were unified through World War II, when the Gustav Line—a series of barriers set to keep the US and Allied forces from advancing to Rome—cut through their towns and destroyed their main train line. In 1943, after finishing harvest, the Ciavolich family in the town of Miglianico hid in their underground cellar; by December of that year, they were forced to evacuate to safety. It wasn't until after the winter of 1944 that the Gustav Line fell, and thousands of soldiers on both sides died from cold, exhaustion, and hunger. On May 3, 1945, the *New York Times* described the situation on the ground as an "Italian Valley Forge high in the cruel Apennines on a 'forgotten front.'" The combination of brutal winters and the challenge of rebuilding in the mountains forced residents to move closer to the sea. The modern, coastal city of Pescara is the region's largest. Farmers replanted vines in flatter areas along the sea, which were easier to tend and produced more grapes at harvest. These vineyards were also closer to main roads, making transportation easier. Soon, the southeastern province of Chieti was booming with bulk wine production. Many Abruzzese winemakers today had family members in the 1960s and '70s who either worked in or grew grapes for wine co-ops.

The rediscovery of native vines in the 1990s started to shift some of Abruzzo's production toward more artisan bottles. There was a lot to learn. In the

Winemaker Cristiana Tiberio and her *pastore Abruzzese*
(Abruzzese sheepdog), Quarmari.

1990s, Ofena winemaker Luigi Cataldi Madonna put the name of an obscure white grape called Pecorino on the label. In the same decade, Cristiana Tiberio's father bought the Fonte Canale vineyard and, with Cristiana, began studying Trebbiano Abruzzese vines, realizing that the variety had much more to offer than making simple everyday white wine. They also found that seven of the vines identified as Trebbiano Abruzzese were actually Pecorino, and they transplanted them to another vineyard. Both white varieties make special vines, but while Pecorino had been growing in obscurity in the mountains, Trebbiano Abruzzese had been misidentified in plant nurseries as Trebbiano Toscano and other unrelated white grapes.

Another shift in favor of quality wine production happened around the turn of the twenty-first century, when more families started to bottle their own wines instead of selling off their grapes. After World War II, the Ciavolich family resettled in Loreto Aprutino and grew grapes for bulk wine. In 2004, Chiara Ciavolich began to bottle wine under the family's name. Made from Trebbiano Abruzzese grapes and aged in amphorae (terracotta vessels) and Slavonian oak barrels, Ciavolich's "Fosso Cancelli" is a layered, golden white wine with subtle notes of herbs and wildflowers.

Through the twentieth century, Abruzzo had outliers, winemakers who became well known despite making wine in a region rarely mentioned by wine writers. Enigmatic producer Edoardo Valentini became famous for a white wine so memorable that no one believed it was made with Trebbiano, a grape that experts deemed mediocre. (This was before many realized that Trebbiano Abruzzese was unrelated to Trebbiano Toscano.) Valentini taught his methods to his son, Francesco, who has made wine at the estate ever since his father passed away in 2006. Like his father, if a vintage doesn't meet his standards, he sells his grapes and skips making wine that year. Valentini's Trebbiano d'Abruzzo continues to be one of Italy's most revered white wines. The flavors—mandarin, yellow wax bean, sunbaked hay, sage, and apple—come together in complex layers.

Then there's Emidio Pepe, who has been making wine the same hands-on, old-fashioned way his grandparents did: no chemicals in the vineyards, grapes picked by hand and crushed by foot, juices fermented with native yeasts, and wines aged in glass-lined tanks before being decanted into bottles by hand. To replicate Pepe's method anywhere else would be next to impossible; it's a product of history and years spent working with the same grapes on the same land. Today, his daughters Daniela and Sofia run the winery, while his granddaughter, Chiara, works on the export side. Each year, the family releases only half of a current vintage so they can continue to age their wines in their cellar, and collectors around the world have bottles of Montepulciano from Emidio Pepe dating back years. If there was any question about the ability of Montepulciano to make age-worthy wines, the Pepe estate has proven the answer is a resounding yes.

Land and Wines

You could argue that Abruzzo has everything one could want in an Italian countryside: mountains, hills, and beaches compacted into an area smaller than Connecticut. In the summer, the coast fills with beach umbrellas stretching out across the sandy shore. It's only forty minutes from there to the foothills and another hour from there to reach the Gran Sasso National Park, home of the Corno Grande, the tallest peak in the Apennines. It's in the hills and mountains where the region has the most promising raw materials for wine.

Abruzzo has four provinces, and all of them grow Montepulciano as well as a small handful of native white grapes. To the north bordering Le Marche, the coastal province of Teramo has mild weather year-round. The best Montepulciano wines from the area are balanced, like those from Emidio Pepe in Torano Nuovo, a commune near the Le Marche border. Yet some areas are warmer and richer in clay, so red wines from this province can show a bigger, bolder side of Montepulciano. The DOCG here, Colline Teramane Montepulciano d'Abruzzo, requires wines to be aged in barrels, making these bottles even richer, perfect for fans of California Cabernet and similar big reds.

To the west, the mountainous L'Aquila province has the fewest vineyards. Its key areas are Ofena, an agricultural valley more than a thousand feet above sea level nicknamed *il forno dell'Abruzzo* (the oven of Abruzzo) because of its intense summer heat. South of Ofena but still in the mountains is Valle Peligna, the birthplace of the Montepulciano grape. To the southeast, the coastal Chieti province makes the most wine and grows the widest variety of grapes, including many international varieties. Around the town of Tollo, the Terre Tollesi (also known as Tullum) growing area is Abruzzo's second DOCG. Granted in 2019, it sits within the larger Tullum DOC in Chieti and focuses on wines made with Montepulciano, Pecorino, and Passerina grapes.

Sandwiched in the middle is the province of Pescara, which includes Apennine foothills as well as the coastal city of Pescara. It's a bit of a Goldilocks area, receiving enough breezes from the mountains to keep things cool in the summer, but it is close enough to the coast to avoid the same kind of weather extremes found in L'Aquila. The province can be divided into two areas: the Vestina, an area of gentle hills that includes the wine villages of Loreto Aprutino and Rosciano; and the sub-area of Casauria, which is hillier and breezier, with a bigger temperature swing between day and night, and includes the village of Cugnoli. In this province, you get mineral-rich wines that can age for years, like those of Valentini, Ciavolich, and De Fermo in Loreto Aprutino and Tiberio in Cugnoli.

Since Montepulciano d'Abruzzo DOC wines can come from all wine-producing parts of the region, it is impossible to describe the overarching characteristics of the wine. A better way to understand Abruzzo is to sample wines from producers from different areas who have taken the trouble to understand their raw material of land and grapes.

Abruzzo Grapes

While white grapes are important, the region is best known for Montepulciano, a red grape planted across the region.

White

Cococciola

Cococciola has long been part of the field blend that went into light, crisp Trebbiano d'Abruzzo DOC wines. Unfortunately, it was common for these grapes to be confused with other local white varieties, and it's been studied on its own only recently. According to Ian D'Agata's book *Native Wine Grapes of Italy*, Cococciola could be related to Puglian grape Bombino Bianco (page 167). It's an easygoing, productive grape that grows well in Abruzzo and delivers plenty of bright acidity and herbal tanginess—as long as it doesn't get too ripe. Its acidity lends itself to sparkling wine, like the *col fondo* Cococciola made by Cingilia, an estate in Pescara that also makes a lovely still wine with the grape. (*Col fondo* is a traditional style of Prosecco in which the spent yeast cells left in the bottle give the wine a cloudy appearance; see page 263.) Cococciola also shows promise in Molise and northern Puglia, though it's still not easy to find Cococciola wines there—or anywhere, for now.

Passerina
(see Le Marche chapter, page 109)

Pecorino
Some say the grape Pecorino got its name from the shape of its grape clusters, which look like sheep heads (*pecora* is "sheep" in Italian); others say it's because sheep liked to eat this vine's leaves. Cristiana Tiberio, who has grown Pecorino for years, finds both stories suspect—whoever said sheep were so selective with their grapevines? A more likely story is that the vine originated in the

A glass of Tiberio Cerasuolo d'Abruzzo.

Cerasuolo d'Abruzzo and Italian *Rosati*

Rosati (rosé wines) are an important part of Italian wine history. In Abruzzo, before the advent of modern winemaking, Montepulciano grapes growing in the mountains didn't ripen easily. Even when harvested as late as November, the wines it made were light and cherry colored (*cerasuolo* means "cherry"). With a warming climate and modern vine management, Montepulciano ripens just fine today, but the tradition of making Cerasuolo continues.

There are a few ways that producers make this deep rosy wine. The oldest way, called *svacata*, involved adding a bit of Montepulciano wine fermenting on its grape skins to the (skinless) Cerasuolo wine before it finished fermenting. This served to darken the Cerasuolo and give it more structure than it would otherwise have. But today, most producers macerate the Montepulciano grape skins with the juices early in the winemaking process, just long enough to extract a cherry color, and then remove the skins. Using this method, it doesn't take long for the wine to turn a deep, pink-ruby hue. There are other techniques as well. Cristiana Tiberio uses only the free-run juice from Montepulciano grapes to make her Cerasuolo. The wine gets its deep color without maceration, she explains, because the fruit comes from a south-facing vineyard with more clay in the soil, allowing the grapes to ripen faster while still maintaining the balance between acidity and fruit flavors. In fact, all good Cerasuolo d'Abruzzo finds balance. Even though the wine is darker than most *rosati* in Italy—or rosé around the world—the color belies its red-fruit brightness and mineral complexity. All of this makes it an extremely food-friendly wine, capable of pairing equally with lighter and richer fare.

Other regions in Italy make vibrant, food-friendly *rosati*. Along the southern part of Lake Garda, there are two types of *rosato*, and both are called Chiaretto. Bardolino, a wine area along the southeastern shores of lake in Veneto, makes Chiaretto from the grapes used in Valpolicella wines. Meanwhile, Valténesi Chiaretto comes from the southwestern shores in Lombardy and is made with Groppello and Marzemino. Both are lighter in color than Abruzzo's Cerasuolo. Puglia, Sicily, and Calabria also have strong *rosato* traditions.

Rosati All Over Italy

- Alberto Graci Etna Rosato, Sicily
- Bonavita Rosato, Sicily
- Castello di Ama "Purple Rose," Tuscany
- De Fermo "Le Cince" Cerasuolo d'Abruzzo, Abruzzo
- G. D. Vajra "Rosabella" Nebbiolo Rosato, Piedmont
- Giovanni Montisci "Barrosu" Rosato, Sardinia
- Girolamo Russo, Etna Rosato, Sicily
- Grosjean Premetta (not technically *rosato*, but it is so light in color that it looks like one), Valle d'Aosta
- I Vigneri "Vinudilice," Sicily
- Le Fraghe "Ròdon" Bardolino Chiaretto, Veneto
- Marisa Cuomo Costa d'Amalfi Rosato, Campania
- Nusserhof Südtirol Lagrein Kretzer, Trentino–Alto Adige
- Praesidium Cerasuolo d'Abruzzo, Abruzzo
- Rosa Del Golfo Rosato, Puglia
- Sartori "Mont'Albano" Bardolino Chiaretto, Veneto
- Sergio Arcuri "Il Marinetto" Rosato, Calabria
- Tormaresca "Calafuria" Rosato, Puglia
- Torrevento "Primaronda" Castel del Monte Rosato, Puglia
- Valentini Cerasuolo d'Abruzzo, Abruzzo

mountains where shepherds kept their flocks. The grape grows well there, too. Its small, round leaves don't shade the grapes, allowing the fruit to get enough sun to ripen in colder climates. The result is a variety with unusually high levels of malic acid, yielding wines that taste bright and fresh, belying their relatively high alcohol content (around 14 percent). Among Italy's native white grapes, Pecorino has been a breakout success. In 1987 in Le Marche, Guido Cocci Grifoni found an abandoned vineyard in the mountains and replanted a few of the vines at his estate following the advice of sommelier Teodoro Bugari. The Conegliano wine school in Veneto and the Agrarian Institute of Ascoli Piceno in Le Marche also took an interest in Grifoni's finds, helping him make the first Pecorino wine. In Abruzzo, winemaker Luigi Cataldi Madonna in Ofena also worked with the variety. In 1996, Cataldi Madonna became the first estate to bottle wine with "Pecorino" on the label. Today, the variety is grown throughout Abruzzo and southern Le Marche. At its best it yields textured wines with a mineral, zesty elegance—like lemon drops infused with a dash of rosemary and thyme.

Trebbiano Abruzzese

Not too long ago, the reputation of Trebbiano Abruzzese was questionable thanks to a mix-up in identity: The vines were often mistaken for Trebbiano Toscano, Mostosa, Bombino Bianco, or Cococciola. Even today, someone can go to a nursery and buy Trebbiano Abruzzese vines and end up with something else. Even more confusing, all those grapes can be used to make Trebbiano d'Abruzzo DOC wines. (Trebbiano d'Abruzzo and Trebbiano Abruzzese are *not* the same: the former is the wine, the latter the grape variety.) While the DOC had a modest reputation, there were always a few standout bottles, most notably those from Valentini. Today the grape is considered a premier white variety. Trebbiano Abruzzese grapes grow large but have thin, sensitive skins. They do best with some shade from the vine canopy, protecting the fruit so they can ripen longer on the vine. The best Trebbiano Abruzzese wines are subtle but spectacular, with

delicate notes of honey and lemon peel balanced with herbs and the local ginestra flower, delivering mild to bright acidity. When made well, they are among the best white wines in Italy.

Red

Montepulciano

Montepulciano is among Italy's five most-planted grape varieties. It grows in Puglia, Molise, Le Marche, Lazio, and Umbria as well as all over Abruzzo. While Montepulciano had a reputation for making cheap, everyday red, it is capable of so much more. Emidio Pepe's Montepulciano is one of the most singular reds in Italy, aging for decades and evolving to express deep red berries, orange peel, and forest floor. At its best, Montepulciano tastes elegant, with fresh brightness reminiscent of sour cherries, pomegranate, and raspberries coupled with accents of oregano and a grip of tannins. Montepulciano is also the base of one of Italy's most beguiling *rosato* wines, Cerasuolo d'Abruzzo (page 39).

Like Pecorino, Montepulciano is a mountain variety, and it does best with a long growing season that gives time for its skins and seeds to ripen while the sugars develop. In a too-hot area, it accumulates sugars quickly, making it hard for the other parts of the grape to mature in time for harvest. In the rocky, calcareous clay soils of Valle Peligna, where the grape originated, Praesidium makes high-altitude Montepulciano and Cerasuolo wines with refreshing acidity and elegant richness. In Le Marche, look for bottles from Rosso Conero, an area near Ancona, and Offida near Ascoli Piceno. (Side note: Montepulciano the grape has nothing to do with Montepulciano, the town in Tuscany. It doesn't grow there, and it's not used to make Vino Nobile di Montepulciano, a Sangiovese-based wine.)

Regional Foods

Agnello all'arrabiata
lamb sauce for pasta seasoned with chiles

Arrosticini
grilled lamb skewers

Brodetto alla vastese
seafood stew with tomatoes and peppers from Vasto

Capra alla neretese
goat stew from Teramo

Cheese
caciocavallo, aged cows' or goats' milk cheese; *pecorino*, sheep's milk cheese; *ricotta*, sometimes smoked with juniper wood; *stracciata*, a fresh cows' milk cheese

Diavolicchio
chiles used in pasta and 'ndocca 'ndocca (described below)

Ferratelle
wafer cookies made with anise

Le Virtu
a soup of lentils and spring vegetables

Licorice

'Ndocca 'ndocca
whole pig cut into chunks and cooked with rosemary, bay leaves, and garlic

Olive oil

Parrozzo
traditional dome-shaped Christmas cake with almonds

Pasta
al ceppo, short pasta strands wrapped around a wooden stick

Cannarozzetti allo zafferano, pasta with saffron

fazzoletti, handkerchief pasta

Sagne e fagioli, pasta made with beans and tomato sauce

spaghetti alla chitarra, spaghetti cut with wires stretched across a wooden frame

Porchetta
roasted suckling pig

Saffron

Salsiccia di fegato
liver sausage

Scapece
pickled fish

Torrone
nougat made with egg white, honey, and nuts; in L'Aquila, it's made with chocolate and nuts; in Chieti, with candied fruit and cinnamon

Recommended Producers

Amorotti

Cataldi Madonna

Centorame

Ciavolich

Cingilia

Cirelli

Colle Trotta

Contesa

De Fermo

Emidio Pepe

Il Feuduccio

Illuminati

Indigeno

La Quercia

La Valentina

Masciarelli

Nicodemi

Pasetti

Plasma

Praesidium

Scarpone

Talamonti

Tiberio

Torre Dei Beati

Valentini

Vini Rabasco

Basilicata

If you were to set a movie in preindustrial times, Basilicata would be a good choice. Consider the scenery: sandstone-hued homes built against a craggy landscape without a single *autostrada* to break the scene. Matera, a city with *sassi*—caves that date back to the Paleolithic era—feels like a place from another time. People lived in the caves until the mid-twentieth century, when the government relocated them to stop the spread of malaria. Today, with hotels and restaurants occupying many of the caves, Matera feels a little less forgotten about. In 1993, UNESCO granted the city World Heritage status; in 2019, it was Europe's Capital of Culture; in 2021, it was the backdrop of the opening scene of the James Bond movie *No Time to Die*. Yet while Matera has gained more attention from outsiders, most of Basilicata is free from tourists. Campania, with Naples and Capri, is more famous, and Puglia, with its flat, endless coastline, is easier to reach. Compared to its regional neighbors, Basilicata has a sense of timelessness: a Santa Fe, not a San Francisco.

The best wines from the region are also timeless. This isn't a place for trendy bottles; people here stick with the old ways. Plus, Basilicata doesn't make a lot of wine. In 2020, the region made 2.4 million gallons (91,000 hectoliters), the third lowest in Italy after Liguria and Valle d'Aosta. Eighty percent of production is red, and the best comes from Mount Vulture, a volcano that, unlike Mount Vesuvius to the west, has not been active in human history. Here, Aglianico grapes are turned into long-lived mountain wines with dusty undertones, the kind that all lovers of aged reds should have in their cellars.

In the 1990s, a wave of investment rushed into Vulture, yet the boom soon ebbed; a Michelin-starred restaurant came and went; a few historic wineries and vineyards changed hands. Yet some managed to keep their prized land in the family. Elena Fucci's grandfather bought vineyards in the 1960s and sold grapes even though his vines were on Contrada Solagna del Titolo, which is prized land. In 2000, the family planned on selling the vineyard, but Elena made an argument for keeping it by studying agriculture at the University of Pisa and starting her namesake winery. For years she made only one wine: a smooth, layered expression of Aglianico named Titolo, after the vineyard itself. Since then, she's branched out slowly, making a version of Titolo aged in amphorae (terracotta vessels) as well as a Titolo *rosato*.

Over the years, a few outsiders have broken into the insular wine community in Vulture. Seeking a quieter life, Fabrizio Piccin and his wife, Cecilia

Naldoni, sold their Tuscan winery, Salcheto, and started over in Vulture with a winery called Grifalco. Fabrizio Piccin has since passed away, but Cecilia and their sons, Lorenzo and Andrea, tend the family's four plots around the towns of Ginestra and Maschito. Their wines range from bold, everyday wines to complex bottles layered with licorice, red fruits, and spice. Lorenzo Piccin also makes his own wine under the label San Martino, giving the bottles names in Arbëresh, the dialect spoken by descendants of Albanians who fled the Balkans in the fifteenth century. Viviana Malafarina, who came to Barile in 2011, is another relative newcomer to Vulture. As the general manager and winemaker at Basilisco, a historic winery owned by Campania-based winery Feudi di San Gregorio, she has access to the estate's Storico vineyard, where octogenarian Aglianico vines grow ungrafted.

Elena, Lorenzo, Andrea, Viviana, and others are part of the Generazione Vulture, an informal group of winemakers founded after an initial push from Italian wine expert Ian D'Agata. The winemakers come together to support each other and promote the area's wines farther afield. But mostly, Vulture doesn't get a lot of outside attention, staying off the radar of most wine lovers. This is despite having all the ingredients for great red wine: an incredibly long growing season, cool nights, volcanic soil, and old vines that are still going strong.

History

When the ancient Greeks colonized the southern Italian peninsula from Calabria to Puglia, they named the land Oenotria, meaning "land of vine poles" or, more commonly, "land of wine." The theory goes that the Greeks were impressed by the native Enotrians, who already grew vines before the Greeks arrived. In Basilicata, the Enotrians were then pushed out by the Lucanians, and for most of written history, Basilicata was called Lucania. After the fall of Rome,

Basilicata was shuffled between outside powers. Among rulers, Frederick II, the thirteenth-century Holy Roman Emperor, was a local favorite, building castles in Lagopesole and Melfi, and his name lingers in landmarks. His son, Manfred, inspired the name of Vulture's Re Manfredi winery: "Re" for "king," "Manfredi" for "Manfred."

The nineteenth century ushered in turbulent times. After King Victor Emmanuel II proclaimed Italy united in 1861, revolts broke out in southern Italy that evolved into civil war, and resentment toward the north lingered for decades after. In 1935, during Mussolini's reign, Carlo Levi, an antifascist doctor and painter from Turin, was exiled to Basilicata. While living in the poor village of Aliano, Levi wrote down his observations. Unlike in the north, no photos of Garibaldi, the nineteenth-century champion of Italy's unification movement, hung on walls, though some villagers posted pictures of President Franklin D. Roosevelt. To Aliano residents, "Italy" was an entity that collected taxes, not a national identity. Levi documented the poverty he witnessed in *Cristo si è fermato a Eboli* (*Christ Stopped at Eboli*), a fictionalized story based on his time there. (Eboli, a town in Campania, was the closest train stop to Aliano.) The book became a hit, inspiring movies and later a TV miniseries, yet it also cemented Basilicata's reputation in Italy as a place of poverty.

Some of that reputation is warranted—people lived in Matera's caves without running water or electricity in the mid-twentieth century because they didn't have options. Yet good wine existed in Basilicata in small pockets. In 1925, Anselmo Paternoster started selling wines from Mount Vulture under the family name, an uncommon move at a time when most people sent grapes to co-ops or wineries in northern Italy. Today, the Paternoster winery is owned by the Venetian wine group Tommasi, but it continues to make wine in the Vulture area under the Paternoster name. The winery's flagship wine. "Don Anselmo," is named after the patriarch. Made from old-vine Aglianico and aged in a combination of Slavonian and French oak, the wine combines flavors of dusty red plum, iron, and wet rock with brooding tannins that allow it to age for years.

Land and Wines

Set in the instep of Italy's boot, Basilicata is hard to reach. The region touches both the Ionian and Tyrrhenian coasts, but only enough to provide small, delightful beaches, not ports with large boats or ferries. The roads are slow, winding their ways around hills and mountains. Less than 10 percent of Basilicata is flat. In the spring, the wild grasses turn emerald, dotted with yellow ginestra flowers, and by summer they are gold. Winter brings snow to the higher elevations. At 2,687 feet (818 meters) above sea level, Basilicata's largest city, Potenza, is one of Italy's coldest.

The focal point of Basilicata's wine world is Mount Vulture, a volcano on the northern reaches of the region made up of seven peaks. From a distance (and using some imagination), it resembles what a mountain peak would look like centuries after an eruption. Mount Vulture's vineyards face east, toward the cooler Adriatic side of the Italian peninsula rather than the warmer Tyrrhenian Sea on the west. The soils vary from volcanic, calcareous clay to sand, and grapes grow at high altitudes between 656 and 2625 feet (200 to 800 meters) above sea level. Here, harvest can wrap up in November, often later than anywhere else in Italy. (It's an informal competition among Valtellina in Lombardy, Taurasi in Campania, and Mount Vulture for who picks their grapes last.)

When grown in the right place and put in the right hands, Aglianico del Vulture is one of the best red wines in Italy. These are deep, dark wines, broody and dusty yet layered with enough minerality and acidity to be great with food. The tannins help these wines age for years, though some bottles are made in a more forward way and can be opened sooner to drink alongside sausages imbued with peppers, roast lamb, and local cheeses. The tricky part is the Vulture area is quite large, and the soil and elevation vary quite a bit. Locals divide the areas into *contrade*, administrative rural subdivisions bigger than a single vineyard but smaller than a town. In Vulture, the best districts are called prime zones and are sometimes found on labels, like Elena Fucci's Titolo. The problem is that if you don't live in Vulture, you're not likely to know the names of any of the *contrade*. If we were to go by the town names—as Ian D'Agata argues in his book *Italy's Native Wine Grape Terroirs*—it would be easier for us to decipher what we're drinking. In a general sense, the towns of Maschito, Barile, and Venosa, which are closest to the summit, are more likely to have the most volcanic soils. Next come the towns of Atella, Forenza, Ginestra, and Ripacandida, followed by Melfi, Lavello, and Maschito. The farther from the summit, the less volcanic soil. Still, each site has its own soil mix, exposure, and altitude, so proximity to the summit doesn't determine the best sites.

Aglianico del Vulture became Basilicata's first DOC in 1971. In 2010, the government granted the Aglianico del Vulture Superiore DOCG designation to recognize *riserva* wines (those made with longer aging periods as determined by DOP guidelines). As far as what makes Aglianico del Vulture a DOC versus a DOCG, it's only a matter of winemaking. At minimum, Aglianico del Vulture DOC ages for a year, while Aglianico del Vulture DOCG Superiore must be aged at least a year in oak and another in bottle before being released. The Aglianico del Vulture Riserva DOCG spends two years in oak and two in bottle, and the earliest it can be released is five years after its vintage. Making DOCG wine in Vulture means a lot of time and money tied up in barrels and inventory, and extra effort may not result in a better wine. (It's why you should never buy wine based solely by its government-issued quality designation.)

Outside Vulture, Basilicata is still all about red wine. Primitivo grows in the Matera DOC along the border of Puglia. Close to the Gulf of Taranto is the Parco dei Monaci (Monk Park), one of the largest monasteries in Italy, which dates to 1532. The Benedictines turn their Primitivo into deep, toasty wines that are perfect for pairing with grilled meat. International grapes also grow in Basilicata as IGT wines (if the name of the grape is on the label, the bottle contains at least 85 percent of that variety). For now, white wines are a minor part of Basilicata's repertoire.

While Matera is an international travel destination, the rest of Basilicata is still Basilicata. The mountain cuisine remains rustic and satisfying, with specialties such as *caciocavallo* cheese, made from the milk of Podolico cows who live in the mountains, and red Senise peppers. The peppers are harvested and strung up to dry like spiky beads on a necklace. Once dried, they are fried and eaten like potato chips or crumbled onto chewy, hand-shaped pasta cooked with a little garlic and toasted bread crumbs, a recipe called *strascinati con i peperoni cruschi*.

That leads us to this point: there's a lot more to Basilicata than Matera's caves, and more depth to the wine and food than many have experienced. Even if a trip is not in the cards for you, Basilicata is where to find some of the best values among Italian red wines for cellaring.

Basilicata Grapes

While there is some white wine made here, Basilicata is primarily a place for red wines, especially Aglianico.

White

Bombino Bianco
(See Puglia chapter, page 167)

Fiano
(See Campania chapter, page 62)

Greco Bianco
(See Calabria chapter, page 53)

Malvasia Bianca di Basilicata
Although the late journalist Luigi Veronelli praised a white Malvasia from Basilicata, the grape was always blended into other wines until the early 2000s when Ian D'Agata encouraged Cantina di Venosa,

a co-op in the province of Potenza, to try it on its own. Today the co-op makes a couple of Malvasia di Basilicata wines aged in stainless steel for a fresh, full expression of the variety. Ian tells us that he's really the one who's grateful for Luigi Cantatore, the winemaker at Cantina di Venosa, who was willing to resurrect an old grape and go through the trouble of making wine with it. Sparkling Matera DOC also often contains Malvasia Bianca di Basilicata, which lends acidity and aromatics to the wines.

Red

Aglianico
Aglianico most likely originated in Campania, but in the altitude and climate of Mount Vulture, the late-ripening grape takes even longer to mature. This leads to red wines with higher acidity than those made with Aglianico grown at sea level in sandy, warm soils. The best Vulture bottles are filled with red cherry or plum, spices, licorice, and tar, carrying plenty of acidity so it tastes livelier than you might expect from a full-bodied red wine. Compared with Aglianico from Campania, Aglianico from Vulture leans more mineral and floral. When young, these wines have spice, such as clove, star anise, cardamom, and juniper berries. (For more on Aglianico, see Campania chapter, page 63.)

Primitivo
(See Puglia chapter, page 168)

Malvasia Nera
(See Puglia chapter, page 168)

Tamurro
We first mentioned this grape in our book *A16: Food + Wine* as one to watch in 2008, figuring that by now it would have become a bit more common in Basilicata. That hasn't really been the case. Producer Tenuta Le Querce makes a very concentrated Tamurro aged in French oak, with gripping tannins that are stronger than those of Aglianico. But for now, this wine remains more of a local curiosity.

Regional Foods

Baccala all'Aviglianese
salt cod with *cruschi* from Avigliano

Baccalà con le patate
salt cod baked with potatoes

Cheese
caciocavallo, aged cows' or goats' milk cheese

fior di latte, mozzarella made with cows' milk

pallone di gravina, a cows' or goats' milk cheese shaped like a ball

pecorino, sheep's milk cheese

provolone, a mild cows' milk cheese used in many baked dishes

ricotta and *ricotta salata* (salted ricotta)

Crapiata
a soup of beans, chickpeas, and lentils

Fucuazza
focaccia topped with olive oil, oregano, and tomato

Lucanica di Picerno
cured sausages with fennel and pepper

Melanzana rossa di rotonda
round eggplant

Olive oil

Panella
whole-wheat bread

Pasta
cavatelli, small curled pasta shaped by pressing and dragging two fingers across the dough

orecchiette, small chunky pasta whose name means "little ears"

strascinati, small chunky pasta similar to orecchiette served with *cruschi*, dried red peppers

Peperonata
fresh peppers cooked in garlic, oregano, and sometimes tomatoes

Peperone di Senise
red semi-spicy peppers, dried and crushed (also called *cruschi*)

Ragù alla potentina
pork ragù

Strazzata
doughnut-shaped bread filled with peppers, prosciutto, and caciocavallo cheese

Recommended Producers

600 Grotte

Alovini

Basilisco

Basilium

Bisceglia Cantina di Venosa

Carbone

D'Angelo

Elena Fucci

Giannattasio

Grifalco

Macarico

Mastrodomenico

Musto Carmelitano

Notaio

Parco dei Monaci

Paternoster

Re Manfredi

San Martino

Tenuta Le Querce

Terre degli Svevi

Villa Rotondo

Calabria

A collection of coiled grapevines grew in a spiral at the base of a hill at the Librandi family's Ponte Duca Sanfelice estate. In the cold January sun, the vines looked wild next to the tidy rows of Gaglioppo vines lining the surrounding hills, but they were there on purpose, explained Nicodemo Librandi. The cofounder of the Librandi winery began planting the vineyard in 1993 to study native Calabrian grapes. With help from the regional agricultural government agency, the experimental vineyard had become something of a living vine bank for the region. Today, the project has expanded to nine vineyards growing around two hundred native grapes. It's been invaluable for studying Magliocco Dolce, a red grape that goes into Librandi's "Magno Megonio." The velvety wine expresses black plums and cocoa nibs, a cuvée that is complex yet still able to complement seafood or 'nduja, a spicy spreadable sausage.

The night before visiting the vineyard, we checked in at a hotel in Cirò Marina, a beach town on Calabria's Ionian coast. An eerie quiet had fallen around the town; half of it looked like an abandoned construction site while the other half appeared to be hibernating for the winter. The next morning, we left the empty beaches and drove inland to the town of Cirò. In the distance, the Ionian Sea stretched out in a blue calm and lemon trees were full of fruit. Recent rains had turned the hills green, and it felt like a typical winter day in Northern California: sunny but crisp, the ocean and mountains never too far away.

For those of us who have tried Calabrian wine, the first bottle almost always comes from Cirò. The best-known wine zone in a little-known region, it makes up nearly half of the region's wine output. The twentieth century wasn't easy on Cirò's wine industry—or any industry in Calabria. In the 1960s, local growers were trapped in a quantity-over-quality cycle, selling fruit in bulk to co-ops. Cirò's main grape, Gaglioppo, was harvested underripe, yielding harsh wines that hurt Cirò's reputation. Gaglioppo's perceived faults were one of the reasons the Librandi family started growing Cabernet Sauvignon, Chardonnay, and Sauvignon Blanc, showing that this corner of southern Italy could compete in a global market. The strategy worked: "Gravello," a Gaglioppo–Cabernet Sauvignon blend; and "Critone," a Chardonnay–Sauvignon Blanc blend, helped international wine buyers become familiar with the region. Meanwhile, strong sales provided the financial resources to invest in native grape research. Today, the project is ongoing. According to Paolo Librandi, Nicodemo's son, the

Mantonico, Castiglione, and Greco Nero grapes also show a lot of promise.

Even with native grapes and a temperate climate, the region's potential is untapped. There are only about two hundred wineries in Calabria, and commercial successes have been limited to a handful of estates. In 2020, Calabria made just over 7.39 million gallons (280,000 hectoliters) of wine, the fourth-lowest yield in Italy (in comparison, that same year, Sicily made 117.9 million gallons—4.46 million hectoliters). From a wine-history perspective, however, Calabria is incredibly valuable and ancient. Some say Cirò is the modern-day incarnation of Krimisa, the wine the ancient Greeks used to toast Olympic athletes. When A16 opened in 2004, we took pride in pouring wines like Ippolito 1845's "Colli di Mancuso," a Cirò Rosso Superiore Riserva that carried the Gaglioppo grape's signature flavors of tomato leaf, dusty rose, and ripe strawberry. We could get only a few bottles into the restaurant at a time, but it was an important wine for us, an indication that there was much more to discover in Italy's deep south. There's a way to go until winemakers figure out the nuances of these grapes and how to best leverage their quality, but times are changing. There's promise in Calabria's hinterlands, areas once left fallow that are free of pesticide residue. And within Cirò, the next generation is taking over family farms, researching deeper into the past to rethink what Gaglioppo wines should taste like.

History

Some say you've never truly experienced Italy until you've been to the south and that you've never truly experienced the south until you've spent time in Calabria. Called "Italia" in the fifth century BC, Calabria *is* the original Italy. When the Greeks annexed Calabria as part of Magna Graecia (Greater Greece), they built cities along Calabria's Ionian coast, from Reggio Calabria at the southern tip of the region to Crotone and Sibari in the north. After the Greeks, Calabria was ruled by a who's who of Mediterranean powers, including the Romans, Byzantines, Arabs, Normans, Swabians, Spanish, and Bourbons. Remnants of the past are preserved in language: in a few pockets of Calabria, a Byzantine version of Greek is spoken, while descendants of Albanian refugees who fled the Balkans in the fifteenth century and resettled in Calabria and Basilicata speak Arbëresh. At the time of the Risorgimento (page 11) in the mid-nineteenth century, a hundred thousand people of Albanian heritage lived in Italy.

Starting in the fifteenth century, Spain ruled Calabria, introducing crops from the Americas such as tomatoes, potatoes, red peppers, and prickly pear. These ingredients grew easily in Calabria's hilly terrain and mild climate and became invaluable parts of the diet. Today, no regional cuisine in Italy is as fiery as Calabrese cooking, whether it's 'nduja or pickled Calabrian chiles, which spice up vegetables or fish. Other classic dishes include peppers and potatoes cooked and served together in simple, satisfying ways. For the most part, Calabrian wines can put up with heat, countering the burn of chiles with herbaceous tang.

An oft-told story about southern Italy is how Garibaldi freed Italians from the oppressive rule of outsiders, thus uniting Italy. Today, however, scholars are revisiting the official histories of southern regions after unification. The former view was that *latifondi*, large estates with a variety of crops and livestock, were run by absentee landowners who didn't have an interest in improving the local conditions. So when these estates were broken up, the local population benefited. That may have been true in some places, but many *latifondi* offered stability. The Barracco family, who owned a large *latifondo* in Calabria, exported olive oil, wool, and caciocavallo cheese and supported those who worked the land with steady employment and housing. When the Italian government broke up *latifondi* after unification, Calabria's economy collapsed. Nearly a million Calabrese left between the late nineteenth and early twentieth centuries, with the majority resettling in North and South America. Later, World War II further emptied out the towns. While quality of life started to improve in the 1960s, depopulation remains a problem today.

There were some bright spots after unification. In 1866, a new train route along the Ionian coast connected Reggio Calabria to Brindisi in Puglia, a breakthrough in transportation for southern Italy. Trains also helped haul grapes and bulk wine to areas farther north. After World War II, *autostrade* (highways) made it easier for Italians to get around their country. In the 1950s, Vincenzo Ippolito climbed into his Fiat and drove north, observing how the wine business was evolving in Tuscany and Piedmont. Farmers were starting to making their own wines and put their names on the bottle, so when he got back home, he vowed to do the same. In 1956, he bottled a Cirò Rosso and a Cirò Riserva, aging the latter in wooden casks, just like they did in Piedmont (today, the *riserva* is called "Ripe del Falco"). The estate's name—Ippolito 1845—indicates the year that the first Vincenzo Ippolito carved his initials and the date into a stone on the family house, marking the beginning of his family's farming story. But it wasn't until the mid-twentieth century that the family started bottling their own wine under their name.

For the most part, infrastructure in Calabria lagged behind northern regions. Inland areas remained isolated, and getting from one town to the next often required going by foot or mule. Some farmers stopped making local cheeses and wines because it was too hard to sell their products without access to paved roads. An *autostrada* connecting Calabria to Naples opened as recently as 1974, so it's no wonder that enological and viticultural breakthroughs were late to take root.

Land and Wines

In his history book *The Pursuit of Italy*, writer David Gilmour describes a moment in which Garibaldi's soldiers climb Aspromonte, a mountain in Reggio Calabria at the southern tip of the region, to collect snow as a refreshment. It's this proximity to the mountains and sea that gives Calabria its potential for great wine. If mainland Italy is a boot, Calabria is its toe. In the north, Campania shares the Pollino mountain range with Basilicata, while farther down, the Sila Mountains fill with skiers in the winter and mushroom foragers in the summer. At sea level, the coastline is endless, wrapping around the toe and touching both the Tyrrhenian and Ionian Seas. The region produces some of the best peppers, olive oil, and citrus fruit in Italy, and it's especially known for bergamot, the signature aroma in Earl Grey tea and many perfumes. The day–night temperature changes combined with the tempering effects of the sea can make parts of this region cooler than many expect this far south in Europe. (Though the coast *does* get hot: in Cirò Marina, temperatures can soar above 95°F/35°C in July and August.) In October, long after harvest is finished along the coast, it may just be getting started in the cooler hills. Drought is also a problem; while it rains more inland, the coast can go six months without rain, forcing vines to seek out water held in the soil.

Carved into five provinces, the region is half hills and nearly half mountains. The northern province of Cosenza has the Terre di Cosenza DOC, a sprawling area incorporating the Pollino Mountains, the Riviera dei Cedri along the Tyrrhenian coast to the west, and the Piana di Sibari, one of the few flat areas in the region, between the Pollino and Silla Mountains. Along the west coast, there are the Savuto and Lamezia DOCs, which face the Tyrrhenian Sea and have a mix of mountain and maritime influences. But most wines are made along the east coast facing the Ionian Sea—from Greco di Bianco, a small area dedicated to *passito* (dessert wine), to Cirò, by far the largest DOC in the region.

Calabria's best wines carry acidity and citrus notes, all of which pair well with the local, spicy food.

In many parts of Italy, you hear a common story: A family has a tradition of growing grapes. The next generation leaves the farm for university or work. Later, they come home, decide to reinvent the business, and start making wine with their family's grapes. In Piedmont, this happened a generation or two ago. In Calabria, it's happening now, and many who return focus on low-intervention wine. In Cirò, it's called *Cirò dei nonni*, wine made how their grandparents used to. Cataldo Calabretta studied winemaking in Milan and worked for other wineries before returning to Cirò with the intention of refurbishing the family business. Today, he harvests grapes manually, relies on spontaneous fermentation rather than commercial yeasts to ferment his wines, and minimizes the use of sulfur at bottling. Sergio Arcuri also takes a natural stance with Gaglioppo, growing the vines in the traditional *alberello* ("little tree") style, which gives Gaglioppo grown in a dry climate the best chance of surviving. Farmers can trim the vines so that extra leaves add shade, shielding grapes from the strong midday sun while the sturdy vines can withstand strong winds from the sea. (The wind also prevents mildew, so winemakers don't have to spray vines as often.) Acuri's "Aris," a Cirò aged in cement, is benchmark Gaglioppo, expressing cranberry, red plum, sage, and graphite.

The countryside exodus that left abandoned farms in its wake is now a benefit to winemakers looking for land unexposed to pesticides or herbicides. After learning how to make wine in southern Campania with winemakers like Bruno De Conciliis, former historian Dino Briglio returned to Calabria, starting L'Acino in the mountain town of San Marco Argentano with a couple of friends. They searched for underused plots of land next to the Pollino National Park, starting with 2.5 acres (1 hectare) of Mantonico grapes before gradually adding other plots of land, some with vines fifty to eighty years old once used by farmers to grow grapes for homemade wine. This was what Dino's grandfather did, and whatever he couldn't keep, he sold to friends, filling up a *damigiana* (demijohn) straight from the barrel. While Dino's friends have since moved on from L'Acino, Dino has slowly expanded vineyard land and planted more native grapes. Some of his vines grow ungrafted in sandy soils, where phylloxera can't spread as easily. He grows two different Magliocco grapes, making old-vine wines filled with notes of brambly berries, red currants, and forest floor. The clean soil and air of Calabria also attracted others, like Giampiero Ventura and Daniela De Marco, who started making low-intervention wine in 2015 at Pasquale Perugini's century-old farm under the label Masseria Perugini. "The lack of industries, which was a measure of our poverty, turned out to be a wealth for us," Briglio explains.

Still, nothing comes easy in Calabria. The 'Ndrangheta, a notorious organized crime syndicate from the region, is still active, and the region sees less investment in infrastructure than other parts of the country. Yet there's something about the new energy in Calabria today that reminds us of Campania in the 1990s—a pretty place with great food and great potential for wine. Campania now makes some of Italy's top white and red wines, and perhaps the same will be true for Calabria. For now, away from the spotlight, Calabrese winemakers are free to do their own thing.

Calabria Grapes

While the region grows several native white grapes, nearly three-fourths of the wine made here is red, and most of it includes Gaglioppo.

White

Greco Bianco

If you're drinking a white wine from Calabria, chances are it's one of many local white grapes called Greco "something," after the ancient Greeks. In other words, Greco Bianco is a source of profound confusion. We know Greco Bianco is not related to Greco grown in Campania (the one used in Greco di Tufo wines, page 63), nor is it the same as the Greco Bianco grown in Alto Piemonte (which is Erbaluce, page 149). There are also a handful of grapes called Greco Bianco within Calabria that aren't related. A little-known variety called Guardavalle is the "Greco Bianco" of the Bivongi DOC. But for the most part, the Greco Bianco we're talking about is the main grape of Cirò Bianco DOC, a white wine with fruity, fresh aromas that goes down easy. For wines that can age, turn to the Greco di Bianco DOC, an area on the Ionian coast south of Cirò that specializes in a honeyed *passito* (try a bottle from Ceratti). Actually, that grape may be a local biotype of Malvasia di Lipari (page 196) of Sicily's Aeolian Islands. The lesson is that since there are so many grapes called Greco Bianco, and most are distinctly different, it can take some digging to figure out exactly which Greco you're getting in the glass.

Mantonico Bianco

This might be Calabria's future white wine star. Thanks to high acidity, tannins, and resistance to drought, it is easy for farmers and winemakers to grow and like. Mantonico can make everything from lean, refreshing wine with key lime and honeysuckle aromatics to richer styles, carrying notes of ginger and tropical fruit, that would please Viognier fans.

It even makes good sweet wines. Mantonico grows along the Ionian coast as well as in pockets inland. L'Acino makes it in a couple of ways: blending it with Guarnaccia Bianca (the local name for Campania's Coda di Volpe grape, page 61) for "Chora," a fresh wine; and "Mantonicoz," a richer skin-contact wine made by macerating Mantonico grapes for a handful of days before pressing. After aging the wine on the lees (the spent yeast cells left after fermentation), the wine takes on a deeper flavor and hue.

Pecorello Bianco

The grape's name means "little sheep," and it's one of the region's more recently rediscovered native varieties, yielding refreshing herbal white wines. In the past decade, plantings have increased tenfold, with producers trying their hand at the high-acid grape. These are the wines to pair with the kinds of vegetable-driven dishes you want to eat straight from spring through early fall. Pecorello grapes have brighter acidity when grown in mountain areas and more salinity when grown on the coast.

Red

Castiglione

Grown around the toe of the region in Reggio Calabria and Cosenza, this little-known grape has thick skins and is primarily used for blending, though Paolo Librandi of the Librandi estate says it's one worth a closer look. (It's been growing in Librandi's experimental vineyards.) Ian D'Agata describes the grape in *Native Wine Grapes of Italy* as having thick skins and large fruit nearly black in color, though we've yet to try a pure Castiglione wine.

Gaglioppo

With a nose of summer-ripe tomatoes, oregano, and orange rind paired with flavors of cranberry and tart red cherries, this Mediterranean wine is easy to get hooked on. The most important red grape in Calabria, Gaglioppo also may be one of its oldest, going back to the time of the ancient Greeks. Its genetics show that it is a cross between Sangiovese and Mantonico, making us wonder if Sangiovese's origins come from farther south than Tuscany. It is slow ripening and high in acid and tannins, needing a long growing season and knowledgeable hands in the cellar to ensure its tannins don't overwhelm the wine. Yet these tannins allow Gaglioppo to age and evolve, giving the best versions of this wine a long life in the cellar. A lot of work is still being done to sort out the best Gaglioppo cuttings, since many vines were selected in the twentieth century for bulk wine production. Gaglioppo skews light in color; its wines evolve quickly from ruby red to garnet with age. As a wine, Gaglioppo exhibits fresh red fruit, earthiness, and a touch of citrus rind. The grape is also used in *rosati* to drink chilled with spicy Calabrese food. While Gaglioppo is grown all over Calabria, it's easiest to come across in Cirò, where it makes up 90 percent of the red wines produced.

Greco Nero

Greco Nero has the same issues as Greco Bianco: many unrelated grapes share this name. Greco Nero di Verbicaro is from the inland town of Verbicaro near the Sila National Park, while Greco Nero di Sibari comes from the coast. Unrelated to those specific grapes, Greco Nero from Cirò is occasionally blended with Gaglioppo, because it gives the Gaglioppo wines more color without adding tannins; Ippolito 1845 makes a deep-pink Greco Nero *rosato*. There are likely a lot more interesting things to find in the world of the Greco Neros, so we'll do as we do with the red Castiglione grape and keep an eye out.

Magliocco (Magliocco Dolce/Magliocco Tondo)

With tightly packed round berries and deeply purple skins, Magliocco makes wines that are silkier than Gaglioppo, with dark plum and cherry notes layered with spices and gentle tannins. With a long growing season, the grape yields wines imbued with blackberries and black cherries, which would please any lover of Malbec or Garnacha. The grape is grown all over Calabria under various names, most significantly Magliocco Tondo and Magliocco Dolce but also Arvino and Guarnaccia Nera, Terravecchia,

Merigallo, and Maglioccuni. It also shares its name with unrelated grapes, like Magliocco Canino. Going on decades, Librandi has made age-worthy "Magno Megonio," a wine made of Magliocco Dolce grown in limestone-clay soils near the Ionian coast. Magliocco Dolce is also an important grape in inland mountain areas of Lamezia Terme, where it yields more red-fruit flavors and minerality.

Magliocco Canino

Not as common as other Magliocco, Magliocco Canino is an inky-purple grape that imparts a good amount of color when used in red blends or alone for a deeply colored *rosato*. Grown primarily in between the provinces of Catanzaro and Cosenza, it's quite different from the better-known Magliocco. Its clusters are bigger and less compact, and it ripens a few weeks before the other Magliocco, with higher levels of acidity. Despite all this, the Ministry of Agriculture insists it's a synonym for Magliocco. To quietly protest this error, L'Acino makes a Magliocco Canino wine called "Ceci n'est pas un Magliocco" (French for "This is not a Magliocco"). Dino Briglio of L'Acino says his grandfather called the grape simply "Canino," and it was one of his most cherished varieties.

Zibibbo

(see Sicily chapter, page 196)

Regional Foods

Black olives

Calabrian chiles

Cheese
caciocavallo, aged cows' or goats' milk cheese

Caprino d'Aspromonte, aged goats' milk cheese

fior di latte, mozzarella made with cows' milk

pecorino, sheep's milk cheese
ricotta and *ricotta affumicata* (smoked ricotta)

Cipolle Rosse di Tropea
red Tropea onions

Citrus fruits
especially bergamot

Eggplant
agrodolce, a sweet-sour side dish

alla parmigiana with tomatoes, mozzarella, and Parmesan

fried

stuffed

Licorice

Mushrooms

'Nduja
spicy spreadable sausage

Olive oil

Pasta
cavatelli, curled pasta shaped by pressing and dragging fingers across the dough

lagane e cicciari, layered pasta of chickpeas, garlic, and parsley

lagane larghe, a ribbony pasta similar to tagliatelle

Pitta pizzulata
unleavened flatbread made with wine, eggs, pecorino, and crushed red pepper

Ragù made with pork

Seafood
tuna, sardines, and anchovies

Tomatoes

Zippuli
savory doughnuts filled with mozzarella and either anchovies or sardines

Recommended Producers

A Vita

Antonella Lombarda

Benvenuto

Cantina di Bova

Cantina Enotria

Cantine Viola

Caparra & Siciliani

Capoano

Casa Comerci

Cataldo Calabretta

Cerrati

Du Cropio

Ferrocinto

Feudo di Sanseverino

Giuseppe Calabrese

iGreco

Ippolito 1845

Iuzzolini

L'Acino

Lento

Librandi

Malaspina

Odoardi

Poderi Marini

Roberto Ceraudo

San Francesco

Scala

Sergio Arcuri

Serracavallo

Spiriti Ebbri

Statti

Terre del Gufo

Terre di Balbia

Zito

Campania

Separated from the Tyrrhenian Sea by a thin strip of land, Lago Fusaro is a coastal lagoon north of Naples. A half mile away, the Roman town of Baiae, once known for extravagant parties, wealth, and scandal, sits underwater. At some point, volcanic activity shifted the earth and submerged the Palm Beach of antiquity under the sea. The suburb of Bacoli sits between the lake and the underwater city, where the Di Meo family has made wine for five generations. Luigi Di Meo works in the vineyards, his forearms deeply tanned below the elbows. His son Vincenzo, the winemaker, and his wife live up the hill next to a Roman aqueduct. Climb up the hill and you can get an expansive view of Lago Fusaro. Turn and you'll see where Baiae sits submerged. There are so many houses and apartment buildings in between, it's a miracle there is room for vines. Campania has the largest population in southern Italy, and Naples is the third-largest city in the country. There are so many people here that even though Bacoli is under twenty miles away from the center of Naples, it can take two hours to get there with traffic.

It's here where the family grows Falanghina Flegrea and Piedirosso vines in the area's signature sandy soils. Some of the vineyards have a thermal underground river covered by a layer of *tufa giallo*, Neapolitan yellow tuff composed of volcanic rocks embedded with fragments of crystals, glass, and ash. The underground river is so close to the sea that it gives the wines what Vincenzo calls a *salata* quality, a note of salinity, and some of the vines are so old that their roots go as deep as the family's origins in Bacoli. Nearby sits a cluster of calderas (depressions formed after a volcanic eruption) called the Campi Flegrei, meaning "fiery fields." The area has shown signs of volcanic unrest since the 1950s, a frequent reminder that life can change in an instant around here. On our visit, we harvested San Marzano tomatoes in a garden with soil as loose as sand and ate them that night with fish, olive oil, herbs, and potatoes. Instead of tasting more Falanghina, though, the Di Meos opened a *metodo classico* Blanc de Morgex et de La Salle wine from Cave Mont Blanc in Valle d'Aosta and a bottle from Sicily made with the red grape Perricone. Under a trellis, we feasted, shared opinions about capers (the best, we agreed, are from Pantelleria), and celebrated la dolce vita—enjoying today because no one knows what can happen tomorrow.

There are times when Campania feels like one giant volcano. Eruptions over history have ended life—burying Pompeii, sinking Baiae—but have also preserved it, enriching soils for vine growing and preventing phylloxera from destroying vine roots. Relics from Campania's winemaking past are also integrated into its present, from vines growing on aqueducts to its *viti maritate*, a vine-training system inherited by the Etruscans. While Campania's wines were celebrated by the ancients, the industry was sidelined by twentieth-century industrial production. Yet this century, Campanian wine is in the hands of artisans who leverage their native-grape advantage with exciting results. Without Campania, Shelley may never have decided to dedicate the wine list at A16 to southern Italian wines. In fact, the restaurant A16 was named after the *autostrada* (highway) that cuts through the province of Avellino, where some of Campania's most prized wines are made. In 2004, when A16 opened, we knew the wines from Campania were special. Since then, they have only improved as more winemakers learn the nuances of Fiano, Piedirosso, Greco, Coda di Volpe, Casavecchia, and so many other revitalized native grapes.

Campania makes about 37 million gallons (1.4 million hectoliters) of wine a year, ranking eleventh in production: a little more than Trentino–Alto Adige and a little less than Lazio. More than half the wine made is red, but the region is best known for its native white grapes. Campania has long been a haven for vines, but it's only been in the past couple of decades that the region has gained the recognition it deserves for quality wine.

History

A stop along the Mediterranean trade route since ancient times, Campania has a long history of growing grapes and making wine. The ancient Greeks and Romans praised the wines made near Naples. At Pompeii, amphorae (terracotta vessels) buried in the ground offer evidence of how wine was stored before Vesuvius erupted in AD 79. Excavations in

Pompeii also unearthed a tavern advertising the wine Falernian (*Falernum* in Latin), a favorite of Pliny the Elder that spun off imitators. Believed to be from a vineyard on Mount Massico in northern Campania, Falernian is still a bit of a mystery; no one is quite sure what grapes were used and exactly where it was made. (And no one knows whether the tavern served actual Falernian or a counterfeit.)

During the Middle Ages, Campania continued to make quality wine to sell abroad. In the eleventh century, the wealthy Republic of Amalfi traded its Tramonti wine far and wide, and the Amalfi coast retained its epicurean values long after the republic's fall. In the seventeenth and eighteenth centuries, under the rule of the Bourbons, Naples grew to half a million people, and by the nineteenth century, Naples was the third-largest city in Europe after London and Paris. The city had a grand opera house, and the royal summer palace in Caserta was compared to Versailles. By 1855, a few years before the founding of the new Kingdom of Italy, Naples was booming. Neapolitan trade with Britain was three times that of other Italian states combined. Neapolitans built the first railroad and first suspension bridge on mainland Italy. At a time when Rome was still dark at night, Naples's narrow streets were illuminated with gas lighting. Amid the wealth were also thousands of poor citizens who lived without kitchens and got by eating pasta and pizza made on the street.

After unification in 1861, Naples lost its footing in international trade, so Campanians adapted, sharing their foods throughout the new Kingdom of Italy. Methods for cooking tomatoes, boiling spaghetti, frying anchovies, and baking pizza spread north. Among these foods, the pizza margherita is the most recognizable: A world-famous combination of tomato, basil, and mozzarella baked on thinly stretched dough, the pizza was invented by a local Neapolitan to honor his queen (though it's unlikely she ever tried it). Even before unification, Campanian cooks documented their work. In his book *A Mediterranean Feast*, Clifford A. Wright mentions *brodecto de li dicti pisci*, a recipe published in an anonymous fifteenth-century southern

Italian cookbook that called for boiling sardines and anchovies in "*vino greco*." Exactly what this "greco" wine was is impossible to say, though the old recipe shows that food and wine have been taken seriously in Campania for centuries.

In the second half of the twentieth century, Campania was stuck, like much of the south, in a cycle of growing grapes for the bulk wine market as the region recovered from World War II. In the 1950s, Antonio Mastroberardino was one of the few wine-makers giving native grapes any attention, caring for Aglianico and Fiano vines instead of planting international varieties. In the 1990s, though, more winemakers began to recognize the potential of native grapes and land. Forgotten varieties from Caserta were studied, and families in the Avellino hills began to give Fiano and Aglianico more attention. With the rediscovery and tending of its native grapes, Campania has emerged as a treasure trove of white grapes such as Asprinio d'Aversa, Biancolella, Pallagrello Bianco, Coda di Volpe, Greco di Tufo, Fiano, and two distinct types of Falanghina. The reds are also memorable, especially Aglianico, but also Piedirosso, Casavecchia, and Pallagrello Nero, all of which are notable for delivering site-specific wines that reflect the soil and microclimates of Campania.

Land and Wines

Campania has five provinces: Napoli, Caserta, Benevento, Avellino, and Salerno. Along the coast, the province of Napoli makes up islands and small peninsulas that are connected by ferries crisscross-ing the Gulf of Naples. The northern coasts have the volcanic soils of Campi Flegrei, where Falanghina and Piedirosso thrive, while to the east—next to Mount Vesuvius—fertile farmland spreads out for growing San Marzano tomatoes. East of Naples, the Avellino province encompasses the forested Irpinian hills. Here, it's noticeably cooler than on

the coast, with wider shifts in temperatures from day to night. North of Avellino, the Benevento and Caserta provinces grow grapes that are rarely found anywhere else.

Coastal Campania, including Amalfi, Vesuvius, Campi Flegrei, and the islands

Vesuvius is one of Campania's most recogniz-able sites as well as one of Campania's oldest wine regions. Winemaker Andrea Matrone of Cantine Matrone can trace his family's roots on the volcano to the eighteenth century. Though it hasn't erupted since 1944, the volcano is still active. The key for opti-mal grape growth after an eruption is how the lava cools. When it cools quickly, it turns to sand, cre-ating soil that can be planted with vines for wines that have elegance and minerality. But when it cools slowly, it hardens and crystalizes, making it impos-sible to replant in the same place. Fortunately for Matrone, the family land has plenty of the former type of terrain, which is where he plants Piedirosso for the estate's Lacryma Christi del Vesuvio Rosso. A handful of other grapes grow amid the volcanic soil of Vesuvius, the most notable being Coda di Volpe, Falanghina, and Aglianico.

West and south of Naples, the Gulf of Naples and the Amalfi Coast offer postcard-perfect vistas of rocky beaches and villas growing citrus trees and herbs. A short ferry ride from Naples, the island of Ischia has been recognized for wine since the time of the ancient Greeks. Like so much of Campania, it is rich in volcanic rock, though its specific kind of rock—green tuff—is unique to the island, giving Ischia's white wines (made with Biancolella and Forastera grapes) refreshing minerality. Along the Amalfi Coast and on Capri, white wines are also made with blends of local grapes: Fenile, Ginestra, and Ripoli. Some of these wines can be quite spe-cial, such as "Fiorduva" from the Marisa Cuomo estate in Furore, where pergola-trained vines shel-ter grapes from the strong winds and sun. The wine itself has austere minerality balanced by layers of nectarine, apricot, orange blossoms, and lemon pith. Inland from the coast, the hilly town of Tramonti, set against the Lattari Mountains, also uses pergolas to grow its Tintore di Tramonti vines, some of which are among Campania's oldest (see Tintore di Tramonti, page 64). On the other side of the mountains, the town of Gragnano has a namesake sparkler, a cheerful wine made with Piedirosso, Aglianico, and the local grape Sciascinoso. Low in alcohol and high in acid, it is near perfect with pizza.

South of Amalfi, the large province of Salerno includes Cilento, home to Paestum, a famous site of ancient Greek temples, and excellent mozzarella di bufala. Here, the mild climate and calcareous-clay soils are best for red and *rosato* production, though sparkling wine, like De Conciliis's "Selim," made with Aglianico and Fiano, and Casebianche's "La Matta," made with Fiano, show that Cilento can also yield brisk, mouthwatering bubbles.

Avellino, including Fiano di Avellino, Greco di Tufo, and Taurasi

East of Naples, the hills of Avellino are cooler and rainier, and it snows at higher elevations. Compared to the Mediterranean vistas from the Amalfi Coast, here the landscape is green and filled with forests of chestnut and oak trees. The food is also different from coastal cuisine: instead of seafood, pork and rabbit are typical, as are caciocavallo cheeses, salumi, and rich ragùs. It's here where you'll find Campania's best-known wines: Taurasi (named after the town of Taurasi), Fiano di Avellino (named after the province of Avellino), and Greco di Tufo (named after the town of Tufo). Many top winemakers make them all, harvesting Greco first, Fiano after, and Aglianico as late as early December—sometimes in the snow. (Pietracupa, Vadiaperti, I Favati, Quintodecimo, Benito Ferrara, and Clelia Romana make all three.) Vineyards in the Irpinian hills have a mix of hard limestones, sand and marl, clay, and, in some places, ashes from Vesuvius. Taurasi's pockets of volcanic soil have protected Aglianico vines from phylloxera, some of the vines are more than a century old (see Aglianico, page 63). Meanwhile, the town of Tufo has veins of sulfur in its limestone soils, further adding nuance to the Greco wines from here. When enology professor Luigi Moio of the University of Naples and his wife decided to start Quintodecimo, they picked the Irpinian hills because the area reminded Moio of parts of France where winemakers lived among their vines. With the concentration of quality vineyards, grapes, and makers, Avellino's wines are only getting better.

Northern Campania, including Benevento, Caserta, and Aversa

North of Avellino in the province of Benevento, Mount Taburno has soils that are similar to Taurasi's. However, the climate can be rainier, creating more restrained Aglianico with higher acidity. The broader Taburno IGT designation encompasses a wide range of native grapes, such as Pallagrello Bianco, Casavecchia, and Coda di Pecora. North of Taburno, the Sannio area borders Molise, with limestone and sandstone soils conducive to growing a range of grapes, from Coda di Volpe and Fiano to Aglianico. To the west, the Caserta province is home of the Falerno del Massico DOC, which some believe is the origin of the ancient wine Falernian. Here, the climate is mostly warm and dry. Closer to the city of Caserta, the commune of Aversa specializes in Asprinio, a white variety that is "married" to trees, a method called *viti maritate*.

Campania white wines can be fruity and near decadent or rich in minerals and acidity. The reds range from simple table wines served chilled to big reds that are best after several years of aging. In between, there's a wide range to choose from, many from grapes that don't grow anywhere else. For wine drinkers who feel stuck trying the same bottles, exploring Campanian wines will break anyone out of a rut.

Campania Grapes

With few international varieties grown in the region, Campania is all about native grapes, especially its wide range of white varieties.

White

Asprinio

Some jokes could be made about drinking Asprinio for a headache in place of aspirin—or taking aspirin after drinking too much Asprinio. In truth, you're unlikely to come across enough Asprinio for either situation. When you do find a bottle of Asprinio d'Aversa, expect it to be lean and crisp, with notes of lemon, and drink it young. It comes from the Caserta province, where the Asprinio d'Aversa DOC is dedicated to the grape. Because the vines are trained up trees, harvest requires ladders. Producer Nanni-Copé's "Polveri della Scarrupata" Fiano wine adds a splash of Asprinio to the blend for acidity. On its own, the grape makes tart, low-alcohol wines, the kind that are thirst quenching on hot summer days. Sparkling Asprinio is also made, though bottles can be hard to track down.

Biancolella

Biancolella is, plainly, one of our favorite grapes. It may be that when we think about the variety, we can't help but envision Ischia, a beautiful island in the Gulf of Naples. Biancolella expresses these surroundings with mineral, saline complexity in the best bottles. Cultivated on steep hillsides made of green tuff (a volcanic rock unique to the island), the vineyards are close to the sea, and the heroics it takes to work harvest here—picking by hand on steep slopes—belie easy-to-love Biancolella wines. Another reason we love Biancolella may come down to Pasquale Cenatiempo, whose family goes back so many generations on the island that he estimates they were originally Greek. His Biancolella wines are filled with notes of ripe stone fruit followed by a zesty finish, the kind of thoughtful bottles to open with fish or rabbit, both common meals on the island. Typically vinified without skin contact and in stainless steel, these wines yield bright flavors of white flowers and citrus with underlying notes of salt. For Ischia Bianco DOC wines, Biancolella is blended with Forastera (page 63) and occasionally hyperlocal grapes, like San Lunardo. (Producer Casa d'Ambra was the first to document the San Lunardo grape,

which could be related to Biancolella.) Biancolella is also grown on Capri, the Amalfi Coast, and the Sorrentine peninsula, where it is used in blends.

Coda di Pecora

Grown primarily for Terre del Volturno IGT wines, Coda di Pecora is unrelated to Coda di Volpe, and it's rare, even in Campania. Il Verro makes a Coda di Pecora wine called "Sheep" (the name of the grape means "sheep's tail"), and it's an herbal, fresh wine, with an elegant bouquet recalling thyme, sage, and citrus peel. A glass of it is a perfect start to a southern Italian meal of vegetables and seafood.

Coda di Volpe

The name Coda di Volpe—tail of a fox—is catchy and practical: it describes the shape of the grape's bunches, which have a cute curve at the bottom. More important to know for wine drinkers is that the grape mirrors its surroundings, adapting to volcanic or calcareous soils and different climates with ease. Coda di Volpe becomes leaner with delicate aromas when grown in cool areas with volcanic soils or ripe with tropical fruit notes when grown in warmer climates with richer soils. The grape is used in the northeast Sannio DOC as well as the Irpinia DOC, and it's one of many white varieties permitted in Lacryma Christi Bianco, a blended wine from Mount Vesuvius. Some find that Coda di Volpe ages remarkably well, putting the variety in company with Fiano and Greco, Campania's other age-worthy white wines. In Castelfranci, Michele Perillo makes a fresh but intense Coda di Volpe from eighty-plus-year-old vines, expressing citrus, wet stone, and stone fruit, while Vadiaperti makes high-altitude Coda di Volpe that also carries the grape's signature wet stone nuance accented with honey.

Costa d'Amalfi Bianco Grapes: Fenile, Ginestra, Pepella, and Ripoli

For its small size, popular tourist destination the Amalfi Coast is home to an incredible amount of grape biodiversity. White wines from around the towns of Positano, Furore, Amalfi, Ravello, and Tramonti are made by blending grapes grown only there. While each grape is a little different—for example, Ginestra, named after the wildflower it resembles in color and aroma, is vigorous and Ripoli is not—the grapes are at their best when grown close to the sea in a dry, temperate climate. Look for these grapes in the Costa d'Amalfi Bianco wines, such as San Francesco's "Per Eva," a blend of Falanghina, Ginestra, and Pepella from the estate's Vigna dei Preti (Priests' Vineyard) located in the Tramonti DOC, and Marisa Cuomo's Costa d'Amalfi DOC. The best of these wines bring to mind freesia, white peach, green almonds, and wet rock, making them perfect with coastal Mediterranean meals.

Falanghina Group

One of the most popular white wines from Campania, Falanghina is made of two unrelated grapes. Some link the name to the ancient wine Falernian, though the connection has yet to be proven. Luigi Moio, an enology professor at the University of Naples who makes wine at his Quintodecimo estate, has long championed Falanghina, a grape his father grew in Falerno (the wine zone named after Falernian). It is hard to differentiate between the two types, since most bottles simply say "Falanghina" on the label. Either will appeal to those who love Sauvignon Blanc, thanks to the wines' high acidity and herbal, green accents.

- **Falanghina Beneventana:** Benevento Falanghina is grown throughout northern Campania. It was differentiated from the other Falanghina in the 1970s by Leonardo Mustilli, who believed his vines were different from Falanghina on the coast. With high acidity, notes of apple and apricot, and hints of mint, it's used in the DOCs of Falanghina del Sannio and Falerno del Massico. Genetically, it has more in common with Biancolella.

- **Falanghina Flegrea:** Grown in Campi Flegrei, Capri, Falerno del Massico, and the Sorrentine peninsula, Falanghina Flegrea makes an excellent aperitivo wine, with zesty citrus and herbal flavors mixed with green apple. The

La Sibilla estate grows ungrafted Falanghina Flegrea vines in the sandy soils of Campi Flegrei, and the result is a complex Falanghina wine with deep golden color and notes of white flowers, ripe apple, and citrus zest.

Fiano

With its near-perfect balance of acidity, minerality, and body, Fiano is—without hyperbole—one of the world's best white wine grapes. A glass of Fiano can evoke hazelnuts and honey or taste like pears and flint. The wines can be dry, sweet, earthy, or even smoky, all balanced by minerality. A well-made Fiano can age for years. Folklore attributes its discovery to the Greeks. The legend goes that the vine was found near the Sabato River in present-day Avellino and taken as a sign from the god Dionysus. Even so, the variety was nearly lost in the twentieth century thanks to phylloxera and changes in fashion. Fortunately, the Mastroberardino family, who had made wine in the Avellino hills for centuries, kept the heritage vine alive.

While Fiano grows well in other parts of southern Italy, it's synonymous with Avellino. Within the Fiano di Avellino DOCG, variations in soils and microclimates yield a range of Fiano styles, yet all offer acidity and body. In general, the towns of Cesinali and Santo Stefano del Sole in the southern part of Avellino make lighter-bodied wines while in northern Avellino around the town of Summonte the wines are richer. In some pockets, volcanic ash gives wines a smoky quality. The Clelia Romano estate takes advantage of its historic vineyards around the village of Lapio that some called Fiano's *grand cru*. These are elegant, layered white wines that make the most of fruit, acidity, and minerality. Meanwhile, the I Favati estate makes Fiano di Avellino with notes of lemon, pear, and white flowers while Ciro Picariello's Fiano di Avellino wines have notes of citrus and green apple. Picariello also takes advantage of Fiano's natural acidity to make a small amount of the delicious sparkling wine "Brut Contadino." (In 2014, Veuve Clicquot asked Picariello to change his orange label for "Brut Contadino" because the parent company of the Champagne house felt it was too similar to its label's signature hue. This only served in bringing more attention to the wine.)

Forastera

Grown on the islands of Ischia and Procida, and also in a small amount on the mainland, Forastera is a coastal grape that benefits from sea breezes to keep it free of vine diseases, like bunch rot. When blended with Biancolella for wines such as Ischia Bianco, it offers a savory counterpoint to complement the Biancolella's easygoing citrus flavors.

Greco

Italy has several wine grapes named "Greco," a tribute to their presumed link to the ancient Greeks, yet most Grecos have nothing in common. For instance, the Greco of Campania has nothing to do with Greco Bianco of Calabria (page 53). While Greco grows throughout Campania, it's most associated with the town of Tufo in Avellino. When grown in limestone and clay soils, Greco yields elegant and nutty wines, and when grown in sandier soils, it imparts more exuberant aromas. Benito Ferrara's "Vigna Cicogna" is a benchmark Greco di Tufo, showcasing Bosc pear, green almond, white pepper, and rosemary combined with brisk acidity and talcum powder–like minerality. The Greco di Tufo from Sabino Loffredo at Pietracupa is another favorite, with soaring acidity (think of biting into a gooseberry), and notes of lemon peel, white grapefruit, and golden apple.

Pallagrello Bianco

In the 1990s, Alberto Barletta and Peppe Mancini founded the Vestini Campagnano estate to focus on the development of rare, native grapes rediscovered in the region. Together, the two rehabilitated Pallagrello Bianco (as well as the red grapes Pallagrello Nero and Casavecchia) with some help from enologist Luigi Moio. While Mancini left the estate in 2003 to create Terre del Principe with Manuela Piancastelli, both estates still focus on those rare native grapes. Part of the intrigue behind Pallagrello Bianco, Pallagrello Nero, and Casavecchia comes from history: during Bourbon rule, these were the varieties planted at the royal

palace in Caserta. Then the grapes were nearly lost due to phylloxera, war, and wine trends. Today, several producers around Caserta grow the varieties in the area's mix of sand, clay, and volcanic ash soils. Its name comes from the local dialect term for "small ball," since the grapes are round and small. Pallagrello makes aromatic and bright wines, though if the fruit is harvested too ripe, the wines can be flabby. A good Pallagrello Bianco, like the version from Alois, is filled with notes of apples and pears with a smooth finish. It can handle meals with a lot of spice or chiles, which can often be tricky for pairings. Pallagrello Bianco wines most often fall under the Terre del Volturno IGT.

Red

Aglianico

If Fiano is one of Italy's best white grapes, then Aglianico is one of Italy's best reds. The old story was that the grape came from the Greeks, though others dispute that claim. Regardless of its origin, Aglianico has grown in Campania for centuries and continues to be the most-planted grape in the region. Some of the oldest vines in Italy are the Patriarchs, treelike ungrafted Aglianico vines in Taurasi dating back more than 150 years. Owned by the Feudi di San Gregorio estate, the vines are being studied by Attilio Scienza, professor of viticulture at the University of Milan, and Luigi Moio, professor of viticulture at the University of Naples, to glean more about the region's viticulture history.

Aglianico wines range from medium bodied (especially when blended with Piedirosso) to weighty and tannic. While it is grown in coastal areas, it is best suited for inland, where it ripens slower, creating wines rich in black fruit, black pepper, and leather. Around Taurasi, harvest can be as late as the end of November or even early December. All Taurasi vineyards have a decent amount of altitude, but Aglianico from Taurasi's lower elevations tends to be the ripest and highest in alcohol, while that from higher elevations is higher in acid. Luigi Tecce makes distinctive Taurasi from eighty-year-old vines at the high-altitude farm that was once his grandfather's. His wines—with notes of blackberry, mission figs, mint, licorice, leather, and red currants—show his affinity for the land that he is dedicated to preserve. Taburno is also an important Aglianico growing area. Its calcareous and sandstone soils yield wines with more acidity, less power, and a more savory flavor than Taurasi.

All DOCG Aglianico wines benefit from aging. Concentrated and structured, they are the kind of wine to pair with a rich ragù or braised meatballs. Young Aglianico has more mint and black pepper, while older Aglianico gradually unveils gravelly, mineral notes.

Casavecchia

Named for the old house where the grape was rediscovered in the early twentieth century, Casavecchia was one of three heritage grapes from Caserta brought back into circulation through the efforts of the Vestini Campagnano estate in the 1990s. Casavecchia isn't an easy grape to grow. Its bunches allow for a lot of space between the grapes, and the sizes of the grapes also vary. Some wonder if the grape still has too rustic of a finish or not enough acid, while others think the tannins have an attractive smoothness.

The variety has its own DOC: Casavecchia di Pontelatone, which is where the Alois estate is located. Look for Casavecchia wines from Alois, Il Verro, I Viticoltori del Casavecchia, Terre del Principe, and Vestini Campagnano.

Pallagrello Nero

Despite the name, this grape is unrelated to Pallagrello Bianco, though both grow in the same area around Caserta thanks to the initiatives started by the Vestini Campagnano estate in the 1990s (see Pallagrello Bianco, page 63). It is a vigorous vine that yields thick-skinned, sweet grapes, and its wines are all about ripe fruit, with notes of black cherry and blackberry. Compared with Casavecchia, it's the more aromatic grape, though the two are often together. Among other producers in Caserta, Vestini Campagnano, Alois, and Il Verro make pure

Pallagrello Nero wine while Nanni-Copé's "Sabbie di Sopra il Bosco" Terre del Volturno IGT is mostly Pallagrello Nero, with a touch of Aglianico and Casavecchia.

Piedirosso

The grape's name means "red foot" and refers to its stem, which resembles the red feet of rock pigeons. Vincenzo Di Meo of La Sibilla says that when the stems turn red, the grapes are ready to harvest. After Aglianico, Piedirosso is the most important local red variety of Campania, thriving in coastal areas and in volcanic soil.

It is common in Aglianico blends, where it helps round out the other grape's tannins, and it plays a significant role in the red wines from Mount Vesuvius. There, winemaker Andrea Matrone of Cantine Matrone is training Piedirosso in an *alberello* ("little tree") style inspired by what he saw on Etna. An ancient variety, Piedirosso is also one of the grapes Mastroberardino is using to restore the vineyards at the archaeological site of Pompeii.

On its own, the grape makes medium-bodied wines with gentle tannins and a spicy, strawberry or red berry character. It's a versatile red wine that pairs with a range of meals, from vegetables and seafood to meat. Near the Amalfi coast, Piedirosso is used in a sparkling wine called Gragnano, named for the town from which it comes. Blended with Aglianico and other local grapes, such as Sciascinoso, Gragnano is the perfect pizza wine and best served chilled.

Tintore di Tramonti

In the Lattari Mountains up the coast from Amalfi, the town of Tramonti has grown Tintore for as long as anyone can remember. Vines from the Monte di Grazia estate run by Alfonso Arpino and his children, Olivia and Fortunato, may be up to three hundred years old. The family bought the property around the turn of the twentieth century, and the vines were already old by then. It's hard to determine their age because of the unique way they grow. The mother vine sends out branches, which farmers

train overhead in a tall pergola style. Instead of pruning the branches when they get too long, they bury the tips, causing a new vine to grow. Over time, the pergola becomes a web of new and old vines growing together. Centuries ago, vines were grown this way so farmers could use the space under the vines to grow vegetables or graze livestock. Today it's still the best way to grow Tintore in Tramonti, since the area can get strong winds and the stable pergola structure protects the vines.

Tintore makes a dark, deep-purple wine with jammy, spicy accents and high levels of acidity. Somewhat reminiscent of Amarone, Tintore can be filled with notes of black plum, maraschino cherry, and dried fig. Tintore is also found in the Colli Salerno DOC wines as well as the Campania IGT, where it's blended with Piedirosso.

Regional Foods

Anchovies

Bruschetta
toasted or grilled bread topped with tomato, anchovy, and/or mozzarella

Cheese
caciocavallo, aged cows' or goats' milk cheese

fior di latte, mozzarella made with cows' milk

mozzarella di bufala, buffalo milk mozzarella

pecorino, sheep's milk cheese

provolone, a mild cows' milk cheese used in many baked dishes

ricotta and *ricotta salata* (salted ricotta)

scamorza, semisoft cows' milk cheese

Chestnuts

Coniglio all' Ischitana
rabbit in the style of Ischia, braised with tomato, wine, garlic, and chile

Gelato

Hazelnuts

Insalata caprese
salad of sliced mozzarella, tomato, and basil

Minestra maritata
a soup of greens and meatballs

Pasta
capellini, angel-hair pasta

bucatini, like spaghetti but hollow inside

linguine, often served with clams (*vongole*)

maccaronara, thick, chewy fresh strands

paccheri, large, hollow tubes

spaghetti, often served with anchovies and/or tomatoes

tubetti, small tubes

Pizza alla napoletana
thin-crust pizza cooked for only ninety seconds in a hot oven

Polpettone alla napoletana
Neapolitan meatloaf filled with egg

Ragù alla napoletana
meat simmered for hours in a rich tomato sauce; the sauce is used to dress pasta, and the meat is eaten separately

San Marzano tomatoes

Sfogliatelle
flaky cone-shaped pastry filled with sweetened ricotta and candied orange

Sfusato limone di Amalfi
aromatic, not-too-tart lemon from Amalfi

Timballo
an elaborate filled and baked pasta dish that varies from maker to maker

Torta di verdure
vegetable pie with ricotta and eggs binding the vegetable filling

Recommended Producers

Coastal Campania, including Amalfi, Vesuvius, Campi Flegrei, and islands

Agnanum

Bosco de' Medici

Cantine Astroni

Cantine Farro

Cantine Matrone

Casa d'Ambra

Cenatiempo

Contrada Salandra

Farro

Federiciane Monteleone

Giuseppe Apicella

Iovine

La Rivolta

La Sibilla

Marisa Cuomo

Monte di Grazia

Olivella

Pietratorcia

Reale

San Francesco

Tommasone

Villa Dora

Cilento

Casebianche

De Conciliis

San Salvatore

Tempa di Zoè

Avellino, including Fiano di Avellino, Greco di Tufo, Taurasi

Antonio Caggiano

Benito Ferrara

Boccella

Cantine Lonardo

Ciro Picariello

Clelia Romano

D'Antiche

Di Prisco

Feudi di San Gregorio

Giardino

Guastaferro

Guido Marsella

I Favati

Il Tufiello

La Rivolta

Lonardo

Luigi Tecce

Mastroberardino

Ognostro

Perillo

Pietracupa

Quintodecimo

Rocca del Principe

Salvatore Molettieri

Sarno 1860

Stefania Barbot

Tenuta Ponte

Torricino

Vadiaperti

Northern Campania, including Benevento, Caserta, and Aversa

Alois

Bellus

Cantina del Taburno

Capolino Perlingieri

Crapareccia

Felicia

Fontanavecchia

Gaia Felix

Galardi

I Cacciagalli

I Pentri

I Viticoltori del Casavecchia

Il Verro

La Rivolta

Luigi Maffini

Montevetrano

Mustilli

Nanni-Copé

Nifo-Sarrapochiello

Perlingieri Poderi Foglia

Quintale

Terre del Principe

Terre Stregate

Venditti

Vestini Campagnano

Villa Carafa

Villa Matilde

Emilia-Romagna

Country roads wrap around the Colli Piacentini, a ruffle of hills crossed by rivers on the far-west side of Emilia-Romagna. It's only an hour to Milan, but it feels like a different planet, with hamlets scattered among the hillsides. In the spring, the hills are emerald green, and by summer, insects hover in the middle of the road, unbothered by traffic. A short drive away, the Trebbia River slices through the Apennine foothills. Locals say Ernest Hemingway called Val Trebbia the prettiest valley in the world, though exactly when and where he may have written it we couldn't say. From the city of Piacenza, it's not far to the Ligurian coast. The Via Aemilia, the old Roman road that runs through Emilia-Romagna, links the west side of the Italian peninsula to the east. The region's main *autostrada* runs parallel to it, and, without traffic, it's only three hours to Rimini, a city on the far-east side of Emilia-Romagna along the Adriatic.

Over the past several centuries, winemaking in Piacenza's hills has been influenced by everyone from the ancient Ligurians and Romans to the French. Pinot Nero (Pinot Noir), Merlot, and Cabernet Sauvignon have grown here for at least a couple of centuries. In the nineteenth century, Giancarlo Ageno, a lawyer from Genoa, founded the

La Stoppa estate and planted Merlot, Marsanne, and Pinot Nero. In the 1970s, Rafael Pantaleoni bought the estate and added the Italian grapes Barbera and Croatina with guidance from the viticulture university in Piacenza. Gradually, though, La Stoppa shifted its focus from French to Italian varieties. In 1980, Giulio Armani came from the university to work as a winemaker. A decade later, Elena Pantaleoni joined the estate after her father passed away, working with Giulio to rethink what a wine from Colli Piacentini should taste like. Pinot Nero was a lovely grape, but maybe not for their area, they decided. They then decided to concentrate on Barbera, Croatina, and the white grape Malvasia di Candia Aromatica.

The Emilia side of Emilia-Romagna is best known for *frizzante* wines—mainly Lambrusco—but La Stoppa's soils are more suited for still production. Inspired by the oxidized style of winemaking of the Jura, a region in France known for deep golden *vin jaune* (yellow wine), Pantaleoni and Armani began letting Malvasia grape skins stay with the wine for longer stretches of time before removing them. The experiments led to "Ageno," a skin-contact Malvasia-based wine named after the estate's founder. (Skin-contact white wines are also called orange wines; see page 84.) When Pantaleoni introduced the wine in 2003, most people thought she was crazy; today, the wine is an iconic skin-contact white, a perfect balance of tannins and savory sweetness. Armani also started his own label, Denavolo, bringing forth more skin-contact white wines and honing the identity of Colli Piacentini wines.

Skin-contact white wines are not unique to Emilia-Romagna, but their spread in the region shows the character of a place that is known for progressive experimentation. Once praised by Mussolini for its loyalty to fascism, Emilia-Romagna went to the other extreme after World War II, becoming known for its strong communist leanings. Its capital, Bologna, was called the buckle of Italy's red belt, and today it remains one of the country's most progressive cities. Thanks to its prosperous cities, flat land, and proximity to Milan, Emilia-Romagna also became one of Italy's wealthiest regions. Modena became a hub for the automotive industry and is still home to exotic car makers such as Ferrari. Some of the region's most innovative winemakers had other careers at first, taking up winemaking as a hobby.

Go to Barolo and people have expectations. Go to the Colli Piacentini or other places in Emilia-Romagna not known for Lambrusco, and outsiders don't know enough about the wines to have strong opinions or question experimental styles. Even Lambrusco, the region's calling card, has been tinkered with as more winemakers return to making it the old-fashioned way, letting it finish fermenting in the bottle. Without the scrutiny of rating systems or fear of financial risks, winemakers have been able to push Emilia-Romagna to the forefront of Italy's winemaking experimentation.

History

Although joined with a hyphen, Emilia and Romagna differ in history and culture. While remnants of ancient Rome are everywhere, particularly in Romagna, both sides went down different paths after the fall of Rome. Following the decline of the Byzantine Empire, Romagna and a few places in Emilia became part of the Papal States, a collection of territories controlled by the pope. The territories remained unsettled, with constant battles among the interests of the Papacy, the Venetians, and powerful families such as the Malatestas of Rimini. There were some bright spots under papal rule: in the Middle Ages, Bologna established a university, now the oldest in the Western world. Meanwhile, Emilia's eastern cities prospered, with productive, large-scale farms. During the Renaissance, the crafts of making prosciutto, Parmigiano-Reggiano, and Lambrusco became established in cities along the Po River, and after the Renaissance, Emilia made advances in farming. In the seventeenth century, the Po River basin became one of the first farming areas in north-central Italy to phase out sharecropping, using paid day laborers instead. Meanwhile, the arts flourished. Born in the village of Busseto in Parma in the early nineteenth century, Giuseppe Verdi became *il maestro della rivoluzione italiana*, the man who made the soundtrack to Italy's unification movement.

In 1860, when Garibaldi was waging battles to unite Italy, commercial Lambrusco production started in earnest. After serving his own wine at his restaurant Osteria dell'Artigliere in Modena for a decade, Cleto Chiarli began putting the wine in bottles and letting it finish fermenting there to capture the bubbles. The company evolved into Chiarli 1860, adopted the metodo Martinotti method (see Italy's Sparkling Wines, page 262), and grew into the largest privately owned producer of Lambrusco. At the turn of the twenty-first century, the family went back to its roots with a new company called Cleto Chiarli. Today, their signature bottle is Lambrusco di

Sorbara del Fondatore, with Lambrusco fermented in the bottle, just like their founder had once done.

There were business reasons to return to an artisanal approach with Lambrusco. In the early 1980s, three out of every ten bottles of wine imported into the United States came from Emilia (and most of it was sweet Lambrusco). But by the late 1980s, Lambrusco had lost market share to wine coolers and other beverages, and the wine had become the butt of jokes. In Burton Anderson's 1980 book *Vino*, a Tuscan winemaker quipped: "Americans gave us Italians Coca-Cola and now we're repaying the debt with Lambrusco." Yet in Emilia, Lambrusco has always been the favorite daily wine, appreciated for how its deep-purple froth and slight bitterness cleanse the palate. And while some argue that the *amabile* (sweet) Lambrusco was made solely to export, the truth is that some Lambrusco fermented the old way could be slightly sweet on occasion. Today, though, most artisanal Lambruscos have a bone-dry finish.

There's more to Emilia-Romagna bubbles than Lambrusco. Nearly every part of Emilia and some areas in Romagna make sparkling wines. In some places, it's because of the soil. Massimiliano Croci, who makes sparkling wine in the Val d'Arda in the Colli Piacentini, believes the lack of nitrogen in his vineyard soil makes fermentation more difficult. Stuck fermentations (when wines stop fermenting midway through) resulted in sugars and yeasts remaining in the wine. When the weather warmed up the following spring, the fermentation would start again, making the wine fizzy. Instead of fighting it, Croci makes bottle-fermented *frizzante* wines from blends of Malvasia, Ortrugo, Trebbiano, Barbera, and Croatina grapes.

Land and Wines

Emilia-Romagna looks like a band stretching across the Italian peninsula. The Po River forms its northern border with Lombardy and Veneto, and the Apennines shape it to the south along Tuscany and Le Marche. A quarter of the region comprises mountains, another quarter is hills, and the rest is the Po River basin, a long stretch of flat, fertile farmland. This topography is what makes Emilia-Romagna one of Italy's largest wine regions by output. In 2020, it produced 175.91 million gallons (6.65 million hectoliters), ranking third in volume behind only Veneto and Puglia.

While Emilia has more in common with Lombardy and Milan—more people, more industry, and more liberal politics—Romagna feels more like central Italy. The wines reflect the differences. Emilia is the land of brambly Lambrusco, skin-contact Malvasia, and a range of sparkling and still white and red wines. Meanwhile, Romagna is known for robust Sangiovese as well as subtler white wines made with the Albana grape.

In Emilia, winters are cold, with fog and frost blanketing the plains, while the summers can be scorching. The hills of Piacenza, Parma, Reggio Emilia, and Bologna spread west and south of the Po River, broken up by tributaries. The hillsides tend to be cooler, with more variation in temperatures. Piacenza and Bologna are the only two provinces in Emilia where Lambrusco isn't made, and vineyards there focus on different grapes. Around Piacenza, white wines are made with Malvasia, Ortrugo, and Trebbiano while Barbera, Croatia, and Pinot Nero go into reds. Meanwhile, the hills around Bologna are known for Pignoletto, which is identical to the grape Grechetto di Todi, grown in Umbria. Unlike in Umbria, where the grape is used to grow a straw-hued still wine, in Emilia, it is often used to make a light, fizzy wine. Meanwhile, the provinces of Reggio Emilia, Modena, and Parma are all about Lambrusco. Each area has its preferred Lambrusco grape, but most are made from a blend since each grape offers something different, from color to tannins and aroma.

Like Emilia, Romagna is split between hills and plains, but its climate is milder and more Mediterranean, thanks to the Adriatic Sea. In the northeast corner where the Po meets the Adriatic, sprawling vineyards of Trebbiano Romagnolo cover the plains. To the south are the Apennine foothills, where Sangiovese and Albana grapes grow. For years Sangiovese from Romagna was considered inferior to the Sangiovese made elsewhere, but extensive work rehabilitating vineyards on the hillsides has changed its reputation for the better. Today, Romagna Sangiovese varies from light and easy to structured and meaty, with deeper color than Tuscan Sangiovese. On the other hand, the Albana grape grows only in Romagna, where some say it's been cultivated since Roman times. The best sites for the grape are the fossil-rich, calcareous-clay soils between Forlì and Cesena, and it's made in still, sparkling, and *passito* styles.

In a region that brought us Parmigiano-Reggiano and prosciutto di Parma, tortellini *en brodo* (in broth), and *aceto balsamico*, it's easy for wine to get overlooked. The city of Parma has been recognized as a UNESCO Creative City of Gastronomy, and it's also the headquarters of the EU's European Food Safety Authority. This is a place where cooks specify the precise age of Parmigiano to use in a recipe. Consequently, the role of wine in Emilia-Romagna is usually about fitting in, not standing out. Yet with so many producers pushing their craft in new directions, wine is no longer a second act at the table.

Emilia-Romagna Grapes

The grapes in this region can be confusing because many go by the same name as others. For instance, Malvasia here has nothing to do with the Malvasia in Lazio, and "Lambrusco" is not one grape but an entire family of grapes.

White

Albana

This grape made a stir in 1987, when the Italian government granted its first white wine DOCG to Albana di Romagna. Many were dismayed that out of all of Italy's white wines, watery Albana was the first to gain elevated status. Like many things in Italian politics, most suspected an inside job. Now that there are many other DOCG white wines—and many winemakers that prefer to ignore the whole system—Albana's status is no longer scandalous. Today, rebranded as Romagna Albana, the wine is known for understated elegance and versatility. The Albana grape itself grows well in limestone soils around Forlì, Cesena, and Ravenna. Its vines are trained on tall pergolas so its long, heavy grape bunches have plenty of clearance from the ground. The Zeoli family of Fattoria Monticino Rosso leverages the grape in different ways, sometimes harvesting as early as August to make bright sparkling wines and as late as November to make rich, botrytis-affected *passito*. Dry Albana exhibits notes of honey, apricot, white flowers, and a hint of Mediterranean herbs, while Albana *passito* is sweet but structured, with notes of tropical fruit.

Malvasia di Candia Aromatica

"Malvasia" is a name shared by a collection of unrelated grapes. The Venetians traded a wine called Malvasia far and wide, so it's no wonder that several white grapes bear that name. Among the Malvasias, Malvasia di Candia Aromatica is one of the best. The elegant grape is one of Emilia's most important, especially in Colli Piacentini, Colli di Parma, and Reggio Emilia, though it also grows in Lombardy and Lazio. True to its *aromatica* descriptor, it evokes aromas of flowers, citrus, ginger, and cinnamon balanced by acidity, and its tannic skins also do well in skin-contact wines. In Emilia, Malvasia can be light and fresh, with bright citrus notes, like Camillo Donati's bottle-fermented sparkling Malvasia, or it can be complex and savory, like La Stoppa's "Ageno." Made by macerating Malvasia (as well as local grapes Ortrugo and Trebbiano) on its skins for four months before aging, the iconic Emilian wine offers notes of dried flowers, honey, and orange peel.

Ortrugo

While it grows in both Emilia and Romagna, Ortrugo is especially important around the Trebbia Valley and the hills around Piacenza in Emilia. It's often blended with Malvasia di Candia Aromatica, and this is how Ortrugo got its original name—*altruga* meaning "other grape." Like many varieties in Emilia-Romagna, Ortrugo is a vigorous vine and does best when its growth is limited by poor soils and sloped hills. As a wine, it's light and minerally, often accented with orange blossom, green apple, and lime. It also makes refreshing sparkling wines. Massimiliano Croci not only blends Ortrugo into a bottle-fermented sparkling wine but also makes "Alfieri," a bone-dry *metodo classico* Ortrugo with subtle fruity notes. (See Italy's Sparkling Wines, page 262.)

Pagadebit (Mostosa)

In the past, farmers occasionally named productive vines after the quantity of grapes they yielded. Piedmont has Carica l'Asino, which means "load up the donkey," and Sicily grows Carricante, which comes from *carrico*, meaning "loaded." In the case of Pagadebit, the name stems from "pay the debts" since the variety was friendly to a farmer's bottom line. To be clear, Pagadebit is not a specific grape. Instead, it's either the local Mostosa grape or the Bombino Bianco grape from Puglia (page 167). The Romagna Pagadebit DOC requires a minimum of 85 percent Bombino Bianco, though Romagna producers interchange Bombino Bianco with Mostosa. For all anyone knows, the two grapes are one in the same. The Trerè estate in Faenza makes "Giòja," a dry, savory *frizzante* Romagna Pagadebit DOC. More than anything, Pagadebit is a fun story about how Italian grape names came about way back when.

Pignoletto (Grechetto di Todi)

Pignoletto's name means "little pine cone," and this refers to the shape of the grape bunches. A historic grape from the limestone-clay soils in the hills around Bologna, Pignoletto makes a saline, light wine with hints of lime, chamomile, and ripe apple. Like most of the region's other varieties, it can be made as a sparkling wine (like Tre Monti's "Doppio Bianco") or a light-to-medium still wine. Some producers, like Alberto Tedeschi, make richer, nuttier versions with extended skin contact. In Umbria, the grape goes under the name Grechetto di Todi and is one of the varieties used in the white wines of Orvieto (page 238).

Spergola

Once a favorite in Reggio Emilia in the nineteenth century, Spergola fell out of favor as vine diseases and mechanization became more common in the area. Spergola needs a fair amount of ventilation to avoid mildew; plus, the grape's thin skins don't do well with machine harvesting. In addition to this, Spergola grew in the same places as Lambrusco grapes, and Lambrusco was a far more popular wine. Fortunately, Spergola didn't disappear entirely. Since the 1990s, brothers Giovanni and Alberto Masini of Ca' de Noci have focused on little-known varieties from Reggio Emilia. Their original Spergola vines were planted in the 1970s, which they use to make "Querciole," a sparkling wine that goes through a second fermentation in bottle. The result is a naturally fizzy wine with the kind of acidity needed for an Emilia-style meal. The brothers also work with other rare, local grapes, such as Malbo Gentile, Sgavetta, and Termarina.

Trebbiano Romagnolo

Trebbiano Romagnolo is heavily planted in Romagna's western plains near the Adriatic because it's a hardy vine, capable of producing a lot of grapes with low risk of mildew or botrytis. It is also grown to make concentrated grape must (juice) and brandy. Trebbiano Romagnolo has been grown in Romagna since at least the fourteenth century. Some grapes can take on golden or red skins when ripe, and these vines are considered higher quality than run-of-the-mill Trebbiano. From this grape, expect a light, everyday wine, the kind to drink chilled in the summer. A lot of Trebbiano wines from Romagna also contain Trebbiano Toscano (see Tuscany chapter, page 230), though it's hard to tell from taste alone. A final note: Trebbiano Modenese, not Trebbiano Romagnolo, is the grape used for Aceto Balsamico Tradizionale di Modena.

Verdea
(see Lombardy chapter, page 129)

Red

Ancellotta
Planted on the plains of Emilia-Romagna, especially around Reggio Emilia, this is an inky, juicy grape that can boost color in Lambrusco and all sorts of wines (and other products). For that reason, it's the fourth-most-planted grape in the region. Ancellotta makes a very "grapey" wine, with a sweet, rich body and aromas of ripe black fruits, but it's not easy to find a pure Ancellotta wine. To do so, we went outside Emilia-Romagna to the northeast corner of Le Marche. There, Fattoria Mancini makes a wine called "Blu" from an old Ancellotta vineyard on its property—its name comes from the deep-blue stain the grape's juices left on the winery's floor.

Barbera
(see Piedmont chapter, page 153)

Croatina
(see Piedmont chapter, page 153)

Lambrusco Family
First, a little plant science: cultivated vines are hermaphrodites; wild vines are dioecious. To bear fruit, wild female vines are pollinated by wild male vines. In the Lambrusco family of grapes, this wild ancestry lingers. To get Lambrusco di Sorbara to produce grapes, its flowers must be pollinated with another type of Lambrusco—mostly Lambrusco Salamino. Many believe the Lambrusco family comes from vines domesticated by ancient people on the Italian peninsula. There are more than a dozen Lambrusco grapes, and they are often blended together.

Here are the most common varieties:

- **Lambrusco di Sorbara:** This variety from Modena is elegant, yielding strawberry-hued, aromatic wines with distinct floral notes. Cleto Chiarli's "Lambrusco del Fondatore," which finishes fermentation in bottle, is a benchmark Lambrusco di Sorbara wine.

- **Lambrusco Grasparossa:** From the town of Castelvetro in Modena, the Grasparossa variety is the only Lambrusco adapted to grow on hillsides, yielding big, tannic, deep-purple wines with notes of violet. Compared with other Lambrusco varieties, it has thicker skins, leading to more tannic wines. Zanasi makes an intense, deeply hued version of Lambrusco Grasparossa di Castelvetro.

- **Lambrusco Maestri:** From Parma, this variety is the most versatile. Easier to grow and more resistant to disease, it gives color, fruit, and structure to Lambrusco wines. At Quarticello, winemaker Roberto Maestri makes a low-intervention "Neromaestri," a Lambrusco made mostly with Maestri and some Grasparossa.

- **Lambrusco Salamino:** From the town of Santa Croce in Reggio Emilia, the Salamino variety gets its name because its grape bunches look like salami. In style, Salamino splits the difference between Sorbara and Grasparossa, bringing richness and structure as well as more delicate nuance. It is the most planted Lambrusco variety. Luciano Saetti of Vigneto Saetti makes a *rosato* and *rosso* Lambrusco with Salamino, both of which go through second fermentation in bottle.

Sangiovese
(see Tuscany chapter, page 231)

Regional Foods

Aceto balsamico tradizionale
traditional balsamic vinegar from Modena and Reggio Emilia

Brodetto
Adriatic seafood stew with tomatoes, garlic, and onions

Butter

Cheese
casatella romagnola, fresh cows' milk cheese from Romagna

Formaggio di Fossa, a cheese aged in tuffaceous rock

Grana Padano, aged cows' milk cheese from the Po river valley

Parmigiano-Reggiano, aged cows' milk cheese for grating

Gnocco fritto
fried bread from Emilia

Cotechino con lenticchie
cotechino sausage with lentils

Cured meats and sausages
Culatello

Mortadella

Prosciutto di Parma

Eels
from Romagna's Comacchio Lagoon

Olive oil

Pasta
anolini, small half-moon-shaped filled pasta

cappelletti, filled pasta

tagliatelle, fresh pasta strands

tortelli, filled pasta shaped in many ways

tortellini en brodo, tortellini in broth

Piadina
flatbread

Porcini mushrooms

Prosciutto di Parma

Ragù alla Bolognese
rich sauce of meat with onion, carrot, celery, prosciutto, and sometimes a tiny amount of tomatoes; its recipe is officially codified by the Chamber of Commerce of Bologna

Recommended Producers

Emilia

Barbolini

Bulli

Denavolo

Ca' de Noci

Camillo Donati

Cleto Chiarli

Croci

La Collina

La Stoppa

Lini 910

Lusenti

Medici Ermete

Monte Rodano

Opera 02

Paltrinieri

Podere il Saliceto

Saetti

Villa di Corlo

Vittorio Graziano

Zanasi

Romagna

Fattoria Monticino Rosso

Fattoria Zerbina

Leone Conti

Mirco Mariotti

San Patrignano

Tre Monti

Friuli Venezia Giulia

With its bright buildings painted in primary colors lining canals filled with boats, the city of Grado looks like a blue-collar Venice, where fishermen haul their catch to restaurants and shops along the water. On weekends, the men head to their *casoni*, cabins on tiny islands in the Grado Lagoon. On one spring Saturday, we joined fisherman Roberto Camotto on his island. On the way, he stopped the boat briefly, scooping up shrimp the size of a thumbnail from the water. In his cabin's minimalist kitchen, he cooked the shrimp in a pan with a little tomato paste and then passed everything—shells and all—through a food mill. At a picnic table on the water, we ate the spaghetti coated in the briny sauce while Roberto poured everyone a glass of Friulano (and shots of grappa for anyone who asked). From the warm lagoon, the mountains felt like a million miles away. Yet by that evening, we were at La Subida, a restaurant in Cormons, a commune within cycling distance of the Italian-Slovenian border. Instead of shrimp, we ate prosciutto made by the D'Osvaldo family and polenta cooked over an open fire. For drink, orange wine was on the table.

Set at the northeast corner of the country between the Carnic and Julian Alps and the top of the Adriatic Sea, Friuli Venezia Giulia stands out from mainland Italy, feeling less like another Italian region and more like a crossroads between the Mediterranean world and eastern Europe. Its split identity goes back generations, with borders in flux until the mid-twentieth century. Trieste, the last piece added, is the farthest city from Rome on mainland Italy. In its previous incarnation under the Austro-Hungarian Empire, Trieste was in the center of action. Starting in the eighteenth century, the Habsburgs transformed the fishing village into a thriving, diverse port city, home to Armenians, Egyptians, Jews, Greeks, Italians, Slovenes, and Austrians. Coffeehouse culture blossomed and spices such as caraway, paprika, and ginger permeated the local cooking. Cultural ties to the Austrians go beyond Trieste, too. Austro-Hungarian influences can be seen in the food of the region, with goulash, dumplings, and *blècs* (buckwheat noodles) served next to prosciutto and polenta. Consider that in 2019, the town of Cormons hosted a festival in honor of Maximilian I of Habsburg, including a reenactment of the jousting tournaments the Austrian emperor loved.

There are also language differences between the rest of Italy and Friuli Venezia Giulia. Near the Slovenian border, families speak Slovene at home.

Elsewhere in the region, they speak Friulian, an officially recognized language in Italy. The word *ronc* means "hills" in Friulano, and wine labels from the area often include *ronc* to define a vineyard or an estate. Federico De Luca, a winemaker from Faedis, a town in the eastern hills of Friuli Venezia Giulia, grew up speaking Italian in school but Friulan at home. His family has lived in the area for more than 260 years, and the name of his family winery, Ronc dai Luchis, means "hillside of the De Luca family." The way he explains it, the language has a word for every tool and every situation, making it a good match for working as an artisan. That kind of focus on craft and efficiency permeates the wine culture in Friuli Venezia Giulia.

Despite its differences from the rest of the country, Friuli Venezia Giulia tends to foreshadow Italian wine trends. It was the first region to embrace temperature-controlled, stainless-steel tanks for white wine production, a revelation in the late twentieth century now taken for granted (or lamented thanks to the bland, industrial Pinot Grigio from northeastern Italy). In the 1970s and '80s, some of Friuli Venezia Giulia's winemakers branched out with "Super Whites"—premium blended wines described as the white counterparts to Super Tuscans—that are still popular today, proving that Italian white wines could age for years. While the region has a three-hundred-year track record of making wine with Merlot, Cabernet Franc, and Sauvignon Blanc, it also has immense appreciation for its native grapes. Walk into a local bar (*frasca*) and ask for a *tajut*, the local word for a glass of wine, and 99 percent of the time they'll serve a wine made with one of the region's most beloved grapes, Tocai Friulano. And then there are the region's orange wines. Starting in the 1990s, Oslavia, a town along the Slovenian border, became Italy's spiritual home of these deep, skin-contact white wines. In other words, Friuli Venezia Giulia is like a crystal ball that shows us what we'll want to drink for years to come.

History

Friuli Venezia Giulia has been steeped in wine culture and production since ancient times. Along the northern shores of the Adriatic Sea, Julius Caesar put troops in Aquileia, growing the city into a hub for wine, and built Cividale, which today is the most important city in the Colli Orientali area. The land later fell under the control of the Lombards, who set up their capital at Cividale, and after that it was under the Byzantines and others until the Venetian Republic took control of portions of the region in the fifteenth and sixteenth centuries. They reestablished Aquileia as a destination for wine and annexed other cities, like Grado, Cividale, and Udine, all of which have some Venetian-style flair in architecture and design. When Friuli Venezia Giulia later became part of the Austro-Hungarian Empire at the end of the eighteenth century, it continued to be a place for winemaking. Grapes such as Picolit, one of Italy's oldest native varieties, went into wine for the royal courts of Europe, an equal to Hungarian Tokaji. European royals also loved the region's wines made with Merlot, Pinot Grigio, Pinot Bianco (Pinot Blanc), Sauvignon Blanc, and Cabernet Franc, all of which still grow in the region today.

While Italy unified in the mid-nineteenth century, turbulence swept through the Austro-Hungarian Empire. The Austro-Prussian War divided the region: the western Friuli portion became a part of Italy, and the smaller Venezia Giulia portion remained a part of the empire. Around the turn of the century, diseases took a toll on the vineyards, and in 1907, an antiphylloxera consortium started to select certain grapes worth the effort of replanting. Many of the grapes not on the list disappeared, although a few were left to be rediscovered much later (such as Pignolo, page 88). Yet just as farmers began to replant, World War I started. Nearly every part of Friuli Venezia Giulia became a battleground: farms were ransacked, livestock was slaughtered, and soldiers took all the wine they found in cellars. The Isonzo Valley, now a prime vineyard area, was the setting of twelve gruesome battles between Austrians and Italians. The Italians lost so badly that they were pushed all the way back to the Piave River in the Veneto—it took the Battle of Vittorio Veneto for the Italian army to gain a victory at the tail end of the war. Afterward, vineyard replanting efforts that had started before the war resumed. In Rauscedo, near the border of the Veneto region, a cluster of nurseries sprang up selling cuttings grafted onto disease-resistant rootstock. Today, Vitis Rauscedo is one of the largest grapevine nursery cooperatives in the world, selling vines within Italy and abroad.

Friuli Venezia Giulia was still rebuilding when the Second World War plunged the region into chaos. This time, the outcome not only left behind devastation but also separated families and property. In 1947, the new border between Italy and Yugoslavia placed some of the farms and families behind the Iron Curtain in border towns like Oslavia. Throughout the Cold War, border crossings between Friuli Venezia Giulia and Yugoslavia were done under the scrutiny of the Yugoslavian military. For a brief time, Trieste was unmoored from any governing body until it became a part of Italy in 1954. At that point, Italy had been a unified country for less than a hundred years.

For the first half of the twentieth century, most Friulan farmers grew multiple crops, including cherries, figs, apples, and grapes, all on the same land. When one harvest finished, another began. After the Second World War, with farms destroyed and few jobs at home, many moved away from the countryside to find work. Yet some doubled down on the rural economy. After losing the family land to Yugoslavia when the borders were redrawn, the Felluga family resettled in the Collio, and two Felluga brothers, Livio and Marco, got into wine. In the 1960s Livio began revitalizing a vineyard in Rosazzo in the southern corner of the Colli Orientali in the foothills of the Alps, while Marco started making agreements with Collio growers, forming a consortium. By the 1970s, each brother was bottling more than a hundred thousand bottles annually, as was another pioneer, Mario Schiopetto, an innkeeper in

Udine who is credited with being the first to make modern white wine in Friuli.

This level of production was a rarity for independent winemakers at the time, but their successes helped pave the way for others to make a living in winemaking. In a typical Friulian origin story from that era, a farmer grew multiple crops and made wine on the side to sell by the demijohn. His son returned from studying enology at the viticulture school in Conegliano in Veneto and started introducing new ideas to his father, encouraging him to rethink the family business. In the 1970s, small farmers were helped by a rise in small-scale cooperatives that put the name of the farmer and vineyard on labels instead of blending all farms and vineyards together, an unusual move then and now. In 1976, enologist Giuseppe Lipari opened a mobile bottling center on a truck to help farmers bottle their production, allowing more wines to enter the market. Friulian white wines found a ready audience for their fresh, bright style, a break with the oxidized white wines of Italy's past. In the early 1980s, cement vats were replaced by temperature-controlled, stainless-steel vats. The *metodo friulano* (Friulian method) depended upon fermenting grape juices at low temperatures while reducing exposure to oxygen and grape skins. The result was fruit-forward wines that traveled well, and they became the style associated with the region.

Today, fresh, fruit-forward wines are still a key part of Friuli Venezia Giulia's wine identity. On the northern side of the Collio, Giorgio Venica, who runs the Venica & Venica winery with his brother, Gianni, once described it to us this way: If you bite into a grape, the pulp is the most satisfying part to eat. If you keep chewing, the grape releases more flavors, but if you chew it for too long, it turns bitter. The Venica family tries to capture as much of the grape as they can without the bitterness.

Not everyone was satisfied with crisp white wines to drink young, so some put resources into ambitious white wine blends for aging. In 1975, Silvio Jermann released Vintage Tunina, a blend of Chardonnay, Sauvignon Blanc, Malvasia, Ribolla Gialla, and Picolit that has since been granted more Tre Bicchieri (Three Glass) awards for white wine from Italian wine publication *Gambero Rosso* than nearly any other. In 1981, Livio Felluga released Terre Alte, a blend of Sauvignon Blanc, Pinot Grigio, and Tocai Friulano, that has since shown the ability to age for more than twenty years. This category of wines soon gained the nickname "Super Whites," a nod to the Super Tuscans. (Tuscany took note: the Antinori family, known for Super Tuscan wines Tignanello and Solaia, now owns the Jermann winery.) And then there are the winemakers who have always focused on blends, which was how wines were made before grape varieties were written on bottles. In the Collio along the Slovenian border, the Keber family makes one wine—Collio Bianco DOC—with Tocai Friulano, Malvasia Istriana, and Ribolla Gialla, each grape contributing to making a rich, deep white wine.

Others abandoned the Friulian style of bright, crisp wines entirely, questioning why white grapes couldn't be treated the same way as red grapes, with the juices spending time with the skins and seeds to extract flavor and preserve the wine without added sulfur—essentially, the old ways of making wine before temperature control. These wines—called orange wines, skin-contact wines, or macerated wines (see Orange Wine, page 84)—are most associated with the town of Oslavia along the Slovenian border and the Carso.

Land and Wines

Cradled by the Carnic and Julian Alps, Friuli Venezia Giulia borders Austria to the north, Slovenia to the east, and the Adriatic Sea to the south. The provinces of Udine and Pordenone comprise the larger "Friuli" portion, which spans from the mountains to the Grado Lagoon and across the plains to the border with Veneto. The smaller "Venezia Giulia" side includes the provinces of Gorizia and Trieste and sits in the southeast corner of the region. Throughout Friuli Venezia Giulia, vineyards grow a range of grapes made into an even wider range of wines.

White wines are the main focus of Friuli Venezia Giulia's winemakers. The region ranks eighth in Italy in production, making 42.9 million gallons of wine (1.624 million hectoliters) in 2020, and nearly 80 percent is white. Yet there is growing interest in red wines made with native grapes like Schioppettino and Pignolo. Glera, the main grape of Prosecco (see Veneto chapter, page 266), originated in the Trieste province. Glera plantings ballooned in the region following a major change in the Prosecco DOC territory in 2009, the year the regulations extended the borders to cover a chunk of northeast Italy, including all provinces of Friuli Venezia Giulia. Yet the region's wine identity comes through more clearly in other wines.

In the west, the large, flat Grave DOC sprawls out toward Venice, growing a range of grapes, including a lot of Glera. South of Grave are three flat seaside growing areas—Annia, Aquileia, and Latisana—that make nuanced wines with Malvasia Istriana and Refosco dal Peduncolo Rosso grapes. East of Aquileia, the Isonzo DOC is one of the world's best flat vineyard areas, where vines grow along the alluvial soils of the Isonzo River. There, hot summer temperatures yield some of the region's most concentrated wines. To the east of Isonzo and just north of Trieste, a narrow rocky plateau called the Carso, bordering Slovenia, makes lean, mineral wines with rare grapes Vitovska and Terrano.

There, the roots of vines muscle through cracks in dense rock, and the resulting grapes create austere, elegant wines.

The region's most-prized vineyard areas are concentrated in the eastern hills of the Collio and Colli Orientali. Here, vineyards are renowned for *ponca*, a light-colored, well-draining composite soil made up of alternating layers of hard sandstone and soft marl. Mario Zanusso of I Clivi, who has vineyards in both the Collio and Colli Orientali, says the marl holds on to moisture, hydrating vines in dry seasons, while the sandstone redistributes the moisture so it gets to where it needs to go. While there are differences in *ponca* from site to site, the vineyards that have it tend to yield wines with the kind of salinity more common in coastal wines.

The Colli Orientali is a long strip of land set farther into the foothills north of the Collio. It has the highest concentration of native grapes in the region, including Picolit, Ribolla Gialla, and Verduzzo for whites and Schioppettino, Tazzelenghe, and Refosco di Faedis for reds. (Faedis is also a town in the Colli Orientali.) The most famous subzone is at the southern edge of the Colli Orientali, Rosazzo, where Livio Felluga got his start. Right next to Rosazzo, to the east and south, is where the Collio begins. Compared with the Colli Orientali, the Collio is warmer, yielding riper fruit and richer wines. But thanks to the *ponca* soil, the wines carry remarkable salinity and acidity. Meanwhile, Oslavia, a cooler town within the Collio on the border of Slovenia, is renowned for orange wines.

The combination of wind, rain, and unique soils yields a range of expressive wines. In winter, bone-chilling dry bora winds cut through the Alps at sixty miles an hour toward the sea. In parts of the Carso, the winds can be so strong that trees grow angled toward the sea. In the summer, warm sea air is tempered by cool breezes from the mountains, regulating the weather and prolonging the growing season. More remarkable than the wind is the rain. Parts of Friuli Venezia Giulia are the rainiest in Italy. September may start out sunny, but if it rains, it can rain for days, making it impossible to harvest grapes. Fortunately, the region's soils are uniquely capable of dealing with deluge. In the flat zones, such as the Isonzo Valley, the areas near the lagoon, and parts of the Grave DOC, sand and gravel soils keep vineyards dry enough that you can walk through without muddying your shoes. In the Carso DOC, only a thin layer of iron-rich red topsoil sits on top of a rocky mix of granite and limestone. And in the Collio and Colli Orientali, *ponca* prevents roots from getting waterlogged. The problem with *ponca*, though, is that it crumbles easily, making hillsides fragile. After a landslide in the 1940s, the Venica family planted apple trees to stabilize their hillside vineyard. Today, the Ronco delle Mele (Apple Hill) vineyard, planted with Sauvignon Blanc, creates one of Venica & Venica's best wines.

The best grapes for the region's climates are the ones that tolerate cooler, wet weather, making conventional rich, big red wines a challenge to produce. Even so, the most planted red grape is Merlot, and as tastes change away from heavy, ripe reds and toward lean, spicier bottlings, native red grapes like Schioppettino and Refosco are also coming into their own. While only a small amount of *rosato* is made here, Friuli Venezia Giulia offers beautiful salmon-hued Pinot Grigio in the *ramato* style, which uses a subtle amount of skin contact to give the wine its pink color, as seen in Vie di Romans' "Dessimis" and Attems's Ramato Pinot Grigio.

Most of the time, white wine is made by removing grape skins immediately or soon after crushing to keep the juices light in color and free from bitterness. In comparison, orange wines are made like red wines, allowing juices to ferment with grape skins, giving them a unique color. Some of these white wines sit with their skins for a day or so while others are stored on their skins for months after fermentation.

Orange wine isn't exactly orange; it can be amber or pale gold—or somewhere in between. For this reason, many prefer to call these wines "skin-contact" or *vini macerati*–macerated white wines. Regardless of the name, these wines can be savory, with notes of white cherry, apricot, bergamot, and spice. In some cases, they are layered wines unlike any others.

This is especially the case among the orange wines of Oslavia, a town on the border of Slovenia. In 2005, Oslavia-based winemaker Joško Gravner released his first amphorae-aged orange wines from the 2001 vintage. Gravner's career is like a time capsule of winemaking in Friuli. In the 1970s, after attending enology school, he embraced technology, producing crisp white wines. In the 1980s, he saw the next generation of precision winemaking technology in the Napa Valley. Rather than inspire Gravner, it convinced him that technology made wines taste the same. Back home, he turned to making white wines in barrique (small French barrels). The bottles were met with acclaim, but he still wasn't satisfied. Then in 1996, two hailstorms destroyed the year's crop. With the few white grapes that remained, he macerated them on their skins in wooden vats. The following year, he fermented another portion in amphorae (terracotta vessels) and started studying the winemaking of Georgia.

A former Soviet country, Georgia (along with Armenia and Iran) is believed to be the birthplace of wine, and winemakers continue working in traditional ways. Honey-colored white wines ferment in large clay vessels called qvevri (which resemble amphorae). Starting in 2000, Gravner visited Georgia several times, importing clay vessels from the country to make macerated wines. Today, Gravner's Ribolla Gialla offers a depth of flavor that's hard to describe: layers of walnut, red apple, rosemary, and birch offer a unique perspective and sense of place.

Separately, Stanislao (Stanko) Radikon also started to wonder how skin contact would affect his wines. The winemaker, also in Oslavia, took a cue from his father, who used to macerate Ribolla Gialla on its skins for practical purposes: he didn't have the money to buy sulfur to stabilize the wine but found that the skins acted like a preservative. Through the next couple of decades, he and his son, Saša (who took over winemaking duties after Stanislao passed away in 2016), experimented with the length of time to leave the wine on the skins, finding the sweet spot between two and four months. Today, Saša makes macerated wines with many other white grapes, and there are many others working with this style in the area.

In the Friuli Venezia Giulia, the Carso also excels in making orange wine. Although Sandi Skerk's wine stays in contact with the skins for up to a year, it is very pale–not even remotely orange. Paolo Vodopivec also makes a light-colored Vitovska that happens to be one of the most mineral-intense wines we've tasted. Orange wines are best with savory foods, from sushi to whole-roasted fish and rich braised meats.

Orange Wine

Italian *Vini Macerati*

Abruzzo
- Cirelli Trebbiano d'Abruzzo
- Emidio Pepe Trebbiano d'Abruzzo
- Valentini Trebbiano d'Abruzzo

Calabria
- L'Acino "Giramondo" Malvasia

Campania
- Cantina Giardino "Paski" Coda Di Volpe
- Contrada Salandra Campi Flegrei Falanghina

Emilia-Romagna
- La Stoppa "Ageno"
- Orsi "Vigna del Grotto" Pignoletto
- Podere Pradarolo "Vej" Bianco Antico Riserva

Friuli Venezia Giulia
- Damijan Podversic, Ribolla Gialla
- Josko Gravner Ribolla
- Radikon Ribolla
- Skerk Vitovska
- Vodopivec Vitovska

Lazio
- Le Coste "Bianchetto"
- Monastero Suore Cistercensi "Coenobium"
- Sete "Alimento"

Le Marche
- La Distesa "Gli Eremi"

Liguria
- Stefano Legnani "Bamboo Road"

Puglia
- L'Archetipo "Litro Bianco"
- Guttarolo "Carsia" Verdeca

Sardinia
- Meigamma "Bianco Quarto"
- Giovanni Montisci, "Modestu"

Sicily
- Alessandro Viola Catarratto
- COS "Rami"
- Eduardo Torres Acosta "Versante Nord" "Terre Siciliane Bianco"
- Guccione "C" Catarratto
- Marco De Bartoli "Integer" Zibibbo
- Nino Barraco Grillo
- Vino di Anna Palmen+o Bianco
- Vini Scirto "Don Pippinu" Carricante

Trentino–Alto Adige
- Foradori "Fontanasanta" Nosiola

Tuscany
- I Botri di Ghiaccio Forte "Ghiaccioforte" Bianco di Sansano Maremma
- Massa Vecchia "Ariento" Maremma Bianco

Umbria
- Cantina Fongoli "Biancofongoli" Umbria Trebbiano Spoletino
- Paolo Bea "Arboreus"

Veneto
- La Biancara di Angiolino Maule "Masieri Bianco"

Friuli Venezia Giulia Grapes

Friuli Venezia Giulia has a wealth of native grapes that rarely grow anywhere else and several French grapes that have grown there for more than three hundred years. Apart from blends, most wines indicate the grape variety on the label, making it easy to know what you're drinking.

White

Malvasia Istriana

In a country filled with grapes called Malvasia, Malvasia Istriana stands out. It can be earthy, fruity, floral, salty, and sometimes everything at once. When the Venetians were selling Malvasia throughout the Adriatic, there's a chance that the celebrated wine was Malvasia Istriana, especially since it grows well along the coast. Malvasia Istriana wines are mostly medium- to full-bodied, bone dry, and packed with acidity and salinity. In Friuli, the grape is best in well-draining areas where the vine's vigorous growth is kept in check, like the *ponca* vineyards of the Collio and Colli Orientali or gravelly or sandy soils near the coast. It is made in both fresh and skin-contact versions, and often expresses orange blossoms, peach, and white pepper, with unexpected spicy notes. On the bottle, "Istriana" is often left off the label, but chances are if it's a Malvasia from Friuli Venezia Giulia, it's Malvasia Istriana.

Picolit

Once prized by European royals, Picolit is one of Italy's oldest native grapes. Grown in the Colli Orientali hills, it gets its name from the size of its grape bunches. Since Picolit has trouble pollinating and growing grapes to maturity, a bunch may contain only ten to twenty grapes, so the vines concentrate all their energy into these paltry bunches. (In comparison, a bunch of Chardonnay has one hundred to two hundred grapes.) Picolit grapes hang on the vine late in the year, air-drying before harvest. In Rosazzo, the Livio Felluga estate carries out harvest by hand from October to the end of November. The result is a golden, sweet wine with notes of apricot, ginger, and pear. Victor Hazan, Marcella Hazan's husband and an Italian wine expert, once described Picolit as having an aloof kind of sweetness, which fits its royal lineage.

Pinot Grigio

Since it's grown and sold everywhere, we all think we know Pinot Grigio. Yet when the vines are planted in the *ponca* soils of the eastern hills or the gravelly river rock of the Isarco Valley, Pinot Grigio becomes one of the most expressive white wines around. It takes on the salinity and mouthwatering acidity from the soils, balancing out its ripe melon, pear, and apple accents. When ripe, the grapes' skins take on a rosy hue, and some Friulian winemakers allow these skins to steep in the juices, creating full-bodied Pinot Grigio called *ramato*, meaning "coppery." It was a traditional way of making Pinot Grigio before the dry, light Pinot Grigio (made in Veneto and parts of Trentino–Alto Adige) came to define the wine, and producers such as Vie di Romans, Ferlat, Scarbolo, and Damijan continue to make this style. While orange wines (page 84) are also made with skin contact, *ramato* applies only to Pinot Grigio. Even though there are truly great Pinot Grigios produced in Friuli, local winemakers would love it if Pinot Grigio could share its spotlight with native grapes, such as Tocai Friulano.

Ribolla Gialla

If you encountered a bunch of Ribolla Gialla grapes on someone's table, you'd be pleased with their bright, sweet flavor and notice their thick yellow skins (*gialla* means "yellow" in Italian). Like Tocai Friulano, Ribolla Gialla is one of the region's beloved native grapes. It does best in places that curb its vigor with poor soils, especially in the Colli Orientali and the Collio. As a white wine, Ribolla Gialla is bright and aromatic, with notes of peach and lemon zest and a dry, mineral finish. It is also often used to make orange wines (page 84) from Oslavia, where its thick skins make it resilient to the town's rainy weather. The skins make the grapes tough to crush, but macerating helps soften them, according to Saša Radikon. Joško Gravner finds that a bit of botrytis (a fungus that can grow on grapes and concentrates its sugars) also softens the skins while adding a layer of flavor.

There is also a local tradition of sparkling Ribolla Gialla. In the old days, the wine would stop fermenting in the winter when the weather became too cold and start up again in the spring, leaving bubbles in its wake. Inspired by this heritage, Mario Zanusso of I Clivi created "RBL," a mouthwatering sparkling wine. Made by closing the vat when the wine is nearly finished fermenting, trapping in the bubbles, the unique wine is fresh and salty, with delicate citrus and floral notes. (It is different from most Prosecco and Champagne, where wine goes through a second fermentation to create bubbles; see Italy's Sparkling Wines, page 262.)

Sauvignon Blanc

Like Pinot Grigio, most people know what to expect from Sauvignon Blanc, but Friuli can challenge those preconceived notions. The combination of *ponca* soils and long growing seasons pushes the wine past its signature grassy/green notes and gives it extraordinary nuance while still maintaining the variety's signature acidity. In the Collio, Venica & Venica's Ronco delle Mele vineyard yields a deliciously tart, long-lasting wine, with notes of green apple and passion fruit. Meanwhile, in the Colli Orientali, Serena Palazzolo at Ronco del Gnemiz make the kind of special-occasion long-aging Sauvignon Blanc that will also change your mind on how expressive this wine can get. So will the Sauvignon Blanc from Miani, if you can find it. A note on Sauvignon Blanc in Italy: it's habitually shortened to "Sauvignon," and that's how it's written on Italian labels and wine lists.

Tocai Friulano

First things first: the grape is Tocai Friulano, and the wine it makes is called Friulano. However, the wine used to be called Tocai, and many still call it

that. The confusion was born out of European law. Hungary was admitted to the European Union in 2004, and in 2007, the Hungarian sweet wine Tokaji became a protected name. Other wines with similar names had to be changed, leaving Friulian winemakers to shorten their local wine to "Friulano." (Locals are still frustrated by the mandatory name change, which thwarted a half century's worth of marketing efforts. "Would you change the name of a Ferrari car?" one asked us.) Still, the grape is beloved to the region, where it's been documented since the twelfth century. When someone pours you a *tajut di blanc* (glass of white wine) at a local bar, most of the time it's Friulano—though they'll call it Tocai. Genetically, Tocai Friulano is identical to Sauvignonasse, which grows in Chile. It is a vigorous wine that is lighter, with more saline notes in less sunny, cooler areas, while it becomes richer and higher in alcohol in warm areas. The roundest, richest versions of Friulano come from the Collio, but the grape can yield everything from bright, mineral-accented wines to full-bodied, round wines with notes of apple, almond, and white peach. Some have a funky cave-like aroma, and others are all about wet stone and flint. In the Collio, Venica & Venica makes "Primarul," a full wine with notes of yellow apple and toasted almond balanced by acidity. In the Colli Orientali, Ronc dai Luchis offers a Friulano with ripe stone fruit paired with saline and herbal notes. In the glass, Friulano is pale green to pale straw in color. With pleasant, citrus-like acidity and notes of almonds and white flowers, it is eminently food friendly, a classic pairing with prosciutto di San Daniele.

Verduzzo

Winemakers who work with Verduzzo are up for a challenge: it's not easy balancing the grape's fresh, mineral side with its bitter tannins, which come from the skins *and* pulp. Yet Verduzzo is primed for a breakout as more tinker with its potential, creating wines that combine earthiness with structure and body. Verduzzo is often compared with Picolit, since both are used to make sweet wines and both grow in the Colli Orientali, yet it is a much different kind of grape. Actually, make that two grapes: Verduzzo Verde, which is green and makes a simple, light-bodied white wine; and Verduzzo Giallo, which has yellow grapes and leaves and grows in the Colli Orientali. The latter makes interesting sweet wines in the Ramandolo DOCG. Because of its tannins, vinifying dry Verduzzo requires care. At I Clivi, Mario Zanusso presses the grapes under very low pressure to minimize the bitterness extracted, creating a Verduzzo that has both body and austerity, and that turns a beautiful amber color with age as its tannins oxidize. Meanwhile, Federico De Luca of Ronc dai Luchis has been experimenting with still and sparkling Verduzzo, making white wines that are both golden and have a tannic but enticing edge.

Vitovska

The grape's name has Slovene origins, which makes sense considering its primary growing area—the Carso—is a narrow strip of land between the sea and Slovenia. Related to Malvasia and Prosecco, it's a grape made for a place where the Mediterranean meets the mountains. Lean, rocky soils and chilling bora wind offer plenty of growing challenges for vintners, but the payoff is a lean, mineral-driven wine that is gently floral on the nose. As an orange wine, it has tannic sturdiness, though it is never deeply colored, even after a year of macerating on its skins. Carso producer Paolo Vodopivec grows only Vitovska, and his transluscent wine made in amphorae (terracotta vessels) buried in the ground is brimming with mineral flavor.

Red

Pignolo

Pignolo is named for the pine cone shape of its grape bunches, and it is another native Italian variety that was almost lost for good, like Casavecchia in Campania (page 64). Owned by the archdiocese of Udine, the abandoned Abbazia di Rosazzo in the Colli Orientali had a vineyard with the last couple of Pignolo vines left in existence. In *Native Wine Grapes of Italy*, Ian D'Agata credits three people for

bringing the grape back: a vineyard worker named Casasola, who cared for the vines and ensured they didn't die out; Silvano Zamò, who took an interest in the grape and now has the Vigne di Zamò estate nearby; and winemaker Walter Filiputti, who began rehabilitating the vines, eventually propagating enough to make wine. The vine is quite tricky to grow; it doesn't always adhere to rootstock after grafting and can grow wild without producing any grapes, which may be why it wasn't replanted after phylloxera. In the cellar, it's prone to stuck fermentations (when wine stops fermenting midway through), and it can be brutally tannic. Yet winemakers have learned how to tame Pignolo into structured wines that, once aged, can carry a spicy charm and brawny quality not found often in the region's reds. While Pignolo now grows throughout Friuli Venezia Giulia, it's still at its best in the Colli Orientali, where it makes wines filled with black cherry, licorice, and herbs.

Refosco Group

Wines that have been around a long time—like Malvasia, Greco, Vernaccia, and Refosco—tend to share their names with a lot of grapes. If it's desirable enough, why wouldn't a farmer want to believe he was growing it? However, that means we have to sift through which Refosco is which, and not all are related. While there are many grapes named Refosco out there, here are the most important:

- **Refosco dal Peduncolo Rosso:** With its peppery spice and bright acidity, this Refosco is the most popular. It's all about red cherries, almonds, and fragrant flowers, like violets. "Peduncolo Rosso" means "red stalk." The stalks are reddish violet and resemble the color of the wine. It's the kind of wine for people who love alpine-style reds, like those from Trentino–Alto Adige (which makes sense, since it's related to Teroldego and Lagrein, the main reds of that region). In Friuli Venezia Giulia, it grows in the hills as well as in the sandy flatlands around Aquileia. You can serve the wine from producers like Vignai da Duline slightly chilled.

- **Refosco di Faedis (also called Refosco Nostrano):** This variety is made only in the village of Faedis in the Colli Orientali. It's an ancient grape that has adapted to the eastern hills. With high tannins, structure, and bright red fruits, it maintains notable freshness, even after several years of aging. Incidentally, Federico De Luca of Ronc Dai Luchis says the people of Faedis love their wine—even though they have only a hundred inhabitants, there are a dozen wineries and eight wine bars in town.

- **Terrano (Refosco d'Istria):** The red wine of the Carso area reflects the same sharp edge as the Carso's key white, Vitovska. This grape variety makes a red wine with heightened acidity—think tart blackberries—and intense minerality, the kind of tangy wine to serve with hearty mountain fare when you need something to cut through the richness.

Schioppettino

The grape's name, which stems from the word *scoppiettare* (crackle) was inspired by one of two things: the way its large grapes pop open in your mouth when you eat them or the way the wine caused explosions when unexpected fermentations started in sealed bottles, breaking glass to release pressure. Sometimes referred to as Ribolla Nera, Schioppettino has a story tied to that of the Rapuzzi family of Ronchi di Cialla in the Colli Orientali. The family has worked with the grape for more than four decades now, but when they started planting the variety in Cialla in 1975, Schioppettino was not on the Italian government's list of approved grapes for wine. This was odd: the grape had been popular since the Middle Ages and was replanted after phylloxera. After World War II, however, it fell into decline. According to Italian wine expert Ian D'Agata, Maria Rieppi, who made wine with Schioppettino grown on her family's estate, kept the grape going for a couple of decades. Then in the 1970s, Dina and Paolo Rapuzzi went all in with Schioppettino, planting it even if they couldn't legally bottle and sell Schioppettino wine because the grape wasn't approved for winemaking. In the late 1970s, however, the Nonino family of grappa fame recognized Maria Rieppi's work with Schioppettino, forcing bureaucrats to reconsider. Meanwhile, journalist Luigi Veronelli talked up the Rapuzzis' project. With the pressure on from some of the industry's most influential people, the government changed the rules, allowing Schioppettino, along with Pignolo and Tazzelenghe, onto the list of permitted wine grapes. Now Schioppettino is one of the brightest red-wine stars in Friuli Venezia Giulia. Sons Ivan and Pierpaolo Rapuzzi continue the family project of working with native grapes, and their Ronchi di Cialla Schioppettino is a sought-after bottle. Unusual for a red grape, it grows well in rainy, cool conditions with good ventilation, and prefers shade over direct sun. The most elegant bottles come from the Colli Orientali, where it can carry Syrah-like notes of black pepper paired with black cherries, currants, and aged balsamic vinegar. While not rich in color, it carries significant complexity.

Tazzelenghe

If we ever need one more example of why it's crucial to maintain biodiversity, file away Tazzelenghe. The grape's name comes from "tongue cutter" in local language, likely because the grape made harsh, acidic wines when it was picked before it was ripe. It's a lot easier to get Tazzelenghe to ripen in our warming climate, though, and the variety is primed for a comeback. Grown in the Colli Orientali and often used in blends, it can make an elegant, violet-hued wine on its own, with crisp floral aromas and tart blackberries and currants, all paired with unflagging acidity and tannins. For people looking for wines to pair with rich foods, Tazzelenghe checks all the boxes. Only a handful of winemakers work with the grape in single-variety wines. Lino Casella, La Viarte, and d'Attimis-Maniago are some of the few, and their Tazzelenghe bottles are worth seeking out to get an idea of what the grape is all about.

Regional Foods

Asparagus with prosciutto

Baccalà
salt cod

Blècs
buckwheat noodles

Cevapcici
grilled sausages

Cheese
Carnia, firm, aged cows' milk cheese

Montasio, similar aged cows' milk cheese, its cheesemaking process in is regulated by its own consortium

ricotta affumicata, smoked ricotta

Cjalzòns
stuffed pasta that can be savory or sweet

Frico
crispy potato and Montasio cheese "pancake"

Gnocchi croccanti
gnocchi filled with prosciutto and Montasio cheese

Goulash (or Gulasch)

Gubana
multilayered sweet pastry filled with dried fruits and nuts

Jota triestina
bean and cabbage soup from Trieste

Polenta

Prosciutto di San Danielle

Tiramisù

Toç in braide
creamy polenta with ricotta sauce and brown butter

Torta di mele
apple cake

Recommended Producers

Abbazia di Rosazzo

Bastianich

Damijan

Dario Prinčič

Denis Montanar

Dorigo

Edi Kante

Edi Keber

Ferlat

Gigante

Gravner

I Clivi

Jermann

La Castellada

La Viarte

Le Vigne di Zamò

Lis Neris

Livio Felluga

Marco Felluga

Marco Sara

Miani

Moschioni

Radikon

Ronchi di Cialla

Ronco del Gnemiz

Scarbolo

Scarpetta

Skerk

Skerlj

Venica & Venica

Vie di Romans

Vignai da Duline

Vodopivec

Zidarich

Lazio

The National Archaeological Museum of Cerveteri sits west of Rome in a sixteenth-century castle next to a beach. Well before Rome was much of anything, this was the Etruscan city of Caere, a thriving port that traded wine from all over the Mediterranean. Today, the museum houses a collection of amphorae, the terracotta vessels used to transport wine in ancient times by boat, as relics of those boom years. Once emptied, amphorae were often broken up and used to line roads or tile roofs—it was easier to make new ones than recycle the vessels. A dirt path nearby leads to the Banditaccia Necropolis, a UNESCO World Heritage site of Etruscan tombs, where the first family of Rome lies. The site itself is understated, the tops of the tombs covered in grass, with nettles and lamb's quarters growing along the path. In the United States, anything this remarkable would be walled off, but people in Lazio are used to living alongside ancient history. They don't take this for granted—in Cerveteri, the Etruscans hold more clout than the Romans. Near the museum, the Casale Cento Corvi winery makes wine with a local red grape called Giacchè, which it claims was *nato prima di Roma*, or "born before Rome."

While that might be true, it's taken the twenty-first century for the wines of the region surrounding Rome to come alive. Compared to other parts of Italy, Lazio was slow to shake off its "quantity over quality" wine reputation. But it's not for a lack of good vineyards or grapes or climate. Sandwiched between Campania to the south and Tuscany to the north, with the spine of the Apennines running along its eastern border, Lazio has a warm, dry coast with temperate breezes from the sea, like Tuscany's Maremma. It has plenty of volcanic soil and cool microclimates thanks to its crater lakes and several small mountain chains that connect to the Apennines, giving winemakers everything they need for making lively bottles. And there are a handful of grapes unique to the area. Lazio's muddled identity is also not because of any lack of talent—winemakers such as Marco Carpineti, Damiano Ciolli, Andrea Occhipinti, and many others have understood the potential of their grapes and territory for at least a couple of decades. The biggest obstacle for Lazio wine was, until recently, Rome.

For years, drinking local in Rome meant sipping watered-down white wines sold by the carafe to crowds. Wine either came from a large co-op, which bought grapes in bulk from local farmers, or from Lazio farmers who came to the city to sell their wine in refillable bottles. Romans bought wine in plastic containers for less than the price of Coca-Cola and stored it on their balconies no matter how hot it got outside. If a farmer tried to get serious and put wine in a glass bottle with the family name on the label, Romans and farmers alike would tease him for being egotistical. Important wines came from outside of Lazio or were made with Merlot, Cabernet Sauvignon, or even Petit Manseng. It also helped if you came from an aristocratic family and didn't have to make money from the land. By the 1980s, it was so hard to make a living growing grapes that the next generation left the fields to take jobs in the city, preferring commuting to working the land for low-paying gains. As farmers stopped selling grapes, co-ops closed, leaving behind fleets of mothballed vats.

In the 1990s, things started to change for the better. Some Lazio natives from grape-farming families decided to make something out of their land and wine. Others who were new to the business, either graduates from the enology program at the university in Viterbo or white-collar career changers, moved to the countryside to take over the abandoned vineyards. They learned as they went, while striving for a slower, sustainable life. Compared to land in nearby Tuscany, vineyards in Lazio were affordable and came with old vines. Because Lazio's wine identity was fragmented, winemakers were free to experiment without the pressure of living up to expectations. As opposed to the large fuss made in Barolo in the 1980s when some winemakers started using barrique (small French oak barrels) in place of *botti* (large Slavonian oak barrels), the only people to take notice of changes in Lazio were the old *contadini*, farmers who thought this next generation was crazy—who would really spend more than three euros on a liter of Lazio wine?

Today, Lazio has turned into one of the most experimental wine areas in Italy. Even the region's classics, like Frascati and Est! Est!! Est!!! di Montefiascone, are being rethought, made with care and with better grapes. Roman restaurants pour Cesanese from Piglio and Olevano Romano, Aleatico from Viterbo, and sparkling Bellone from Cori. Giacchè is still rare, but that it even survived the old days is enough reason to celebrate.

History

Rome has always had an outsize impact on Lazio's identity. The city is so famous that it is easy to overlook the region that surrounds it. Visitors may spend decades exploring Rome but rarely venture out to the countryside to discover other ancient cities, such as Cori. South of Rome, Cori was once the capital of the Latini, one of many tribes in Lazio that predated the Romans. The Samnites, Aequi, and Volsci lived in the Apennines, and the Etruscans controlled the area north of the Tiber River. While everything eventually came under Roman control, the region's patchwork identities linger today. The land around Cori in the southwest feels more like northern Campania, the northeast near Lake Bolsena more like Umbria. At times, the only thing that the north and south of Lazio have in common is that they are rural and relaxed, the opposite of Rome.

The Eternal City has been famous forever. By 69 BC, Rome had nearly a million voters listed on the census, the largest number in Europe for any city until the nineteenth century. Yet after the empire's fall, Rome's population plummeted, and the countryside absorbed some of the city. By the middle of the eighth century, the Papacy took control of the land around Rome, which became the Papal States. This band of territories stretched from the Tyrrhenian to Adriatic Sea by way of Umbria and was linked through treacherous roads through the Apennines, so oversight from Rome was limited. Infighting among the ruling classes left much of the city in disrepair until the sixteenth century, when new fountains, churches, and streets were constructed during the High Renaissance. And even then, it was no guarantee that the country's most iconic city would also become its capital. By 1861, when Italian patriots declared they had unified Italy, Rome was still under the power of the pope. French troops surrounded the city to protect the head of the Catholic Church until conflicts elsewhere in Europe in 1870 forced them to leave. Only then did Italians secure Rome, which has been the country's capital ever since.

No matter who was running Rome, wine was on the table for aristocrats and farmers alike. Since ancient times, the Castelli Romani—the picturesque hills south of the city known for being a source of wine—have long been a destination for wealthy families, bishops, and popes, who vacationed and built villas in the towns near Lake Albano. Among these towns, Frascati is the most synonymous with Lazio wine. During the Middle Ages, residents there built simple cabins out of *frascata*, a local wood. When wine was ready to drink, they hung a *frasca*, or branch, outside their door, an invitation that they were open for business. When the last barrel was empty, the *frasca* came down. This tradition spread throughout Lazio, where grottoes, caves, and inns of all kinds served wine straight from the barrel along with bread, cheese, and simple fare. In one of Italy's more whimsical wine origin stories, a traveling German bishop sent his servant ahead to find the inns that served the best wine. If the wine was good, he wrote "Est," Latin for "It is," on the door. By the time the servant reached Montefiascone, a town near Lake Bolsena, he was so appreciative of the wines that he scrawled "Est! Est!! Est!!!" on the door. Today, historians have questioned the story's validity, but it lives on in the Est! Est!! Est!!! di Montefiascone DOC.

The tradition of going to the source for wine continued throughout the twentieth century, especially during *sagras*, or annual festivals. During the Sagra dell'Uva in Marino, a town on the north shore of Lake Albano, wine even flows from the fountain. In the twentieth century, Romans knew that wines always tasted better where they were made. Part of this had to do with the challenges in transportation. Before bottling processes became sophisticated, wines were pumped from barrel to tank for transport and then siphoned into new containers in Rome, exposing the liquid to heat and oxygen. This was especially tough on white wines, which were (and still are) the majority of what Lazio makes and drinks. In Burton Anderson's 1980 book *Vino*, he describes the situation like this: "By the time the last liters were drawn off into carafes, the wine was often flat, sour, clearly off." And sometimes it wasn't all wine in those carafes. On June 30, 1974, the *New York Times*

ran the headline "Fake Wine Stirs Italian Scandal." A mix of water, molasses, coloring agents, and "dregs from pressed grapes" from Sicily had been passed off as Frascati in Rome. Eventually, stainless steel vats, temperature-controlled fermentation, and better bottling processes combated oxidation problems. White wines fermented without their skins were filtered, bottled, and—before more sophisticated bottling technology came along—pasteurized. While these wines were stable for transport, they were also homogenous and industrial, and some lamented the loss of the more nuanced, golden wines served directly from the cask.

Red wines had it even worse. Lazio's best known red, Cesanese, had a reputation for making cheap, off-dry, often fizzy wine. In Robert Camuto's book *South of Somewhere*, he recounts winemaker Damiano Ciolli's story of going to Rome with his father to sell Cesanese door-to-door, filling reusable bottles with wine. When Damiano took over the farm in 2001, he began looking beyond Lazio for ways to make better wine with Cesanese. In the early days, neighbors thought he was foolish to expect more from a common grape. It took him exporting Cesanese abroad to prove that the wine was excellent, and now demand for it outpaces supply. We used to pour his spicy, floral "Silene" by the glass at A16, but now, we fly through our inventory so fast it's hard to keep enough bottles in stock. The wine's versatility lies in its balanced acidity coupled with notes of spice such as clove, nutmeg, and white pepper.

In the twentieth century, there was an outlier amid Lazio's cheap wines. At Fiorano, his estate along the ancient Via Appia, Prince Alberico Boncompagni Ludovisi made singular bottles that he wanted to drink. In addition to Malvasia di Candia, he grew Cabernet, Semillon, and Merlot, never using chemicals or turning to industrial techniques to farm the land. To buy a bottle, people came to the estate and paid with exact change. Over the years, the wines garnered mythical status in Rome for reaching quality levels that most thought impossible for the region. Meanwhile, the prince grew more particular. After his last vintage in 1995, he was so sure no one could continue making wine to his exacting measures that he tore most of the vines out and sold off the rest of his inventory in 2000. Somehow, A16 was lucky to get a few bottles, and we poured them for Italians who said they never could find them in Rome. The Semillon and Malvasia di Candia showed remarkable longevity, with notes of lemon verbena, lavender honey, and nectarine mixed with a dash of petrol. Today, some in the family claim the prince had a change of heart after ripping out the vines. From separate pieces of the prince's land, two different factions are making wines with "Fiorano" in the name: his granddaughters Alessia, Allegra, and Albiera Antinori, who have the "Fattoria di Fiorano" label (and are part of the Antinori family of Tuscany); and a cousin, Alessandrojacopo Boncompagni Ludovisi, who has the "Tenuta di Fiorano" label. Both feuded over who could use the Fiorano name, but that might be how the prince would have liked it.

Land and Wines

Formed by volcanic activity millions of years ago, Lazio is physically a lot like Campania. Instead of having a dramatic coastline, though, its drama lies inland, where hills and mountains surround deep crater lakes. Thanks to elevation and microclimates, many of its best growing areas have cooling breezes and large temperature swings between morning and night. Lazio is 20 percent flat and 26 percent mountainous, with the remainder made up of hills. While it used to pump out more wine than nearly any other region, today its output of around 38.3 million gallons (1.45 million hectoliters) ranks in the middle, between Campania and Lombardy.

While Lazio has five provinces, most of them cover rural areas, with the big exception of the province surrounding Rome that shares the same name. In the north, bordering Tuscany and Umbria, the Viterbo province has become a dynamic place of winemaking experimentation, especially along the shores of Lake Bolsena, Europe's largest crater lake. There, olive trees are just as common as vines, and the soil is rich in volcanic ash and iron. The grapes that grow here, like Sangiovese, Canaiolo, Ciliegiolo, Grechetto, and Procanico (a higher-quality biotype of Trebbiano Toscano), reflect how close the province is to Tuscany and Umbria. (Some, like winemaker Sergio Mottura, work on both sides of the border; see page 238.) In the past, most farmers around the lake had small vineyards and sold their grapes to co-ops. Today, those small plots are being rehabilitated by relative newcomers. On the northern slopes of the lake in the town of Gradoli, low-intervention winemakers such as Gianmarco Antonuzi and Clementine Bouveron make several blends at Le Coste, a cult-favorite winery, while Andrea Occhipinti focuses on the aromatic red grape, Aleatico. Meanwhile, American Joy Kull, who learned how to make wine at Le Coste, has her own low-intervention winery, La Villana. In the old days, vineyards were grown at lower elevations, but now, some are experimenting with planting vines as high as 1,967 feet (600 meters) above sea level.

Some of the new energy from Gradoli has infiltrated the south shore of the lake around Montefiascone. Starting in 2014, friends Marco Fucini, Nicola Brenciaglia, and Daniele Manoni began restoring old Canaiolo vines, later borrowing Andrea Occhipinti's cellar to make their wine. Under the Il Vinco name (after the willow branch used to tie vines to stakes in the vineyard), they make juicy *rosso* and *rosato* Canaiolo wines. Farther south near Viterbo, the Monastero Suore Cistercensi—Sisters of the Cistercian Order—make blends from native grapes. The sisters do everything themselves, from farming organically and harvesting to making the wine. In the early 2000s, Giampaolo Bea, of Paolo Bea in Umbria, began working with the nuns to help them craft gentle skin-contact white wines, like "Coenobium" (for more on skin-contact wines, see Orange Wine, page 84). With notes of cantaloupe, apple, and lemon pith, the wine is incredible with food: the time the grapes spend on the skin imparts a savory note to the wine, allowing it to complement earthy flavors such as saffron, sea urchin, and mushrooms. And with roasted carrots glazed with honey and black pepper, it's also a seamless match.

West of Lake Bolsena along the coast bordering Tuscany lies a warm, dry area where wineries, like Habemus, focus on international grapes Grenache, Syrah, and Tempranillo, which benefit from breezes from the Tolfa hills. To the east of Viterbo bordering Umbria and Abruzzo, the claw-shaped province of Rieti is mostly mountains, with the least amount of vineyard land. South of Viterbo, the province of Rome takes up the largest swath of land in the region, stretching from Rieti to the coast. The coastal hills are warm, with areas like Cerveteri growing a mix of international and local grapes, like Giacchè. But most of the winemaking attention in the province is south of the city, starting with the Castelli Romani.

Surrounding Lake Albano, the hills south of Rome are home to Frascati, Marino, and many other towns that make up Lazio's best-known wine area. Built over centuries with elaborate villas (Sophia Loren once lived here), there are vines everywhere, even at the pope's official summer residence at Castel Gandolfo, where consulting enologist Riccardo Cotarella—known for the modern Falesco winery in Montefiascone—was tapped to make wine for the Vatican. The Castelli Romani DOC comprises the northern side of Lake Albano, while the Colli Albani wines come from the central and southern parts around the lake. Wines from Frascati and Marino now allow Malvasia Puntinata, Bellone, Bombino Bianco, and/or Greco (the same Greco that grows in Campania) into the mix, which has improved the wine's potential. In the Castelli Romani, Casale Marchese uses Malvasia Puntinata in their Frascati Superiore, which makes a wine that conjures a combination of pomelo, green apple, orange blossom, and wax bean. The vineyard land itself has long been recognized for being unusual, with high levels of potassium and sodium in the soft, volcanic soils. As such, the white wines made from here tend to be rich in minerals, giving them complexity even without notable acidity. More important than the soils is the move among winemakers to reclaim the importance of blending local grapes. With Frascati and its neighboring wine areas, the sum is better than its parts.

Within the Alban Hills, there's also a movement to restore the tradition of making wine in chestnut barrels. Farmers planted chestnut trees so they could later harvest the wood for barrels, which were used regularly until around the 1960s. Cantina Ribelà's Chiara Bianchi and Daniele Presutti sought out barrels from Alfredo Sannibale, the last chestnut barrel maker in the area, to age their "Pentima," a rich, skin-contact Malvasia.

East of the Alban Hills, framed by the Ernici Mountains to the east, is the home of the two Cesanese grapes, Comune and di Affile, which are fragrant, fruity, sometimes spicy, and nearly always good with pasta *all'amatriciana*. The commune of Affile (from which Cesanese di Affile takes its name) is higher in altitude than the Olevano Romano and Piglio, but the microclimates are similar in all three areas, with cool nights and warm days. What changes is the soil, which can shift between volcanic to clay from vineyard to vineyard.

The provinces of Latina in the southwest and Frosinone in the southeast make up the southern portion of Lazio. Here, the most notable wine area is Cori, which sits at the edge of the Lepini Mountains. Marco Carpineti, one of the first to champion native grapes such as Bellone and Nero Buono, has a vineyard of volcanic soil called Capolemole, which yields wine with a fresh, mineral edge. Carpineti was once the president of the local co-op, Cincinnato (named after a Roman senator who settled in the area), before going it alone. Today, both Carpineti's winery and Cincinnato make wine with Bellone and Nero Buono, experimenting with the best ways to vinify the varieties that locals believe have been grown there for thousands of years. South of Cori along the hot, dry coastal hills, the town of Terracina has another rare grape, Moscato di Terracina, which is made in both sweet and sparkling styles.

The deeper you look in Lazio, the more stories of reinvention emerge. The one thing that we hope won't change is how well these wines pair with food. Whether it's roadside porchetta in the Alban Hills or fried artichokes at an osteria in Rome or even the squid ink pasta at A16, Lazio wines work with them all. White or red, the best Lazio bottles refresh the palate no matter how rich the meal.

Lazio Grapes

Even though nearly three-quarters of the wine made in Lazio is white, the region has been quietly building up a following for spicy, aromatic red wines.

White

Bellone

Large, thin-skinned Bellone grapes are great to eat, something that isn't the case for all wine grapes. Bellone used to be common in the hills around Lake Albana until it was displaced by Trebbiano Toscano and Malvasia di Candia in the twentieth century. Today what's old is new again, and producers such as Frascati maker Casale Marchese are reintroducing Bellone to their blends. The best place for Bellone is Cori, where the variety grows well in the volcanic-limestone soils and dry, temperate climate. There, farmers never stopped growing the grape (they couldn't afford to rip out vines and start over with imported vines). Bellone from Cori is fresh, filled with accents of stone fruit and green apple or ripe citrus and Mediterranean herbs. The variety has high acidity, allowing it to make balanced sparkling and sweet wines, too. The Cincinnato co-op makes two Bellone wines: a sparkling wine made with the *metodo Martinotti* technique (see Italy's Sparkling Wines, page 262) and a still wine with a longer, fruit-forward finish. Both wines have bright fruit giving way to more complex flavors of herbs and lemon rind. Marco Carpineti also makes a handful of wines with Bellone, including "Capolemole

Bianco," a fresh, floral white wine from grapes grown in volcanic soils; "Kius," the first *metodo classico* sparkling Bellone ever made; and "Nzù," an amphora-aged wine that showcases a richer side of the grape.

Bombino Bianco
(see Puglia chapter, page 167)

Grechetto Group
(see Umbria chapter, page 241)

Greco
(see Campania chapter, page 63)

Malvasia Group

The Malvasias of Italy are a confusing group of grapes; even though they share the same name, most are not related. Some reach great heights; others are more modest in their success. Friuli Venezia Giulia's Malvasia Istriana (page 86) is one of the best, and so is Emilia-Romagna's Malvasia di Candia Aromatica (page 72). Despite the similar name, Lazio's Malvasia Bianca di Candia has no connection to either, as far as we can tell. According to Jancis Robinson's book *Wine Grapes*, "Candia" was an old name for Crete, where these grapes reportedly were transported from. The trickiest part is that labels often say "Malvasia," and it takes a little digging to figure out which Malvasia is used in the wine. Oftentimes producers use a mix, since so many of Lazio's wines are blends.

- **Malvasia Bianca di Candia:** This vigorous variety is known for high yields and high acidity, which makes it a reliable blending grape, though one that may not be ready to stand on its own. One theory on why Frascati and other historic Lazio wines developed a poor reputation in the twentieth century is that the DOC regulations required vintners to use Malvasia Bianca di Candia (and Trebbiano Toscano) in place of Malvasia Puntinata. The regulations finally changed, and more winemakers use Malvasia Puntinata for their DOC and IGT wines today.

Winemaker Damiano Ciolli with his Cesanese vines.

- **Malvasia Puntinata (Malvasia del Lazio):**
Named for the speckled skin of the grapes when ripe (*puntinata* means "spotted"), Malvasia Puntinata used to be the main Malvasia of many of Lazio's historic winemaking areas until it fell out of favor. Compared with Malvasia Bianca di Candia, it has lower yields and is more susceptible to vine diseases, yet today it's recognized as the better wine grape of the two. Lightly aromatic with high acidity if the grapes are picked before they become too ripe, this Malvasia yields rich, almost creamy white wines with light herbal and floral notes. Lorenzo Costantini blends both Malvasia types together in "Borgo del Cedro," a Frascati Superiore. In the Frascati area, Cantina Ribelà makes pure Malvasia Puntinata aged in chestnut barrels, the traditional type of wood used in the Castelli Romani. This Malvasia is also made into a *passito* called Cannellino, in which grapes are left to dry on the vine before being pressed and vinified.

Moscato di Terracina

Italy has a few small towns in warm coastal areas that make historic wines with a Moscato grape, like Moscato di Trani in Puglia. The town of Terracina, an hour's drive south of Rome along the coast, has a warm, breezy maritime climate. There, Moscato di Terracina picks up the salt from the air and soil, helping to balance the fruit-forward flavors in *passito* and sparkling wines made from local producers Terra delle Ginestre and Cantina Villa Gianna. These wines often have both tropical fruits and apricots, with enticing floral aromas. Cantina Sant'Andrea's "Oppidum" is a dry version of Moscato di Terracina. The low-alcohol wine, with bright notes of gooseberry, pairs well with seafood.

Passerina

(see Le Marche chapter, page 109)

Trebbiano Giallo

Named for the golden color of its grapes when ripe (*giallo* means "yellow"), this Trebbiano is a historic grape of Lazio, blended into many of its white wines. Like Malvasia, producers tend to shorten the grape to "Trebbiano" on a label, so it's hard to know whether a wine includes Trebbiano Giallo or the more common Trebbiano Toscano. Around Lake Bolsena and Orvieto, it is often blended with Procanico, a similar grape that is believed to be a higher quality biotype of Trebbiano Toscano.

Trebbiano Toscano

(see Tuscany chapter, page 230)

Red

Aleatico

A close cousin of the aromatic red wine Lacrima di Morro d'Alba (page 110), Aleatico is known for delivering aromas of flowers, cinnamon, and cherry with each glass. Unlike a lot of wine grapes, Aleatico is sweet to eat out of hand thanks to its thin skins. Unfortunately, its thin skins complicate matters in damp years, since they make the grape susceptible to mildew. To preserve its acidity to make dry wine, vintners harvest early. While attending the viticulture and enology program at the university in Viterbo, Andrea Occhipinti became fascinated with Gradoli, studying the land for his thesis. After leaving school, he started making wine there in 2004, experimenting with dry versions of Aleatico, performing blind tastings in which Aleatico was mistaken for white wine. Today, he makes a range of wines with the grape, including "Alter Alea," a white wine, and "Alea Rosa," a *rosato*. With notes of strawberry, black pepper, tangerine, and watermelon, this *rosato* has both everyday appeal and enough structure to stand up to complex fare at the table. Occhipinti's friend Ludovico Botti, who also studied Aleatico at the same university, makes Aleatico close to the Umbrian border at his family's winery, Trebotti. Joy Kull, an American who started the La Villana winery in Gradoli, has a crisp and floral Aleatico with spicy notes. The grape is also grown on the islands of Elba and Capraia off the coast of Tuscany. There, it goes into *passito* with the grape's classic aromas of roses, and violets.

Canaiolo

(see Tuscany chapter, page 230)

Cesanese Group

Grown in or near the Apennine foothills, Cesanese has become Lazio's standout red. In the past, the wines were *amabile*, or semisweet, and slightly fizzy thanks to residual sugar left in the wine. Once sold in refillable containers for a few euros in Rome, the wines are now allocated (sold to key accounts in

limited quantities, which happens when demand outpaces supply). The reason is simple: fruit forward and bright, with light tannins and floral aromas, Cesanese is the kind of red wine that plays well with food, from fennel sausage to nearly anything with capers. Even artichokes, a notorious difficult vegetable pairing, don't clash with this wine. Expect flavors such as cherry, raspberry, spices, and a hint of green pepper. There are two different Cesanese grapes. Wines under the Cesanese del Piglio DOCG or Cesanese di Olevano DOC can contain either, while Cesanese di Affile DOC contains the "di Affile" variety.

- **Cesanese Comune:** With larger grapes than Cesanese di Affile, Cesanese Comune creates juicy, low-tannin wines with accents of spices and even lychees. It grows around the towns of Piglio and Anagni in Frosinone and Olevano Romano in Roma. While it's often described as less important than the di Affile grape, it is easier to work with and imparts a fresh quality to Cesanese wines.

- **Cesanese di Affile:** Named for Affile, a town only a half hour from the regional park of the Simbruini Mountains, this Cesanese does better growing in high elevations compared with its Comune counterpart, gaining in complexity and tannins and allowing more aging time in the cellar. Ciolli makes "Cirsium" with Cesanese di Affile vines planted in 1953 by his grandfather. Expect notes of cassis, loganberry, iron, red plum, and morello cherries.

Ciliegiolo
(see Tuscany chapter, page 231)

Giacchè
Grown around the coastal town of Cerveteri east of Rome, Giacchè is a small grape with a lot of seeds and thick skins that can make it hard for winemakers to love. It fell out of favor in the twentieth century as other grapes became more popular, but the Collacciani family of Casale Cento Corvi is one of the few wineries to take an interest in it. Thanks to the family's history—Giacchè was the wine of their grandparents' generation—Casale Cento Corvi rehabilitated enough vines to make a mildly spiced, slightly tannic wine filled with dark-fruit flavors, like blueberries and blackberries.

Montepulciano
(see Abruzzo chapter, page 40)

Nero Buono
The name means "good black grape," and Nero Buono yields a grapey wine with a deep-purple hue and an herbal nose. It's a grape that would have been forgotten had it not been for the work of the Cincinnato co-op and its then-leader Marco Carpineti (before he left to start his own winery). Locals take pride in the grape, which they believed had been planted in Cori by Cincinnato, an ancient Roman who settled there in the fifth century BCE. It used to be called Nero Buono di Cori—and locals still lament dropping the "Cori" name from the grape. Like the white grape Bellone, it grows well in the volcanic soils and dry, temperate climate around Cori.

Sangiovese
(see Tuscany chapter, page 231)

Regional Foods

Brutti ma buoni
"ugly but delicious" hazelnut cookies

Carciofi alla giudia
"Jewish-style" fried artichokes

Carciofi alla romana
artichokes cooked in olive oil, garlic, and herbs until tender

Carciofi infarinati
artichokes breaded and fried

Cheese
pecorino, sheep's milk cheese

ricotta romano, made with sheep's milk

Coda alla vaccinara
braised oxtail

Coratella d'agnello
cooked lamb innards

Fagioli en purgatorio
beans "in purgatory," cooked with garlic and herbs and served with olive oil

Pasta
alla gricia, pasta tossed in rendered guanciale, grated pecorino, and black pepper

all'amatriciana, tomato-guanciale sauce for pasta

cacio e pepe, pasta tossed in grated pecorino and black pepper

gnocchi alla romana, gnocchi made from semolina flour and sliced into disks

rigatoni con pagliata, rigatoni with intestines

spaghetti alla carbonara, spaghetti tossed in an emulsified sauce of eggs, pepper, guanciale (or pancetta), and grated pecorino

Pizza al taglio
thick-cut pizza in the style of an open-faced sandwich

Pupazza frascatana
doll-shaped cookie with three breasts, two for milk and one for wine

Saltimbocca alla romana
veal cutlets with prosciutto and sage

Trippa alla romana
tripe in tomato sauce

Vignarola
spring stew of peas, artichokes, and fava beans

Recommended Producers

Abbia Nòva

Andrea Occhipinti

Antica Cantina Leonardi

Casale Cento Corvi

Casale del Giglio

Casale della Ioria

Casale Marchese

Castel de Paolis

Cecubi

Cincinnato

Colli di Catone

Cominium

Corte dei Papi

Damiano Ciolli

De Sanctis

Di Palma

Etruscaia

Falesco

Fattoria di Fiorano

Fontana Candida

Formiconi

Il Vinco

L'Olivella

Luca Sbardella

Macciocca

Marco Carpineti

Maria Ernesta Berucci

Monastero Suore Cistercensi

Palazzo Tronconi

Paolo e Noemia d'Amico

Sant'Andrea

Santa Lucia

Sergio Mottura

Stefanoni

Tenuta di Fiorano

Terenzi

Terre dei Rutuli

Tullio

Villa Simone

Le Marche

At four thirty in the morning, a group of bidders sat on the bleachers near a digital screen posting prices as cartons of fish traveled down a conveyor belt. The Mercato Ittico di Pesaro, a local fish auction in northeastern Le Marche, offered sardines, mackerel, and scampi as well as *canocchie* and *baganelli*, local fish once saved for cats until enterprising cooks turned them into delicacies. Other than a burly man who complained the fishermen were roughhousing the daily catch, the mood was subdued, the electronic bidding quietly belying the drama in prices: while some catches were cheap, turbot netted thirty-five euros a kilo. Alberto Taddei, a sommelier who makes wine at his family's Selvagrossa winery nearby, brought us there to catch a glimpse of everyday life along the Adriatic coast. After a round of espresso, we followed Alberto through the coastal city of Pesaro to buy fish to take home to eat with his mom's *passatelli*, an extruded pasta made with eggs, flour, and breadcrumbs and served in a light broth. We chased down the fish and pasta with a glass of Albanella, a saline white wine made from vines grown close to the sea.

Bordering Emilia-Romagna to the north, Abruzzo to the south, and Umbria to the west, with tiny portions grazing Lazio and Tuscany, Le Marche is in the center of Italy, the calf of the boot. Its long coastline makes the region a haven for seafood and beach lovers, but compared to places like Capri that attract international tourists, Le Marche is traveled mostly by Italians. From gentle hills to river valleys and mountains, little of Le Marche is flat, yet its countryside is softer than that of Abruzzo. Le Marche generally feels gentler and less wild, with medieval cities scattered throughout the hilly landscape.

Le Marche's annual wine output is only 35 percent of what Tuscany produces each year. Yet like Tuscany and its most well-known wine, Chianti (see page 221), Le Marche also faced a quality crisis with its main wine, Verdicchio. In the 1960s and '70s, Verdicchio dei Castelli di Jesi was a light, tart mass-market white wine sold in whimsical bottles. To keep up with demand, Verdicchio vines were grown to generate more grapes, diluting quality and character. In the cellar, it wasn't much better. Overly technical winemaking stripped the wines of personality so they all tasted the same. The silver lining was that some companies used their mass-market profits to reinvest in the cellar and vineyards, setting a foundation for more nuanced wines in the future.

Mass-market wine was always at odds with how Le Marche natives did business, according to

Ampelio Bucci, the proprietor of Villa Bucci, one of Le Marche's historic estates, and professor of marketing at the University of Milan. The region is home to small-scale artisans, some of whom weave bags for Prada or Fendi, bind books by hand, or make shoes to order. One handmade pair of shoes from Le Marche–based Bontoni costs a thousand euros. In other words, if you can't make the most in the world, make the best. In 2011, Ampelio explained to us how this played into wine: "I always insist that you have to focus on the indigenous grape because that's the only way a small producer can be more of a craftsman. In Italy, we are not able to make large industry. We are able to make small- and medium-sized businesses."

The Bucci family has had its roots in Le Marche since antiquity; a Roman plaque in the seaside city of Senigallia has "BUCCI" etched into the stone. In 1936, Ampelio's father bought property in Montecarotto, a hill town inland from Ancona, and in the 1970s, Ampelio took over managing the estate, moving away from growing commodity crops and toward growing grapes and olives. He brought in Giorgio Grai, an enologist from Alto Adige, to help establish the estate's wine made from Verdicchio grown in eight plots scattered around the Castelli di Jesi area (mainly in the towns of Montecarotto, Serre de' Conti, and Barbera). He also started collecting vintage typewriters, shoe molds, and screw presses once used to crush grapes—all old things that speak to making handcrafted goods.

With a few exceptions, Le Marche wine is made by small to medium producers that push each other toward quality production. While Verdicchio, Sangiovese, and Montepulciano are the most grown grapes, there's energy being put into lesser-known white and red varieties. For whites, there's Pecorino in the south and Biancame and Albanella in the north. There are also two excellent aromatic reds, Vernaccia Nera in the Serrapetrona DOCG and the Lacrima grape in the Morro d'Alba municipality. Plenty of producers are also making bubbles, from *metodo classico* wines made with Verdicchio to sparkling reds reminiscent of Lambrusco. While not every bottle knocks it out of the park (that's true everywhere), it is hard to find bad wine in Le Marche. And all this—plus the fresh seafood—makes a visit to Italy's eastern coast all the more worthwhile.

History

The ancient Greeks founded Ancona, which is Le Marche's current capital and one of Italy's busiest ports. By the time the Greeks arrived, the Adriatic coast had already been settled by Umbrians and Etruscans. Later, the Romans built up the coast, and even today, the old parts of Senigallia still carry a Roman imprint, with broad boulevards and a large outdoor marketplace. After the fall of Rome, it became dangerous to live along the coast, and inhabitants moved inland, building walled hill towns to stay safe from invaders. Today, one of Le Marche's best-known wine regions, Verdicchio dei Castelli di Jesi, spreads out west of Senigallia amid the hills of the *castelli*, a series of medieval towns.

Le Marche soon became one of the Papal States, a band of territories cutting through the center of the Italian peninsula, including Perugia, Spoleto, Benevento, Ancona, Romagna, and parts of Emilia. From the eighth century until Italy's unification in the mid-nineteenth century, these states found themselves under the rule of the pope, and the Catholic Church held sway over the culture and politics. In Le Marche, the town of Loreto welcomed pilgrims from all over Europe who came to visit the Santa Casa (Holy House), the place—according to legend—where the Virgin Mary raised Jesus. While Italy's unification was not good for all regions, it changed Le Marche for the better when the new government forced the Vatican to sell off land. In the 1870s, Antonio Garofoli bought his own plot in Loreto and soon began selling wine to pilgrims. Today, Garofoli remains an important winery in Le Marche, evolving over generations to make a broad range of wines with the region's key grapes, Verdicchio and Montepulciano.

In the mid-twentieth century, Le Marche's white wines, like most whites across Italy, were modernized for industrial production. Advances in cellar chemistry and a booming export market led to the production of mass-market wines in bottles shaped like fish or amphorae—shapes that became synonymous with Verdicchio wine for years. Gradually, a shift toward quality began as better temperature-controlled systems were introduced into cellars. In 1981, Garofoli released Macrina, a Verdicchio wine sold in a clear Bordeaux bottle, to prove that their Verdicchio could age for a couple of years without browning—a breakthrough at the time (previous bottles were pasteurized for stability). Still, in the wake of the move toward volume production, the heritage of older, less vigorous grapes was lost, as these vines were pulled out and replanted in favor of higher-volume clones. As a result, it's harder to find old vines—such as the kind you see in Vulture in Basilicata or in the Langhe in Piedmont—in Le Marche.

In the past decade, Le Marche wines have become more varied, with second-, third- or even fifth-generation winemakers trying their hand at new ways to think about wine. More wines are certified organic or are grown in an organic way, and some winemakers are breaking free of the DOC system (see Italian Wine Quality Rankings, page 24) to carve their own path. The next generation of winemakers in Le Marche belong to Terroir Marche, a nonprofit consortium that pools resources together to promote each other's work.

Land and Wines

Le Marche is framed by the Apennines to the west and divided by a few river valleys running west to east. Its climate is split between the north and south, with the city of Ancona as the divider. North of Ancona, the climate leans continental, affected by winds blowing across the Adriatic from Friuli and the Balkans. There, cold fronts from the east keep vintners on guard against hail during harvest, just as they are in Piedmont, Lombardy, the Veneto, and Friuli. South of Ancona, the weather becomes more Mediterranean, and instead of storms during harvest, it's a lack of rain that's the concern. On the coast, the sea moderates weather extremes, keeping temperatures from spiking in any one direction.

While plenty of red wine is made here, Le Marche's calling card is white wine made from Verdicchio. Spanning the north and south sides of the Esino River, the Verdicchio dei Castelli di Jesi DOC is broad, comprising twenty-six villages spanning west of the medieval town of Jesi. Made up of a mix of limestone and marly clay, the soils pave the way for wines with bright acidity, and the sea offers a long growing season. Within Jesi, some villages are known for specific nuances. Broadly speaking, Verdicchio can be bolder north of the Esino, while south of the river it can be more perfumed. The differences between the sites are one reason Ampelio Bucci favors blending wines from various plots together for Villa Bucci's Verdicchio dei Castelli di Jesi. Corrado Dottori of La Distesa also blends but within a smaller geographical scope. For his Marche Bianco "Terre Silvate," he takes Verdicchio and Trebbiano Toscano grown in three different sites around the village of Cupramontana, resulting in a vibrant wine with layers of apple, citrus, chamomile, and salt. (Even though these vineyards are within the Verdicchio dei Castelli di Jesi DOC area, Dottori produces the wine as a Le Marche IGT to give him freedom to make the wine as he chooses.)

Compared with the gentle hills of the Jesi area, Matelica is more extreme. A north-south valley within the Apennine foothills, it's shielded from the ocean climate and sits at a higher elevation, resulting in larger temperature swings between night and day and throughout the year, from snowy winters to scorching summers. Here, there is also plenty of marl and sandstone soil, but the soils themselves are geologically older than those of Jesi. The combination lends itself to a longer growing season for Verdicchio, rendering a more structured wine with fresh citrus notes. In comparison, Verdicchio from Jesi is rounder and gentler, showing Mediterranean herbs, dried fruit, wildflowers, and a pinch of spice. No matter where it grows, Verdicchio expresses a characteristic note of bitter almond.

In the north of Le Marche, the wines are more of an even mix of white and red. Pinot Nero (Pinot Noir) has been grown since Napoleon came to Italy, and it's a required red grape in the sparkling wines of Colli Pesaresi DOC. A few Italian varieties are also gaining ground, such as Biancame and Albanella, both of which were frequently thought to be Trebbiano Toscano in the past. Grown along the Metauro River near the cities of Urbino and Pesaro, Biancame is the main variety in the Bianchello del Metauro DOC. In the south around Offida, white grapes Pecorino and Passerina continue to draw interest, particularly Pecorino. This grape was nearly lost until Cocci Grifoni's founder, Guido Cocci Grifoni, discovered a vineyard in the mountains in the 1980s and began studying its vines on advice from the Conegliano wine school in Veneto, the Agrarian Institute of Ascoli Piceno in Le Marche, and master sommelier Teodoro Bugari. The variety became one of the biggest native grape success stories to come out of central Italy, and the original vineyard remains at the winery today.

While white wines in Le Marche are being made in richer styles today compared to the 1970s, the region's red wines are getting lighter. In the 1990s, rich Montepulciano wines aged in French oak barrels, such as Oasi degli Angeli's Kurni, became iconic for their intensity, but today's reds are less concentrated and focused more on fresh aromas. More Sangiovese grows north of Ancona, and more Montepulciano grows to the south, especially in and around the Conero National Park. Within the park,

Montepulciano grapes grow in chalky soils, which can stress vines in years of little rainfall, leading to exceptionally concentrated fruit. Rosso Piceno is the largest DOC of Le Marche, including wide expanses of Ancona, Macerata, and parts of Ascoli Piceno, yielding an easier wine composed of Sangiovese and Montepulciano.

In northern Le Marche, Ciliegiolo, Colorino, and international varieties, such as Cabernet Franc, are commonly grown, along with Sangiovese. In Pesaro at the Taddei family's Selvagrossa winery, Alberto Taddei's grandfather bought Ciliegiolo vines from a nursery years ago to blend with his Sangiovese, thinking they were Colorino vines. According to Alberto, the error has turned out to be a good thing: Selvagrossa now makes a juicy, fresh *rosato* with Ciliegiolo.

Among Le Marche's reds, aromatic varieties Lacrima and Vernaccia Nera make fun, somewhat unusual wines. In 1958, Alberto Quacquarini started reviving an old practice of drying Vernaccia Nera grapes to concentrate the sugars, then adding the dried grapes to the following year's wine after harvest. The result is an ever-changing wine—sometimes dry, sometimes sweet, sometimes gently sparkling. Meanwhile, Lacrima is nearly only grown around Morro d'Alba, a town near the sea. Like the Pecorino grape, it nearly disappeared until Stefano Mancinelli and his family began producing wine with the grapes in the late 1970s. Later, the Marotti Campi family became a major proponent of the grape, becoming the first to bring Lacrima wine to San Francisco.

In the future, Le Marche producers will continue to dig deeper into understanding the differences amid their terrain. With Verdicchio, it's complicated: some producers would rather not be so closely associated with specific Verdicchio DOC or DOCG zones—some in Matelica want to drop "Verdicchio" from their labels and call their white wines "Matelica" so they can draw more attention to their terroir—while others would rather bring back the tradition of using blends of different white grapes and get away from making pure Verdicchio wines. If the climate continues to warm in Le Marche, there may even be a shift toward more red wines and fewer white wines. For now, we're fortunate that there is plenty of nuance to explore.

Le Marche Grapes

Le Marche is mostly known for Verdicchio, so much so that it's easy to overlook local red grapes Vernaccia Nera and Lacrima. The region also grows grapes common in neighboring regions Abruzzo and Tuscany.

White

Albanella

Albanella's story is a classic case of a local white grape getting confused with Trebbiano Toscano through no fault of its own (the same thing happened to Biancame). Around Pesaro, Albanella has long been thought of as another word for Trebbiano, but some scientists and vintners are convinced that it's either a biotype (a genetically identical but different grape, like Vermentino and Pigato, pages 118–119) or a completely unrelated grape. The grape is still around thanks to Fattoria Mancini, which has been making wine with Albanella since the 1970s. The estate also helped establish a subzone within the Colli Pesaresi DOC called Roncaglia, and white wines made in that subzone likely contain Albanella. (To make things more complicated, the DOC also requires the wine to contain 25 percent Pinot Nero—Pinot Noir—vinified as a white wine.) At Selvagrossa, Alberto Taddei started making Albanella from a coastal vineyard close to Roncaglia, and he was so enthused by the grape, he planted more vines. The combination of the maritime climate and the soil composed of limestone, sand, and clay gives the wine a clean, saline, mineral flavor, making it the perfect coastal white to drink alongside fresh seafood.

Biancame

Also known as Bianchello after the Bianchello di Metauro DOC, Biancame was confused with Trebbiano Toscano for years. But if the two vines grew side by side, it would be hard to believe they were the same variety. In *Native Wine Grapes of Italy*, Ian D'Agata describes Biancame as a vine that yields very white grapes, even when they're ripe, while Trebbiano Toscano grapes are golden at harvest. We're hedging that the difference is more than skin deep. Biancame is grown mostly near the cities of Urbino and Pesaro around the Metauro River, as well as around Rimini in Romagna. The wines the grape yields are at once light and fresh as well as round, with pleasant floral and citrus notes. Some also use it in sparkling and *passito* styles.

Cococciola
(see Abruzzo chapter, page 37)

Passerina

This grape is most at home in Le Marche in the Ascoli Piceno province and throughout Abruzzo, though some also grows in Lazio. It is often part of a blend with other local white grapes, though more producers are bottling it now on its own. For pure Le Marche Passerina, look for wines from Offida, a town within Ascoli Piceno, as well as the Terre di Offida DOC, which makes sparkling and *passito* styles. In fact, the grape yields so many styles of wine that it can be hard to pinpoint what a classic Passerina wine should be. In other words, it's too early to crown the white grape the next Pecorino. In the vineyard, it's hardy and disease resistant, and its grapes carry a welcome level of acidity. Some wines are steely, with lemon-lime tartness and flint, while others are richer and rounder, with more apple blossoms and acacia honey than lemon.

Pecorino
(see Abruzzo chapter, page 37)

Ribona (Maceratino Bianco)

This little-known grape, also called Maceratino Bianco, is mostly found in Le Marche's Colli

Maceratesi DOC. Once mistaken for other varieties (a recurring story in Italy, especially among white grapes), it's now understood to be a specific variety. Some say the grape comes from Greece and others think it's related to Verdicchio. It was once best known for fresh, easy white wines, though that is changing as growers and winemakers gain experience working with it. The Boccadigabbia estate makes "Le Grane," a Ribona wine made by adding slightly overripe grapes to the wine after it has been fermented to pass it through a second fermentation. The result is a richer wine with deep, ripe-fruit aromas.

Verdicchio (Trebbiano di Soave, Turbiana)

The likely origin for Verdicchio is the Venetian countryside, where its genetic twin, Trebbiano di Soave, still grows. One theory goes that after plagues swept through the Veneto after the Middle Ages, survivors moved away, taking prized cuttings with them. In Le Marche, the Verdicchio vines adapted readily to the limestone-rich soils and sunny weather.

Because it can create structured wines, Verdicchio is sometimes thought of as a red grape dressed up as a white. It's a productive variety and can produce a generous number of grapes while still maintaining high quality. It even does well with a little shade from its leafy canopy to protect the grapes from getting too much sun, which makes them bitter.

Verdicchio's classic tasting notes are bitter almond and citrus, with delicate floral aromas (it's not known for being very fragrant). Limestone soils add to the minerality and crisp, even vibrant acidity. Close to the coast in the Castelli di Jesi area, the wines can give the perception of scrub brush, while in the cooler, mountain area of Matelica, they carry more citrus fruit. The best renditions of Verdicchio can also age easily for a decade or more, with some of the citrus and herbal flavors giving way to more complex background notes. The grape has also long been used to make *frizzante* and *spumante* wines, and today's fashion for bubbles will bring us more sparkling Verdicchio to sample.

On the southern shores of Lake Garda in Veneto and Lombardy, Verdicchio is called Turbiana, where it's the key grape in the Lugana DOC. In Veneto's Soave area, Trebbiano di Soave is often used to round out Soave's main grape, Garganega.

Red

Ancellotta
(see Emilia-Romagna chapter, page 74)

Ciliegiolo
(see Tuscany chapter, page 231)

Colorino
(see Tuscany chapter, page 231)

Lacrima

Nearly the only place you'll find this grape is in the Lacrima di Morro d'Alba DOC in the Ancona province, where it grows close to the sea. But if you didn't know that this grape was grown in Le Marche, the DOC name can be confusing. To clear it up: Lacrima is not used in the Lacryma Christi wines from Mount Vesuvius, nor is it from Alba, a town in Piedmont. Instead, the name "Lacrima" comes from the Italian word for "tear," and it may have garnered its name for how grape juice teared up on the surface of the grape when ripe due to its thin skins. As for Morro d'Alba, that's the town where this grape grows. The deep purple wine is heavily perfumed, filled with everything from roses and rose geranium to warm baking spices. Like so many native Italian grapes, Lacrima could have disappeared had it not been for the work of local growers. Stefano Mancinelli was the first in recent times to champion the grape; before the DOC was granted in 1985, there were fewer than three acres (one hectare) planted. In 2003, the Mancinelli estate went the extra step to confirm the vines were Lacrima with DNA analysis. Lacrima is made as a dry and off-dry red wine as well as *passito*, which is excellent with chocolate.

Montepulciano
(see Abruzzo chapter, page 40)

Pinot Nero (Pinot Noir)

(see Trentino–Alto Adige chapter, page 214)

Sangiovese

(see Tuscany chapter, page 231)

Vernaccia Nera

While some Vernaccia Nera grows in Umbria, the best grapes come from the mountain village of Serrapetrona, where it is used to make Vernaccia di Serrapetrona DOCG, an unusual but excellent sparkling wine. At least 40 percent of the grapes for this wine are dried for a few months before being crushed. Vernaccia Nera had largely been forgotten about until Alberto Quacquarini revitalized the practice of drying the grapes in the mid-twentieth century, and the Quacquarini family continues the tradition. The concentrated juices from the dried grapes are added to the Vernaccia Nera wine made right after harvest, then it is left to ferment for a couple of months. Later, the wine goes through a third and final fermentation in bottle. The result can be sweet or dry, but it is always effervescent and deeply purple, imbued with aromas of dried rose petals, violets, and berry jam (like Lacrima, Vernaccia Nera is an aromatic grape). To try the grape made as a still wine, look for reds from the Serrapetrona and the I Terreni di Sanseverino DOCs.

Regional Foods

Beans

Brodetto
Adriatic seafood stew with tomatoes, garlic, and onions

Cauliflower
battered and fried

Cheese
caciotta, mild cows' milk cheese

pecorino, sheep's milk cheese

Fennel

Frustenga
raisin, fig, and walnut polenta cake

Olive all'ascolana
deep-fried stuffed olives

Olive oil

Pasta
maccheroncini di Campofilone, square spaghetti from Campofilone

passatelli, an extruded pasta made from bread crumbs and eggs

spaghetti alla chitarra, spaghetti cut with wires stretched across a wooden frame

tagliatelle and other ribbony pasta shapes, made with egg and durum wheat

Piadina
flatbread

Potatoes

Prosciutto di Carpegna

Stoccafisso in umido
fish cooked with tomato, onion, carrots, celery, and sometimes potatoes

Vincisgrassi
delicate layered pasta resembling lasagna with truffle and veal ragù

Recommended Producers

Alberto Quacquarini

Andrea Felici

Aurora

Belisario

Bisci

Boccadigabbia

Bonci

Borgo Paglianetto

Brocani

Bruscia

CasalFarneto

Ciù Ciù

Claudio Morelli

Cocci Grifoni

Colle Stefano

Di Santi

Garofoli

Failoni

La Distesa

La Monacesca

La Staffa

Le Terrazze

Luigi Giusti

Malacari Tavignano

Mancini

Marotti Campi

Oasi degli Angeli

Pievalta

Poderi San Lazzaro

San Lorenzo

Sartarelli

Selvagrossa

Stefano Antonucci

Tavignano

Velenosi

Villa Bucci

Liguria

In 1884, Claude Monet set up an easel in Dolceacqua, a medieval town on the western edge of Liguria, to paint the arched bridge connecting the Doria Castle with the town. The painting lives in the Musée Marmottan Monet in Paris, but for a few months in 2019, it visited Dolceacqua as part of an exhibit of works Monet painted along the French and Italian Riviera. To reach the painting that summer, we hiked up a steep cobblestone path to the top of the castle, where we enjoyed it alone in a small room against a black wall. Monet's signature brushstrokes made the light bounce off the sandstone bridge, and the trees and river softened the small but imposing castle in the backdrop. Later, we stopped for lunch across the river at a café overlooking the bridge. In nearly the same spot where Monet painted the castle, we ate stuffed vegetables topped with breadcrumbs while sharing a carafe of the local red, Rossese.

Dolceacqua was a lucky stop on our itinerary, and we would have missed it entirely had it not been for Marco Foresti, a winemaker we met earlier that day at his cellar down the road. Marco poured us glasses of his Pigato, Vermentino, and Rossese, the grapes of the area. Like most vintners in Liguria, Foresti is a small operation, selling most of its wines locally—either to Italians or to the French who drive over the border to buy it. Marco said wine is cheaper in Liguria than France, so the French come here to stock up. How it's possible for Ligurian wine to be less expensive, though, remains a mystery. While Foresti has twelve vineyards, they span less than seventeen acres (seven hectares) total on terraced hillsides. Marco's mother brought us focaccia dotted with black olives, and the conversation shifted away from wine. When he learned we had driven all the way from Verduno, a village at the northern point of the Barolo wine zone, he asked if we were planning to visit the Monet exhibit up the road. When we admitted that we hadn't heard of it, he shook his head. He'd be happy to talk more about his wines, he said, but it would be a shame if that meant keeping us from seeing the Monet. A cynic might say he had too much to do that day and couldn't afford to spend more time with us, and maybe that was true. A more likely story is that in Liguria, wine is part of life, but it is not all of life.

Lining the northwestern edge of the Italian coast, Liguria is little more than a crescent moon facedown in the Ligurian Sea. Separated from Piedmont by the Ligurian Alps, the small region has so little in common with Piedmont's topography and climate that it feels as if it's a different country. While we were driving there from Barolo, we watched the hills and valleys give way to a mountain highway riddled with switchbacks that ultimately spit us out into the Italian Riviera. Olive orchards, cypress trees, cactus, and palm trees lined the hills as the highway cut along the coast through terracotta-roofed towns that faced the sea.

Bound by mountains, cities, and water, Liguria is a challenging place to make wine. Sixty-five percent of the region's terrain is steep, and what isn't steep is merely hilly. Some of the terraced hillsides are made up of *fasce*, ancient dry-stone walls that have been used in Liguria for centuries, and many are built steep hillsides. During harvest, funiculars transport grapes up or down the hills to the wineries, especially in places where there aren't any roads. When maintained well, these terraces prevent erosion, which is a constant threat. (In 2021, a mudslide near Genoa washed a cliffside cemetery into the sea.) These factors ensure Liguria will never make much wine. In contrast to Piedmont, which produced nearly 67.9 million gallons (2.57 million hectoliters) of wine in 2020, Liguria yielded just over 2 million gallons (79,000 hectoliters). In Italy, only Valle d'Aosta makes less wine. There are easier ways to make money in Liguria—you can get a job in Genoa or go into the tourism industry at resorts along the Riviera. Even growing olive trees is less of a headache. And yet vintners here persevere, harvesting grapes along precarious cliffs and above highway tunnels and anywhere else their ancestors had carved out land to farm.

Take the Ruffino family of Punta Crena, who have tended the same vineyards in the village of Varigotti for more than five hundred years. Made with tart, green Lumassina grapes, their sparkling Colline Savonesi Frizzante is emblematic of Ligurian refreshment, briny and fresh, and just the thing to drink with fresh oysters or roasted vegetables with olives. Other winemakers are relative newcomers, rehabbing neglected family land by growing grapes. In 1975, Laura Aschero began planting vines on her family's land in the hills above Imperia as a hobby, something to do with her husband after he retired. The hobby turned into a namesake winery, which her son, Marco Rizzo, took over after her passing in 2009. He now works with his daughter, Bianca, vinifying Pigato and Vermentino, two genetically identical vines that act more like cousins than twins: both are mineral driven, but Pigato carries extra richness of wildflower honey and white nectarine.

History

This coastal, craggy region takes its name from the ancient Ligurian tribes who once lived and made wine here. In the sixth century BC, Greek merchants arrived with new techniques for growing vines and making wine. Later, the network of Roman roads made it much easier to transport wine from Liguria to other parts of the empire. But while wine has been made in Liguria since ancient times, it was only around the Middle Ages that the region was recognized for it, thanks in large part to the Republic of Genoa. For a couple of centuries, the Genoese controlled the Ligurian and Tyrrhenian Seas and maintained trading outposts as far away as the Black Sea. Only the Venetians could match the strength of the Genoese, and the two maritime republics remained adversaries. By the late fourteenth century, Venice defeated Genoa in a battle over trade in the eastern Mediterranean, causing the Genoese to shift from trade to banking, becoming, for a time, the financial center of western Europe. Throughout it all, wine was big business. The Genoese traded what they called Vernaccia, oxidative wines that Attilio Scienza, professor of viticulture at the University of Milan, believes were made with Vermentino grapes.

Like the Venetian Republic, Genoa couldn't stay independent indefinitely. In the eighteenth century, Liguria became part of the Kingdom of Sardinia, which also included Piedmont, Valle d'Aosta, Sardinia, and parts of present-day France. At the turn of the nineteenth century, Napoleon marched through the Maritime Alps to Genoa and, over several turbulent years, carved up much of Italy. While Napoleon's reign would not hang on for long, those years helped seed the Italian independence movement through the essays of Genovese activist Giuseppe Mazzini, which inspired Italian unification hero Giuseppe Garibaldi to join the cause for independence (see The Risorgimento, page 11).

Land and Wines

Liguria's wine areas are divided into halves with Genoa in the center. The Riviera di Ponente borders France while the Riviera di Levante makes up the eastern side near Tuscany. Liguria makes mostly white wine, but its west side offers some notable reds. Both coastlines contain ancient mixes of clay and sand, all of it sedimentary rock—there are no volcanoes here. Vineyards have a good amount of marl and limestone, with more acidic soils in the eastern stretch of land and neutral soils in the west. Clay soils at the base of a hill may give way to sandy soils on steep hillsides. Along the Tuscan border, Liguria's Colli di Luni DOC is close to Carrera, where Michelangelo sourced his marble. There, flinty, herbal Vermentino and Sangiovese wines share space with other red wines made with a handful of rare grapes, like Barsaglina and Pollera Nera.

Another determining factor in how the grapes do in Liguria is the sea. Grapes that grow here need to tolerate sea breezes or they won't grow well. Most vineyard land is steep and faces the sea. While the sea brings salt to the air, it also insulates the grapes from cold winds coming off the Alps. Grapes here also do best in moderate temperatures—nothing too cold or hot. Then there is the pitch of the vineyards, many of which are on remarkably steep cliffside terraces. In 1537, Italian bishop Agostino Giustiniani credited the genius of human intellect for the terraces in Cinque Terre, which allowed for excellent wine. Named for "five lands" (the villages of Monterosso al Mare, Vernazza, Corniglia,

Manarola, and Riomaggiore) and accessible only by foot, train, or boat, Cinque Terre is now a national park and UNESCO World Heritage site. In the twentieth century, many of Cinque Terre's dry-stone *fasce* were abandoned because it was too much work to make wine without a road to help transport grapes to a winery. Today, however, *fasce* rehabilitation projects are under way to help stem the risk of landslides and preserve native grapevines and other plant life.

Working in a place as beautiful as Cinque Terre has attracted some winemakers from outside the region—Barolo producer Elio Altare makes white wine at five-acre (two hectare) Campogrande. But most of the wine in Liguria is still made by Ligurians, like Samuele Heydi Bonanini of Azienda Agricola Possa in Riomaggiore. Of the seven thousand or so bottles he produces, just over a thousand of them are Sciacchetrà, the area's traditional *passito* made by air-drying Albarola, Bosco, and Vermentino grapes. Samuele dries them for three to four months before singling out the best grapes and pressing them by foot. The traditional wine is a living artifact of Cinque Terre's winemaking heritage. There are countless other examples of microproducers in the region—flip through a copy of *Gambero Rosso*, an annual guide of Italian wines, and you'll see winery after winery with six, four, or even two hectares (between fourteen and five acres) of vineyard land. A large producer in this area makes more than fifty thousand bottles annually. In comparison, a large producer in Veneto makes more than four million each year.

The small quantities wouldn't matter if the wine was bad; tourism would guarantee most of it would be sold one way or another. But pride in the regional winemaking has been reinvigorated. Besides, for all the challenges in maintaining vines on steep terrain, winemakers have the temperate climate on their side. During the day, the stones of the terraces retain heat, acting as insulation on cold evenings. During hot periods, sea breezes help moderate temperatures, while in colder months, they keep the chill from the Alps at bay. Taken together, it's exceptional terroir for white wines with salinity and red wines that favor herbaceous acidity over tannins. In Liguria, you get true Mediterranean wines, the best of which evoke the region's salty olive, basil, and citrus flavors in each glass.

Liguria Grapes

Lucky for us, most Ligurian wines indicate the grape used on the label, except for the blended wines from Cinque Terre.

White

Albarola (Bianchetta Genovese)

Albarola is a pale, green-white grape that delivers good acidity and a salty, herbal edge, yielding the kind of wine that anyone who loves French Muscadet or Portuguese Vinho Verde will also gravitate toward. It makes sense, too—all those wines express the salty flavors of the sea. Grown around Genoa and in the Golfo del Tigullio (where it's called Bianchetta Genovese), as well as Cinque Terre and into Tuscany, Albarola is mostly used as part of a blend. In Cinque Terre, it's paired with Bosco and Vermentino to make both dry and the Sciacchetrà (*passito*) wines. The grape itself has thin skins but tolerates sea breezes well. Starting in the late 1970s, Pierluigi Lugano of the Bisson estate was the first to make pure wine with this grape, though Bisson's labels use the name Bianchetta Genovese (for a long time, the grapes were believed to be different varieties). Bisson's Bianchetta Genovese "U Pastine" embodies the light-bodied, delicately herbal, snappy characteristics of the grape.

Bosco

Another key grape in Cinque Terre wines, Bosco loves growing near the sea—even more than other local vines. The closer it is planted to the shore, the higher its sugars and color, yielding wines with deeper, richer body. This is why it's so well suited to the blends of Cinque Terre: Albarola adds the acidity, Vermentino adds a floral polish, and Bosco provides body. The grape is also essential in the area's special Sciacchetrà (*passito*) wines. It rarely grows anywhere but in Liguria, with plantings concentrated around the Cinque Terre towns of Riomaggiore and Manarola.

Lumassina (Buzzetto, Mataòssu)

It's rare to find this tart green grape growing anywhere but the provinces of Savona. Even though uncommon, it's worth seeking out wines made from this grape, which are delicately floral, zesty, and low in alcohol. A theory behind its name is that it comes from *lumasse* or *lumache*, meaning "snails," since the wine pairs so well with them. The grape does have two other local names, Buzzetto and Mataòssu. Tommaso Ruffino and his family of the Punta Crena estate make a spritzy Lumassina, a perfect wine to drink with the fritto served along the Ligurian coast. Look for Lumassina among Colline Savonesi IGT wines.

Pigato

Pigato, along with Favorita in Piedmont, is a biotype of Vermentino, a grape with a long history and a not-so-clear origin story. Yet all three grapes make very different wines. Over time, the Pigato grape evolved in such a way that it developed spots, which is likely how it got its name (the local word *pigau* means "spotted"). Like most grape varieties that thrive in Liguria, it is happiest by the sea, able to withstand poor, stony soils and sparse rainfall. It also can deliver surprising structure for a coastal white wine, with white stone fruit aromatics and a savory petrol and granite edge—just the kind of thing you find in Riesling. Some producers, like Marco Foresti, say it can be easier these days to sell Pigato than Vermentino because while Vermentino is made in Tuscany, Sardinia, Spain, and France, Pigato is mostly grown only in the Riviera di Ponente, the western side of the region. Try Pigato with Mediterranean meals—think fish with olive oil and lemon and beans with pesto.

Vermentino

Well before opening A16, Shelley fell for the refreshing wines of Vermentino. The white grape grows in Sardinia (page 173) and northern Tuscany (page 221), but it is also the best-known grape variety in Liguria. It spread along the Tyrrhenian coast thanks to the Genovese traders, who called it Vernaccia. Vermentino is allowed in all the main Liguria DOC wines, most importantly Colli di Luni near the border with Tuscany. It is the perfect variety for maritime climates and does best when it never gets too cold. Yet it can withstand strong sea breezes and hot summer sun without overripening. Vermentino is not high in acid (which is one of the reasons it works well in the Cinque Terre blends that contain the higher-acid Albarola grape), instead carrying a saline, mineral verve. Vermentino makes leaner wines than Pigato, though both share a salty quality. Its wines often have delicate citrus aromas, such as grapefruit and lemon, as well as notes of white peach and melon. In the northwest Gallura area of Sardinia, Vermentino grows over pink granite stone, yielding complex, mineral-rich wines that can age for years. Genetically identical to Vermentino, Favorita grows next door in Piedmont. Long a favorite variety in Roero, plantings today have decreased in favor of grapes such as Arneis and Chardonnay. There is also Vermentino Nero, a red grape that grows in Liguria and Tuscany, though it is either a mutation of Vermentino or its own variety. In Colli di Luni, the Bosoni family of Cantine Lunae makes a deep-pink *rosato* with Vermentino Nero, and still and *frizzante* styles can also be found across the border in Tuscany.

Red

Barsaglina (Massaretta)

Found in small pockets of southeast Liguria along the border of Tuscany, Barsaglina (also called Massaretta) is a high-acid, high-color red grape that originated in the Massa Carrara province in Tuscany. It's found in the blends of the Colli di Luna DOC as well as in some Tuscan IGT wines, where it was added to Sangiovese to boost color. According to Professor Attilio Scienza, the grape had a nickname that translated to "smelly" because it was prone to yielding reductive wines, giving off a whiff of rotten egg. It has the propensity to make full, sometimes tannic wines that also taste fresh, thanks to its acidity. Cantine Lunae uses Barsaglina in an IGT Liguria di Levante blend.

Ormeasco (Dolcetto)

Ormeasco is the local name for Piedmont's Dolcetto (page 153). Its name comes from the town of Ormea, which is technically in Piedmont, though so close to the Ligurian border that it feels like it should be Ligurian. At any rate, Ligurians treat this grape as one of their own. When eaten out of hand, the grapes are sweet and low in acid, bearing little resemblance to the resulting wine, which is often pleasantly bitter or tannic. In the Pornassio area, the wines carry the same kind of herbal, saline quality that marks so many Ligurian wines, and it's one of the region's best reds. Pornassio producers also make a deep orange-red *rosato* with Ormeasco called Sciac-trà (not to be confused with the *passito* wine Sciacchetrà from Cinque Terre).

Pollera Nera (Corlaga)

A little-known, deep-blue variety, Pollera Nera, also called Corlaga, used to be common in Cinque Terre. It is still grown along the eastern side of Liguria, namely Colli di Luni, where it's used for blending. Cantine Lunae, one of the largest and most prominent estates in the Colli di Luni area near La Spezia, blends the grape with Sangiovese and Merlot for a Colli di Luni DOC red wine.

Rossese

Cultivated in the western side of Liguria, especially around the Dolceacqua growing area, Rossese makes red wines we could drink every day. The medium-bodied wines have accents of sour cherries and tangerines mixed with Mediterranean scrub brush. This is all balanced by round tannins and Liguria's signature salinity. Think of Rossese as the coastal counterpart to Schiava (Vernatsch) from the Alto

Adige (page 216). The grape is a synonym for the French Tibouren variety, where it's often used in rosé, though it is unclear whether Rossese went to France and became Tibouren or Tibouren wended its way to Dolceacqua and became Rossese. Soldiers from the noble Doria family may have brought back vine cuttings, but none of this is confirmed. Still, there's no doubt that the grape is at home in the rocky vineyards chiseled into the mountainsides that look out over western Liguria.

Regional Foods

Anchovies

Baccalà
salt cod

Cheese
formaggetta savonese, fresh cheese made with goats' milk and cows' milk

stagionato de Vaise, cows' milk cheese from Val di Vara that resembles alpine *toma*

Ciuppin
fish soup made from local seafood

Farinata
a savory crepe made with chickpea flour

Focaccia
di Recco, focaccia from the town of Recco made from thin dough and filled with cheese

with olives and/or onions

piscialandrea, with tomatoes and anchovies

Fritto misto
fried local fish

Olives

Olive oil

Pandolce
Genoese panettone, a sweet, domed bread filled with raisins, pine nuts, and candied citrus

Pasta
corzetti, coin pasta shaped by a stamp

picagge, ribbon pasta

mandìlli de Saea, silk handkerchiefs

Pesto
made with basilico genovese, basil from Genoa

Ripieni di verdura
stuffed vegetables

Torta verde
savory tart of greens

Recommended Producers

Altare-Bonanni

Azienda Agricola Possa

BioVi

Bisson

Cà du Ferrà

Cantine Lunae

Cascina delle Terre Rosse

Cascina Praié

Cian du Ciorgi

C. Vio

Daniele Ronco

Dell'Erba

Durin

Foresti

Ka Mancinè

La Felce

La Ricolla

Laura Aschero

Le Rocche del Gatto

Maccario Dringenberg

Maffone

Maixei

Possa

Punta Crena

Ramoino

Riccardo Bruna

Santa Caterina

Sassarini

Selvadolce

Singhie

Terenzuola

Terra di Bargòn

Testalonga

Lombardy

Lake Iseo is the smallest of Italy's great northern glacial lakes, a deep-blue curl surrounded by steep slopes that contour its shores. Villas and hotels with terracotta roofs cluster around the lake, while a tiny fortress island sits near a larger one with small hotels and a harbor. It's the kind of place anyone would want to visit in the summer, stay a week, and unwind with afternoon swims, boat rides, and beach reads. In our vacation fantasy, each night we'd take a boat to La Foresta, a restaurant on the larger island that serves freshwater fish pickled, dried, and grilled. We'd eat it all with the local sparkling wine, which happens to be Franciacorta. It's hard to argue that it gets much better than this.

Bordering Switzerland to the north, Piedmont to the west, and Trentino–Alto Adige and Veneto to the east, with the Po River framing most of the Emilia-Romagna border, Lombardy is the center of northern Italy, the place where most roads, planes, and trains end up at some point. Yet in the world of Italian wine, it can feel like an outlier. Instead of being rich in native grapes, it's a hub for industry, from fashion to banking to engineering. With Milan in the center, Lombardy is also the most densely populated region in Italy, with more than ten million residents. A lot of Italy's artisan winemakers first took corporate jobs in Milan after university before realizing they wanted to do something else with their life. They left Lombardy, headed back to their region, and applied what they learned about business to the family farm. It's not that Lombardy doesn't make great wine—there are several standout areas—but the economy gets by just fine without it.

Here, you'll find *metodo classico* sparklers from Franciacorta and Oltrepò Pavese as well as mountain Nebbiolo (locally called Chiavennasca) from Valtellina, one of Italy's most extreme and historic areas for viticulture. *Rosato* wines, like Chiaretto, come from the gravelly shores of Lake Garda, and juicy, effervescent reds come from the hills along the border with Emilia-Romagna. Lombardy even has its own Lambrusco as well as a *passito* made with a purple-hued Moscato. It all adds up: in 2020, the region ranked ninth among Italy's twenty regions in volume, producing nearly 38.99 million gallons (1.476 million hectoliters), a bit more than Lazio and a bit less than Friuli Venezia Giulia. While Lombardy's wines are not as well known in the United States as those from Piedmont and Tuscany, they are popular in Italy. Because of their range in styles and price-points, there is something for everyone.

History

Winemaking around Lombardy's lakes and mountains predates the Roman era, with ancient Ligurians bringing grape cultivation and terracing techniques to the hillsides. Roman infrastructure grew the winemaking trade, creating the roads that connected the east and west sides of northern Italy. The fall of Rome opened the region up to tribes who came from north of the Julian Alps. First came the Ostrogoths, who ruled until conflicts with the Byzantine Empire provided an opportunity for the Lombards to take over. The "Long Beards" (who wore their hair short in the back and long in the front) took over much of northern Italy and other parts of the Italian peninsula from about AD 568 until Charlemagne conquered them in 773. The legacy of the Lombards endures in the region's name as well as in contemporary politics. In the twelfth century, a band of northern cities came together and called themselves the Lombard League. Their unified strength helped defeat an army sent by Frederick I, the Holy Roman Emperor, in the Battle of Legnano. Centuries later, the battle was recast as a key moment in Italy's history, giving rise to myths supporting everything from the Italian unification in the nineteenth century to the promotion of fascism in the 1930s. Today, the Lombard League is synonymous with a radical right-leaning political organization that, at one point, threatened to secede from the country.

Lombardy is the birthplace of Italy's most prosperous modern city, Milan. Surrounded by hills, mountains, and fertile farmland, the region has long excelled in cheesemaking, from alpine cheeses to fresh ricotta made with cows' milk. By the fifteenth century, Milan was one of the richest cities on the Italian peninsula. In 1482, Leonardo da Vinci arrived in Milan to paint frescoes, acquiring a garden with a small vineyard. The grapes Da Vinci grew remained a mystery for years—a fire destroyed the garden, and whatever remained was bombed during World War II. Yet this century, scientists extracted DNA from roots dug from the rubble and found remnants of a grape that was a 90 percent match with Malvasia di Candia Aromatica (see page 72). Scientists recreated the garden vineyard, which is now a museum. If Leonardo was drinking Malvasia in Milan around the turn of the sixteenth century, the grape could have also been the wine of choice of Matteo Bandello, a novelist who lived around the same time. In *A Mediterranean Feast*, Clifford A. Wright shares that Bandello espoused the joys of spending a hot summer day in Milan drinking *un generoso e preziosissimo vino bianco* (a fine and full-bodied white wine).

By the nineteenth century, the arrival of phylloxera hit Lombardy's vineyards hard. In 1879, it was the first Italian region to document the insect. When it was time to replant, many farmers went with French grapes, since there was already a tradition of growing French varieties dating back to Napoleon's short-lived rule. After World War II, the region's economy rebounded rapidly, and some entrepreneurs took their newfound wealth and invested in sparkling wine made near Lake Iseo. Today, Franciacorta is one of the newest commercial wine successes in the region. On the opposite side of the spectrum, Lombardy's Valtellina area is one of the oldest, a wine region on the steep, stony terraces near the Swiss border that goes back two millennia.

Land and Wines

Lombardy's collection of glacier lakes, mountains, hills, and plains creates pockets of diverse winemaking styles. As a landlocked region framed by the Alps to the north and the humid plains in the center, it has a continental climate. Nearly half of Lombardy comprises mountains, and most of the rest of it is flat save for hilly sections near Lakes Iseo and Como and in the southwest near Emilia-Romagna. The primary grapes grown in the region are Croatina and Barbera as well as Pinot Nero

(Pinot Noir) and Chardonnay. A collection of red Groppello and Lambrusco grapes, as well as the white grape Turbiana (Verdicchio), grow in flatter areas around the southern tip of Lake Garda. Meanwhile, Chiavennasca, the Lombard word for "Nebbiolo," is the primary grape in Valtellina.

Franciacorta

Franciacorta spreads from the southern side of Lake Iseo; out to the east to the hills of Monticelli Brusati, Ome, and Gussago; to the west from the city of Erbusco; and to the base of Monte Orfano. Lake breezes cool the vines in the summer, and hills protect the area from the warm, humid air from Milan. In the winter, the lake works in reverse, warming the area and insulating the shores. Formed by glaciers, the morainic soil, rich in sand and silt and poor in clay, is conducive to growing grapes with the acidity needed for sparkling wine production.

Wine has been made here since at least the sixteenth century, and much of it was sparkling. In 1570, Girolamo Conforti, a physician from Brescia, documented the local wines in *Libellus de vino mordaci* (*Dissertation on Sparkling Wine*). Italian sparkling wine enthusiasts today point out that Conforti's work came out a century before an abbot named Dom Pérignon put bubbles into Champagne, but it's likely that both wine regions had sparkling wine simply due to weather. If fermentation stops in winter and restarts in spring, a wine will have bubbles. Conforti also noted that Franciacorta wines had acidity—something he described as "a piquant or biting flavor that does not dry out the palate like wines that are immature and austere, and that does not make the tongue soft like sweet wines." Still, the Franciacorta that we know today is very new. In 1961, fresh out of enology school in Alba, Franco Ziliani wanted to work to recreate an Italian sparkling wine that could meet the finesse of Champagne. Through a family friend, he met Guido Berlucchi, who had bottling problems with his dry white wine. Ziliani convinced him to make a sparkling wine as they do in Champagne, with a secondary fermentation in the bottle. Made with Pinot Bianco (Pinot Blanc),

which used to be the main grape of the area, "Pinot di Franciacorta" from the Guido Berlucchi winery was the first modern *metodo classico* sparkling wine in the area. By 1967, Pinot di Franciacorta had gained a DOC and wines could contain Pinot Grigio, Pinot Nero, and Pinot Bianco. Today, the guidelines are much stricter. Pinot Grigio is no longer allowed; most plantings are Chardonnay, and Pinot Bianco comprises only about 5 percent of the vines.

Ziliani and Berlucchi's gambit ushered in a wave of entrepreneurs, many of whom made money from other industries in nearby Milan and wanted to have some fun with their fortunes. Some already had land in the area, such as Maurizio Zanella, who got into wine as a teenager after being sent to live on the family's hobby farm near Lake Iseo to stay out of trouble. The intervention succeeded in inspiring an interest in making premium sparkling wine. Ca' del Bosco means "house of the woods," but today's winery is more like a Willy Wonka wine factory complete with sculptures in the cellar and innumerable patents, like a "Grape Jacuzzi," which washes all the grapes before press. Made only in exceptional vintages, Ca' de Bosco's flagship, "Anna Maria Clementi," has delicate bubbles with notes of orange blossom, lemon verbena, and brioche. With a backbone of acidity and a long-lasting finish, it's a beautiful, meticulous wine. Bellavista, another top producer in Erbusco, has a sleek facility that looks pulled out of a James Bond movie, and built with deep pockets. And it makes sense: the sparkling wine dreams of Zanella and Vittorio Moretti, the founder of Bellavista, were fueled by Italy's economic boom in the mid-twentieth century. Zanella's father, a successful entrepreneur, guaranteed the loans for Zanella to build a cellar, while Moretti built his dream winery with the healthy profits from his construction business.

In the 1970s, however, the region nevertheless had a long way to go. It was still hard to source specific vines for replanting vineyards. A nursery may have sold dozens of vines as Pinot Bianco, but once the vines matured, it was clear they were different varieties, creating unintentional field blends. Over the years—and unlike in most other areas in

Italy—the producers in Franciacorta worked together to increase quality standards, which are now among the strictest in Europe. Today, Franciacorta, Champagne, and Cava are the only European wines that do not have to print *spumante* on the label to indicate a sparkling wine—if you see Franciacorta, you know you're getting bubbles. There are guidelines on vine density (vines need to be planted very close together), harvest (grapes must be picked by hand), and how long the wines must age before release (no less than eighteen months but often longer). It's also a leading area in Italy for organic farming. Franciacorta also has the Curtefranca DOC, a still wine made with the same grapes and Sebino IGT, which encompasses native or international grapes that grow in the area.

As far as how it compares with Champagne, Franciacorta can be rounder and more fruit forward, with creamy bubbles and nutty complexity in older wines. It's not a matter of one being superior to the other but appreciating both as different wines. Yet like Champagne, new winemakers are rethinking how best to express a sense of place in Franciacorta, such as Cà de Vént and Divella Gussago eschewing dosage (the sweetness added at the end of the sparkling winemaking process) for leaner, more site-expressive wines.

Oltrepò Pavese, Lake Garda, and Lugana

If it took the 1960s for an interest in sparkling wine to reawaken in Franciacorta, it was already going strong in Oltrepò Pavese. In 1865, Carlo Gancia and Count Carlo Giorgi di Vistarino began to produce what they called "Italian champagne." Two years later, Domenico Mazza di Codevilla, an engineer, brought in an enologist from Reims in France to improve his *spumante* wine. Early successes led more producers to make sparkling wine, and today the region makes more Pinot Nero *spumante* than anywhere else in Italy, using both tank and *metodo classico* techniques. In fact, Oltrepò Pavese seems to make every shade of sparkling, *frizzante* (semi-sparkling), and still wines possible. Some wines

bring to mind Emilia-Romagna's Lambrusco, while others are red wines that age for years.

The vibe here is that of a quiet farming community. Some of Italy's most iconoclastic natural wine producers are in Oltrepò Pavese and across the border in Emilia-Romagna's Colli Piacentini. Near Bronti, the Maga family has made wine from Barbacarlo and Montebuono, two iconic hillside vineyards, since the nineteenth century. The wine is a field blend of Croatina, Uva Rara, and Vespolina grapes, fermented with native yeasts and bottled without filtering. Sometimes the wines finish fermenting in the bottle, making them fizzy in an uncontrolled way, a throwback to preindustrial sparkling wines. Meanwhile, the Castello di Luzzano estate spans both Colli Piacentini and Oltrepò Pavese, growing red grapes Croatina and Barbera in both areas. Once owned by the Catholic Church, the property now belongs to the Fugazza family, who runs Castello di Luzzano and an *agriturismo* (farm stay) on the property. Roman terracotta amphorae found on the property are on display at the castle, and the former customs house is a restaurant that makes country dishes, such as roasted pork with apples and sage served with slightly chilled and easygoing, deep-red sparkling wines.

The shores of Lake Garda, Italy's largest lake, are also a significant source of wines, though they come in a broader range of styles. The climate around the lake is warm, giving the area more of a Mediterranean feel than the rest of Lombardy. The Lugana DOC, which spills into the Veneto next door, is primarily centered around the Turbiana grape (the local name for Verdicchio), which yields fresh white wines with subtle notes of citrus zest, stone fruit, and almonds from the warm, calcareous clay soils. Alessandro Cutolo of Marangona uses Turbiana to make a fresh, bright Lugana wine that is versatile at the table, pairing especially well with vegetables.

Rosato production is also an important part of Lake Garda's wine identity, though here it's called Chiaretto. Made with a blend of Groppello, Marzemino, Sangiovese, and Barbera, Costaripa's Valtènesi Chiaretto "Molmenti" convinced the editors of wine guide *Gambero Rosso* to add a *rosato* category for its "wine of the year" awards. (The wine won it in 2019.) Meanwhile, south of Lake Garda around the city of Mantua, Lambrusco Mantovano is the only Lambrusco made outside Emilia-Romagna. The main grape is Lambrusco Viadanese (also called Lambrusco Mantovano as well as Groppello Ruperti), and the result is a cheerful, easy drinking sparkler.

Valtellina

In northern Lombardy, the Valtellina Valley traces the Adda River, running from the Stelvio Pass west into Lake Como. Centered around the town of Sondrio, the area is remarkable for its altitude; vines grow between 985 and 2,295 feet (300 to 700 meters) above sea level. Valtellina viticulture is what Italians call "heroic." Vineyards comprise a serpentine of stone terraces that, if unfurled, would stretch for more than 1,550 miles (2,500 kilometers). Here, vines grow in topsoil brought up from the river, mostly made of a mix of sand and silt. Some terraces require stepladders to get from row to row, and most everything must be done by hand. To work one hectare (2.47 acres) of vines at Ar.Pe.Pe., her family's estate, Isabella Pelizzatti Perego estimates it takes fifteen hundred hours a year. In comparison, it's about one hundred hours in a flat vineyard and around four hundred hours in a hilly area.

The time and effort required to maintain vines is one of the reasons the area has seen a dramatic decline in vines over the past century. At the turn of the twentieth century, there were 12,360 acres (5,000 hectares) of vineyards in Valtellina. Today it is slightly more than 2,000 acres (850 hectares), with only about fifty producers. Yet the stone terraces shore up hillsides from erosion and absorb heat during the day to keep vines from getting too cold at night. When combined with a south-facing exposure, which maximizes the sunlight; a range of mountains sheltering the valley from cold air from the north; and the warm *breva* winds from Lake Como, which thaw the ground in the spring, you can get a late-ripening grape like Nebbiolo to thrive in the mountains.

Within Valtellina, five subzones are singled out for being the best spots. The most notable are Grumello, Sassella, and Inferno. Of the remaining, Maroggia is the smallest, and Valgella is the largest. The richest wine is the DOCG Sforzato di Valtellina, made by air-drying Nebbiolo grapes after harvest before pressing them, adding an extra layer of flavor from the raisined grapes, like a mountain-style Amarone. There are different ways of making Sforzato. Producers like Nino Negri select grapes prior to harvest and dry them in small crates slowly for one hundred days before making the wine, while Ar.Pe.Pe. lets the fruit dry on the vine before harvesting it. No matter how it's made, Sforzato (sometimes called Sfursat) is a luxurious wine, with the acidity of Nebbiolo combined with darker fruit flavors such as black plum, spicy star anise, and bittersweet dark chocolate.

On the opposite side of Sforzato is Rosso di Valtellina DOC, wines to drink on the younger side—though in reality, the "younger side" for Valtellina can still be several years old. During the challenging harvest of 2014, Ar.Pe.Pe. skipped making any *riserva* wines and instead created a regular *rosso*, red but with grapes blended from their best plots within Sassella, Grumello, and Inferno. Isabella nicknamed the wine, released in 2016, a "super Rosso."

The Five Subzones of Valtellina

Inferno

The name implies it's a hot area, and it is—mostly because it has a lot of rocks, which help reflect the alpine sunshine and heat things up. The soil is also chalkier, giving the wines a mineral edge. In some cases, the heat comes through in the glass, with notes of balsamic or prune. These wines are meant to be aged.

Grumello

Taking the name of the Grumello Castle at the top of the vineyard, Grumello has slightly richer and sandier soils than other areas, yielding wines that are a little plusher and easier to drink at younger ages than other vineyards. The wines can be lighter and more fruit forward.

Maroggia

Located on the far west side of Valtellina around the commune of Berbenno di Valtellina, Maroggia is the smallest growing area—only 62 acres (25 hectares) of terraced land. In comparison, Grumello is nearly 200 acres (80 hectares). It is also the newest subzone, recognized in 2002, so it's not easy to find pure Maroggia wines abroad.

Sassella

On the west side of Sondrio, this steep and sunny vineyard area is the second largest. The western side is warm, while the eastern side is cooler and breezier. Top producers frequently use Sassella grapes for their best wines, which provide more structure and potential for aging. Wines from Sassella can start out a little closed when young but evolve to have complexity, with more minerality than Grumello.

Valgella

On the easternmost side of the area and farther from Como, Valgella is cooler and rainier, with sandy soils with some granite. The wines are a bit like Grumello in that they are more approachable when young. Sandro Fay is the best-known wine producer in the area.

Lombardy Grapes

Two of the most-planted grapes in Lombardy are international varieties: Chardonnay and Pinot Nero (Pinot Noir) for the sparkling wines of Franciacorta and Oltrepò Pavese. The region also has a handful of native grapes, most of which also grow in other northern regions.

White

Chardonnay
(see Trentino–Alto Adige chapter, page 211)

Erbamat
In an era when climate change is already impacting vines, some forgotten grapes could come to the rescue. At least that's the case Ian D'Agata makes for Erbamat in his book *Italy's Native Wine Grape Terroirs*. As regions get warmer, Franciacorta may reach a point where it can't achieve the acidity it needs from French grapes (a cool climate preserves acidity). Enter Erbamat, a grape with off-the-charts levels of malic acid, the kind found in tart green apples. The grape was once written off for its propensity to ripen as late as November, if at all. As harvests start earlier, it's no longer as challenging to get the grape to reach optimal ripeness. Today up to 10 percent can be used in Franciacorta cuvées (blends), and it's a grape to follow to see whether interest in it as a standalone variety develops. Some are already adding it to their wines: Barone Pizzini "Animante" Franciacorta includes 3 percent Erbamat in the Chardonnay, Pinot Nero, and Pinot Bianco blend.

Turbiana
(see Verdicchio, Le Marche chaper, page 110)

Verdea
Also grown in Emilia-Romagna and Tuscany, Verdea is an underexplored grape that has the potential to break out for its ability to yield light, mineral, floral wines with notes of apple and pear—just the kind of food-friendly, everyday bottles we love to find. It grows around Milan and Pavia and its bunches produce large green grapes that are eaten as table grapes in Tuscany and Emilia-Romagna. It also is made into *passito* wines. Look for bottles labeled "Verdea" when seeking it out.

Red

Barbera
(see Piedmont chapter, page 153)

Chiavennasca (Nebbiolo)
While Nebbiolo is mostly known as the famous grape of Piedmont, its birthplace is likely in or near Valtellina, where it's called Chiavennasca (a local word that means "best for wine"). There, historic estates like Ar.Pe.Pe. preserve biodiversity by replanting using only local vines. When grown at a high altitude with large temperature swings between day and night, Chiavennasca obtains thick skins, allowing for extended contact with the skins during the winemaking process. Despite lengthy maceration times, the high-acid, high-tannin wine takes on a lighter hue than Nebbiolo wines grown at lower altitude. With fresh notes of strawberries and rose, Chiavennasca-based wines are versatile with food. A well-made wine from one of the specific subzones like Sassella or Inferno can age for decades. (For more on the variety, see Nebbiolo, Piedmont chapter, page 154.)

Croatina (Bonarda)
(See Piedmont chapter, page 153)

Groppello Group
Groppello isn't a single grape but a group that shares the same name. There's Groppello Gentile, the main

grape, but also Groppello di Mocasina (also called Groppello di Santo Stefano) and Groppello di Revò, which is more common in Trentino. Gentile and Mocasina are often blended together for the Riviera del Garda Classico DOC. The most important area for Groppello grapes is Valtènesi, a subzone of the Riviera del Garda Classico area, which has gravelly, well-draining soils to keep the vigorous vines from overproducing. The Mocasina variety has smaller grapes and lends more of a vegetal edge than the Gentile variety, which has larger grapes. As a red wine, Groppello is juicy, spicy, and medium bodied, with notes of black pepper and green herbs. Groppello is often blended with Marzemino, Barbera, Sangiovese, and other grapes that also grow around the lake. It's also used in Chiaretto, a traditional *rosato* from Lake Garda.

Moscato di Scanzo

A grape grown in the hills around Bergamo, Moscato di Scanzo is one of the few native grapes in an area with mostly French varieties. When Romans settled in Scanzo, they reportedly produced a Moscato wine that was held in high regard. Whether this is the exact same Moscato grape or not, it makes for a good story. This is a truly special kind of red Moscato: sweet to eat out of hand, the inky-purple grapes made into *passito*-style wines are velvety and lush, with aromas of violets and spices. Few Moscato di Scanzo DOCG wines are made from this small zone, so never pass up the opportunity to taste it if one comes your way.

Pinot Nero (Pinot Noir)

(see Trentino–Alto Adige chapter, page 214)

Uva Rara

This "rare grape" is best known in blended wines from Lombardy and Piedmont. It's "rare" (*rara*) because of the way the bunches form with gaps between the large grapes, allowing for air circulation and making it challenging for bunch rot to form. This was a beneficial trait in Lombardy's sometimes damp continental climate. Plus, Uva Rara is easy to grow and can be harvested very late in the year, after the rest of the grapes have been picked. In Oltrepò Pavese, it is used to make *novello* (Beaujolais nouveau–style wine) and *rosato* wines as well as reds, the most famous of which comes from Barbacarlo, an iconic vineyard parcel near Broni. There, the Maga family uses the grape in a field blend that also includes the Croatina and Ughetta grapes. There is a tiny bit of Uva Rara in Alto Piemonte, and once in a while it's blended with Nebbiolo, though most winemakers feel it's best for simple table wines—the kind to bring on a picnic with some salami and cheese—not wines designed for aging.

Vespolina (Ughetta)

More commonly known as Vespolina (though Ughetta is how it's referred to in Lombardy), this grape is part of a stellar class of native red varieties from northwestern Italy. It grows in small bunches spread out through the vines, and often the grape skins are ripe when the seeds are still green. The result is a red wine with high acidity and noticeable white pepper aroma on the nose, with elegant notes of raspberries and green tea leaves. It is not easy to find a pure Vespolina wine (you'll most likely encounter it when blended into reds from Oltrepò Pavese or Alto Piemonte), though Gilberto Boniperti makes "Favolalunga," a 100 percent Vespolina from the Colline Novaresi DOC in Piedmont.

Regional Foods

Bresaola
air-cured beef

Blueberries

Butter

Cheese
Crescenza, soft cows' milk cheese

Grana Padano, aged cows' milk cheese for grating (similar to Parmigiano-Reggiano)

Gorgonzola, cows' milk blue cheese

Robiola, soft-ripened cows' milk cheese

Taleggio, semisoft washed-rind cows' milk cheese

Valtellina Casera, a semi-hard or hard cow's milk cheese

Minestrone

Ossobuco
braised veal shank topped with gremolata, a mix of parsley, garlic, and lemon zest

Pasta
anolini, small half-moon-shaped filled pasta

ravioli di zucca, pumpkin-stuffed ravioli

tortelli, filled pasta shaped in many ways

Pizzocheri
buckwheat pasta with butter, potatoes, cabbage, and Valtellina Casera cheese

Polenta

Risotto alla milanese
risotto with saffron

Vitello tonnato
veal served cold with a sauce made from preserved tuna, capers, lemon juice, and mayonnaise

Recommended Producers

Franciacorta

Alessandra Divella

Arcari + Danesi

Barone Pizzini

Bellavista

Berlucchi

Ca' del Bosco

Cà del Vént

Contadi Castaldi

Corte Fusia

Divella Gussago

Il Mosnel

Il Pendio

Le Marchesine

Nicola Gatta

Villa Crespia

Oltrepò Pavese, Lake Garda, and Lugana

Cà Maiol

Castello di Cigognola

Castello di Luzzano

Frecciarossa

Lino Maga (Barbacarlo and Montebuono wines)

Marangona

Zuliani

Valtellina

Ar.Pe.Pe.

Balgera

Barbacàn

Dirupi

Dislivelli

Fay

Mamete Prevostini

Nino Negri

Scerscé

Molise

A woman with curly brown hair placed a board filled with cured meats on the red-checked table, then headed back to the kitchen to get the rest of our order. The restaurant was large enough to hold a wedding reception, but that afternoon, only a few men sat in the back, quietly chatting. The street in front of the restaurant was just as quiet, the sidewalk nearly empty. In ancient times, the city of Campobasso was base camp for the Romans. During the Second World War, it became base camp for the Canadians stationed there, earning the nickname "Maple Leaf City." But that was all a long time ago. These days, the capital of Molise feels like a forgotten place.

To be sure, Campobasso has some lovely sites. In the center of the city, you can walk up a winding cobblestone street to a church with beautiful frescoes. From there, an expansive view of Molise's hillsides unfolds. There's also the pasta. The server returned with two plates, one filled with twisted strands flecked with sausage and delicately coated with a puree of green peppers—a signature flavor here—and another of thick noodles bathed in tomato sauce. We drank purple Tintilia with our meal and felt as though we could camp out there the rest of the day.

Southeast of Rome and north of Naples, with Abruzzo to the north and Puglia to the south, Molise is nearly all mountains. Only around three hundred thousand people live here spread across nearly two thousand square miles. (For comparison, around eight hundred thousand people live in San Francisco spread across forty-nine square miles.) Until 1963, Molise was part of Abruzzi e Molise, which combined the region with its larger neighbor, Abruzzo (page 33). Both regions share some of the most spectacular wilderness in the country. The Sulmona-Carpinone train line—"the little Trans-Siberian," a journalist in the 1980s called it—allows you to see it up close. Starting in Sulmona in the mountains of Abruzzo and ending in Carpinone in the mountains of Molise, the old-fashioned train runs through national parks, gorges, nature preserves, and tiny mountain villages. Once used to transport goods during World War II, the rail line was destroyed and then later nearly abandoned. Today, it's found new life in slow tourism, a way that allows visitors to explore local culture while leaving a small environmental footprint. In general, Molise feels primed for the slow-tourism movement. It's a region where villages come together to hunt and butcher wild boar, work a grape harvest, or preserve the summer's crop of tomatoes. Here, people still know how to live off the land.

Despite the region's raw ingredients—unspoiled land and mountain climate with large temperature swings between day and night, both of which benefit viticulture—Molise is a work in progress. In some areas, the mountains are too extreme or cold for grape growing. In other areas, tracts of land are too small to make it worth the bother of growing grapes. Or there's just not enough money for making and selling wine. Like neighboring Abruzzo, the mountainous areas of Molise suffer from depopulation because of lack of work and infrastructure. The factory jobs are along the coast, leaving inland areas desolate. And even when a winery makes a great wine, it's still a challenge to draw any attention to it. The local grape, Tintilia, is Molise's best chance at standing out, but most wine drinkers have never heard of it. The region is also saddled with a legacy of being sidelined within its own country. In Burton Anderson's 1980 Italian wine book, *Vino*, he describes how a taxi driver in Rome who was raised in Molise told him to head to Piedmont if he wanted good wine. Even today, Italians joke that "*Molise non existe*," Molise doesn't exist.

While Molise is a minor player in the modern Italian wine industry, it definitely *exists*. In 2020, the region produced 10.62 million gallons (402,000 hectoliters) of wine—an output higher than that of Calabria, Basilicata, Liguria, or Valle d'Aosta, the lowest-producing regions in the country. The vast majority is table wine made from the ribbon of warm coastline around the city of Termoli, where the land is easier to farm. But experts say the most promising terroir in the region is in the mountains, which happens to be where Tintilia grows the best. The small-but-growing number of producers who make wine that makes it out of the region show that Molise has the potential for something special. Yet, there are still ways to go before this part of Italy becomes a wine destination.

History

It is hard to tell the story of Molise. For most of modern Italian history, it was part of Abruzzi e Molise, so not a lot of historians have delved into Molise's unique past like they have in other parts of Italy. Consider this a thumbnail sketch.

From 1000 BC to about 295 BC, Molise was controlled by the Samnites, a civilization of fierce warriors who readily adapted to its extreme mountain climate. After a series of brutal wars and rebellions, the Samnites fell to Rome, and the land was folded into the Roman Empire. Soon, grape growing flourished, like it did in the rest of the Italian peninsula. Molise had a decent amount of vineyard land well into the nineteenth century. Like the rest of southern Italy, it found itself under Spanish control in the sixteenth century, which is one of the reasons that Tintilia's origin has long been linked to Spain—*vino tinto* means "red wine" in Spanish, and Tintilia is deep in color.

Recent European history has been tough on Molise. Over the past century and a half, thousands emigrated. Those who stayed endured World War II and the fighting along the Gustav Line that destroyed many of Molise's villages as well as the Sulmona-Carpinone train route. Like Abruzzo, most of the postwar rebuilding happened along the coast. In 1972, government incentives encouraged Fiat to open a factory in Molise, making motors in Termoli. Stable factory jobs were a big deal for the region, which had been struggling with 15 percent unemployment, triple the rate of northern regions like Emilia-Romagna. While factory work is still important, the region is also home to artisans. In the town of Agnone, craftsmen cast bronze bells by hand, while in the city of Isernia, women continue a centuries-old tradition of creating elaborate hand-woven lace.

Land and Wines

Like Abruzzo to the north, Molise has the benefits of both mountains and sea, yet the region is smaller, with less coast and more mountains. More than half is mountains, while the rest of the region is hilly, with a few flat areas along the coast. The small region has two provinces: Isernia, in the inland mountains toward the border with Campania, and Campobasso, stretching from the mountains to the coast. Termoli in Campobasso is the region's busiest town, filled with Italians hitting the beach. In winter, the mountains can get several feet of snow, enough for the ski resorts of Campitello Matese and Capracotta to operate. The Biferno River, which runs from the Apennines to Termoli, is one of the region's most important wine areas. There are no DOCGs here and only three DOCs: Pentro di Isernia, which is split north and south of the city of Isernia, near the border with Campania; a Molise DOC; and Tintilia del Molise, which covers the entire region. But DOC wines make up a fraction of the output here. And as in Abruzzo (and, frankly, most of Italy), a DOC label doesn't always guarantee much about the quality inside the bottle.

More than 80 percent of the wine made here is table wine, and most of it is red. Cabernet Sauvignon, Merlot, and Sangiovese grow here, but nearly half of all grapes in Molise are Montepulciano, a variety more associated with Abruzzo. In general, Montepulciano from Molise has an earthy, dusty quality, with more dark fruits and pronounced tannins than in Abruzzo, and some are also quite concentrated. In Campomarino, near the coast just southeast of Termoli, the Di Majo Norante estate is one of the lone producers to have had an international reach for years. The estate's signature wine, Don Luigi, is a powerful, modern Montepulciano, which manages to balance concentration without covering up the nuance of the grape. This wine is all about dark fruits, such as blueberries, coupled with Medjool dates, black licorice, and leather.

While Montepulciano is the most important grape by volume, Tintilia is the most important as a point of identity. Di Majo Norante grows the grape at a slightly higher altitude than Montepulciano, making a Tintilia wine that has supple tannins with accents of red fruits and black pepper. Meanwhile, smaller, newer estates are putting Tintilia at the core of what they do. Farther into the mountains at just under 1,970 feet (600 meters) above sea level, Claudio Cipressi grows Tintilia for sentimental reasons: his grandparents used it to make homemade wine. Cultivating this grape has been a long process—old vines needed to be recuperated and propagated before the yields were large enough to make wine. The endeavor was made more challenging by grapes themselves, which aren't particularly juicy. With the help of enologist Vincenzo Mercurio, Cipressi has made several Tintilia wines, from *spumante* to deep-red "Macchiarossa," which showcases notes of plum, black cherries, and black pepper. Closer to the coast, the Terresacre estate has also deemed Tintilia its flagship bottle, creating a rich red wine with violet-tinged notes of tart black plums. Farther inland, near Campobasso in the small town of Ripalimosani, at around 2,130 feet (650 meters) above sea level, the organic Vinica estate highlights its Lame del Sorbo vineyard, which has grown Tintilia for nearly a century. Aged in stainless steel tanks, Vinica makes both a *rosso* and *rosato* Tintilia named after the vineyard, and both show a fresher side of the grape, with floral aromas and a touch of tannins.

Molise has some white wines—from Cococciola to Falanghina and Sauvignon Blanc—yet even if some of the wines can be quite good, they are hard to track down. The only way Molise is going to prove to the world that it *truly exists* is by getting Tintilia into more of our glasses.

Molise Grapes

The local red Tintilia grape is exclusive to the region.

White

Cococciola

(see Abruzzo chapter, page 37)

Falanghina Group

(see Campania chapter, page 62)

Red

Montepulciano

(see Abruzzo chapter, page 40)

Tintilia

The first written documentation of Tintilia dates to 1800 in Campobasso, where census records indicated it was the most planted grape in the area. For years, Tintilia was believed to be related to Bovale Sardo from Sardinia, but genetic analysis shows no connection. The new hypothesis is that the grape came from the Spanish Bourbons, who ruled southern Italy before unification in the nineteenth century. *Vino tinto* means "red wine" in Spanish; plus, the variety has high levels of anthocyanins, making its wines deep in color. Wherever it came from, it's been grown for centuries in the region. But with three seeds, small berries, and paltry clusters, the variety is not easy to grow—it takes a lot of Tintilia to make a little bit of wine. This explains why the grape fell out of favor in the 1960s, when farmers swapped it out in favor of higher-yielding varieties, like Montepulciano. Yet the grape's high ratio of skins and seeds to juice is also what gives Tintilia its distinctive, tannic character. Its wines are deep purple, with spicy, peppery notes reminiscent of Syrah. If you're a lover of deep brooding reds, Tintilia is worth seeking out (even if it takes a while to find a bottle).

Regional Foods

Agnello all'arrabiata
lamb sauce for pasta seasoned with chiles

Arrosticini
grilled lamb skewers

Brodetto
Adriatic seafood stew with tomatoes, garlic, and onions

Cheese
caciocavallo, aged cows' or goats' milk cheese

pecorino, sheep's milk cheese

ricotta, sometimes smoked with juniper wood

stacciata, a fresh cows' milk cheese

Lentils

Olive oil

Pasta
similar to Abruzzo (page 41), but with more green bell pepper

Scattone
an aperitivo made with pasta cooking water, red wine, and crushed red pepper

Recommended Producers

Borgo di Colloredo

Cianfagna

Claudio Cipressi

Di Majo Norante

Salvatore

Terresacre

Piedmont

Christoph Künzli turned his compact car onto a dirt road and cut through the trees. After a few sharp turns and a short stretch, the trees gave way to an unexpected site: a Nebbiolo vineyard. The vines were trained in the old Gallo-Roman system, in which four poles surround each vine supporting the shoots so that they form an x from above. The practice helps control vigor, Christoph explained, making vines easier to manage by hand. Standing in the vineyard with nothing else visible except forest, we felt as though we were in a wine frontier land. The reality is that the vines were here before the forest encroached. As our shoes crunched over fine gravel soil, Christoph described the difference between Nebbiolo grown in Boca (where it's called "Spanna") and Nebbiolo grown in more famous parts of Piedmont. "In Barolo, you have chalk," he said. "Here, you don't have chalk; you have minerality."

The vineyard was one of a handful that Christoph had rehabilitated for his winery, Le Piane, in the town of Boca. One of a few towns along the Sesia River in Alto Piemonte (High Piedmont, the northern part of the region), Boca saw its prestige plummet in the twentieth century. Yet long before collectors became enamored with the wines in the southeast part of the region, Alto Piemonte made some of the best reds in Europe. Records of Nebbiolo in Boca go back to the fourteenth century. Lessona, a town just west of Boca, started bottling wine in the seventeenth century, around the same time as Burgundy and Bordeaux. Since glass was more valuable than most wine back then, only good wines ever made it into bottles. By the beginning of the nineteenth century, Boca had twice as much vineyard land as Barolo does today.

Major economic and environmental disruptions in the twentieth century pushed Alto Piemonte's wine industry into a steep decline. Vine diseases that arrived at the end of the nineteenth century (downy mildew, powdery mildew, and phylloxera) damaged vineyards, and areas that were spared were pummeled by bad weather. In 1951, a hailstorm ruined most of Boca's remaining vines. Most families had only one or two small plots of land, making it difficult to withstand a few bad years. By the end of that decade, 90 percent of the town's wine economy had collapsed. Meanwhile, Italy's textile industry exploded, and locals left to take jobs in nearby factories. As a result, family ties to the land were severed, and younger generations grew up without a connection to any sort of winemaking heritage. As more vineyards went untended, the forest crept in.

By the late 1980s, Boca had only three wine producers left.

It was in this state that Christoph, a Swiss wine merchant traveling with enologist Alexander Trolf, first saw Boca. Of the remaining producers, Antonio Cerri made wine so incredible that Christoph changed his life, came to Boca, and, with Alexander, learned how to make wine from the octogenarian before he passed away. Christoph eventually took over Antonio's 1.2-acre (0.5 hectare) vineyard and began to cobble together more parcels, removing trees so Nebbiolo, Croatina, and Vespolina vines could flourish. Compared with Nebbiolo wines from elsewhere, Alto Piemonte wines are traditionally blends. According to Christoph, Vespolina acts like seasoning, drawing out Nebbiolo's qualities. For the past couple of decades, others have also started to bring viticulture back to the town. Today, Boca has around a dozen winemakers, and while it's nothing like the old days, it's a start.

Wine drinkers around the world love Piedmont, yet most of their love is focused on the Langhe, a wine area encompassing Barolo and Barbaresco. Say either zone to anyone interested in wine, and they'll know you're talking about the good stuff. Say Boca and you might get someone thinking about a city in Florida. Yet the Italian town of Boca is a reminder that nearly every part of Piedmont is filled with wine tradition.

Piedmont can keep wine lovers engaged for a lifetime thanks to its long list of grapes and high-quality standards. Professor Anna Schneider, a renowned ampelographer (a specialist of grape varieties), estimates that around two hundred grapes originated in northwestern Italy. While Nebbiolo likely came from Valtellina in neighboring Lombardy (page 127), it spread throughout Piedmont and Valle d'Aosta (page 247). Nebbiolo is one of Italy's oldest vines, documented in Turin as early as 1266. Nebbiolo also spawned other grape varieties, including Vespolina, Freisa, Grignolino, and Arneis. Its list of siblings and half siblings is even longer, including Pignola, Refosco, and Teroldego. Beyond the Nebbiolo family tree, Piedmont grows many other grapes, from Barbera, Dolcetto, Ruchè, and Pelaverga among the reds to Cortese, Erbaluce, Favorita, Nascetta, and Timorasso among the whites.

In 2020, the region made 67.91 million gallons (2.57 million hectoliters), seventh in production overall, and just behind Tuscany. Slightly more is red, but white wines are also important. Vineyard land in the Langhe is at such a premium that some hazelnut groves and forests have been pulled out and replanted with vines. There have been consequences—hillside erosion where trees have been removed for instance. Yet the biggest concern is about climate change. Winemakers formerly concentrated on doing everything they could to get grapes to ripen now worry more about preserving acidity as summers get hotter and weather becomes more extreme.

Back at Le Piane's tasting room, Christophe showed us an aerial shot of Boca at the turn of the twentieth century, with hills carved up into tidy vineyard plots. Today, the same shot shows mostly forest. Yet as grape growers in southern Piedmont grapple with warmer vintages, Boca is well positioned to weather a changing climate. Protected from alpine winds in the winter by Mount Fenera and from heat in the summer by the Sesia River, the town's climate preserves high acidity and crunchy red-fruit flavors in wines that can age for years.

History

Piedmont's history diverges from that of the rest of the Italian peninsula. Rather than being ruled by the popes or Spanish and Austrian royals, the region fell under the control of the House of Savoy, a dynasty based in Turin with territories that reached present-day France as well as Liguria and Sardinia. It had a reputation for oppressive cultural conservatism until 1796, when the region fell under Napoleonic rule, which brought in land reform and enlightened thinking. When the House of Savoy regained control in 1815, it retained some French influences, and its realm—the Kingdom of Sardinia—became the center of the unification movement of Italy.

Winemaking here is thought to have begun with the ancient Ligurians, who brought grape cultivation to the region. The Romans, who arrived around the second century BC, expanded the wine trade in the territory, building the city that became present-day Alba. After the fall of Rome, most of Piedmont fell into dark times except for areas around Carema and Gattinara, which were controlled by the Church. There, monks refined viticulture practices, determining the best ways to grow grapes, when to harvest them, and how to turn them into wine.

French culture influenced the House of Savoy. The Count of Cavour, Camillo Benso—the future first prime minister of Italy—deferred to France for culture cues his entire life. Giulia Falletti, who became the Marchesa di Barolo, was French, born as Juliette Colbert de Maulévrier. The marchesa strategized that good wine could help her raise money for charity, explains Kerin O'Keefe in her book *Barolo and Barbaresco: The King and Queen of Italian Wine*. At the time, most wine in the area was fizzy and sweet, a product of stuck fermentation due to cold weather in the fall. (When too cold, yeasts in wine go dormant, though fermentation restarts when they warm up.) The wine from the marchesa's estate was a step above the local production, and in the 1830s, she introduced her Barolo to King Carlo Alberto, head of the House of Savoy. It was so good that it prompted the king and his son, Victor Emmanuel II (the future king of Italy), to make their own Barolo. From this connection, we get Barolo's slogan "King of Wines, Wine of Kings."

Most of the improvements in Barolo's cellars during this time came from General Paolo Francesco Staglieno. The general insisted on fermenting wines dry before bottling so they could age. He also upgraded cellar hygiene, destemmed grapes to remove excess tannins, and created a time frame for aging. While making wine for the king, he lived at Castello di Verduno. (Today, you can stay in the castle or its *agriturismo* down the road.) Staglieno outlined his methods in an 1837 book that set standards for the era, yet for years, his contributions

to Barolo were overlooked, writes O'Keefe. Instead, Barolo's improvements were attributed to a French enologist and merchant named Louis Oudart. While the Count of Cavour did hire Oudart to work on the wines at his Grinzane Cavour estate, it was after he had hired Staglieno.

Even though Piedmont had noble families and good wine, most of the region's countryside was poor up through the twentieth century. As more jobs opened in factories in Turin and elsewhere, people moved to cities for work. Those who stayed grew grapes for negociants, wine merchants who made their own wine. Most Barolo and Barbaresco estates blended grapes from vineyards throughout the areas. In the 1960s, a few winemakers, like Beppe Colla and Bruno Giacosa in Barbaresco and Barolo and Angelo Gaja in Barbaresco, began bottling wines from single vineyards, but the idea for cru (single-vineyard) wines in the Langhe didn't take off until 1975. That year, winemaker Renato Ratti, the head of the enological institute in Alba, began mapping the historic vineyards of Barolo and Barbaresco. Years later, these vineyards would inform the *menzioni geografiche aggiuntive* (MGA) system. (See The Villages of Barolo and Barbaresco, page 147.) Even so, some of the Langhe's best wines are still blends. The historic Francesco Rinaldi estate makes a Barolo blended from vineyards in the towns of Barolo and La Morra as well as cru wines from prized vineyards Cannubi and Brunate. All these wines show traits of classic-old world Barolo: dark red fruit, subtle notes of spice, and a long, satisfying finish.

The 1980s brought upheaval to winemaking in Barolo and Barbaresco. Younger winemakers (the "modernists") wanted to make sleeker wines using barrique (small French oak barrels) that were more approachable when young. Meanwhile, the "traditionalists" advocated for aging wines in *botti* (large barrels) and making vintages that required years of aging before drinking. The early fights—called the Barolo Wars—were intense, but disagreements over barrel type, aging, and other processes are now old news. Over time, modernists became more restrained with oak, while traditionalists changed out old barrels and aging infrastructure in the cellars. Some opted for middle ground. Sergio Germano, whose winery, Ettore Germano (named after his father), will try out everything—large barrels, small barrels, amphorae (terracotta vessels)—and then taste, assess, and analyze what will make the best wines from his Serralunga vineyards. When we visited, his daughter was preparing for exams to study enology and follow in her dad's footsteps.

In the Langhe and the rest of Piedmont, the late 1990s was the turning point when warmer weather began to impact vineyard work. Quality measures adopted in the 1970s and '80s, such as green harvesting (trimming away some unripe bunches to encourage ripening), started to make fruit that was too concentrated. Winemakers used to determine harvest based on a Brix measurement—higher Brix meant higher sugars and a better vintage, though that is changing. Mario Andrion, winemaker at Castello di Verduno, focuses instead on pH. For him, acidity is the essential ingredient when making wines for that can age.

Today, Piedmont is a global destination for wine, though fame come with challenges. Fewer natives can afford to live in the region's premier wine regions. Harvest requires bringing workers from Macedonia or elsewhere because there aren't enough locals to do the job like the old days. There are also many more wineries than before. In 1962, the village of La Morra had seven wineries; now there are many. As trees are removed to make room for more Nebbiolo, concerns about biodiversity are growing. Yet not everywhere. In the Alto Piemonte, it's unlikely that overproduction will become a problem. Maybe all that forest isn't so bad after all.

Land and Wines

Located in the top western corner of Italy, Piedmont is cradled by the Alps, which separate it from France and Switzerland. Its name means "foot of the Alps," and the mountains influence the weather and climate across the region. Within Italy, it borders tiny Valle d'Aosta in the far north and Lombardy to the east. A corner touches the westernmost tip of Emilia-Romagna, while to the south, it's separated from Liguria by the Maritime Alps. Only about a quarter of the region is flat, while the rest is divided between mountains and hills. While red wine gets all the attention, the town of Asti is synonymous with sparkling wines, like brightly fizzy Moscato d'Asti and sparkling Asti Spumante. South of Asti, the town of Canelli has one of Italy's oldest *metodo classico* sparkling wine companies, Contratto.

Piedmont can be divided into three general areas: Alto Piemonte, the provinces of Asti and Alessandria, and the Langhe. While Nebbiolo gets the most attention, the most-planted grape in the region is Barbera, followed by Moscato Bianco—thanks to the popularity of Asti Spumante and Moscato d'Asti.

Alto Piemonte

Alto Piemonte includes Turin and the growing areas within the five provinces scattered east, west, and north of the region's capital. Most of the winemaking is centered around either side of the Sesia River. The west side—the Coste della Sesia—has the towns of Lessona, Bramaterra, and Gattinara, the last of which made wines praised by Thomas Jefferson. The east side of the river, the Colline Novaresi, includes the towns of Boca, Ghemme, Sizzano, and Fara. In general, Boca, Gattinara, and Bramaterra contain ancient volcanic soils derived from the formation of the Alps; Lessona has marly sand; and Ghemme, Fara, and Sizzano are made up of glacial moraine. Besides soil, Nebbiolo wines from Alto Piemonte stand apart from Langhe Nebbiolo because they're typically a blend of grapes, with Vespolina adding spiciness and Croatina or Uva Rara bumping up fruit and color.

There is also alpine winemaking near the western border with Valle d'Aosta. The Produttori di Carema, a local co-op, sources fruit from seventy-one small growers in Carema. Here, grapes grow on steep stone terraces overlooking the Dora Baltea valley. Pergola-like trellises called *topie* train the vines

The traditional *botte* in the cellars of
Francesco Rinaldi in Barolo.

Winemaker Mario Andrion of Castello di Verduno makes Barolo and
Barbaresco and works with local grape Pelaverga.

to protect them from damage from strong winds. Nebbiolo takes longer to ripen in the area's granite soils, but the cooler climate yields garnet-hued wines with plenty of perfume. Nearby Caluso and the Canavese areas also use the *topie* technique to protect high-acid white Erbaluce grapes from hail (the grapes stay safe below the canopy of leaves). These wines are bright and chalky, with a delicate aroma of white flowers. The area also makes a couple of aromatic red Malvasia wines.

Asti and Alessandria

Southeast of Turin, the Asti province is the center for Piedmont's sparkling wine production. The local name for the Moscato Bianco vine is Moscato Canelli, which comes from the town of Canelli. It's the grape that makes Asti Spumante and Moscato d'Asti, the former more bubbly and dry made with *metodo Martinotti*, while the latter is softer and sweeter, often finishing fermentation in the bottle (see Italy's Sparkling Wines, page 262). The production area for these wines is broad, stretching from the provinces of Cuneo to Asti and Alessandria. The best vineyards within this zone are rich in limestone, bringing forth expressive aromas of orange blossoms and white peach. Canelli also represents the northern edge of the Alta Langa DOCG, a zone dedicated to *metodo classico* sparkling wine made with Chardonnay and Pinot Nero (Pinot Noir).

The Monferrato hills stretch over a wide area encompassing the province of Asti and Alessandria and spanning southeast to the town of Tortona. The idiosyncratic grape Ruchè comes into its own in Castagnole Monferrato. Grignolino also grows here, as does Barbera, which originated in the Monferrato area. There is also a pocket of Nebbiolo grown around the town of Albugnano. In general, vineyards in the Asti province have more sand, giving wines more aromas with lighter body, while Alessandria has more calcareous-clay soils, yielding slightly richer wines. Meanwhile, the Colli Tortonesi (hills of Tortona) is home to Cortese, the white grape used in Gavi wines. Made in the mildest and driest part in the region, Gavi is near Mediterranean in style, with a mineral,

chalky freshness that is similar to white wines from Liguria. In nearby Ovada, Dolcetto is a historic grape, turning out rustic, full-bodied red wines.

The Langhe, including Barolo and Barbaresco

The Langhe (also called Langa) is in the southern Cuneo province. "Langhe" comes from a word with Celtic origins roughly meaning "land tongues." From the air, hills stretch in bands toward the southwest. Barolo and Barbaresco sit on the east side of the Tanaro River, while Roero sits on the west. Meanwhile, the Alta Langa spreads out in the hills between Asti, Alessandria, and Cuneo.

Barolo and Barbaresco's soils are divided into two main types. There's Tortonian, which is a gray-blue color made from a mix of calcareous sand and marls known for aromatic, floral Nebbiolo. Some villages also have Sant'Agata soils, a subset of Tortonian soil that provides even more aromatic wines. Other villages have Serravallian soil, which is lighter in color, with more limestone and sandstone, creating structured, stern wines. (See The Villages of Barolo and Barbaresco, page 147, for more details.)

Due to similar soils, grapes, and winemaking styles, Barolo and Barbaresco are endlessly compared. In the old days, people liked to say Barolo made "masculine" wines and Barbaresco made "feminine" wines, gentler and more approachable than Barolo. That description is not only insulting but also inaccurate. Barbaresco is closer to the Tanaro River and has a slightly milder climate than Barolo. In some areas, grapes grow with thinner skins, yielding wines that are ready to drink sooner than Barolo. This isn't always the case, though, and both zones have vineyards that create structured wines and vineyards that yield rounder wines. Take Castello di Verduno's output, for example. One of its Barolos comes from the Monvigliero vineyard, a Verduno cru known for finesse and aromas of strawberries and red currant. Compared to a wine from Serralunga, another town in Barolo, it's brighter and lighter. Yet Castello di Verduno also makes Barbaresco from Rabajà, a cru yielding wines that are often broader.

Across the Tanaro, the Roero remains a bit wild, with forests as well as fruit orchards breaking up vineyard land. The area's sandier soils, rich in minerals and salts, create a spectrum of wines ranging from sturdy to light, with fragrance and freshness. Freisa, Nebbiolo's closest relative, grows here, as does Arneis, a white grape that makes delicately floral wines. Plenty of Moscato Bianco comes from here, too. When vinified dry, it becomes the Langhe answer to Sauvignon Blanc.

The Langhe also is known for Dogliani, the prime zone for Dolcetto, as well as Barbera d'Alba,

Dolcetto d'Alba, and Pelaverga, among others. To the north in the Alta Langa, the focus shifts to *metodo classico* sparkling wine with Chardonnay and Pinot Nero. The Rivetti family (of Barbaresco's La Spinetta) runs the historic Contratto estate in Canelli, where the underground limestone cellars are a UNESCO World Heritage site. Winemakers throughout the region have also played around with sparkling wines made with native grapes, such as Ettore Germano's "Rosanna," a savory, sparkling Nebbiolo. In essence, Piedmont has more to offer than red wine for collectors.

The Villages of Barolo and Barbaresco

A wine lover can spend a lifetime tasting the terroir of Barolo and Barbaresco by studying the various vineyards and still not learn it all. Case in point: the Barolo area has 181 MGAs—*menzioni geografiche aggiuntive*, or additional geographic mentions—170 are vineyards and 11 are villages. Meanwhile, Barbaresco has 66 MGAs, including its 4 villages. MGAs are allowed on labels in both zones. For clarity, the names Barolo and Barbaresco are both villages as well as larger growing zones that include other villages.

Barolo Villages

Barolo
Barolo vines grow in Sant'Agata soils, comprising a mix of clay and sand with a high percentage of limestone. Expect wines from this village to be structured, though some can be perfumed and velvety. Of the village's thirty MGAs, Cannubi gets the most attention. Since gracing labels in 1752, the vineyard has been recognized for quality well before the village of Barolo. However, while Cannubi indicates the historic vineyard of a large hillside, Cannubi Boschis, Cannubi Muscatel, Cannubi Valletta, and Cannubi San Lorenzo are vineyards that make up the rest of the hill. In fact, the use of "Cannubi" on the label became contentious because of all the other so-called Cannubis, and some argued that the original "Cannubi" represented the best part of the hill. All this is to say that not all Cannubi is the same.

Main MGAs: Bricco delle Viole, Brunate, Cannubi, Cannubi Boschis, Cannubi Muscatel, Cannubi San Lorenzo, Cannubi Valletta, Cerequio, Le Coste, Sarmassa

Castiglione Falletto
Loaded with winemaking talent, this village also has one of Barolo's most famous crus—Monprivato, which is synonymous with famed producer Giuseppe Mascarello. Some of the soils around this village contain more sand than the rest of the area. Castiglione Falletto Barolos are balanced, structured, and can age quite well.

Main MGAs: Bricco Boschis, Fiasco, Monprivato, Pira, Rocche di Castiglione, Vignolo, Villero

La Morra
With its Sant'Agata soils, the village is most known for its floral, perfumed wines that also convey earthiness—they're broader than Verduno Barolos but with similar charming aromas. Wines from Brunate and Cerequio (which are shared with the village of Barolo) fall on the more powerful side of the spectrum for La Morra wines.

Main MGAs: Arborina, Brunate, Cerequio, La Serra, Rocche dell'Annunziata

Monforte d'Alba
Monforte d'Alba had the opposite problem of Barolo with its too many Cannubis. Instead, they made their MGAs so big, the vineyard meaning diminished. Some parts of the area have more sand than clay, allowing vineyards to drain better in rainy years. On average, these are round, ripe wines that pack some power. (The MGA Ginestra also is a special vineyard for Barbera grapes.)

Main MGAs: Bussia, Ginestra, Gramolere

Novello
Wines from Novello are often blended with wines from other villages in Barolo; on their own, they can be big and tannic.

Main MGAs: Bergera-Pezzole, Ravera

Serralunga d'Alba
Located in the southeast corner of the Barolo area, Serralunga d'Alba is also where King Victor Emmanuel II had his hunting estate, Fontanafredda. The soils in this area have high amounts of calcium carbonate, yielding slow-aging, complex wines.

Some fall on the austere side, while others are powerful, full of tar and licorice.

Main MGAs: Arione, Boscareto, Cerretta, Falletto, Fontanafredda, Francia, Gabutti, Lazzarito, Ornato, Parafada, Prapò, Vignarionda

Verduno
In the far north corner of the Barolo area, the quiet village of Verduno grows Nebbiolo in Sant'Agata soils, though, compared with Barolo and La Morra, Verduno soils have more chalk. Its wines are elegant, lightly structured, and quite food friendly.

Main MGAs: Massara, Monvigliero

Other Villages to Know: Cherasco, Diano d'Alba, Grinzane Cavour, and Roddi
The remaining villages in the Barolo zone can range from producing wines that have a lot of structure to those that are fleshy and broad. Grinzane Cavour is known for its repository of heritage vines, which are maintained to preserve the genetic diversity of Piedmont's main grapes. The Diano d'Alba village is better known for its Dolcetto. Cherasco is one of the few villages that grows the white grape Nascetta.

Main MGAs: Bricco Ambrogio (in Roddi)

Barbaresco Villages

Barbaresco
The namesake of the wine zone also has some of the best vineyard land for Nebbiolo, period. Nearly all the wines are balanced, though some crus, like Rabajà, produce richer wines than cooler sites, like Asili. (Gaja's San Lorenzo vineyard is also in the village of Barbaresco.) In addition to the Langhe's usual limestone, some vineyards have more sand, leading to wines that are more approachable. The Produttori di Barbaresco makes cru wines from some of Barbaresco's best areas, offering a chance to taste the difference between Pora from Barbaresco, Santo Stefano from Neive, and so on.

Main MGAs: Asili, Martinenga, Montefico, Montestefano, Ovello, Pora, Rabajà, Rio Sordo Roncaglie, Tre Stelle

Neive
In addition to limestone, the vineyards around this town have pockets of clay, which lends itself to bigger styles of Barbaresco. Within the Albesani cru, legendary producer Bruno Giacosa bought grapes for his Santo Stefano wines, a portion of the vineyard owned by the Castello di Neive.

Main MGAs: Albesani, Basarin, Cottà, Gallina, Serraboella

San Rocco Seno d'Elvio
Once part of Treiso, this tiny town is easy to overlook and once grew several other grapes before Nebbiolo became so popular. The town has only four crus, and three are shared by Treiso.

Main MGAs: Rocche Massalupo

Treiso
Up until the 1980s, many of Treiso's best vineyards grew Dolcetto, Moscato, and Barbera. (The village still makes outstanding Dolcetto.) The area is cooler than other parts of Barbaresco and is known for austere, powerful, elegant wines thanks to its marl-limestone soils.

Main MGAs: Bernadot, Nervo, Pajorè, Rizzi

Piedmont Grapes

Nebbiolo (rightfully) gets a lot of attention in Piedmont, but it's worth appreciating the breadth and depth of all the native grapes that grow in the region, from lithe Arneis to misunderstood Freisa.

White

Arneis

You wouldn't think that Arneis, a low-acid white grape, would be related to the high-acid, high-tannin red grapes like Nebbiolo, but the two are part of the same family tree. Scientists modeled a genotype that could be the extinct parent of Arneis and red grape Grignolino; if the genotype is accurate, Arneis is the grandchild of Nebbiolo.

Like so many grapes in Italy, Arneis could have become extinct had it not been for a few people who took pains to keep it going. In the 1970s, influential estates Vietti and Bruno Giacosa took an interest, paving the way for the grape's popularity at the end of the twentieth century. The name may come from a local word for a temperamental, difficult person, though winemakers such as Domenico Almondo of Giovanni Almondo have learned how to overcome the challenges it presents in the vineyard. Arneis is most at home in the sandy soils of the Roero, especially in the vineyards of Bric Renesio, Castellinaldo, and Canale. As a wine, Arneis is all about fresh white peach or apricot, pear, white flowers, and almond. It's a subtle, elegant wine, one worth slowing down to taste so you don't overlook its delicate flavors and aromas.

Carica l'Asino

Many Italian grapes are named for their bounty. Emilia-Romagna has Pagadebit (page 73), which means "pays the bills." Piedmont has Carica l'Asino, which means "load the donkey," either because the vine has high yields that allow farmers to load up the donkey with a lot of grapes or because donkeys were required to navigate the terrain. At any rate, it's rare to come across the variety apart from the wines that Bruna Ferro and her sons make at Carussin, their family winery in San Marzano Oliveto in Monferrato. Often blended with local white grapes, such as Favorita and Cortese, this grape yields a wine that is all about the countryside: honeycomb, grass, and stone fruit.

Cortese

Almost everyone's first experience of Cortese comes in a glass of crisp, pale Gavi. Gavi became one of Italy's most popular white wines in the 1960s, but popularity brings problems, namely too many people making the wine in less-than-stellar ways. Today, the redemption story is about reclaiming the characteristics of Cortese. First documented in the seventeenth century at the Casale Monferrato, the grape is native to southern Piedmont.

It's a thin-skinned variety but tolerant of cold weather, and it is always high in acidity as tasted in the wines from La Morella in the Colli Tortonesi, which carry notes of lime and herbs. While "crisp" and "racy" are still common descriptors for Cortese wines, the variety has a richer side. The late Stefano Bellotti of Cascina degli Ulivi, an early adopter of biodynamic methods, showed how the wine could be richer and rounder, with notes of golden apple and honey.

Erbaluce

At the Paris Exhibition of 1855, Erbaluce took home the gold medal, but the grape from the foothills of the Alps just north of Turin doesn't garner as much attention today. Even so, it grows pretty much in the same place as it did back then: northern Piedmont, especially around the commune of Caluso as well as farther east along the Sesia River.

On the vine, the grape is starkly pale in color until it is ripe, which is where it gets its name (*luce* means "light" and *alba* means "sunrise"). Like Cortese, Erbaluce has high acidity, yielding fresh, mineral-driven wines. Its searing acidity works well in sparkling wines, and it occasionally goes into a hard-to-find *passito* (the grape's thick skins dry well for this type of dessert wine). Like Arneis, Cortese wines will never hit you over the head with aromatics, but expect delicate notes of white flowers, grass, and stone fruit. (Side note: while it is sometimes called "Greco," it is of no relation to Greco Bianco in Calabria, page 53, or Greco in Campania, page 63.)

Favorita

(see Vermentino, Liguria chapter, page 119)

Moscato Bianco (Muscat)

Moscato Bianco may have been born in Greece or elsewhere, but no matter its origins, it's been in Italy for a very long time. While Moscato Bianco production extends to nearly every Italian region, it has long been associated with Piedmont, becoming popular in Asti and growing especially well around Canelli, Santo Stefano Belbo, and Loazzolo, just south of the city. Even before the advent of the autoclave for making tank-method sparkling wine (see *metodo Martinotti*, page 262), the grape was known for sweet, fizzy wines.

Today, Moscato d'Asti and Asti Spumante are the best-known Moscato wines from Italy. Made by cold-fermenting the juices so that half the sugar remains, Moscato d'Asti is the sweeter sparkling wine and only gently bubbly—a wine that smells (and tastes) like tangy peaches and cream. Asti Spumante goes through two fermentations, so it has a more forceful bubble and is drier. In Piedmont and other parts of northern Italy, Moscato Bianco almost always means bubbles. The Bera estate in Canelli makes lovely low-intervention Moscato d'Asti with native yeasts. In 2019, they also started making an unfiltered dry Moscato. Elsewhere in the country it is just as often a dry or *passito* (dessert) wine. From Puglia, Moscato di Trani is a rare, fragrant *passito* made with the local type of Moscato Bianco called Moscato Reale.

No matter the wine, Moscato Bianco always has a distinct floral-fruity aroma, making it easy to pick out in a blind tasting.

Nascetta

Once used in church wines, this semiaromatic white variety is a historic grape in Barolo, documented by the enology school in Conegliano (in Veneto) soon after the school's founding in the late nineteenth century. Today, after a lot of work by producers in the town of Novello, it is showing true potential. In the early 1990s, it was rediscovered in a defunct winery and propagated. Like the rest of the Barolo area, most wines made in Novello are red, so Nascetta was a rare opportunity to make white wine with a native variety. The grape also was a historic variety in the towns of Cherasco, in the Barolo area, and Mondovi, a commune south of there. In Novello, it thrives in the town's limestone soils.

The sensitive variety has lower-than-average acidity, but it makes a pleasant fruity wine with a distinctly saline finish—the kind that would appeal to those who love Vermentino.

Timorasso

If Nascetta is emerging as a new favorite white wine grape, then Timorasso paved the way. A nearly forgotten grape from the Colli Tortonesi area, Timorasso exists today thanks to the efforts of local winemaker Walter Massa, whose work rehabilitating and replanting the grape not only saved it from extinction but also drew international attention to the grape. Today it still grows mostly around the hills of Tortona. (Many producers add "Derthona," Tortona's Roman name, on their Timorasso labels.)

Timorasso makes layered white wines with notes of honey and toasted nuts, distinct mineral undertones, and acidity on a par with Riesling. Timorasso wines are on the richer end of the spectrum and can be high in alcohol. Like Riesling, they are capable of aging for years.

Early spring Nebbiolo vines.

Red

Barbera

This bright, fruity grape is easy to love, which makes it no wonder that it is one of the most-planted red grapes in Italy, behind Sangiovese and Montepulciano. While its origins are murky, its modern-day home is in northern Italy, especially the areas around Alba, Asti, and Alessandria. In general, it does better in vineyards with a higher percentage of clay in the soil, compared with Nebbiolo, which does better in vineyards with a higher percentage of limestone. For Barbera, this has been a good thing: in an era where Nebbiolo commands higher prices, winemakers aren't ripping out Barbera and replanting with Nebbiolo because each has different soil requirements. Barbera's history is not spotless: in the 1980s, cost-cutting producers added methanol to enrich Barbera, resulting in several deaths. That tragic event is fortunately well in the past, and Barbera producers today embrace all the styles of wines that the grape can yield, including picnic-ready lighter wines, bright, food-friendly wines that carry distinct red-fruit notes, and rich versions aged in oak (though the characteristics of Barbera are less about oak and more about acidity, fruitiness, and a dry, mouthwatering finish). In general, Barbera from Alba tends to be bigger in style than Barbera from Asti. Barbera also forms an important part of blends in Lombardy's Oltrepò Pavese area as well as across the border in Emilia-Romagna. Because of the variety's high acidity and low tannins, it offers balance to grapey field blends of Croatina and Vespolina.

Brachetto

Grown in Asti and Alessandria, this aromatic grape creates a wild mix of flowers and spice in the glass. In the nineteenth century, with the efforts of Arturo Bersano, it became popular as an aromatic sparkling wine. Sparkling Brachetto continues to be popular in Italy, but still Brachetto wines offer a deeper way to explore the grape's aromas of wild rose and baking spices. As a wine, it is lighter in alcohol than other reds and floral-fruity, the kind of wine that pairs well with dessert—even challenging pairings like chocolate. Slightly sweet, low in alcohol, and gently fizzy, the Brachetto d'Acqui from Braida di Giacomo Bologna is a refreshing after-dinner palate cleanser.

Croatina (Bonarda)

There is overlap between the grapes grown in Alto Piemonte and those grown in Lombardy's Oltrepò Pavese region and across the border in Emilia-Romagna. The overlap can cause confusion between grape names and wine names. Even though Croatina is not a synonym for a grape called Bonarda, the wines made with Croatina are often called Bonarda, as in "Oltrepò Pavese Bonarda" (in Lombardy), "Colli Piacentini Bonarda" (in Emilia-Romagna), and "Collina Torinese Bonarda" (around Turin). In Alto Piemonte, Croatina can be blended with Nebbiolo and Vespolina, and in Emilia-Romagna it's paired with Barbera. The variety's tannins are more rustic than Barbera or Nebbiolo, yet it is also capable of adding deep, dark fruit and a dash of minerality to a blend.

Dolcetto

First, an explanation about the name: while "Dolcetto" means "little sweet one," the grape makes quite dry, tart wines. The name applies to how the grape tastes when eaten—its flesh is sweet and low in acidity. Dolcetto has the misfortune of growing well in places where Nebbiolo also grows. Because Nebbiolo commands the most money and interest, Dolcetto plantings are down. Plus, the grape can be fussy, growing unevenly throughout the season. The exception is Dogliani, a town in the Langhe where Dolcetto has always been the most important grape (and therefore grown in prime spots). As a vine, it ripens early, an advantage for winemakers who also grow Nebbiolo, since they can harvest Dolcetto while Nebbiolo is still on the vine. Even though Dolcetto is low in acid, it's high in tannins, so the best Dolcetto wines can taste fresh, with herbal or lavender edges coupled with raspberries or cherries. In Liguria, Dolcetto is called Ormeasco, and it's also used to make Sciac-trà, a Ligurian *rosato* wine.

Freisa

Named after its aroma, which resembles strawberries, Freisa is one of Nebbiolo's closest relatives. Yet even with this distinction, it was another almost-forgotten Piemontese grape. Like Dolcetto and Grignolino, Freisa grows well in the same vineyard areas that Nebbiolo grows. It's a challenge to vinify because instead of getting its tannins from the skins, like most grapes, the tannins are mostly in the seeds. Balancing its tannins and acidity takes practice, and not everyone has cracked the code, or cares to. Wines made with the grape tend to be more angular than round and plush, which for years went against the trends. Winemakers have bills to pay, and it's way easier to sell people on Nebbiolo (or Barbera or even Dolcetto). Today, though, trends are swinging back in Freisa's favor. Yielding light red wines with acidity coupled with complex aromas of strawberry and citrus, Freisa feels right for modern times.

Grignolino

This native Piedmont grape is the grandchild of Nebbiolo, and it shares family characteristics with Nebbiolo and Freisa. None of the varieties produce wines with strong, pronounced color, and all contain a fair bit of acidity and tannins. In Grignolino's case, the grape yields wines that taste fresh and somewhat lean, and are filled with the taste of sour cherries, red plums, and pepper. In his book *Native Wine Grapes of Italy*, Ian D'Agata calls Grignolino one of his favorite wines, "a misunderstood but lovely variety" that was once widely loved by Piedmont's noblemen. What happened? Tastes changed, and the grape's delicate aromas and color fell out of favor. Like Dolcetto and Freisa, Grignolino grows best where Nebbiolo grows, so farmers selected the better-known grape to plant. Today, its main areas are in the Asti and Alessandria provinces. Grignolino also has a lot of seeds, so it won't yield as much juice as other grapes, and the tannins can be bitter if the wine is not made carefully. Still, the perfumed, bright wines are eminently food friendly.

Malvasia di Casorzo

Casorzo is a town east of Turin within the province of Asti, and it's pretty much the only place you'll find wines made with this aromatic red Malvasia grape. The thick-skinned jammy grape makes sweet or nearly sweet wines in a sparkling or *passito* style, and it is set apart from other sweet wines by its notable tannins and acidity.

Malvasia di Schierano

Grown around Turin, Malvasia di Schierano is an even more aromatic and refined Malvasia than Malvasia di Casorzo, expressing aromas of strawberries and rose geranium. It too is made either as a sweet, gently sparkling or still wine that is typically low in alcohol, expressing red-fruit flavors in each glass.

Nebbiolo

Officially documented in Turin in 1266, Nebbiolo is the quintessential Piedmont grape. Its cradle of origin is somewhere in the foothills of the Alps, perhaps in or near Valtellina in Lombardy. Professor Anna Schneider, the renowned ampelographer (a specialist of grape varieties), describes it as a non-migrating grape, a variety that has stayed where it was born. Head to other parts of Italy, or even across the border to Switzerland or France, and you won't find any native vines related to it. All the grapes it is linked to—like Freisa, Vespolina, Grignolino, and others—are also from northwestern Italy, further proof that Nebbiolo's home has always been in the space between the Alps and the Apennines.

There is a lot of diversity among Nebbiolo local names with Picotener in Valle d'Aosta, Chiavennasca in Lombardy, and Spanna in Alto Piemonte. Among the vines, there's also diversity in biotypes, which can vary in everything from the color, size of the grapes, and shape of the leaves. Yet all Nebbiolo is legendary for how it expresses the place where it grows, from the sun exposure and altitude to the exact mix of soil. Vineyard cartographer Alessandro Masnaghetti delineated the specific vineyards of the MGAs (*menzioni geografiche aggiuntive*, or additional geographic mentions), showing the variations in terrain.

Even though Barolo and Barbaresco command the most attention and highest prices for Nebbiolo wine, people who love the grape also look farther afield, to the Alto Piemonte towns of Gattinara, Ghemme, and Boca, as well as to Valtellina and Valle d'Aosta. Wine made with Nebbiolo carries a medium garnet color, which is lighter in cooler climates. Expect Nebbiolo wines to have noticeable acidity and tannins, which allow them to age. Yet they are equally known for their aromas, a varied blend of roses, spices, leather, and sour cherry. Ethereal or grounded, austere or floral, good wines made with Nebbiolo are captivating.

Nebbiolo Rosé

It's easy to think that this variety is another biotype of Nebbiolo, but Anna Schneider and her colleagues insist that Nebbiolo Rosé is a separate variety. In Valtellina, the grape is called Chiavennaschino (little Chiavennasca), and compared with Nebbiolo, its color is much paler, as you'd expect with the "rosé" name. This hue belies its alcohol and tannins, which can be high, though the grape has lower acidity than its sibling. Like Nebbiolo, it delivers memorable aromas of roses and red fruits. It's hard to find the grape vinified solo, but it can be used to boost the perfume in blends.

Pelaverga Group

There are two Pelavergas: Pelaverga Grosso, which has large bunches and grapes, and Pelaverga Piccolo, which has small bunches and medium-size grapes. The one to remember is Pelaverga Piccolo, which grows only around Verduno, the northernmost town in the Barolo area. Pelaverga vines have been grown in Verduno since the sixteenth century because the thick-skinned grape was sweet to eat and made decent church wine. For whatever reason, though, the grape didn't spread to other parts of the Langhe. Gabrielle Burlotto, one of the first female sommeliers in Italy, decided to try making a wine with Pelaverga in the late 1960s, and by 1973, she felt she had completed enough experiments to make a decent wine with the variety. Yet it's only been recently that Pelaverga has been in demand, especially abroad. Mario Andrion, winemaker at Castello di Verduno,

notes that it grows best in places where Nebbiolo doesn't, such as the base of a slope. It is also harvested earlier, as early as August for sparkling Pelaverga and early September for still wine. With silky tannins, bright red fruit, and herbal aromas, it is an easy grape to like. Pelaverga Grosso is unrelated and grows around Turin, where it is used in the wines of the Colline Torinesi and Colline Saluzzesi. The variety offers high acidity and strawberry aromas. Like Pelaverga Piccolo, the Grosso variety is found only in Piedmont (as far as we know).

Ruchè

Home in the Monferrato hills, Ruchè is a unique red grape. Like Brachetto, it's aromatic, but in a way that makes it easy to mistake for a white wine in a blind tasting. That is, until you get that tannic bite. In the mid-twentieth century, Don Giacomo Cauda, a town priest, began making wine with Ruchè. Like the aromatic grape Gewürztraminer, it gives off aromas of spices and rose petals, and it has relatively low acidity, especially when compared to Barbera and Nebbiolo. For years, Ruchè received little attention until California winemaker Randall Grahm tasted Luca Ferraris's spicy Ruchè at Vinitaly, the annual Italian wine trade show in Verona, and loved it so much he began importing the wine. This gave Ruchè exposure in the US, and while that partnership has dissolved, this rare aromatic red grape continues to gain interest among anyone who loves wines with intricate aromas.

Uva Rara

(see Lombardy chapter, page 130)

Vespolina (Ughetta)

(see Lombardy chapter, page 130)

Regional Foods

Agnolotti del plin
delicate stuffed pasta

Asparagus

Bagna cauda
buttery, anchovy-infused dipping sauce served with vegetables

Bollito misto
stew with at least five different cuts of meat

Cannelloni
savory filled crepes

Cardoons
spring vegetable, similar to celery and artichokes, often served with bagna cauda

Carne cruda
beef tartare

Cheese
fontina

Gorgonzola, cows' milk blue cheese

ricotta made with cows' milk

Robiola, soft-ripened cows' milk cheese

toma

Fonduta
melted cheese (mostly fontina) made into sauce for dipping (Italy's fondue)

Gianduja
chocolate-hazelnut blend

Hazelnuts

Risotto

Truffles

Tajarin
Piemontese-style tagliatelle

Vitello tonnato
veal served cold with a sauce made from preserved tuna, capers, lemon juice, and mayonnaise

Zabaglione
dessert cream made by whisking egg yolks and sugar with Marsala

Recommended Producers

Alto Piemonte

Antichi Vigneti di Cantalupo

Antoniolo

Boniperti

Castello di Conti

Dessilani

Francesco Brigatti

Il Sorpasso

La Prevostura

Le Piane

Le Pianelle

Nervi

Monsecco

Orsolani

Paolo Saracco

Paride Iaretti

Produttori di Carema

Tenute Sella

Travaglini

Umberto Fiore

Asti and Alessandria

Agostino Pavia

Bera

Boveri

Braida di Giacomo Bologna

Carussin

Cascina degli Ulivi

Cascina 'Tavijn

Cerruti

DeGiorgis

Ezio Trinchero

Il Mongetto

La Caudrina

La Colombera

La Ghibellina

La Morella

Luca Ferraris Agricola

Ricci

San Fereolo

Sant'Agata

Tenuta Grillo

Vittorio Bera & Figli

The Langhe, including Barolo and Barbaresco

499

Aldo Conterno

Anna Maria Abbona

Armando Parusso

Bartolo Mascarello

Borgogno

Brezza

Brovia

Bruno Giacosa

Cantina del Glicine

Cantina del Pino

Cappellano

Ca' del Baio

Ca' del Prete

Ca' Rossa

Cascina delle RoseCascina Roccalini

Cascina Val del Prete

Castello di Verduno

Cavallotto

Chiara Boschis

Cigliuti

Elio Altare

Ettore Germano

Einaudi

Francesco Rinaldi

Francone

Fratelli Alessandria

Giacomo Borgogno

Giacomo Conterno

Giacomo Fenocchio

Gianfranco Bovio

Giovanni Almondo

Giuseppe Rinaldi

Gaja

G.D. Vajra

La Spinetta

Lorenzo Accomasso

Manzone

Michele Chiarlo

Marchesi di Barolo

Marchesi di Grésy

Oddero

Paitin

Pelissero

Produttori del Barbaresco

Prunotto

Rizzi

Roagna

Sottimano

Taliano Michele

Val del Prete

Vietti

Viglione

Alessandra Bera of Bera in Canelli

Puglia

The pot was already boiling with orecchiette when we stuck our heads into the small kitchen. The cook dropped in a heap of leafy broccoli rabe, but before we could see the rest of the process, we were directed to a dining room full of crown molding and gold paint. "Do you speak Italian?" the family patriarch asked. Badly, we admitted. "French?" Unfortunately, worse than Italian. We must have been unclear, so the patriarch continued in French until an underwhelming-looking mix of army-green vegetables and pale pasta nubs hit the table. But then we took a bite: with punchy olive oil infused with garlic and red pepper flakes, the flavor more than made up for the pasta's appearance, creating a meal that tasted richer than seemed possible from so few ingredients. In a way, that lunch in a gilded room encapsulates Puglia, a region that is over-the-top in some ways but down-to-earth underneath it all. Its wines also fluctuate—they can be layered and (sometimes) overly complex or plain and honest. At their best, they surprise with simplicity and freshness.

Earlier that day, we had arrived in Trani, a pretty fishing port, to visit one of the few remaining producers of Moscato di Trani, a late-harvest wine that is golden, honeyed, and just about everything you could want in a dessert wine. Before our appointment, we checked into a convent converted into a hotel, which overlooked the small harbor. Across the water, the cathedral's bell tower looked like a Venetian campanile, a trick of the eye that could make you believe you were no longer in Italy's deep south. Puglia often gives off this otherworldliness, populated by whoever blew in from the greater Mediterranean. *Va dove ti porta il vento,* a local saying goes. Go where the wind takes you.

Since the region has a long coast and is relatively flat (only 2 percent is mountains), Puglia was easy to conquer and colonize but hard to control. Greeks, Saracens, Romans, Byzantines, Swabians, Normans, Spanish, and others came and went, all leaving traces behind. The city of Brindisi came of age in Roman times, marking the end of the Appian Way, the ancient road that connected Rome to the coast. After the fall of Rome, Puglia's other main coastal city, Bari, grew under the influence of the Byzantines. Later, the city of Lecce acquired its stunning Baroque architecture during the sixteenth and seventeenth centuries. But some pieces don't fit neatly into history. Castel del Monte, the octagonal castle dreamed up by Emperor Frederick II in the thirteenth century, still looks futuristic. In comparison, the towns of Alberobello and Locorotondo, which are filled with white-washed, conical homes called *trulli*, feel pulled from prehistory. Puglia's food is also different from any other region in Italy. Home to burrata, the creamy filled mozzarella now beloved around the world, it is also the place for a sharp dried fava bean puree served with dandelion greens, a combination that brings to mind Egyptian *ful medames*.

There's truth to the saying about the wind, though. Puglia is nearly always windy. No more than forty miles wide at the most, the flat Salento peninsula gets breezes from both the Ionian and the Adriatic Seas, while the entire region contends with the tramontana, a cold, strong winter wind, and the sirocco, whose hot gusts arrive in spring and fall from the Sahara. While staying in the town of Manfredonia, Norman Douglas, an early-twentieth-century British writer, heard that the sirocco blew so hard that it broke all the lampposts between the town and the train station. He checked it out for himself, writing: "It must have been a respectable gale, since the cast-iron supports are snapped in half, every one of them."

For grapevines, wind can be good and bad. It can prevent disease by keeping vines dry in cool areas and cool in hot areas. Yet winds are also drying, which can be challenging in an already arid place. Still, making wine in Puglia means making peace with the wind. Marianna Annio and Raffaelo Leo, a husband-wife team making wine in Gioia del Colle, went a step further, naming their winery Pietraventosa (Windy Stone). The couple got serious about wine in the early 2000s when they decided to make something for themselves rather than work for others. But they weren't winemakers by trade, so they learned as they went, gradually establishing a reputation for their lithe, endlessly drinkable Primitivo. In the beginning, they had to give away their wine, but finding buyers these days for the thirty thousand or so bottles they make annually isn't a problem anymore. In this case, the wind has treated them well.

Pietraventosa represents one side of Puglia's winemaking, in which local people, many of whom were raised around farming but became cops or mechanics or bookkeepers, decided to go back to the land, making wine on a shoestring budget while working to overcome the stereotype that all wines here taste cooked, made in a too-hot climate. The other side of Puglia is industrial-scale production. Making nearly 257.9 million gallons (9.76 million hectoliters) in 2020, Puglia is second only to Veneto. While Veneto makes the most DOC wine in Italy, Puglia leads the nation in table wine production, considered the lowest category on the quality spectrum. Volume is why Puglia's wines are hard to sort out from afar, especially when you're looking for bottles with a sense of somewhereness.

A few estates represent the middle ground between scrappy entrepreneurs and industrial producers. Some started making wine in bulk for northern wineries before shifting to bottling their own wine. Some larger producers have found ways to balance quantity with quality, pushing for better standards in the vineyards and cellars. In Guagnano, a small town on the Salento peninsula near Lecce, Cosimo Taurino stands out for quality and consistency through the years. The Taurino family has been making wine since World War II. In the 1970s, Cosimo Taurino took over from his father and worked with enologist Severino Garofano to make a wine purely from local Negroamaro grapes, aging it in barrique (small French oak barrels) and showing the potential that the grape had for quality red wine. Today, the estate has tamped down its reliance on barrique, and its Negroamaro wines remain benchmarks for southern Puglia.

Not too far away, a small winery has stuck it out for multiple generations surrounded by much larger players. Natalino del Prete grows a grab bag of native grapes in the *alberello* ("little tree") style used by the ancient Greeks. Some of his Negroamaro vines are more than fifty years old, and all are grown as hands-off as possible, slowly and without chemicals. His daughter, Mina, also works with him, and the wines themselves fall into the same camp as our orecchiette lunch: grounded, deceptively simple, and greater than the sum of their parts. In other words, the gems stand out from the sea of production, showing what's possible in one of the warmest parts of Italy's south.

Negroamaro vines at the Natalino Del Prete farm.

History

On the southern section of the Murge, a breezy high-altitude plateau, Gioia del Colle is one of Puglia's best winemaking territories. It's known for Primitivo, the same grape that Americans call Zinfandel. The story goes that a seventeenth-century monk named Don Francesco Filippo Indellicati noticed a small vine with grapes that ripened earlier than others. He named the vine "Primitivo," meaning "early" or "first," and its cuttings spread throughout Gioia del Colle and later Manduria farther south in the region. Primitivo became important in brandy production until phylloxera and higher alcohol taxes stopped the brandy trade. It was also one of many grapes shipped north to use in bulk wines and vermouth. In the 1980s—when Zinfandel became popular in California—a few Gioia del Colle winemakers started bottling their wine under their own name, capitalizing on the grape's tie-in with a California wine. But at that time, few thought of Puglia as a place for quality wine.

This wasn't the case in ancient times. The empires that controlled Puglia drank local wine, at least dating back as far as the ancient Greeks, who colonized the region. The flat stretches of land, abundant sunshine, and dry summers made vineyards easier to work than those in mountain areas, with more consistent results. During Roman times, the wine trade passed through Brindisi. Exactly what Puglian wine was like in Greek or Roman times is impossible to say, though it's likely that the grapes we associate with Puglia today came later. In 1996, UC Davis professor Carole Meredith, an expert on wine grape DNA profiling (who proved that Primitivo and Zinfandel were genetically identical) identified Tribidrag, a local Croatian grape, as the original vine. Historians then found records showing that a barrel of Tribidrag had been sent to Puglia in 1488. Others say Slavic refugees who resettled in Puglia brought the vine with them. Regardless, Primitivo spread throughout the region and remains one of Puglia's most identifiable wines.

By the turn of the twentieth century, local wine in Puglia was good for everyday drinking. After his visit to Manfredonia, Norman Douglas traveled to the hill town of Monte Sant'Angelo on the southern side of the Gargano Promontory. The town was a pilgrimage site where Christian tourists came to see a cave allegedly visited by the archangel Michael. To escape the crowds, Douglas found a subterranean wine bar where he delighted in tasting "a divine product: a *vino di montagna* of noble pedigree." The wine was one of the few things that pleased him on his visit to the town, which was otherwise packed with sweaty pilgrims (even back then, tourists complained about other tourists). Douglas also wrote about the Castel del Monte, an octagonal castle built on the Murge in the thirteenth century by Frederick II of Hohenstaufen, the Holy Roman Emperor. Yet while today the area around Castel del Monte is known for wine, Douglas never made that connection. His glass of wine must have come from somewhere near Manfredonia.

Modern Puglian wine got its start around Castel del Monte. The castle, a UNESCO World Heritage site once used as a base for Frederick II's favorite hobby, falconry, shows up on some wine labels. In the twentieth century, the de Corato family grew grapes in the stony land around the castle, making wine to ship north for blending. One day, Carlo de Corato wondered if the *rosato* he was making with Bombino Nero grapes could stand up to wines from more prestigious areas. He set up a blind tasting with an expert wine-tasting friend, mixing in bottles from northern Italy and France. When it turned out that their favorite was his own wine, he figured it was worth the risk to try bottling and selling it himself. Today, the de Corato family's Rivera estate has helped make a name for Castel del Monte wines internationally.

Farther south, on the Salento peninsula, the Leone de Castris estate is credited with being the first to bottle *rosato* in Italy, starting in the 1930s. After World War II, Americans who tried the "Five Roses" wine loved it so much that the family began exporting the *rosato* to the United States. By the late 1970s, Leone de Castris was the largest private winery in Puglia. Today, the company makes more than forty wines over 740 acres (300 hectares) of vineyards, yet it still bottles "Five Roses," a wine that the guide *Gambero Rosso* described as a "sapid, fresh, long and pleasant wine."

Land and Wines

Puglia offers long, flat stretches of land, an anomaly in Italy outside the Po River basin. Parts of the region resemble California's Central Valley, with large-scale farms growing grains and produce. Yet while Puglia is stereotyped as a one-dimensional, sunbaked land, not all of it is hot and flat. Some areas can be much cooler thanks to north-facing vineyards and altitude.

The province of Foggia makes up the far north, bordering Molise (page 133), and it's still finding its way in the quality wine world. Years ago, we met the owner of an estate in Lucera who hoped to rehabilitate the near-forgotten Cacc'e Mmitte di Lucera DOC (in dialect, the name means "to drink and refill," a reference to adding more grapes to a fermenting vat of wine so you can drink the excess). The estate's Uva di Troia wine was good, yet it eventually lost its distributor because it was tough to sell abroad. Foggia's vineyards compete with large grain farms, and most of the grapes that grow here go into table wines. East of Foggia, the Gargano Promontory—the spur of Italy's boot—which comprises woods and rocky coastlines, is best known for seaside vacations and hiking. South of there is the Barletta-Andria-Trani province, which is known for the wines of Castel del Monte. The castle itself is on the northern part of the Murge, a large, limestone plateau with hills stretching south through the province of Bari. Portions of it range from 650 to 1,970 feet (200 to 600 meters) high. Around the castle, Uva di Troia and Bombino Nero are planted in rocky vineyards with shallow topsoil and red soils. Among white grapes, Bombino Bianco grows along with Pampanuto, a rare local variety. On the coast near Andria and Trani, a small amount of Moscato Reale is still propagated for Moscato di Trani, a dessert wine that dates to the Middle Ages.

South of Bari on the Murge, Gioia del Colle is known for Primitivo, though growers also work with Malvasia Nera, Negroamaro, Aglianico, and Sangiovese. There, Cristiano Guttarolo inherited his grandmother's farm, turning it into a low-intervention winery growing a range of southern Italian grapes and aging wines in amphorae (terracotta vessels), including the rare red grape Susumaniello, which is slowly gaining ground in Puglia. The windswept area has soils streaked with iron-rich red clay and limestone, which provide beneficial nutrients to vines. Southeast of Gioia del Colle, the vineyards switch to white grapes in the Itria Valley. There, Martina Franca, Locorotondo, and Alberobello are favorite areas to visit for tourists looking for baroque architecture and UNESCO-recognized *trulli*.

In the southern part of the region, the Murge gives way to the flat Salento peninsula. Iron-rich red clay supports the vineyards and olive trees. In Taranto, the town of Manduria makes a richer, riper style of Primitivo than in Gioia del Colle. Phylloxera wiped out most of the Primitivo vines here around the turn of the twentieth century, but vineyards were replanted with cuttings from Gioia del Colle. Closer to Brindisi, the wines are lighter in style, with many *rosati* made with Malvasia Nera and Negroamaro. East of Manduria, in the Salice Salentino area, the wines are mostly made of Negroamaro, with some Aleatico. Farther south and closer to Lecce, Negroamaro is joined by Malvasia, Susumaniello, and a bit of Sangiovese. For producers in southern Puglia like Natalino del Prete, growing a range of grapes helps workflow during harvest: the family starts with Primitivo in early September and ends with Malvasia Nera at the beginning of October, picking Negroamaro, Susumaniello, and Aleatico in between.

In Puglia, especially on its southern side, vines are faced with the elements: limited by water and challenged by sun, heat, and wind. It's true not all of Puglia's wines are good—there's still a heavy use of chemicals on industrial farms, and environmental

Winemaker Natalino Del Prete in his
Salice Salentino vineyard.

activists point to a deadly disease that spread through olive groves in the Salento peninsula as an example of what can happen when the environment is knocked out of balance. Yet the winemakers in Puglia who have learned how to handle the terrain have found ways to make wine that varies from powerful to quirky to eminently drinkable. As the world faces climate change at an accelerating pace and as wine-producing regions become hotter and drier, Puglia's successes may show a way forward for others.

Puglia Grapes

While red grapes dominate Puglia's wines, interest in white grapes like crisp Verdeca and Bombino Bianco is growing. Puglia also makes some of Italy's best *rosati*, a style perfectly suited for local grapes Bombino Nero and Negroamaro.

White

Bombino Bianco

Traditionally used in blends, Bombino Bianco grows throughout Puglia, Abruzzo (where it is permitted in the Trebbiano d'Abruzzo DOC wines), and parts of Lazio. It is also the main grape used in the Pagadebit wines of Emilia-Romagna (page 73). "Pagadebit" means "pay the debts," and vines were so generous that they gave farmers enough grapes to pay off whatever they owed. In recent years, the variety has become better understood for qualities like high acidity and a somewhat creamy texture (think honeydew melon). It also often has anise and bitter almond accents. At its best, it is a bright, charming wine, something to drink chilled on a hot day or at the beginning of a meal. (By the way, it is an excellent match with burrata, Puglia's prized creamy mozzarella.)

Fiano
(see Campania chapter, page 62)

Malvasia di Candia
(see Lazio chapter, page 100)

Minutolo

For years, Minutolo was misclassified as a subvariety of Fiano, yet the only thing the grape has in common with the more famous variety from Campania is that they both make white wine. To be fair, some Puglian producers feel that Minutolo has untapped potential, like Fiano did a few decades ago. Unlike Fiano, Minutolo is aromatic, so much so that wine descriptions often liken it to Moscato. Like most white varieties in Puglia, it is used in blends, though renewed interest in indigenous vines has some exploring Minutolo as a standalone wine. So far, the wines range from neutral and brisk to layered, with citrus zest, honey, thyme, and the kind of aromas that bring to mind Torrontés from Argentina. (For the latter example, try I Pàstini's "Rampone" Valle d'Itria IGP Minutolo.) Minutolo is also often in the blends of Martina Franca and Locorotondo DOCs.

Moscato Reale
(see Moscato Bianco, Piedmont chapter, page 150)

Pampanuto

One of the white grapes that grow around the *trulli* towns of Locorotondo and Alberobello, Pampanuto is used in the white wine blends from central Puglia. It's a low-acid grape, but it is also resistant to diseases and generates dependable yields in the vineyard. It hasn't been studied enough to understand what its potential would be in the long run, but the current evidence suggests it makes a light, delicate white wine that deserves more interest.

Verdeca

Grown in the heart of *trulli* country around the town of Locorotondo, Verdeca has long been a key grape in vermouth production. Named for its green color in the vineyard (*verde* is "green" in Italian), Verdeca wines are straw-colored with a hint of green. With high acidity, accents of grapefruit and lemon, and subtle mineral/flinty notes (like examples from the producer Li Veli), Verdeca will appeal to anyone looking to switch up their Pinot Grigio game. For a different approach, Macchiarola makes a skin-fermented Verdeca, an orange wine (page 84) with notes of honey, spices, and dried apricot.

Red

Aglianico
(see Campania chapter, page 63)

Aleatico
(see Lazio chapter, page 100)

Bombino Nero
There is no relation between Bombino Bianco (page 167) and Bombino Nero—they just share a name. While Bombino Bianco grows in vineyards all along the Adriatic coast, Bombino Nero grows only in Puglia, especially in the area around Castel del Monte near Bari. The drought-tolerant variety plays an important role as a blending grape in many Puglian red wines and is added to Primitivo, Negroamaro, and occasionally Uva di Troia wines to polish tannic edges or lend freshness. While it can make a standalone red wine, it's better known for *rosato*, yielding elegant, salmon-hued wines. Its grape bunches ripen unevenly, leaving some green when others are ready to go, and while this isn't ideal for red wines, it can be beneficial for *rosato*. The less-ripe grapes add acidity, balancing the strawberry and raspberry flavors with zippy tartness. Compared with Negroamaro, Bombino Nero makes lighter, brighter pinks, though both are quintessential Puglian *rosati* and just the kinds of bottles to drink chilled with a summery southern Italian meal.

Malvasia Nera Family
According to Ian D'Agata's *Native Wine Grapes of Italy*, there are two Malvasia Neras from Puglia: Malvasia Nera di Brindisi and Malvasia Nera di Lecce. While DNA tests show them to be identical, they are different enough from one another that it's more likely they're biotypes of the same grape rather than identical grapes. The Brindisi variety ripens early and is aromatic, while the Lecce variety ripens late and is not aromatic. The former is also much more common than the latter, but neither is particularly reliable for making wines that can age (they both oxidize easily). When it comes down to drinking them, most Malvasia Nera from Puglia is blended with Negroamaro or another red grape, so exactly which grape is in the glass isn't as important as what it's being blended with.

Negroamaro
For years we thought "Negroamaro" meant "black bitter," but when we had lunch in Brindisi years ago with the team behind Tormaresca (the Antinori family's Puglia estates), we were gently corrected: "Negroamaro" means "black black," derived from both Greek and Latin words for the color. Perfectly suited for the warm Salento peninsula, the grape is drought tolerant, important in one of Italy's driest climates (and something that has caught the attention of winemakers in other drought-prone areas, like California). It also does well in hot weather, maintaining acidity all the way to harvest. Finally, it's adaptable, growing well in a range of vineyard areas. The skins of the grape are deep in color, though its wines aren't nearly as dark as you might expect, except for its *rosato*—a few hours of skin contact gives the wine a deep-pink hue similar to what you find in Cerasuolo d'Abruzzo (page 39). As a red wine, it has plummy notes balanced by acidity, sometimes with orange peel and red-fruit accents. It can also have a bit of fennel, bell pepper, or other herbaceous notes. Blending it with a touch of Malvasia Nera helps round out its tannic edges.

Primitivo
Everyone who has tasted California Zinfandel thinks they know Primitivo, and to some extent they're right. In 1996, thanks to advancements in DNA profiling, Professor Carole Meredith of UC Davis proved that Zinfandel and Primitivo were the same variety. The grape's name refers to how it ripens early. At harvest,

it reaches unusually high sugar levels—leading to more alcohol—and it also is quite deep in color. For years, these attributes made Primitivo the ultimate blending wine for anemic wines made in cooler climates. Yet once the connection between the Italian grape and Zinfandel was made, interest in Primitivo as a standalone wine took off.

The Manduria zone is warmer and lower in altitude, with iron-rich red-clay soils leading to richer, jammier versions of Primitivo, with hints of dark chocolate and sweet cherry. Primitivo from Gioia del Colle tends to be more elegant with higher acidity thanks to higher altitude, lower temperatures, and calcareous soils. It's not a tannic variety, which is one of the reasons many assume Primitvo wines can't age. Yet Pasquale Petrera of Fatalone, an estate in Gioia del Colle that started bottling its own wines in the late 1980s, believes that high acidity can give the wines a long life. Fatalone sits in one of the windiest parts of Gioia del Colle, and it's common for the last grapes of the harvest to have dried on the vine. Rather than making the wines taste overripe, however, it gives them what Petrera describes as a toasted almond accent, a characteristic specific to Gioia del Colle Primitivo bottles.

Susumaniello

This is another productive "pay the debts" or "load the donkey" kind of grape, the kind that yields so many bunches that farmers in the old days must have loved growing it. Yet it's quite rare and nearly only found in Puglia. Mostly used with Negroamaro, Susumaniello can be hard to drink on its own, and its tannic load can require lengthy aging before it mellows out. Producers who like it have learned how to work with it, not against it. Susumaniello wines from I Pástini or Li Veli are tart and almost savory but also packed with notes of fruit, from deep cherry and red currant to blackberry. Meanwhile, the Susumaniello from Guttarolo in Gioia del Colle is almost wild, redolent of blackberry and blackcurrants.

Uva di Troia (Nero di Troia)

This grape, sometimes called Nero di Troia, is synonymous with Castel del Monte, which is why Frederick II's octagonal castle graces more than a few Uva di Troia wine labels. The grape is fussy to deal with in the vineyard—it sunburns easily and takes forever to ripen—but the hard work pays off in wines with finesse. In an era when blockbuster reds have fallen out of favor in exchange for reds that show a sense of place, Uva di Troia is well positioned as one of southern Italy's most elegant reds. The wines often express notes of violet and fennel. Never strong in color, it's more of a ruby-hued wine, with notes of tart red currant and raspberry. It's not a high-acid variety, but its tannins can be rough if not handled well. Like Primitivo, Bombino Nero, and Negroamaro, Uva di Troia also makes delightful *rosato*—full of rhubarb, cranberries, and spice.

Regional Foods

Brodetto
Adriatic seafood stew with tomatoes, garlic, and onions

Cheese
burrata, creamy cows' milk mozzarella filled with cream and curds

caciocavallo, aged cows' or goats' milk cheese

fior di latte, mozzarella made with cows' milk

pecorino, sheep's milk cheese

provolone, mild cows' milk cheese used in many baked dishes

ricotta and *ricotta salata* (salted ricotta)

Chickpeas

Dried fava bean puree with dandelion greens

Eggplant

Lamb with rosemary

Lampascioni
wild hyacinth bulbs

Olive oil

Olives

Pasta
cavatelli, small curled pasta shaped by pressing and dragging two fingers across the dough

orecchiette, small, chunky pasta whose name means "little ears"

Tiella di pesce
fish pie layered with potatoes, mussels, and herbs

Taralli
ring-shaped crackers

Tomatoes

Recommended Producers

Alberto Longo

Botromagno

Cantele

Cantina Sociale Cooperativa

Castello Monaci

Cosimo Taurino

Cristiano Guttarolo

d'Aprì

Due Palme

Fatalone

Felline

Gianfranco Fino

Girolamo

I Pástini

Jorche

L'Archetipo

Leone de Castris

Li Veli

Macchiarola

Masseria Altemura

Masseria Furfante

Melillo

Menhir

Morella

Natalino del Prete

Palamà

Paololeo

Paradiso

Perrini

Petrelli

Pietraventosa

Polvanera

Risveglio

Rivera

Rosa del Golfo

Rubino

Schola Sarmenti

Tenuta Chiaromonte

Terrecarsiche 1939

Torleanzi

Tormaresca

Torrevento

Tre Pini

Vallone

Vetrere

Viglione

Villa Schinosa

Zecca

Sardinia

In February 2019, Sardinian shepherds dumped canisters of sheep's milk onto highways and streets, painting them white. This was an act of protest against the price of sheep's milk, the main ingredient in one of Sardinia's most important exports: pecorino cheese. Milk prices hadn't been so low since the 1970s, and for a shepherd, the devaluation of milk wouldn't just hurt business, it could end a way of life.

It's impossible to imagine Sardinia without sheep or shepherds. Most of the island's mountainous inland is too sparse to support cattle, but sheep can live off whatever grows in the craggy landscape. Sheep outnumber people here, and shepherds often use main roads to move herds from mountains to valleys. (Fortunately for the animals, Sardinia is the only Italian region without an *autostrada*.) A few weeks after the protests, the government reached an agreement with the shepherds for a higher price per liter, stabilizing the industry for the time being. Around the same time, Shelley visited Sardinia, staying at an *agriturismo* (farm stay) near Oristano owned by dairy farmer Michele Cuscusa. There, she saw cheesemakers culture pecorino and watched shepherds shear herds, leaving piles of wool next to the road. In the middle of it, Cuscusa did it all—cared

for sheep, kept bees, made cheese, ran a cheese-making school, and even made a little bit of wine. He focuses on sustainable living and taking a stand against monocultures, but when it's a day-long ferry ride to the mainland, it makes sense to guarantee your supply of wine and cheese.

Besides, Sardinians tend to go it alone. If mainland Italy is a boot and Sicily is the ball being kicked by it, Sardinia isn't even on the same playing field. The island sits 120 miles (200 kilometers) west of the Italian peninsula, an isolation that makes it feel like its own tiny country. Inhabited since prehistoric times, Sardinia never became part of Magna Graecia (the Greater Greece of antiquity), and it played a minor role within the Roman Empire. Its most lasting influence from outsiders came from Spain. For four centuries, Sardinia fell under the Spanish Aragon dynasty. One of Sardinia's most traditional wines, Vernaccia di Oristano, is a close cousin to Spanish sherry. Still, the island has always had its own culture and history. About a million people speak Sardo (also spelled "Sardu"), one of the few official non-Italian languages recognized in the country. There are also the mysterious Nuraghi, cone-shaped stone fortresses made by an ancient people who disappeared without leaving clues as to what happened to them. The Nuraghi's existence is one of the reasons Sardinia is often linked to Plato's legend of the lost city of Atlantis. But the island was never truly lost—rather, it existed in its own insular world.

While Sardinia's past is mysterious, its present is less so. Now it's about continuing an agricultural way of life, whether that's a shepherd making pecorino cheese or a winemaker vinifying wine. Part of Sardinia is what is called a Blue Zone: a region where an unusually high number of residents live beyond one hundred years. The reason is complicated and goes beyond the good genes, time spent outdoors, and a diet filled with olive oil, whole grains, and beans that would help anyone age well. Factors also include friendship, extended family, and the habit of spending time together at the table. Some of Sardinia's plant life also lives much longer. Ungrafted vines of Carignano ("Carignan" in French) that date back to the early twentieth century make some of the island's most expressive red wines. Even more impressive is the Patriarch, an olive tree in the town of Cuglieri that is between eighteen hundred and two thousand years old. In the summer of 2021, it caught fire in a blaze that torched the town. The news spread through Sardinian media, prompting a team led by a University of Cagliari botany professor to protect what remained of the tree's roots and trunk. After months of effort, the rescue mission worked: new shoots emerged the following spring, another Sardinian symbol of resilience.

History

In 1974, a farmer stumbled upon something in the ground while plowing a field west of Oristano. It turned out to be an archaeological find of a lifetime: a necropolis filled with stone statues of warriors, archers, and boxers dating back to the Iron Age. The Giants of Mont'e Prama, as they came to be called, are some of the oldest statues found in the Mediterranean, relics from an ancient, advanced society. At some point, the civilization disappeared, leaving the island sprinkled with Nuraghi stone fortresses and a lot of questions about what happened to the people who built them.

The civilization's downfall could have been a case of unlucky geography. Sitting in the middle of the Mediterranean, Sardinia was vulnerable to coastal attacks. Phoenicians, Carthaginians, Romans, Byzantines, and Arabs—whoever was in control of the Mediterranean at the time—raided the island, enslaving Sardinians who lived near the water. Those who remained relocated inland. On the eastern side of the island, the ghost village of Tiscali is accessible only through a steep, rocky hike. The village sits in what looks like a cave and was prime real estate for anyone wanting to stay hidden from the Roman army. Today, locals say if you can make the hike from Tiscali and back, you have what it takes to be a shepherd.

This insular nature affected Sardinia's wine traditions. Some Sardinians point to grape seeds found in a Nuragic settlement as proof that winemaking on the island predates outside influences. Others are more convinced that grapes were brought to the island by the Phoenicians, who founded the trading port that later became Cagliari, the region's capital. Wine may have always been made on the island, but it didn't take hold in the same way that it did in other parts of Italy. During Roman times, the island became an important source of wheat, not wine. (The Romans never quite controlled the island like they did other parts of Italy.) That changed when the Aragonese of Spain took over.

Starting in the fourteenth century, Sardinia was under Spanish rule for four centuries. The Spanish especially influenced the west side of the island's architecture and culture. As they do in Spain, Sardinians cook with saffron, though few other parts of Italy use it, except for Sicily. And then there's Vernaccia di Oristano, an oxidized wine that many compare to Spanish sherry. It's made by filling barrels partially so the wine is exposed to air. This encourages a thin layer of yeast to form on its surface. While too much oxygen turns wine to vinegar, the yeast, called *flor*, protects it, while imparting notes of toasted nuts, bread, and orange rind. Historic Oristano producer Contini makes three versions: one aged for four years; one for twenty; and "Antico Gregori," otherwise known as a *vino perpetuo*, a wine made by adding new wine to older vintages, some of which go back to the winery's early days at the turn of the twentieth century. The wine's high alcohol level (16 to 18 percent) makes it stable for long aging, and it's one of Sardinia's most iconic bottles.

In 1708, the island briefly became an Austrian territory before falling under the control of the Turin-based House of Savoy. A century and a half later, Sardinia became part of the new Kingdom of Italy. Italy's unification hero Giuseppe Garibaldi later retired to the island of Caprera, part of an archipelago off the northeastern coast of Sardinia, where he lived for the rest of his life. This northeast coast was once a quiet part of the island until the 1960s, when the Aga Khan, one of the world's wealthiest investors, and other developers built up beach resorts along the coast, quickly attracting celebrities such as Ingrid Bergman and Princess Anne. Today, the glitzy emerald coast remains an anomaly for the down-to-earth island.

For the first half of the twentieth century, winemaking in Sardinia was carried out by small family businesses. Phylloxera (page 12) had wiped out many of the island's vineyards, and replanting efforts were slow until the 1950s, when the Italian government incentivized farmers to plant more vines. The mass plantings that resulted produced grapes for co-ops that turned it into *vino da taglio*, bulk wine sent to mainland Italy and France to beef up lighter wines. While *vino da taglio* production was common in Italy's south, Sardinian co-ops realized that making less but better wine could net them more money. They pulled out inferior vines and concentrated on the vines better suited for an island with low rainfall and poor soils. Today, the region makes around 15.9 million gallons (602,000 hectoliters) a year. Five regions—Molise, Calabria, Basilicata, Liguria, and tiny Valle d'Aosta—make less, but Sardinia has the lowest yield per hectare of vines in the country.

Land and Wines

With long, warm summers and mild winters, Sardinia's climate is pure Mediterranean. The grapes that grow well here are heat loving and tolerant of drought but sensitive to freezing temperatures and rain. Consequently, the same grapes that grow well here also tend to grow in other parts of the Mediterranean, like Liguria, coastal Tuscany, Corsica, the South of France, and many parts of Spain. Yet the island has its own unique flora and fauna. Thousands of pink flamingos live in the marshes around the Golfo di Cagliari. There is also *miele di corbezzolo*, a bitter honey made by bees that pollinate the flowers of the corbezzolo tree, known as the strawberry tree (*Arbutus unedo*), which blooms for three months a year. In the Gallura area, cork forests produce most of the corks used to stopper bottles. The cork forms as tree bark and can be cut off with a pocketknife.

Less than a fifth of Sardinia is flat, with the rest made up of hills and mountains. The Gennargentu ranges run through the center-east part of the island, providing the highest peak on the island, Punta La Marmora, at 6,017 feet (1,834 meters) above sea level. Inland from there is the wild, sparse Barbagia, a part of the island better known for shepherds, which also has some of the best land for Sardinia's signature red grape, Cannonau. The flatter areas around Alghero in the northwest and the Campidano in the southwest have the highest density of vines on the island. Sardinia wines are nearly half-red and half-white, with some *rosato*, sparkling, and sweet wines rounding out the rest of the production.

The northern Sassari province spans two distinct wine areas. To the northwest, above the Costa Smeralda, the Gallura area yields special Vermentino. Vineyards have a unique pink granite stone covered with meager topsoil, lending minerality to the wines as well as complexity, austerity, and ability to age. The Ragnedda family of the Capichera estate, who focused on Vermentino well before the area became famous for it, makes a beguiling version, with notes of peach, apricot, citrus peel, and raw almonds. Meanwhile, Surraru, a younger estate in the heart of the Gallura area, also makes Vermentino that exhibits freshness but enough complexity and backbone to age. Vermentino di Gallura wines—and much of the Vermentino made throughout Sardinia—is perfect seafood wine. Capichera and Cantina Gallura also make remarkable *vendemmia tardiva* (late harvest) wines with Vermentino, and for all their sweetness, they are surprisingly versatile, with enough mineral depth to stand up to just about anything.

On the northwestern side of the island around the city of Sassari, the yellow-white soils (a mix of limestone, clay, sandstone, and other conglomerates) turn out a Vermentino that's more fruit forward, with notes of lemon peel and Mediterranean herbs. Beyond Vermentino, the Sassari area excels in Cagnulari, a once-overlooked red grape that has rebounded, yielding medium-bodied red wines with aromas of sour cherries and scrub brush, a contrast to the richer Cannonau wines from the island. Along with elegant Cagnulari and Vermentino wines, Giovanna Chessa makes a fragrant *passito* (sweet wine) with Moscato in this area. Meanwhile, the Dettori estate focuses on single-vineyard wines from grapes like Monica, Pascale, Cannonau, Vermentino, and Moscato. South of Sassari, the diverse Alghero area has nearly every grape on the island, from ever-present Cannonau to Torbato, a rare white grape grown by Sella & Mosca, one of the largest private wineries in Europe.

In the center, stretching from west to east, are the provinces of Oristano and Nuoro. To the west, around the city of Oristano, the weather is hot, dry, and breezy. Prickly pear cactus grows on the edges of vineyards, while vines growing near the coast pick up saline notes influenced by the sea. The Tirso River valley is home to Vernaccia di Oristano, where the white grapes grow in stony alluvial soils, becoming concentrated with sugars before harvest. The Sardinian version of Malvasia di Lipari also grows here, especially around the town of Bosa (just north of Oristano). There, terraced vineyards face the sea, and the wine gets similarly concentrated and rich in flavor. Some are made in an oxidative style like Vernaccia di Oristano, though production has dropped off as popularity wanes.

East of Oristano, the province of Nuoro is larger but wilder. The inland vineyard areas in the foothills of the Gennargentu ranges have higher altitudes than elsewhere on the island, and the vines enjoy a cooler, breezier climate than they do farther south. It's in the wild Barbagian inland where some of the best Cannonau comes from. There, Giuseppe Gabbas makes Cannonau with a mix of tart red fruit and acidity balanced by the grape's round, juicy character. The town of Mamoiada is another sweet spot for Cannonau, where Giuseppe Gungui of Berteru grows the grape at 2,130 to 2,295 feet (650 to 700 meters) above sea level in granite soils. In this area, Cannonau becomes a medium-bodied, bright wine with notes of wild raspberries and blackberries. Along the east coast in Ogliastra, Cannonau vines benefit from sea breezes that give the wine a touch of salinity, which you taste in the still and sparkling Cannonau from the co-op Cantina Dorgali.

The southern part of the island comprises two provinces: the larger, Sud Sardegna, sits below Oristano and Nuoro and hugs the smaller, Cagliari, which encompasses the region's capital and its surrounding area. Sud Sardegna is one of the most productive wine areas, encompassing the Campidano plains as well as the Sulcis at the southern tip of the island. The warm vineyard areas have mixes of sand, clay, and loam. (Confusingly, the enormous Cagliari DOC covers both provinces as well as Oristano.) White grapes Nuragus and Nasco as well as red grapes Monica and others grow throughout the southern part of the island, which is also the hottest portion, receiving the brunt of the sirocco winds from the south. Here, Cannonau takes on rich notes of pepper and black fruits. While it's common for these wines to reach 15 percent alcohol, the best are balanced with well-integrated acidity. Part of Sud Sardegna is known as Terralba, or "white earth," so named for the white sands in the soil. While the red grape Bovale Sardo grows elsewhere on the island, it's most at home in these warm, sandy soils.

The most historical winemaking corner of the island is the southern tip of Sardinia and the surrounding islands of Sant'Antioco and San Pietro. This area, the Sulcis, is often one of the hottest growing areas in Italy, but it is also one of the world's great terroirs for Carignano. Cantina Giba (formerly known as 6Mura) is a joint venture between the Santadi co-op and Tenuta San Guido, the Tuscan estate best known for the Bordeaux-style wine Sassicaia. The co-op Sardus Pater also makes Carignano with red cherry fruit and creamy complexity. The Sulcis is known for sandy soils, which protected the area's oldest vines from phylloxera. While not all Carignano vines are ungrafted here, the oldest have grown on their original rootstock for more than a hundred years.

Despite Sardinia's insularity, the best of its wines translate well to the mainland, and the more we taste, the more we realize we're only starting to explore what the island has to offer. It stands apart from the pack in many ways. Its signature bread, *pane carasau*, is paper-thin, like Armenian lavash crossed with Greek phyllo—and unlike any bread found on the Italian mainland. Its durum wheat *fregola* pasta has more in common with Israeli couscous, while *malloreddus* is like cavatelli turned gold with saffron. The fact that the region happens to be making wines that have outlasted trends is a testament to the pride Sardinians have in their way of life and their stubborn determination to protect it.

Sardinia Grapes

While Sardinia's best-known grapes, Vermentino and Cannonau (known as Garnacha in Spain and Grenache in France), grow elsewhere in the world, Sardinia's terrain also boasts several native grapes that aren't found anywhere else.

White

Nuragus
Nuragus is now the second most-planted white grape on the island after Vermentino. Hardy, vigorous, and tolerant of drought, the variety grows mostly around Cagliari. In Sardinia's bulk wine days, it was one of the most-planted grapes on the island before falling out of favor. In *Vino Italiano*, David Lynch and Joe Bastianich quote a co-op director who claimed that plenty of Roman Frascati contained Sardinian Nuragus in the old days. When the island shifted toward higher-quality winemaking, Nuragus was left behind. Recently, though, that's starting to change. Thanks to the influence from the sea, Nuragus wines tend to be lean, saline, and low in alcohol, with notes of white peach and Mediterranean herbs—a wine to drink on a beach vacation or whenever seafood is on the menu. Some winemakers are exploring the grape's more nuanced side, like Antonella Corda, whose Nuragus di Cagliari from the southern part of the Campidano expresses nuanced notes of pear and apple accented with sea salt.

Vermentino
(See Liguria chapter, page 119)

Vernaccia di Oristano
Vernaccia di Oristano is the name of a grape and a unique oxidized wine that reminds many of Spanish sherry. Grown in the warm Tirso River valley near Oristano, the grapes get generously

ripe, and their high sugar levels leads to wines with higher-than-average alcohol levels. Under the right circumstances, a thin veil of yeast called *flor* forms on the surface of the wine, giving it complex notes of apricot, bitter orange, toasted nuts, and even a bit of brine. Aged for at least four years but often many more, these are special-occasion wines, the kind to serve at the end of a meal in small glasses with cheese. (Beware of their higher alcohol content.) Contini's Vernaccia di Oristano's "Antico Gregori" is the benchmark of the style. Other versions of Vernaccia di Oristano can be fortified (when a spirit is added, look for *liquoriso* on the label), and they can be sweet or dry. When made as a straightforward white, or when it's blended with Vermentino, Vernaccia di Oristano is bright and refreshing to drink with seafood.

Sardinia's Other Native White Grapes: Nasco, Semidano, Torbato

Sardinia grows a handful of other grapes that make refreshing Mediterranean-style white wines. The Nasco grape yields a light, herbal-accented white wine and is mostly grown in the southern part of the island. Occasionally used to make *passito*, it's also found blended with Semidano, another local white grape that offers rounder notes of white flowers and stone fruit. A small amount of Torbato grows in northwest Sardinia in the Alghero area, where Sella & Mosca makes "Terra Bianche," one of the only pure Torbato wines found on the island. It's a rich, elegant white wine with notes of green apple, pear, and white flowers. Like Vermentino, these other white wines complement seafood- and vegetable-forward meals.

Red

Bovale Sardo

A relative of Cagnulari, another Sardinian native grape, Bovale Sardo does well in sandy soils and hot climates in the southern part of the island. It's a stingy vine, and it can be tricky in the cellar. But in the right hands, it generates wines with notes of herbs, plum, and cherry coupled with assertive tannins. The Pala winery is one of the best-known producers of Bovale Sardo, making wine from decades-old ungrafted vines growing in sandy, phylloxera-resistant soils.

Cagnulari

Cagnulari isn't the easiest grape for farmers to love. Late ripening and sensitive to disease, it fell out of favor years ago. Fortunately, it has made a comeback in the Sassari province, yielding perfumed, medium-bodied red wines with bright notes of raspberries or blackberries, just the kind of wine to drink with a Mediterranean meal. In Usini, a town north of the city of Sassari, the Giovanni Maria Cherchi estate was one of the first to take the grape seriously, leveraging the limestone-clay soils to create bright, elegant red wines accented with red fruits and notes of mint and spice.

Cannonau (Garnacha, Grenache)

In Spain, the grape is called Garnacha, though it's better known around the world by its French name, Grenache. Sardinians point to archaeological findings of grape seeds dating back well before the Spanish arrived as proof that Cannonau has been on the island for centuries, but a more accepted theory is that the grape arrived during Spanish rule. No matter who grew it first, Cannonau is Sardinia's most important red grape. Growing in the *alberello* ("little tree") training system, Cannonau can withstand dry weather and hot summers, producing black-hued grapes filled with red and black fruit flavors. The best wines balance the rich fruit flavors with acidity and structure. Grown at higher altitudes, the wines express notes of strawberries, blackberries, and herbs. The center of the island also has century-old Cannonau vines, some of which go into the deep wines of Bentu Luna, an estate founded by Lombardy sparkling winemaker Gabriele Moratti. In the warmer, flatter southern part of the island, the these wines can be strong (and high in alcohol) but they can still taste balanced, with notes of blackberries and a spicy nose of pepper.

Carignano (Carignan)

Grown all over the wine-growing world and more commonly known as Carignan, this international variety has a long history in Sardinia, especially in the southwestern Sulcis district. There, it makes some of the best wines on the island. In the dry, warm climate, the vine produces thick-skinned grapes that acquire an intense depth of flavor, delivering balanced, earthy wines with long finishes. The Sulcis area is especially important to the grape because it's where Carignano withstood phylloxera. Cantina Giba's Carignano del Sulcis "6Mura" Rosso is what century-old Carignano tastes like: balanced, with Mediterranean scrub brush, deep-purple plums, and a touch of savory smoke. Wines from La Sabbiosa and Enrico Esu are both deep wines, with sun-ripened flavors of boysenberry and black licorice accented by clay.

Monica

One of the most planted grapes in Sardinia, Monica has a somewhat murky identity—Italian wine expert Ian D'Agata suggests there are many local grapes with that name, and they are not necessarily related. For most of modern history, Monica was typically used in blends with other red grapes. On its own, it's a fresh, medium- to light-style red, with bright fruit, soft tannins, and floral aromas. Panevino's "Box' e Croxu" wine, a Monica-Carignano blend, expresses macerated strawberries accented with mint, oregano, and a hint of balsamic. It's the type of wine that works well with Sardinian flavors, like vegetables cooked gently in olive oil or spaghetti with bottarga grated on top.

Regional Foods

Anchovies

Beans

Bottarga
cured mullet or tuna roe, often served grated over spaghetti

Braised lamb

Capers

Cassòla
Sardinian fish casserole

Cheese
pecorino, sheep's milk cheese

ricotta

Chestnuts

Fennel

Miele di corbezzolo
bitter honey made by bees pollinating the corbezzolo tree (also called the strawberry tree, *Arbutus unedo*)

Mirto
A digestivo (after-dinner) liqueur made from myrtle berries

Olive oil

Olive oil–preserved tuna

Olives

Pane carasau
paper-thin traditional bread, sometimes called *carta di musica* or "music sheet"

Pasta
fregola, pellet-size semolina pasta, often cooked with clams

malloreddus, short cavatelli-like pasta flavored with saffron, sometimes called Sardinian gnocchi

culurzones, a filled pasta similar to ravioli

Saffron
harvested on the island and used in cooking

Sea urchin

Suckling pig

Recommended Producers

Alberto Loi

Antonella Corda

Argiolas

Buio

Cantina del Bovale

Cantina Gallura

Cantina Giba (Formerly 6Mura)

Cantine di Dolianova

Cantine Surrau

Capichera

Cardedu

Chessa

Cherchi

Contini

Deperu Holler

Dettori

Enrico Esu

Ferruccio Deiana

Feudi della Medusa

Giovanna Chessa

Giuseppe Gabbas

Costolai

Cungui

Jankara

La Sabbiosa

Meigamma

Mandrolisai

Mesa

Olianas

Pala

Panevino

Pedra Majore

Pedres

Piero Mancini

Punica

Santa Maria La Palma

Santadi

Sardus Pater

Silvio Carta

Soletta

Sorso Sennori

Surrau

Templum

Trexenta

Vigne Rada Alghero

Sicily

Black volcanic rock breaks up scrub brush, olive trees, and vines along the stretch of land from the tip of Mount Etna to the Passopisciaro Circumetnea train station. Most of the time, the volcano avoids massive eruptions, giving off plumes of smoke and small tremors to release pressure. Occasionally, though, it lets off a lot more steam—each *sciara* (lava flow) on the mountain is a souvenir of past destruction. Benjamin North Spencer's book *The New Wines of Mount Etna* recounts some of Etna's most memorable eruptions, like the one in 1928 that buried vineyards, orchards, roads, train tracks, and most of the coastal town of Mascali under lava. Still, those who live here are used to geological drama. Moving away would mean missing out on one of the most dynamic vineyard areas in the world.

It didn't seem all that dynamic at the turn of this century. Back then, most grapes from Etna were sold as bulk wine. Sicilian winemakers focused on Nero d'Avola, a native red grape that grew easily across the island and sold well abroad. In contrast, few outsiders had heard of Nerello Mascalese, the main red of northeastern Sicily, named after lava-scarred Mascali. Plus, growing grapes on the volcano required a lot of effort. The traditional vineyard system used on the volcano is the *alberello* method, where vines are propped up on poles and grow independent of wire supports. *Alberello* vines required a lot of hands-on work. Additionally, farmers worked at high altitude, since the best vineyards on the volcano sit at more than 1,312 feet (400 meters) above sea level. The cost to harvest grapes for bulk wine didn't add up, so vineyards fell into disrepair. There were some exceptions— local businessman Giuseppe Benanti and enologist Salvo Foti began working together in the late 1980s to prove that great wine could be made on Etna— but for the most part, farmers on the volcano made wine for family, friends, and the osteria down the road. That was the environment in 2005 when pianist Giuseppe Russo returned to his family's 37-acre (15 hectares) property, a short walk from the Passopisciaro train station. He restored the old cellar, rehabilitated vineyards, and taught himself how to make wine by phone, he joked to us, referring to his constant calls to his friend, Tuscan enologist Emiliano Falsini. When he was finally happy with the results, he began bottling the wine under the name of his late father, Girolamo Russo, who had worked the same land.

The village of Passopisciaro is on Mount Etna's "Costa d'Oro" (Gold Coast), a stretch of land on the north side of the volcano between the towns of Linguaglossa and Randazzo. The area yields elegant Etna Rosso wines made (mostly) with Nerello Mascalese. Between Etna and the Nebrodi Mountains to the northwest, the Alcantara Valley forms a wind tunnel, channeling the tramontana winds from the north as well as winds from the east, keeping the vines dry and cool. The north side of the volcano also gets the equivalent of three more weeks of sun than the rest of the Etna DOC, helping late-ripening Nerello Mascalese mature. Despite this setting, when Giuseppe set out to make great wine, no one was sure he'd be able to sell it. That's not the case now. Demand for Giuseppe's Etna Rosso wines, including three made from distinct *contrade*, vineyard areas that loosely translate to "neighborhoods," outstrips supply. Meanwhile, his enologist friend Emiliano began making his own wine on Etna, unable to resist working in a geological hotspot.

Italians love Sicily. The largest island in the Mediterranean Sea is known for its food—sweet-sour caponata, *pasta con le sarde* (pasta with sardines), and gelati made in a rainbow of flavors—all of which is paired with warm hospitality. To the east, the island landscape is punctuated by Mount Etna, the tallest Italian peak south of the Alps. To the west are windswept lands and the cities of Palermo, Trapani, and Marsala. Sicilian wines are also well loved across Italy, not only those from Etna but also Vittoria in the southeast, Faro in the northeast, Marsala in the far west, and the island of Pantelleria, which sits closer to Africa than to mainland Italy.

Even though Sicily is physically large, it is not Italy's biggest wine supplier—Veneto, Puglia, and Emilia-Romagna each make more than the island's annual 117.9 million or so gallons (4.46 million hectoliters). Yet Sicily comes close to first in wine diversity. Along the coast, vines pick up saltiness from wind and salt in the soil, seasoning everything from breezy coastal whites; amber, ageable Marsala; and rich, sweet *passito*. An arid climate keeps vine diseases

in check and restricts yields by stressing the vines from lack of water. Meanwhile, Mount Etna provides options at higher altitudes—where vines experience wide temperature swings from day to night—as well as soils filled with ash and pumice. It's the range, depth, and history within Sicily's viticultural past that makes it feel like an entire country of wine rather than solely a region.

History

Sicily may be one of the oldest winemaking centers in the world. In 2017, on the southwestern side of the island, archaeologists found six-thousand-year-old grape residue in a hot sulfurous cave within Mount Kronio. The archaeologists claimed they found wine; others were skeptical and requested more proof before adding Sicily to the list of the oldest centers of grape-based wine production, alongside Armenia, Georgia, and Iran. Regardless, wild grapes likely grew on the island for centuries before the arrival of the Greeks in the eighth century BC. On Mount Etna, the earliest winemakers vinified grapes with *palmenti*, vats made of lava rock. Each *palmento* had a vat for crushing grapes and another for fermenting juices. Powered by gravity, the ancient low-tech system was ahead of its time. Today, *palmenti* are scattered around the volcano like artifacts and some have been restored.

The island originally had two native tribes: the Sicels in the east and the Sicani in the west. When the Greeks arrived, they brought their winemaking techniques with them, as they did elsewhere in southern Italy. When the Romans came to control the island, however, winemaking took a back seat to grain production, and Sicily's countryside grew wheat for bread. After the fall of Rome, agricultural diversity on the island rebounded. In the ninth century, the Arabs took control of the island, bringing back small-scale farms and ushering in two hundred years of agricultural advancements. Arabs built reservoirs and water towers on the island and introduced the concept of irrigation. New crops arrived, from sugarcane to citrus fruits, apples, quince, and pomegranates. To make raisins, Arabs dried the sweet, fragrant Zibibbo grapes, which are best known today for making the *passito* wines from the island of Pantelleria. The Arabs also built circular gardens on the island surrounded by stone walls. Inside, citrus trees grew protected from the island's strong winds; some of the gardens are still in use today.

While wine culture diminished during Arab rule, Sicilians didn't abstain completely. In Clifford A. Wright's *A Mediterranean Feast*, he notes that Ali al-Ballanubi, a Sicilian Muslim poet of the era, wrote about drinking wine, and minority religions were permitted to make wine for sacramental purposes. After Arab rule came the Norman kings, the mercenary soldiers who fought the Byzantines for the popes, and agricultural advancements continued. Roger II, who spoke Greek and Arabic, presided over a cosmopolitan court tolerant of different religions and ethnicities, while the rest of the island flourished economically and culturally. This was the last time that Sicily ruled itself. After the thirteenth century, the island came under the domain of the Aragonese of Spain, who controlled the island as well as Italy's other large island, Sardinia, for four hundred years.

Sardinia and Sicily are quite distinct from one another, though the island regions share a couple of similarities that were enhanced during Spanish rule. As in Spain, both islands cook with saffron, which is not as common on the Italian mainland. Both also make *vino perpetuo*, "perpetual wine" made by adding new wine to older vintages, like how sherry is made in Spain. Most wine turns to vinegar if exposed to too much air, but these wines are protected by high alcohol levels. On the warm west coast of both islands, grapes can get extremely ripe, and wines can reach alcohol levels between 16 and 18 percent. (In comparison, typical bottles span from 11 to 14.5 percent alcohol.) These "perpetual wines" are savory and somewhat oxidized, with notes of toasted nuts, citrus peel, and spices.

When English businessman John Woodhouse arrived in the port city of Marsala in 1770, he tasted *vino perpetuo*, which inspired him to create a fortified version for export. The new wine that had an added distilled spirit was named after the city and became so popular that more British traders set up Marsala houses, lending money to farmers, building roads, and improving other infrastructure to facilitate trade. In the early nineteenth century, a trade embargo between France and Britain grew Marsala sales even more, and by the mid-nineteenth century, land for Marsala grapes expanded throughout the western side of the island. By fortifying a base wine, Marsala was no longer strictly a *vino perpetuo*, and Marsala makers made a range of styles (see Dessert Wines: Passito and Marsala, page 190).

The nineteenth century brought prosperity to brokers selling Etna wine. In the 1860s, when northern European vines were destroyed by phylloxera (page 12), foreign wine merchants began buying wine from Etna. Vineyards were planted more extensively around the volcano than they are today, with vines reaching sea level. But when phylloxera finally hit the island, most of these vines were destroyed except for those planted at higher altitudes and in sandier soil. In places like Enna, a dry inland province west of Mount Etna, most vineyards were never replanted. Phylloxera also affected vineyards in western Sicily. Without a local supply of grapes, Marsala houses had to buy grapes from elsewhere, which began a decline in quality that still affects Marsala's reputation. A few places in western Sicily emerged unscathed. On the island of Mozia, for instance, there are Grillo vines that are more than a century old.

Apart from the wine trade around Etna and Marsala, most Sicilians in the nineteenth century were sharecroppers who faced high rents and unfair taxes. Absentee royals owned the land, and to ensure that rent was paid, they hired *gambelloti*, men who extracted payments for security, laying the groundwork for the Sicilian Mafia. The unification of Italy in the mid-nineteenth century made things worse for rural Sicilians. The new government increased taxes on Marsala exports, softening the market for fortified wines right when phylloxera depressed the island's wine trade. Without jobs or stability, thousands of Sicilians left the island by the turn of the twentieth century.

In the 1950s, the Italian government incentivized farmers to plant more vines, encouraging the following business model: grow as many grapes as you can and sell them to co-ops. In Sicily, there were few exceptions to the quantity-over-quality model until the 1970s. That's when Cantine Settesoli, based in Menfi on the west side of the island, began planting Chardonnay, Syrah, and Merlot at the request of co-op president Diego Planeta. Planeta also brought in consulting enologists, notably Bordeaux expert Giacomo Tachis, who advocated for blending French grapes with native varieties to boost color and texture. Sicily was too hot for most French grapes, yet the experiment prompted foreign wine buyers to consider importing Sicilian wines. Planeta also served as president of the Istituto Regionale della Vite e del Vino (Regional Institute of Vine and Wine), an institution focused on making and marketing wine from Sicily. The promotional efforts of both organizations paid off, and even today, Italians from elsewhere marvel at the marketing skills of Sicilians. The Planeta family also started its own winery, which today remains one of Sicily's largest, making 3.5 million bottles annually. Eventually they hedged away from international grapes, making wines like "Santa Cecilia," a spicy, balsamic-like Nero d'Avola from Noto, a city on the island's southeast horn.

There were other twentieth-century innovators. In the late 1970s, when former race car driver Marco De Bartoli returned home to Marsala, he began questioning the authenticity of the Marsala his family produced. By the late twentieth century, Marsala had devolved into a cheap cooking wine, and De Bartoli wanted to return to the old tradition of making *vino perpetuo*. The result—"Vecchio Samperi," made from ripe Grillo grapes—is not technically Marsala because it is not fortified, but it became a symbol of Marsala that predated the British. De Bartoli also explored Pantelleria, buying Zibibbo in 1984 from the Bukkuram *contrada* to make a rich, honeyed *passito*. Since De Bartoli's passing in 2012, the winery

has been run by his children, Renato, Sebastiano, and Giusippina, who make other wines with Grillo as well as unique Zibibbo wines from Pantelleria, including "Integer," which has at least twenty days of skin contact, and "Pietranera," a dry, herbal-accented Zibibbo.

While other parts of the island were experimenting and expanding in the twentieth century, Etna remained off the radar. In 1988, local businessman Giuseppe Benanti hired enologist Salvo Foti, an Etna native, to make wine on his property. Benanti and Foti brought in experts and conducted a series of experiments across the volcano to better understand the land and what kinds of wines it could produce. One result was the creation of "Pietra Marina," a white wine made with Carricante grapes from Milo, a town on the east side of the volcano. The wine, an Etna Bianco Superiore, went on to convince skeptics that a local white grape from Etna could make one of Italy's best, most age-worthy white wines. Foti, who left Benanti in 2011, is Sicily's most important homegrown enologist. Today he consults for other wineries and makes his own wine at I Vigneri di Salvo Foti, continuing to explore the possibilities for local grapes Carricante, Nerello Mascalese, and Nerello Cappuccio.

The 1990s saw the beginning of outside investment on Etna. Tuscan producer Andrea Franchetti broke ground on Passopisciaro, and American wine importer Marc de Grazia started Terre Nere. Later, Belgian Frank Cornelissen began making low-intervention Etna wines, and others have followed. While some long for the old days, this new time on Etna is marked by experimentation. Unlike Barolo and Barbaresco in Piedmont, or Chianti Classico in Tuscany, Etna winemakers don't have a strict style guide to follow. Even Benanti's three decades of vintages aren't a big enough sample size to say definitively what Etna wine should taste like. And in a place as unpredictable as an active volcano, it may be a while before we have an answer.

Alberello training at I Vigneri in Milo,
a commune on Mount Etna.

Andrea Foti in the I Vigneri cellar.

Land and Wines

Sicily's climate revolves around hot, dry summers and cool, rainy winters. In August 2021, the southeastern town of Floridia clocked in at 119.24°F (48.4°C), the hottest temperature ever recorded in Europe up to that point. Not all parts of the island are equally scorching, though. The far northeast corner around Messina is the rainiest. To the south, Mount Etna protects the volcano's west side from rain while funneling it to the east side, which is wetter and cooler. In contrast, on the warm, windy west coast and islands, it's normal to go for months without any rain at all. More than half the island is hilly, a quarter is mountainous, and the remainder is flat. In the hottest areas, north- and east-facing vineyards are better than south- or west-facing sites, which get the hot sirocco winds from Africa. On Etna, high altitude and exposure impact weather, creating microclimates that are much cooler than at sea level. Soils also vary throughout the island. In the south and west, there is some clay, sand, and quite a bit of limestone. In the southeast in the provinces of Ragusa and Syracuse, volcanic rock from the extinct volcano Mount Lauro is mixed into the soil. Meanwhile, Etna, Pantelleria, and the Aeolian Islands are primarily volcanic.

West Side, including Marsala, Trapani, Alcamo, Palermo, Menfi, and Agrigento

Around the cities of Trapani and Marsala, most of the vineyards grow grapes for Marsala. Amid large farms, small producers show a different side to these grapes. In the hills outside of Alcamo between Palermo and Trapani, brothers Alessandro and Aldo Viola grew up in a winemaking family, and today work separately on their own wine labels. They grow similar varieties, such as Grillo, Catarratto, and Grecanico (a Sicilian synonym of Veneto's Garganega grape), and Nero d'Avola, creating their own low-intervention interpretations of

their terrain. In Marsala, Nino Barraco grows vines so close to the sea in sandy and red clay soils that they pick up salt from the soil and wind, seasoning his natural wines made with Zibibbo, Catarratto, Grillo, and Nero d'Avola, as well as Perricone, a red grape found mostly on the west side of the island.

Southeast Side, including Vittoria and Noto

The Cerasuolo di Vittoria DOCG zone sits in the southeast between the communes of Gela, Caltagirone, and Vittoria. In the summer, the ground can get so hot that you can feel the heat seeping through the soles of your shoes. But from the blindingly white limestone rock and red sand soils, the grapes produce lithe, strawberry-imbued wines. Cerasuolo di Vittoria itself is a blend of strawberry-scented Frappato and plum-red Nero d'Avola. (*Cerasuolo* means "cherry," referring to the wine's color. It is not related to the Cerasuolo made in Abruzzo.) The zone was on the decline until the early 1980s when COS cofounder Giusto Occhipinti, with Giambattista Cilia and Cirino Strano, began making wine for fun with local grapes. Over the years, they got more serious, slowly revitalizing the reputation of the area as a place for quality wine and experimenting with amphorae (terracotta vessels). "Pithos Rosso," a Nero d'Avola wine, and "Pithos Bianco," a Grecanico wine, are both fermented and aged in amphorae buried in the ground, which provides insulation from the heat.

Giusto's niece Arianna Occhipinti started working at COS at sixteen, founding her estate when she finished university in 2004. In international wine circles, her name has become synonymous with Frappato, the lighter and more delicate of the two Cerasuolo di Vittoria grapes. She makes single-vineyard Frappato accented by strawberry but contrasted by a more savory, slightly wilder side of the grape. She also grows Zibibbo and a local white grape called Albanello, both of which she blends into an lush, floral "SP68 Bianco" wine named after the main road near her vineyard. Her fragrant "SP68 Rosso" is mostly Frappato, with a touch of Nero

All Italian *passiti* are made from dried grapes. *Appassimento*, the Italian technique of drying grapes before they're pressed, concentrates the sugars and makes a richer wine. While you can find *passiti* all over Italy, the style is most associated with Sicily. To make Passito di Pantelleria and Malvasia delle Lipari, grapes start to dry on the vine or are picked and then dried. Made with Zibibbo grapes, *passito* from Pantelleria tends to be richer, with notes of dried fruit and apricot. Made from Malvasia di Lipari grapes, Malvasia delle Lipari is slightly lighter with spicy notes of ginger. In the southeastern corner of the island, Moscato di Noto *passito* comes from Moscato Bianco grapes. Of the three, it's more delicate, with notes of orange blossoms and preserved lemon. The natural sugars and acidity in all these *passiti* enable them to age for years.

Marsala also benefits from Sicily's warm, dry weather, which helps grapes get extra ripe and reach higher levels of alcohol. Even so, Marsala is a fortified wine classified for color, sweetness, and age. *Oro* and *ambra* Marsala are made with white grapes (such as Catarratto, Inzolia, and Grillo), while the less common *rubino* Marsala comes from red grapes (such as Perricone, Nero d'Avola, and Nerello Mascalese). Next, Marsala can be *secco* (dry), *semi-seco* (semisweet), or *dolce* (sweet). For age, *fine* is set aside for one year, *superiore* for two, *superiore riserva* for four, *vergine* for five, and *vergine stravecchio* for 10 or more years. Some Marsala is also made via the *solera* method, the technique used to make Spanish sherry, blending younger wines with older wines for a consistent house style.

Serve *passito* and Marsala in small pours with a slight chill to mellow their higher alcohol content.

Italian Dessert Wines

Basilicata
- Cantine del Notaio "L'Autentica" Passito di Moscato
- Gioia al Negro "Fabula" Passito

Calabria
- Cantine Viola, Moscato Passito di Saracena
- Ceratti Greco di Bianco Passito

Campania
- I Pentri "ISS" Passito
- Luigi Maffini Passito

Emilia-Romagna
- Maria Galassi "Stramat" Passito Rosso
- Poderi dal Nespoli "Bradamante" Vino Bianco da Uve Stramature
- Zerbina Romagna Albana Passito

Friuli
- Conte d'Attimis Maniago Colli Orientali del Friuli Picolit
- Girolamo Dorigo Colli Orientali del Friuli Picolit
- Rocca Bernarda Colli Orientali del Friuli Picolit
- Scubla "Cràtis" Verduzzo Friuli Colli Orientali

Lazio
- Casale Cento Corvi Giacchè Passito
- Cantina Sant'Andrea "Capitolium" Moscato di Terracina Passito
- Donato Giangirolami "Apricor" Passito
- Sergio Mottura "Muffo" Grechetto di Civitella d'Agliano

Dessert Wines

Passito and Marsala

Le Marche
- La Montata "Santo" Passito
- Luciano Landi Lacrima di Morro d'Alba Passito
- Sartarelli Verdicchio dei Castelli di Jesi Passito

Liguria
- Azienda Agricola Possa Cinque Terre Sciacchetrà
- Bisson Acinirari Passito
- Walter de Batte Cinque Terre Sciacchetrà

Lombardy
- Castello di Grumello Valcalepio Moscato Passito

Molise
- Di Majo Norante "Apianae" Moscato del Molise

Piedmont
- La Spinetta "Oro" Moscato Passito
- Orsolani Erbaluce di Caluso Passito

Puglia
- Li Veli Aleatico Passito
- Villa Schinosa Moscato di Trani

Sardinia
- Cantine di Dolianova Moscato di Sardegna Passito
- Contini Vernaccia di Oristano
- Giovanni Battista Columbu Malvasia di Bosa

Sicily
- Arianna Occhipinti "Passo Nero" Passito
- Colosi Malvasia delle Lipari Passito
- Donnafugata "Ben Rye" Passito di Pantelleria
- Ferrandes Passito di Pantelleria
- Hauner Malvasia delle Lipari Passito
- Marco De Bartoli "Bukkuram" Passito di Pantelleria
- Marco De Bartoli Riserva Marsala Vergine "1988"
- Planeta Passito di Noto
- Virgona Malvasia delle Lipari Passito

Trentino–Alto Adige
- Cantina Valle Isarco "Nectaris" Kerner Passito
- Zeni "Rosa" Moscato Rosa Passito

Tuscany
- Avignonesi Vin Santo di Montepulciano
- Badia di Coltibuono Vin Santo del Chianti Classico
- Capezzana Vin Santo Carmignano DOC
- Massa Vecchia Aleatico Passito
- Panizzi Passito di Toscana
- Torre a Cona "Merlaia" Vin Santo del Chianti

Umbria
- Barberani Moscato Passito
- Paolo Bea Montefalco Sagrantino Passito

Valle d'Aosta
- Ermes Pavese "Ninive" Blanc de Morgex et de La Salle Vino da Uve Stramatura
- Ezio Voyat "Le Muraglie Ambrato" Moscato Chambave Passito

Veneto
- Giuseppe Quintarelli Recioto della Valpolicella Classico
- La Montecchia "Donna Daria" Fior d'Arancio Passito Colli Euganei
- Pieropan "Le Colombare" Recioto di Soave

Arianna Occhipinti in her vineyard in Vittoria.

d'Avola. (Since Shelley's restaurant A16 was named after a road in Campania, we have a special affinity with these wines.) On the east side of the island's southern horn, the Val di Noto area grows plenty of Nero d'Avola and Grillo as well as Moscato Bianco, which goes into the aromatic dry, sparkling, and sweet wines of Moscato di Noto.

Northeast Side, including Messina, Faro, and Enna

In contrast to all the white wine made on the west side of the island, the far northeast corner is all about red wines. In the small Faro DOC, Salvatore Geraci makes his elegant Palari wines, showing what Nerello Mascalese grown in sandy soils by the sea can taste like. Of Sicily's nine provinces, only Enna in the center is not known for vines. An exception to this is Nicolò Grippaldi's vineyard, planted in 2015 in Gagliano Castelferrato. In the past, the commune had lost its vines to phylloxera.

Etna

Set within the province of Catania, Mount Etna's vineyard areas form a backward *C*, hugging the volcano. Vines grow on the north, east, and south slopes, while the hot, dry west side is planted with pistachio trees. While all the vineyards are volcanic, the soil is anything but uniform. Each *contrada* (one of 133 officially recognized "neighborhoods" for Etna wines) contains lava in different stages of erosion: some with more rocks and others with more sand. The north side focuses on Etna Rosso (red wines made predominantly with Nerello Mascalese), while the cooler east side around the town of Milo is renowned for Etna Bianco (white wines made mostly with Carricante). The south slope feels more impact from the hot sirocco winds, but it, too, stays cooler than the rest of the island, and white and red grapes both grow well. Even though Nerello Mascalese and Carricante are the main grapes of the volcano, they are often blended with other grapes, including Catarratto and the local white Minnella for white wines and Nerello Cappuccio for red. Yet many other grapes grow on the volcano, and many wines are made outside the Etna DOC rules. Frank Cornelissen has been finding a way to make wine that—in his words—is like liquid rock. He mixes and matches white and red grapes in sought-after wines like "Susucaru"; constantly reevaluates wine-making methods, aging in both terracotta amphorae and fiberglass containers; and rethinks his hard-line stance against using sulfur to help preserve his wines. Ongoing experiments reveal what is possible working on such unique land.

Pantelleria and the Aeolian Islands

Warm and arid, Sicily's satellite islands are places where time slows down. Zibibbo and Malvasia di Lipari thrive in the volcanic terrain and are well-suited to making passito. (See Dessert Wines, pages 190–191.) In addition to specializing in wines made mostly from dried grapes, the islands (especially Pantelleria) produce some of the Mediterranean's best capers and dried oregano.

In truth, nearly all Sicily is special in some way, and nearly every corner has wine to seek out. If things keep moving forward like they have been, the island will draw us in for years to come.

Sicily Grapes

Most of Sicily's output is white wine from the west side of the island. The east side also makes plenty of white, but it is more known for its reds, namely Etna Rosso, Faro, and Cerasuolo di Vittoria.

White

Carricante

Grown on Mount Etna, Carricante goes into some of Italy's most age-worthy white wines, like Benanti's now-iconic "Pietra Marina." The grape's name comes from its generous yields—*caricare* means "to load" in Italian. (Filippo Grasso's delightful blended white wine "Carrico 68.8" takes it a step further: *carrico* means "loaded," and 68.8 kilos was the maximum a donkey could carry.) Even so, Carricante wasn't as well known as Sicily's other white grapes until a surge of interest in Etna wines brought attention to the variety. Carricante sunburns easily, making it tough to grow in warmer parts of the island, but it is fantastic at high altitude, especially on the cooler, foggy eastern slope of Etna around the town of Milo. (All Etna Bianco Superiore must come from there.) To Salvo Foti, renowned Etna winemaker and founder of I Vigneri di Salvo Foti based in Milo, Carricante is endlessly fascinating. At its best, Carricante yields lemony wines with notable amounts of malic acid (the same acidity found in green apple). With their acidity and surprisingly pleasant aromas of petrol, some Carricante wines suggest Riesling. Carricante also makes appearances in white blends from the volcano, pairing up with little-known local grape Minella and others. Carricante, whether blended or not, is always brilliant with food thanks to its subtle, herbal notes and acidity.

Catarratto Family

Accustomed to hot, dry island weather, Catarratto is the most common white grape in all of Sicily. To be more precise, *grapes*: there is more than one Catarratto biotype (genetically identical vine), and they behave differently enough to carry specific names. Catarratto Comune (the most-planted grape in Sicily) and Catarratto Lucido are the most common, with Lucido offering more acidity and aroma and Comune bringing more sugar. Grown mostly on the west side of Sicily, Catarratto vines generate a lot of grapes at harvest, which made them popular for mass-produced Marsala. By the 2000s, as interest in Sicilian-grown Chardonnay receded, Catarratto began getting more critical praise. Some great Carricante-based Etna Bianco wines have a touch of Catarratto blended in, rounding the Carricante's sharper corners. With its high sugar content, Catarratto wines can be high in alcohol. On the west side of Sicily in Alcamo, brothers Aldo and Alessandro Viola make wine separately under their own names and both make skin-contact wines that show Catarratto's complex, savory side. Without skin contact, Catarratto wines are straw yellow in the glass and have a mildly fruity, herbal nose and subtle, salty finish—just the wine to drink with Mediterranean seafood.

Grecanico Dorato

(See Garganega, Veneto chapter, page 265)

Grillo

Grown on the west coast of Sicily, Grillo is a happy accident, a grape that came out of a natural cross between Catarratto Lucido and Zibibbo. It's a variety born for a hot, dry climate, especially in the sandy soils around Marsala and the island of Mozia. There, the vine's vigor is held in check, allowing the grapes to become more concentrated in flavor, and the grape's thick skins protect it from the hot sirocco winds. It is also drought tolerant and resistant to phylloxera. When harvested super ripe, Grillo can make wines high in alcohol—as much as 18 percent. This is perfect for *vino perpetuo*, a "perpetual wine" that combines new vintages with old. The Marco De

Bartoli estate is synonymous with the oxidized style; its Grillo-based "Vecchio Samperi," aged for a year in amphorae (terracotta vessels) and later in barrel, is nutty, savory, and slightly hazy, with delicate notes of orange peel. Yet most Grillo is simpler and breezier. Valle dell'Acate's "Zagra" is named after orange blossoms, and it's zesty, with lemony-almond flavors and a distinct salty note. The Marco De Bartoli estate also makes a few other Grillo wines, including the refreshing sparkler "Terzavia" and the still white "Grappoli del Grillo," which express notes of salt and yellow apple. Grillo carries more weight and aroma than Carricante, and it easily wins over fans of Sauvignon Blanc.

Inzolia (Ansonica)

Once blended into Marsala, Inzolia fell out of favor in the second half of the nineteenth century when it was hit with powdery mildew, a new disease on the island at the time. In the 1990s, it rebounded in a big way as winemakers rendered it into plush, juicy wines. While the variety is drought tolerant, it's sensitive to heat. Its thin skins sunburn easily, causing grapes to split. It also isn't high in acidity, so in the wrong hands, Inzolia can taste flat. When all goes well, though, the wine has a lightly herbal, floral nose and subtle notes of stone fruit and pear, as shown in Menfi-based Cantine Barbera's Inzolia. In Tuscany, the same grape is called Ansonica, and it's an important variety on the island of Elba. Sometimes Sicilian wineries use "Ansonica" on the label instead of "Inzolia."

Malvasia di Lipari

While there are many grapes called "Malvasia" (thanks to the work of Venetian merchants who traded the wine throughout the Mediterranean), most are unrelated, and some are better than others. Count Malvasia di Lipari is one of the good ones, yielding one of Italy's most distinguished *passiti*. Malvasia di Lipari has some cousins, including Calabria's Greco Bianco and Malvasia di Sardegna, all of which make distinct sweet wines. While the grape is named after Lipari, it grows throughout the Aeolian Islands off the northern coast of Sicily, especially on Salina.

From these volcanic vineyards, the low-yielding vines offer concentrated, sweet grapes ideal for Malvasia delle Lipari. ("Malvasia *di* Lipari" is the name of the grape; "Malvasia *delle* Lipari" is the name of the *passito*.) Some producers make dry Malvasia di Lipari (look for wines labeled IGT Salina). These wines are often easygoing, with notes of mandarin, lemon peel, and honey, though traditionalists argue that sweet wines are better for showing off the grape's character. Carlo Hauner, who vacationed on Salina in the 1960s and later returned to start a business and help revitalize the island's flagging wine trade, makes a deeply honeyed Malvasia delle Lipari *passito*. Also from the island of Salina, Virgona makes a Malvasia delle Lipari that pairs perfectly with ricotta, cheese, or any fruit dessert.

Moscato Bianco

(see Piedmont chapter, page 150)

Zibibbo (Moscato di Alessandria)

Called "Zibibbo" in Sicily and "Muscat of Alexandria" or "Moscato di Alessandria" elsewhere, this grape may have come from Egypt before spreading throughout the Mediterranean and far beyond. (In Arabic, *zabib* means "raisin.") Zibibbo is synonymous with Passito di Pantelleria, a specialty of Sicily's southern island. It is not easy to make *passito* anywhere, but Pantelleria's vineyards are extreme. The vines grow in an *alberello* ("little tree") format much closer to the ground than elsewhere to better endure the island's constant winds. At Abbazia San Giorgio, the shoots, weeds, and dirt are cleared around the base of each vine in winter so the grapes will have enough room to hang without touching the ground. Some vines grow on steep terraces supported by dry-stone walls, adding another physical challenge of working the land. The vine training, which goes back to the ancient Greeks, is so specific to the island that it is on UNESCO's list of Intangible Cultural Heritage. To make the wine, grapes are dried to about 60 percent before they are crushed (so it takes a lot of grapes to make a little wine). Still, Zibibbo's thick skins allow the grapes to dry in the sun without too much damage, and the drying concentrates flavor and sweetness, creating a layered wine with notes of orange blossom, spices, and dried apricot.

Donnafugata's "Ben Ryé," with notes of raisin, orange peel, and brown sugar, is a classic example. The grape also goes into Bianco di Pantelleria, a dry white wine, as well as some more experimental wines, like Marco De Bartoli's "Integer" Zibibbo, a skin-contact wine fermented in amphorae (terracotta vessels) and wooden casks with the exuberant aroma you expect from Moscato. Outside Pantelleria, Zibibbo is also popular, often blended with other local grapes. Arianna Occhipinti's food-friendly "SP68 Bianco" blends Zibibbo with Albanello, a rare white grape grown mostly around Syracuse and Ragusa.

Red

Frappato

This strawberry-scented, delicate red grape deserves to be better known. Ideal for the sandy and *terra-rossa* (red sand over limestone) soils in the southeastern corner of Sicily, Frappato makes delicate, cherry-colored wines. They are lighter in color than most red grapes, with fresh aromatics and a tart, strawberry-like finish. Frappato is best known as part of the blend with Nero d'Avola in Cerasuolo di Vittoria, a red wine named after its cherry color (*Cerasuolo* means "cherry"). Compared with Nero d'Avola, Frappato's grape bunches are smaller, its yields lower, and its skins more fragile, creating low-tannin red wines with a light, fresh finish. Light- to medium-bodied Frappato from Valle dell'Acate is a perfect warm-weather red, with bright notes of strawberries and raspberries and subtle tannins, perfect for drinking slightly chilled. Meanwhile, Arianna Occhipinti's "Il Frappato" offers a deeper, savory interpretation of the variety, with hints of iron and leather.

Nerello Cappuccio

Etna grape Nerello Cappuccio's leaves shade its grapes like a cloak. (Some say the name comes from the Capuchin monks, who wore hooded robes.) On Etna, it's a workhorse red, with low acidity, good color, and pleasant red fruit that makes it useful for blending with Nerello Mascalese, rounding out the latter's sharp edges in Etna Rosso wines. Tuscan consulting enologist Emiliano Falsini, who makes a tiny amount of wine on Etna under his own name, feels its use as a blending grape was more important in the days when farmers harvested Nerello Mascalese too early, making a wine that was too astringent (like when winemakers in Tuscany used to blend Merlot into Sangiovese to take the edge off). Others feel that Mascalese and Cappuccio have evolved to complement each other, and some go as far as to make wines showcasing Cappuccio on its own. Benanti makes a lively pure Nerello Cappuccio wine redolent of red fruits.

Nero d'Avola (Calabrese)

In the 1980s and '90s, the Sicilian wine community put its marketing power into Nero d'Avola. Pitched as the wine to drink for those who loved big wines like Syrah, Nero d'Avola became an export hit. As a result, the vine was planted nearly everywhere on the island and was blended with international grapes to make it taste big and bold. Now Sicily's second-most planted grape (after Catarratto Comune) is back to its roots, yielding medium-bodied, food-friendly reds. Named after Avola, a port city in the southeast, Nero d'Avola is an important grape throughout Sicily. (Considering the grape's synonym, Calabrese, it may have come from Calabria.) It's a hardy vine that produces grapes in loose bunches, yielding wines with aromas of blackberries. With moderate alcohol, plush texture, and high acidity, it blends well with light Frappato in Cerasuolo di Vittoria DOCG wines. Centopassi, a co-op on a plateau outside Palermo, comprises vineyard land seized from convicted members of the Mafia. Today, it's a symbol of freedom from organized crime. The co-op's Nero d'Avola "Agrille di Tagghia Via" is dedicated to a man killed by mob violence in the late 1970s. It's a spicy red that pairs perfectly with caponata or *pasta alla norma*. In the southwest, the Gulfi winery in Ragusa grows Nero d'Avola in limestone-clay soils, yielding a rich, cherry-plum wine. The Aeolian

Islands also grow a small amount of Nero d'Avola, which Tenuta di Castellaro blends with the rare red grape Corinto for "Nero Ossidana," a deep, volcanic red from Lipari.

Nerello Mascalese

Twenty years ago, Nerello Mascalese was known outside Sicily for a couple of interesting reds from the Faro DOC, a town in Italy's northeast corner near Messina, and little from anywhere else. Today, thanks to Mount Etna, winemakers from around the world have become captivated by the native variety, likening it to Pinot Noir. For some, it's up there with Nebbiolo and Sangiovese as one of Italy's great red grapes. It's a fair comparison. Like Nebbiolo in northwestern Italy and Sangiovese in central Italy, Nerello Mascalese expresses the place in which it is grown, yielding elegant, long-aging reds that have finesse and structure. Like Nebbiolo and Sangiovese, Nerello Mascalese requires a lot of time in the vineyard pruning and managing vines. It also ripens late—if you want great Nerello Mascalese, you'll harvest around the end of October and cross your fingers that the rain doesn't get there first. All the efforts are worth it because of what it brings to the glass: acidity, vibrancy, elegance, and capacity to age gracefully.

The grape is named for the town of Mascali, located at the base of the volcano. Most of Sicily's Nerello Mascalese grows in the province of Catania, though the northern side of the volcano is where it's most established. There, some vines, like those on the Terre Nere estate, are more than a hundred years old. The standard recipe for Etna Rosso wines is at least 80 percent Nerello Mascalese, with some Nerello Cappuccio rounding out the rest. This is because Nerello Mascalese is light in color, and Cappuccio boosts the fruit flavors. The three *contrade*-based wines from Girolamo Russo on the north side of Etna all have a splash of Nerello Cappuccio. In comparison, Salvo Foti plays with a wide array of red blends with Nerello Mascalese. Meanwhile, Frank Cornelissen's brooding "MunJebel Rosso" is pure Nerello Mascalese from the north side of the volcano. Nerello Mascalese also goes into many of Etna's *metodo classico* sparkling wines, such as those from Murgo (the grape's affinity for sparkling wines is another reason people like to compare it to Pinot Noir). In the glass, Nerello Mascalese looks vibrant but never deep in color, with aromas of violets, cherries, and spices and a long finish.

Perricone

Grown mostly on the west side of the island in the provinces of Trapani and Palermo, Perricone was once popular as the base of *rubino* Marsala. (In Marsala, the grape is also called Pignatello.) Hit hard during the phylloxera outbreak, the variety never really rebounded in vineyard acreages, but it hasn't gone away. As an everyday red to serve with a Sicilian meal, it's hard to go wrong with Perricone. Everyday Perricone is fruit forward and juicy, with notes of dark red cherries, spice, and a touch of tannins, but some producers give the grape more attention. Gaetano and Nicoletta Gargano of Il Censo, an estate on the west side of Sicily near the town where *Cinema Paradiso* was filmed, demonstrate Perricone's elegant side. Although the estate had been in Gaetano's family for generations—mostly growing grains, beans, and a few vines—it had largely been abandoned. A few decades ago, Gaetano met Giampiero Bea, the groundbreaking winemaker behind Umbria's standout estate Paolo Bea, and was inspired to reinvigorate his land. Bea worked with the estate on its Perricone wine, "Njuro," a deep-hued wine that expresses blackberries, pomegranate, and gentle mineral notes.

Regional Foods

Arancini
saffron-infused fried rice balls filled with meat, cheese, or vegetables

Artichokes

Bottarga
cured mullet or tuna roe, often served grated over spaghetti

Cannoli

Capers and caper leaves

Caponata
eggplant with sweet-sour sauce, can include potatoes, tomatoes, and green peppers

Chickpeas

Cipolle all'agrodolce
onions cooked in a sweet-sour style

Citrus
lemons, tangerines, citrons, oranges (rinds are also candied)

Dried fava beans

Gelato
especially pistachio flavor

Granita
shaved ice in citrus or coffee flavors

Insalata di mare
seafood salad

Nuts
almonds

pistachios

Olive oil

Olives

Pasta
busiate (corkscrew pasta)

pasta al forno, baked pasta, like manicotti

pasta alla Norma, pasta with a tomato-eggplant sauce topped with grated ricotta salata

pasta con le sarde, pasta with sardines, fennel, pine nuts, and raisins

pasta con tonno sott'olio, pasta with oil-packed tuna

tagghiateddi, Sicilian-style tagliatelle pasta

Pesto alla Trapanese
pesto made with almonds and tomatoes

Raisins, dried apricots, and other dried fruit

Salmoriglio
olive oil, lemon, and garlic vinaigrette served with swordfish, tuna, or other seafood

Semifreddo
semifrozen creamy dessert flavored with almond or chocolate

Sfincione
Sicilian-style pizza sliced thick and topped with tomato, onion, and anchovies

Recommended Producers

West Side, including Marsala, Trapani, Alcamo, Palermo, Menfi, and Agrigento

---

Aldo Viola

Alessandro di Camporeale

Alessandro Viola

Assuli

Baglio di Pianetto

Cantine Barbera

Caruso & Minini

Centonze

Centopassi

Di Giovanna

Elios

Feudo Disisa

Feudo Montoni

Firriato

Cuccione

Gueli

Il Censo

Marco De Bartoli

Nino Barraco

Planeta

Principi di Butera

Rallo

Tasca d'Almerita

Southeast Side, including Vittoria and Noto

Arianna Occhipinti

ArmosA

Centonze

COS

Curto

Feudi del Pisciotto

Gulfi

Lamoresca

Manenti

Mortellito

Paolo Calì

Poggio di Bortolone

Riofavara

Tami

Tenuta del Nanfro

Tenuta La Lumia

Valle dell'Acate

Northeast Side, including Messina, Faro, and Enna

Bonavita

Enza La Fauci

Le Casematte

Nicolò Grippaldi

Palari

Etna

Ayunta

Barone di Villagrande

Benanti

Biondi

Calabretta

Calcaneus

Ciro Biondi

Cottanera

Eduardo Torres Acosta

Emanuele Scammacca del Murgo

Emiliano Falsini

Etnella

Federico Curtaz

Fessina

Filippo Grasso

Frank Cornelissen

Girolamo Russo

Graci

I Custodi e Vigne dell'Etna

I Vigneri di Salvo Foti

Monteleone

Monterosso

Nicosia

Palmento Costanzo

Passopisciaro

Pietradolce

Pietro Caciorgna

Romeo del Castello

Scilio

Scirto

Tenuta Boccarossa

Terrazze dell'Etna

Terre Nere

Tornatore

Vigneti Vecchio

Vino di Anna

Pantelleria

Abbazia San Giorgio

Donnafugata

Ferrandes

Terre di Pantelleria

Aeolian Islands

Cantine Colosi

Caravaglio

Carlo Hauner

Lantieri

Tenuta di Castellaro

Virgona

Trentino–Alto Adige

In 2006 when Florian Gojer interned at a couple of wineries on California's central coast, he encountered a world of winemaking that was entirely different from what he knew back home. It wasn't so much the wine styles—though those were different, too—but rather the predictability and vastness of California agriculture. On the central coast, grapes ripened amid a pattern of rainless hot days and cool, foggy nights. Vineyards were easier to farm, lining gentle hillsides, and the change in soil and altitude was subtle. To be sure, California winemakers had their own challenges, but they weren't the same ones that Gojer had back in Alto Adige, the German-speaking half of Trentino–Alto Adige. There, the Dolomite Mountains frame the landscape, and rivers slice through narrow valleys, feeding into a funnel between the Brenner Pass on the Austrian border and Lake Garda. In Alto Adige, the Adige and Isarco Rivers form a V before merging south of Bolzano and flowing down to Trentino, the southern half of the region, and past the city of Trento. On valley floors, apple orchards claim the best land, and bike routes cut through the trees, making the region a destination for cycling vacations. On the hillsides, pergola vines are trained in an upside-down L-shape pointing out from the steep slopes, exposing the grapes to cooling breezes. Farmers own small plots of land—each parcel is often not larger than four or five acres (a couple of hectares), and each plot has its own unique combination of altitude, soil, and grape. It's an intricate network of vineyards, and no vintage is the same.

Gojer now works at his family's Franz Gojer/ Glögglhof estate based in Santa Maddalena, a historic vineyard near Bolzano. At around ten thirty every morning, the lazy, warm Ora wind arrives, replacing the cool breezes from the Valle Isarco to the east. Facing south, with rocky glacial moraine—rocks, dirt, and sediment deposited as glaciers pushed into the earth—Santa Maddalena is a warm site, which is why it's one of the best-known sub-zones within the Alto Adige DOC for red wines. (In German, St. Magdalena is the name of the town and St. Magdalener is the name of the wine; in Italian, the place and wine are both called Santa Maddalena.) At Glögglhof, the Gojer family grows red grapes Schiava and Lagrein, and their Santa Maddalena wines express Schiava's characteristic red-fruit flavor, with a little tannin. Florian and his father, Franz, also have a cooler vineyard close by in Cornedo all'Iscarco ("Karneid" in German) where they grew old-vine Schiava. It's a high-altitude spot, and its soil is completely different—volcanic rock, with thin, sandy topsoil. Schiava doesn't ripen quickly here, but when it does, it makes wines that are lighter and brighter, with flavors of crunchy strawberries and herbs. These differences—even among vineyards that are relatively close to each other—are repeated throughout Trentino–Alto Adige.

Even though the Italian government counts Trentino–Alto Adige as a single region, it might as well be two. Both provinces operate independently. Bolzano is the de facto capital of Alto Adige, while Trento, the region's official capital, focuses on Trentino. The two sides have divergent histories dating back to (at least) the Middle Ages. Culturally, Trentino leans closer to Italy, while Alto Adige—"Südtirol" (South Tyrol) in German—looks north to Austria. The cultural differences are also reflected in the food. There are a few similarities: both provinces make *canederli* (*knödel* in German), a dumpling made of bread; eat speck, a cured ham similar to prosciutto; make cows' milk alpine cheeses; and harvest apples, but that's where the similarities end. Trentino has a northern Italian feel, with polenta or pasta on the table, often served with local mushrooms. Meanwhile, Alto Adige feels more like Austria, turning out rye bread and desserts like strudel with custard and poppy seeds.

With wines, the divide is the same: some similarities and many differences. Both provinces grow a lot of Pinot Grigio and Chardonnay; both have unusually high success with Müller-Thurgau, a grape used for table wine in Germany; and both make ruby-red wines with Schiava grapes (called "Vernatsch" in Alto Adige). That's more or less where the similarities stop. Trentino excels in making classic-method sparkling wine, deep reds from native red grape Teroldego, and nutty, rare *vino santo* from the white Nosiola grape. Meanwhile, Alto Adige is all about still alpine whites—Pinot Bianco, Kerner, Gewürztraminer, Riesling, Veltliner—that would feel more at home in northern Europe than in an Italian enoteca.

While Trentino–Alto Adige has a reputation for making a lot of Pinot Grigio for the export market, its total production is nowhere near the top in Italy. In 2020, the region made 29.93 million gallons (1.13 million hectoliters), just 2 percent of Italy's total production. Trentino makes slightly more wine than Alto Adige, and both provinces make more white than red. What binds the two are the rivers, the mountains, and the warm Ora winds, which create a unique set of microclimates for vines to thrive.

History

When hikers trekked in the Ötztal Alps on the border between Austria and Italy in 1991, they came upon a frozen arm and called a rescue team. They knew something had gone wrong, but they never expected that the man had been murdered more than five thousand years ago and preserved in ice. Before he met his demise, Ötzi the Iceman, as he came to be called, lived in the Adige Valley during the Copper Age. His mummified corpse now lies in the Südtirol Museum of Archaeology in Bolzano. Even back in Ötzi's era, the Adige River valley was a good place to live. Fresh water and food sources sustained ancient humans, who could travel back and forth between the Alps along the Brenner Pass, the lowest passageway through the mountains. Ötzi may not have been drinking wine, but wine also has a long history here, dating to 500 BC. When the Romans arrived, in 15 BC, they built upon the local wine culture. In Burton Anderson's *Wine Atlas of Italy*, he writes that wooden barrels were used for wine transport here instead of terracotta amphorae, since wood was plentiful, and barrels were easier to move through the mountains.

Yet even though the Romans settled in the Adige Valley, the region always had stronger ties to Germanic cultures north of the Alps than it did to Rome. During the Middle Ages, Trento became the capital of powerful prince-bishops, and its position in the middle of the Adige Valley made it a natural place for Italian- and German-speaking people to meet. Venetians also passed through Rovereto, today Trentino's second-largest city, on their way to the

The pergola system used to train vines at J. Hofstätter.

Cantina Terlano is known for its long-aging white
wines made with the Stocker method.

Brenner Pass, and the city's architecture still reflects Venetian influence. In comparison, Alto Adige was staunchly aligned with the north. It had a German name—Südtirol—and was part of the Austrian state of Tyrol for centuries until 1919. During the Middle Ages, German and Swiss monks established monasteries in Alto Adige and sent wine north, where it was harder for grapes to ripen. Some of these monasteries are still making wine today. In the northern reaches of Valle Isarco, the Abbazia di Novacella is one of the longest continuously operating wineries in the world, with records dating back to 1142. The Muri-Gries monastery's presence in Alto Adige is more recent, established in 1845 when Benedictine monks from Muri in Switzerland moved to Gries, a hamlet outside of Bolzano. Today, the hamlet has been engulfed by the city, but Klosteranger, the monastery's walled vineyard and a historic home of the native red grape Lagrein, remains.

In the early nineteenth century after the Napoleonic Wars, Austria annexed Trentino, folding it into the Austrian state of Tyrol and officially connecting it to Alto Adige. Italian-speaking Trentino and German-speaking Alto Adige remained part of Tyrol until the end of World War I, when Italy was given both territories. Under Mussolini, Italian became the only official language permitted, and schools were forbidden from teaching German. Natives of Alto Adige—who still thought of themselves as Tyrolean—were forced to choose between forgoing their culture or immigrating to Austria. Distrust in the Italian government continued after World War II. To quell separatist tensions, the Italian government made Trentino–Alto Adige autonomous, giving them more power to govern themselves and select their own languages. (Sardinia, Sicily, Valle d'Aosta, and Friuli Venezia Giulia have the same special status.) Today, most residents in Alto Adige speak German first and Italian second, and cities, wineries, and wines have both German and Italian names. "Südtirol" is just as common on wine labels as "Alto Adige."

Trentino–Alto Adige's ties to Tyrol also made lasting impacts on the area's wine education. In 1874, the Tyrolean parliament approved a plan to open an agricultural school and research center in the former monastery of San Michele all'Adige for the study of winemaking. Istituto Agrario di San Michele was later renamed Fondazione Edmund Mach (the Edmund Mach Foundation) after its first director, and it's not only Italy's oldest viticulture and enology school but also one of its most influential.

Born in 1879, Trentino native Giulio Ferrari graduated from San Michele before heading north to study winemaking. Inspired by Champagne, he sought to make sparkling wine from Chardonnay grown in the mountains. Ferrari made his first vintage in 1902. He continued to refine his technique for fifty years before selling the business to local businessman Bruno Lunelli in 1952, though he stayed on as technical manager until he passed away in 1965. As a tribute to the founder, the Lunelli family created "Riserva del Fondatore Giulio Ferrari." A long-aging *metodo classico* that layers the acidity from mountain-grown Chardonnay with notes of lemon and bread crumbs, it is one of Italy's best sparkling wines. The Lunelli family has grown production substantially, working with about five hundred local growers, many of whom have handshake deals to sell their grapes to the company. Following Ferrari's lead, Trentino has grown into one of Italy's best centers for sparkling wines, which now fall under the umbrella of the Trento DOC. Reflecting the mountains, Trento's *metodo classico* wines are clean and precise, with acidity and a mineral finish that keep you returning to the glass.

Most people who own vineyards in Trentino–Alto Adige have plots that are too small to support a winery. For this reason, wines made here often come from co-ops. Yet while co-op wine is associated with quality degradation in much of Italy, the same wasn't true here. Part of the reason is that the co-op system arose here much earlier than elsewhere. In 1893, local growers in Alto Adige pooled their resources to found Cantina Terlano (Kellerei Terlan). In 1898, Cantina Tramin (Kellerei Tramin) followed, and many more came after. Between the agriculture and enology studies at San Michele all'Adige and the investments in cellars from the co-ops, Alto Adige winemakers had more resources to study their craft. In the 1950s, Cantina Terlano's cellarmaster Sebastian Stocker start developed a method for creating long-lived white wines by aging the wine on the lees (spent yeast cells) in steel tanks for 10 to 30 years. The lees, he hypothesized, were a natural preservative, keeping white wine from oxidizing.

As white wines gained recognition, the reputation for red wines suffered. Schiava, the region's most important red for most of the twentieth century, was made in bulk and shipped to Switzerland and Germany, where markets wanted cheap, light red wines. Often farmers made more money growing apples than grapes. In the 1980s, a winemaker wanting to break out of the bulk market had better success using international grapes. J. Hofstätter was one of the first estates to make vineyard-specific wines: Kolbenhof, a vineyard once owned by Jesuits from Innsbruck, is renowned for Gewürztraminer that strikes a balance between mineral complexity and aroma, finishing completely dry. Meanwhile, "Barthenau Vigna S. Urbano" comes from Mazon, one of the best areas in Italy for Pinot Nero (Pinot Noir). Today, both wines remain some of Alto Adige's most iconic bottles. Winemakers Alois Lageder and Elena Walch also were early to identify special sites and made Chardonnay, Sauvignon Blanc, and other wines from international grapes, demonstrating to the export market that fine wine could come from Alto Adige.

Today, the focus has shifted to native grapes as the next generation embraces Lagrein, Nosiola, and others. Winemakers who didn't experience the old days of bulk Schiava is rehabilitating the variety's old pergola-grained vines (look for *alte reben*, "old vines," on the label). The results are elegant, accessible, food-friendly reds, the kind that nearly all wine drinkers love.

Land and Wines

Walled off from the coldest northern air by the Dolomites but open to the south where the warm Ora winds travel up from Lake Garda, Trentino–Alto Adige avoids extreme cold. In the summer, Bolzano rivals Sicily as the hottest place in Italy thanks to the volcanic porphyry mountains that surround it, absorbing heat and baking the city. It's as though the region is one part continental and one part Mediterranean, where cool-climate Gewürztraminer and Pinot Bianco grow next to cypress and palm trees. It's the only region in Italy where vines easily grow between 650 and 3,280 feet (200 to 1,000 meters) above sea level, with some growing even higher. The nights do get cold and higher elevations can get frost, yet it's the constant tension between cold and hot that gives the wines from this region their signature acidity and aroma.

The northernmost part of Alto Adige includes the high-altitude vineyards of Valle Isarco (Eisacktal) to the east and the Val Venosta (Vinschgau) to the far northwest. Both focus on aromatic, refreshing white wines made with grapes such as Kerner, Riesling, Veltliner, and Sylvaner. With the volcanic soils, these wines tend to have a mineral undertone that grounds their accents of white flowers and delicate fruit aromas. The Pliger family of Kuenhof makes flinty white wines with notes like pear and orange blossoms coupled with high acidity, allowing them to pair well with a range of foods from around the world. Between Val Venosta and Valle Isarco, the town of Merano (Meran) has a warmer climate perfect for reds, mostly peppery, bright Schiava wines. Down valley from Merano, the Santa Maddalena vineyards spread out along warm, south-facing hills surrounding Bolzano. Most of the grapes grown here are Schiava, but Lagrein also performs well in the heat.

South of Bolzano, the Adige River passes through Terlano (Terlan). Cantina Terlano's (Kellerei Terlan's) "Terlaner," a blend of Pinot Bianco, Chardonnay, and Sauvignon, produced since the co-op's early

The Alto-Adige town of Termeno.

years, evokes white peach, chamomile, and stone. Farther down from Terlano, Lake Caldaro (Kaltern) is another warm area tempered by the lake. There, Schiava thrives along with Chardonnay, Sauvignon Blanc, and a handful of other international varieties. Just south of the lake, the town of Termeno (Tramin), is the historic home of Gewürztraminer, and Cantina Tramin (Kellerei Tramin) makes "Nussbaumer," a heralded Gewürztraminer known for acidity in what is typically low-acid variety. East of Tramin on the other side of the Adige River, Pinot Nero grows in the Mazon area.

When the Adige River enters Trentino, it widens before funneling down toward Trento, and the soil types lean more toward limestone and yellow clay, which impart a different kind of minerality to the wines. Like Alto Adige, Trentino's production is dominated by co-ops, but Trentino's are much larger—Cavit and Mezzocorona make millions of bottles annually, mostly for export. Yet the co-ops are owned by small growers (Mezzocorona has around five thousand members), most of whom have 5-acre (2-hectare) plots of land in mountain microclimates. Many Trentino farmers specialize in mountain Chardonnay, the most important grape for Trento DOC wines. What sets apart Trento DOC sparkling wines from other Italian sparklers is altitude—Chardonnay can grow up to 2,500 feet (760 meters) above sea level, resulting in high-acid wines.

Trentino has its share of distinct wine areas. West of the Adige River between the towns of Mezzocorona and Mezzolombardo, the flat, stony Campo Rotaliano is famous for elegant, acidic, long-lived red Teroldego wines from Elisabetta Foradori. Nearby in the hills, Pojer e Sandri makes lithe Müller-Thurgau wines. Farther south, the Vallagarina, a valley stretching from Trento all the way south, is the home of light reds made with Marzemino grapes. Running parallel to the Vallagarina but separated by mountains, the Valle dei Laghi and its chain of small lakes is known for the native Nosiola grape, which historically went into *vino santo*, a *passito* wine. There are also some outliers, like the historic Tenuta San Leonardo estate in the far south corner of Trentino. Owned by the noble Gonzaga family, the estate has been working with Bordeaux grapes, growing Carménère, Cabernet Sauvignon, and Merlot, since the early 1800s. Made from a blend of the three grapes, the estate's namesake wine is exceptionally elegant, with notes of ripe cherries, black currants, and cocoa nibs.

In Trentino and Alto Adige, the traditional way to train vines with pergolas—pointing out from terraced slopes to make it easy to walk underneath and harvest grapes—is suited to the mountains. While pergolas have commonly been criticized because grapes grown this way tend to produce too many bunches, diluting quality, here grape growers stuck with the system because pergolas protect grapes and soils by adding shade, preserving acidity. Generally, maintaining acidity isn't a problem in the region, but it's not immune to the changing climate. More than in other regions, growers in this area are experimenting with hybrid grapes, growing them at higher altitudes and seeing how well they do without any treatments in the vineyard (like spraying with copper to combat mildew). The experiments may feel far-out today (hybrid grapes are a tough sell to wine lovers), but the region has a reputation for taking low-brow grapes (like Müller-Thurgau) and turning them into something special. If hybrids have a future in Italy, it may be in these mountains.

Trentino–Alto Adige Grapes

Trentino and Alto Adige mainly focus on white wines. The labels, which are in both Italian and German, usually note the grape, making it easy to figure out what you're drinking.

White

Chardonnay

Chardonnay has long played a role in Italian *metodo classico* sparkling wines. More than 120 years ago, it was planted in Trentino–Alto Adige, where it became the key white grape for Trento DOC sparkling wines thanks to the work of Giulio Ferrari, who pioneered Trentino's mountain-made sparkling wine production. When grown in the cool mountain terrain, with wide temperature swings between morning and night, Chardonnay becomes stony, with the high amounts of acidity needed to make high-quality sparkling wine. In Lombardy, Chardonnay is most associated with the *metodo classico* wines of Franciacorta, where it is by far the main grape. In a general sense, the wines of Franciacorta, an area with a mild climate and soils that vary between sand, gravel, and clay, can be rounder than the Chardonnay-based sparkling wines from Trento DOC. Chardonnay is also grown in Alto Adige, where it is made into still wines. Elena Walch's Chardonnay comes from Castel Ringberg, a large vineyard above Lake Caldaro (Kaltern). In the warm microclimate, the grapes get full and ripe, and the result is a full-bodied, rich Chardonnay. Tiefenbrunner's "Vigna AU" also comes from Chardonnay grown in a warm site with high amounts of limestone and salt in the soil, producing an intense, almost spicy white wine with a mineral finish. Franciacorta also makes still Chardonnay under its Curtefranca DOC. Chardonnay grows in the rest of Italy but not always successfully. In Sicily, for example, it's being taken out and replanted with native white grapes that are more drought and heat tolerant.

Gewürztraminer/Traminer Aromatico

Named after the Alto Adige town Termeno (Tramin), Gewürztraminer and Traminer are genetically identical but improbable twins. First documented in the thirteenth century, Traminer came first as a nonaromatic green grape, before traveling elsewhere and mutating into Gewürztraminer, which grew pink grapes laden with aromas. The addition of "Gewürz," given for the grape's aromas, came in the late nineteenth century. Gewürztraminer went on to make some of the most lush, opulent wines in the world, the kind that fills wineglasses with roses, spices, and lychee. Gewürztraminer is not known for acidity, but in Alto Adige, its wines become unusually dry and restrained. Made from a single vineyard in Termeno, J. Hofstätter's "Kolbenhof" is all about Golden Delicious apples, lychees, and preserved lemon, while Tiefenbrunner's Gewürztraminers are beautifully aromatic, with rose petals, jasmine, and honey. Both have a complex honeyed tone with a backbone of gentle acidity to complement local dishes, like dumplings with speck, or schnitzel with poppy seed brown butter. Alto Adige also grows aromatic Goldtraminer, a cross between Trebbiano Toscano and Gewürztraminer used in late-harvest wines.

Kerner

The best vine crossings gain qualities from parent vines but also have their own story to tell. That's the case with Kerner. Made in Germany by crossing Italian Schiava Grossa with Riesling, Kerner offers Riesling-level acidity with an herbal, savory edge. In Alto Adige, it's appreciated for its dependable production, resilience to frost, and ability to grow at high altitude. This practical nature belies its ability to make world-class white wine, especially when grown in the Valle Isarco (Eisacktal) in Alto Adige's far northeast. In the village of San Nicolò (Saint Nikolaus) near Lake Caldaro (Kaltern), the Niklas winery was the first to plant Kerner in the area. Today, Kerner from Niklas is one of the best white wines in the region, its piercing acidity offset with notes of Bartlett pear, lime, and pencil lead. The wines from Köfererhof and Abbazia di Novacella are similarly enticing. Meanwhile, the Kerner from Franz Gojer is fresh and savory, with flinty, herbal notes—a perfect aperitivo wine.

Müller-Thurgau

Developed in 1882 by Swiss botanist and oenologist Hermann Müller, Müller-Thurgau is a cross between Riesling and Madeleine Royale, a table grape that has since disappeared. For most of its existence,

Florian Gojer at his family's Franz Gojer/Glögglhof
winery based in Santa Maddalena.

Müller-Thurgau was pigeonholed as a workhorse variety, a popular grape in mass-produced German wines. However, when grown at altitude in Trentino–Alto Adige, Müller-Thurgau becomes a mouthwatering wine. In Trentino, Corvée cultivates vines at 2,297 feet (700 meters) above the Cembra Valley, yielding an aromatic wine with citrus and white flowers. In Alto Adige, co-op Erste + Neue's Müller-Thurgau comes from vineyards grown at 1,312 feet (400 meters), yielding an aromatic, bone-dry wine filled with lime zest and honeysuckle. Tiefenbrunner's flagship wine, "Feldmarschall," comes from Müller-Thurgau grown at 3,300 feet (1,005 meters)—one of the highest vineyards in Europe. The wine is slightly riper than most Müller-Thurgaus, with graceful, floral aromas and a distinct mineral accent balanced by notes of lemon and white peach. It's one of Alto Adige's iconic bottles, which is all the more impressive considering many had written off Müller-Thurgau as a failed experiment.

Nosiola

Native to Trentino, this local white grape is named either for its nutty aroma (*nocciola* is "hazelnut") or the nutty color of the grapes when they're ripe. Grown mostly in the Valle dei Laghi, it is also one of the most interesting native white grapes in the region. Nosiola is versatile, yielding everything from a bright, refreshing white wine to rich, golden *vino santo*. Made by drying grapes after harvest and pressing them the following spring during Holy Week, *vino santo* is one of Trentino's oldest wines. (Tuscany and a few other regions make similar wine, though in Tuscany it is called Vin Santo and uses different grapes and a slightly different method.) Nosiola is also used to make *vini macerati* (Orange Wine, see page 84). Trentino winemaker Elisabetta Foradori ages Nosiola on its skins in amphorae (terracotta vessels) for half a year or longer, resulting in a nuanced and subtly spicy orange wine with plenty of savory flavor. Pojer e Sandri's Nosiola, with hints of orange zest and hazelnut, is a wine to drink young. For a different take, Marco Zani plays with Nosiola in a bone-dry *frizzante* blend with Sauvignon Blanc and Chardonnay as well as a nutty,

pure Nosiola that expresses orange zest and green apple with a slightly salty finish.

Pinot Bianco (Pinot Blanc, Weissburgunder)

In 1881, Edmund Mach, the first director of the enology school in San Michele all'Adige that now bears his name, recommended planting Pinot Bianco in Alto Adige. The grape used to be grown throughout Champagne and, decades later, Franciacorta, before falling by the wayside in both wine regions. That never happened in Alto Adige. Around the town of Terlano (Terlan), just south of Bolzano, it comes into its own as one of the best long-lived white wines in the region. Cantina Terlano's "Vorberg" is a Pinot Bianco after aging for a year on its lees (spent yeast cells). The wine ages astonishingly well, with rich notes of green apple and pear balanced by flint, limestone, and a touch of citrus zest. The high elevations of the vineyards—it can be planted up to 2,133 feet (650 meters) above sea level—preserve the acidity of the grape.

Pinot Grigio
(see Friuli Venezia Giulia chapter, page 86)

Sauvignon Blanc
(see Friuli Venezia Giulia chapter, page 87)

Sylvaner

Yet another Alto Adige grape that grows best in the cool mountain climate of the Valle Isarco (Eisacktal), Sylvaner (spelled "Silvaner" in Germany, where it's also grown) is one of the area's traditional white grapes. Sylvaner is a mineral-rich wine with the structure and acidity to age. The striking example from Kuenhof is all about cool, rocky alpine terrain with subtle undercurrents of green apple and pear that give the wine an unexpectedly long finish. Nearby, Sylvaner from Abbazia di Novacella is mineral-rich, with a gentle nose of apple and white peach.

Veltliner

Mostly grown in the Valle Isarco (Eisacktal), Veltliner—Alto Adige's shorthand for Austria's main white grape Grüner Veltliner—makes a quintessentially crisp, everyday mineral white. Balanced and easygoing, these are the kinds of wines to drink after a day of trekking around the Dolomites. Cantina Valle Isarco's version is a greenish yellow, apple-like wine with refreshing acidity, while Pacherhof's Veltliner has notes of white pepper, with similar levels of acidity.

Red

Lagrein

Lagrein is hard to grow. If a vine has too many leaves and shoots, it drops its grape bunches. The grape's skins are thin, so if it rains at harvest (which is common), rot sets in quickly. A few things do help: the local pergola system helps manage vine vigor, and breezes from the south or east keep leaves and grapes dry. And then there's the summer heat. Bolzano's soaring temperatures are essential to get Lagrein to ripen—for Lagrein, the hotter the better. In Bolzano, Muri-Gries's Lagrein comes from Klosteranger, its historic walled vineyard. In this warm site, the wine turns meaty, with blackberries and plum layered with smoke, violets, and spice. Never overpowering, Lagrein is a versatile food wine, with sour cherries and blackberries combined with black pepper notes and acidity. When served next to Schiava, the other local red, it is noticeably richer, though some versions can be light, especially when made as Lagrein *kretzer*, a *rosato*. The *kretzer* from Nusserhof is redolent of strawberries, a refreshing drink for hot Bolzano summers.

Marzemino

An offspring of Teroldego, Marzemino is Trentino's lighter red grape, making cheerful, medium-bodied wines with notes of strawberries or cherries countered with an herbal streak. Documented in the fourteenth century, the grape spread throughout the Veneto, Emilia-Romagna, and Lombardy, though it's more common in Trentino, especially around the northern shores of Lake Garda. The grape has thin skins and requires ventilation to prevent vine

disease. Some Marzemino wines can taste too green because they were picked too early; winemaker Eugenio Rosi counters this by letting the grapes ripen as long as possible and then drying them after harvest (like they do to make Amarone). The result is a full, thoughtful Marzemino. Meanwhile, low-tech producer Furlani experiments with sparkling and still Trentino cuvées, blending Marzemino with Teroldego and a handful of obscure local red grapes for bright, tart wines brimming with red-fruit flavors.

Pinot Nero (Pinot Noir, Blauburgunder)

One of the world's most popular wine grapes, Pinot Nero inevitably grows in Italy, especially in Lombardy, where it's used in the *metodo classico* sparkling wines of Oltrepò Pavese and Franciacorta. As a still wine, however, it reaches some of its best expressions in Trentino–Alto Adige. The region's glacial soils, cold nights, and altitude preserve the acidity, creating wines that are a harmonious blend between savory flavors and red fruit. South of Bolzano, the Niedrist family, who has made wine in Alto Adige for nearly two hundred years, has a couple of Pinot Neros: a *riserva* from vines planted in the 1960s in volcanic-glacial soils and "vom Kalk" from vines that grow in gravelly, limestone soils in Appiano Monte. Meanwhile, the J. Hofstätter estate's Barthenau Vigna S. Urbano is an expressive red with notes of red currant, raspberry, and cedar.

Schiava (Vernatsch) Group

There is more than one vine called Schiava ("Vernatsch" in Alto Adige and "Trollinger" in other German-speaking areas). The most common is Schiava Grossa—the parent of white grape Kerner—which has larger grapes and grape bunches than Schiava Gentile or Schiava Grigia. Most of the time, however, a bottle will simply say "Vernatsch" or "Schiava" without being more specific, and all grapes called Schiava produce similarly juicy red wines with low tannins and light color. The Italian name "Schiava" translates to "slave," a degrading term some say came from the ancient Romans, who "enslaved" the vines by tethering them to

Rudi Kofler of Cantina Terlano

poles. Grown in the region for centuries, Schiava from Alto Adige was immensely popular in Austria and Switzerland. After the First World War, when Trentino–Alto Adige became part of Italy, Schiava was important enough that the government allowed it to be sold across the border without restrictions. The historic vineyard for Schiava, Santa Maddalena, once carried an infamous reputation—in 1941, Mussolini's government named it one of the country's best reds, which only served to land Schiava in criticism later for being a favorite wine of fascists. When demand for Schiava softened in the second half of the twentieth century, many vines were ripped out in favor of international grapes. Fortunately, it's making a quality comeback as a younger generation embraces the juicy freshness of the grapes, planting the vines at higher altitude to draw out the aromas of strawberry, almond, and violets. In Santa Maddalena, a south-facing hillside outside Bolzano, the Gojer family make a couple of different Schiava wines, some blended with a splash of Lagrein. South of Bolzano in the village of Cortaccia (Kurtatsch), Andreas Widmann makes Schiava that is at once savory and full of fruit, something you could drink any day. That's the thing about wines made with Schiava: with bright acidity and soft tannins, they are eminently thirst quenching and food friendly, good matches with everything from hearty mountain fare to spicy and savory cuisines from around the world.

Teroldego

The main red variety of Trentino, Teroldego reaches its greatest heights in Campo Rotaliano, a warm, gravelly site along the Noce River in the northeastern corner of Trentino. Once celebrated in royal courts, the grape became another anonymous red grape later on, with a few exceptions. Brothers Leonardo and Michele de Cles of Barone de Cles won a gold medal for their take on it in a national wine competition in 1973, and the Donati family has also long been tied to the variety. Still, in the 1980s, when Elisabetta Foradori began selecting the best Teroldego vines to propagate from existing vines on the family property in Campo Rotaliano, it was the first time in ages that anyone had studied the grape in that level of detail. Foradori released "Granato" in 1986, a peppery red wine with restrained notes of blackberries and black cherries that soon became a benchmark for the grape and granted her the nickname "queen of Teroldego." She and her family continue to evolve how they make wine with Teroldego, converting to biodynamic farming, experimenting with aging wine in amphorae (terracotta vessels) and tanks, and fermenting wines spontaneously (using native yeasts from the vineyard instead of adding commercial yeast). The grape itself yields a darkly colored, fruity wine that is softly tannic and bright.

Regional Foods

Apples
especially from Trentino's Val di Non area

Asparagus

Canederli (knödel)
dumplings made from old bread blended with speck

Cheese
Montasio, aged cows' milk cheese, its cheesemaking process is regulated by its own consortium

Vezzena, alpine cows' milk cheese to be eaten fresh or aged and used for grating

Chestnuts

Kastanientorte
cake made of chestnut puree, butter, flour, sugar, and eggs

Mostarda
piquant fruit preserve with mustard seeds (and sometimes mustard oil)

Mushrooms

Polenta

Poppy seeds

Pork

Potatoes

Rye bread

Salumi

Schlutzkrapfen
half-moon pasta stuffed with cheese and spinach

Speck
cured ham similar to prosciutto

Strudel

Trout

Recommended Producers

Alto Adige

Abbazia di Novacella

Alois Lageder

Baron Widmann

Cantina Cortaccia (Kellerei Kurtatsch)

Cantina San Michele Appiano (Kellerei St. Michael-Eppan)

Cantina Terlano (Kellerei Terlan)

Cantina Tramin (Kellerei Tramin)

Cantina Valle Isarco (Kellerei Eisacktal)

Carlotto

Castel Sallegg

Elena Walch

Erste + Neue

Franz Gojer

Gump Hof

J. Hofstätter

Köfererhof

Kuenhof

Manincor

Muri-Gries

Niedrist

Niklas

Nusserhof

Pacherhof

Pranzegg

Tiefenbrunner

Widmann

Trentino

Cavit

Corvée

De Vescovi Ulzbach

Dorigati

Eugenio Rosi

Ferrari

Foradori

Furlani

Marco Zani

Mezzacorona

Pojer e Sandri

Roberto Zeni

San Leonardo

Tuscany

Only fourteen towers remain in San Gimignano, though at one point they numbered more than seventy. The town, which spreads out around the ridge of a hill in central Tuscany, had an arms race of sorts between the eleventh and thirteenth centuries. Prominent families wanted towers, and each wanted theirs to be taller than their neighbors'. For pilgrims walking the Via Francigena on their way to Rome, San Gimignano loomed from the hill like a medieval metropolis. Over the centuries, San Gimignano's fortunes waned, and it lost some of its structures. Shelling during World War II reduced the number to the fourteen left today.

Within the Tuscan wine world, San Gimignano and its remaining towers, which have been restored to their medieval glory, represent a rare puddle of white wine in a countryside dominated by red. Nearly 90 percent of Tuscan wine is red, and the majority is Sangiovese. Yet San Gimignano's main wine, Vernaccia di San Gimignano, is white and has been made here since the thirteenth century. In 1966, when the government released its inaugural list of DOC wines, Vernaccia di San Gimignano was first to receive the honors, even before Chianti, Brunello, and Barolo. It would be easy to write off Vernaccia di San Gimignano as a historical wine made for tourists, but it can be seriously good. Marine fossils are found in the soils around the town and limestone is everywhere, all of which is ideal for white wine. Elisabetta Fagiuoli, who has made wine at her estate, Montenidoli, for half a century, creates layered Vernaccia di San Gimignano wines with a touch of skin contact, expressing apricots and almond, flint and earth wrapped in a savory tang.

In Tuscany, great wine exists in nearly every corner. The region's wine output in 2020 was 68.76 million gallons (2.6 million hectoliters), ranking sixth in the country and nearly the same as Piedmont. And like Piedmont, Tuscany's winemakers take themselves seriously. The 2019 edition of the Italian wine guide *Gambero Rosso* called Tuscany a battleground in which the country's top enological talent competes. In the past few decades, Tuscan estates have poured resources into their vineyards and cellars, researching ways to handle making wine amid a changing climate. Panzano, a subcommune in the heart of Chianti Classico, has been completely organic for years, and other areas are following suit. The region's wines have rarely been better.

In a way, though, Tuscany has a lot to live up to. When we picture the Italian countryside, we think of cypress trees, olive groves, medieval cities, and a gentle climate—essentially, we imagine Tuscany. This is the home of Dante, the Italian language, and the Renaissance, where people love to take selfies with the Tower of Pisa and the statue of David. Some snicker at the region, calling its countryside "Tuscanshire" from all the vacation villas owned by foreigners and celebrities, like Sting. If you want to see "real" Italy with "real" Italians, they say, it's better to visit Calabria or Molise or Basilicata, which doesn't see nearly the number of tour buses. However, writing off Tuscany for not being Italian enough is absurd, especially with its wine contributions. Its beloved Chianti Classico is likely the oldest-known delineated wine region in Europe. Tuscany was early in establishing a wine commerce that benefited the working classes and the nobles centuries ago. And while Italy's top consulting enologists often emerge from northern regions, like Piedmont and Trentino–Alto Adige, Tuscany has always had a pool of homegrown talent. For the past couple of decades, the debate about the region's top Sangiovese wines isn't whether they're any good but why it's crazy they aren't (usually) as expensive as Barolo.

History

Tuscany's cultural foundations, like those of Lazio to the south, came from the Etruscans and later the Romans. But its true regional identity was shaped by its city-states. While much of the Italian peninsula found itself in a power vacuum after the fall of Rome, the medieval towns of San Gimignano, Siena, Pisa, and Florence governed themselves like mini-republics. The base of their organizational structure came from the ancient Greeks, who established self-governing cities in Sicily in pre-Roman times. Cities were governed either by *contrade* (districts), or guilds representing specific professions. The *contrade* were competitive with one another—Il Palio, a biannual horse race in Siena pitting each

district against each other, started in the Middle Ages and continues today, with each team carrying a flag with its mascot. In Florence, there were guilds for merchants, bankers, doctors, shopkeepers, and seemingly every category of artisan. Some guilds amassed political power, which helped its members, the *popolo*, receive concessions from the noble classes who depended on their skills. The guild system appeared in other parts of Italy, but it was most concentrated and successful in Tuscany. While not everyone was equal in the system, an everyday Florentine in the Middle Ages often had more autonomy than his contemporaries living under a feudal lord elsewhere on the Italian peninsula.

Tuscany's city-states thrived, but they also fought one another for territory and resources. Governed by the de' Medici family, Florence came to dominate the other cities. In 1557, when it gained Siena, the Florentines controlled nearly all of Tuscany, including the area between Florence and Siena that we now call Chianti Classico. The hilly stretch of land had long been recognized for its wine. In 1398, the name "Chianti" appeared in an official document that mentioned wine, and in 1565, the black rooster, which appears on all labels of Chianti Classico today, was chosen to symbolize the wine. Influential families, like the Capponis of Florence—who today make Chianti Classico in Greve under their label Calcinaia—expanded their vineyards and olive orchards into the countryside. Many needed an outlet to sell their wines. To do so without paying taxes, they built *buchette del vino*, or wine windows (literally "small holes for wine"), into their city residences. If a non-noble Florentine wanted wine, he put his jug and money into the window and received a filled jug in return. Later, during the Plague, these windows became important for the contactless exchange of goods. (History repeats itself; in 2020, vendors sold wine and gelato out of *buchette del vino* in the early days of the coronavirus pandemic.)

By the eighteenth century, the noble classes knew where the best wines came from. In 1716— well before the Italian government created its DOC system—Grand Duke of Tuscany Cosimo III de' Medici delineated four areas in Tuscany

Barrels of Chianti Classico at Villa Calcinaia.

that produced the best wine: Chianti (the Chianti Classico of today), Carmignano, Rufina-Pomino, and Valdarno di Sopra. In the century that followed, a political figure who played an important role in Italy's unification, Baron Bettino Ricasoli, documented his ideal blend of Chianti grapes. After the death of Camillo Benso, the Count of Cavour, he became Italy's second prime minister in 1861. Ricasoli had strong patriotic ideas of what it meant to be an Italian citizen, but as a member of one of the oldest winemaking families in Italy, he had equally strong ideas about Chianti. In 1872, he wrote that certain grapes, including the white grape Malvasia, could be blended into Sangiovese to add balance and aromas—though he suggested leaving Malvasia out if the wine was destined to age. Years later, his words were taken out of context and reinterpreted as an official recipe: Chianti should be a blended wine, and that blend needed to include white grapes.

Chianti's identity crisis began in the early twentieth century. Increasingly more wines called "Chianti" were made outside the traditional Chianti area. Instead of pushing back on the inaccurate labels, the government expanded Chianti's boundaries to include a much larger zone, all with different climates, soil types, and Sangiovese biotypes. In 1932, the government issued a decree that Chianti made in the original zone would now be called "Chianti Classico," and the larger area beyond the borders originally drawn by Cosimo III de' Medici would be called "Chianti." By then, however, other problems were brewing.

For centuries, the Tuscan wine industry relied on the *mezzadria* system in which sharecroppers lived on and farmed plots of land, then gave half of what they produced to the landowner. After World War II, the practice was dismantled, but nothing took its place. Farmers, who had decades of experience in the fields, left the countryside for work and housing. Meanwhile, the landowners were left with vineyards and no one to take care of them. By the 1950s, many estates became neglected. To prevent a Tuscan wine collapse, the Italian government showered the region with attention. Landowners were paid to replant vineyards with new clones of

Sangiovese that guaranteed high yields to make cheap Chianti sold abroad in *fiaschi*, straw-covered bottles. Soon, chemical companies arrived, teaching wineries how to use pesticides on their vines. The old ways of farming and making wine were lost, and a new, more industrial system took hold.

The overhaul was made official in 1966, the year that the DOC laws came into effect. The regulations took Ricasoli's suggestion for blending white grapes into Chianti and made it part of the official recipe. If you were a winemaker who wanted to make a pure Sangiovese wine, you couldn't call it Chianti Classico *or* Chianti. To put the word "Chianti" on the label, winemakers needed to add white grapes. Instead of good-quality Malvasia, which Ricasoli had suggested, winemakers could use Trebbiano Toscano. The result was a thin, rusty-red wine with high acidity and little else to offer. Yet this style became synonymous with Tuscan wine.

In the mid-twentieth century, landowners who wanted to make quality wine looked beyond Italy for inspiration. In Maremma, a large area surrounding the southern Tuscan coast, a quiet experiment brewed. Next to the walled village of Bolgheri, the Marchese Mario Incisa della Rocchetta planted French vines on a hillside within his estate, Tenuta San Guido. The Marchese was a fan of Bordeaux, and he reasoned that the stony hillside resembled the gravelly soil of Graves, perfect for growing Bordeaux grapes Cabernet Sauvignon and Cabernet Franc. In 1968, he had his first vintage, blending the two grapes into a wine he called "Sassicaia," meaning a "place of many stones." Within a decade, Sassicaia—a Tuscan wine made with French grapes—had spawned a new wine category: the Super Tuscan. More premier bottles made with French grapes emerged under this new umbrella. Because they didn't follow any DOC guidelines, these wines were classified under the lowest quality tier, *vino da tavola* (table wine). But they were made with higher standards in mind: lower yields in the vineyard, more aging, and more expensive barrels. The success of Super Tuscan wines also led to a lot more vineyards planted with international grapes over local varieties. In 1996, the rules of Chianti Classico were even changed to allow winemakers to blend in international grapes. Soon, Sangiovese was being mixed with Cabernet Sauvignon and Merlot instead of the traditional blending partners Colorino and Canaiolo. Few seemed to believe Sangiovese could ever reach great heights on its own.

Fortunately, there were always a handful of stubborn Sangiovese believers. Around the time that the Marchese was working with enologist Giacomo Tachis on the early vintages of Sassicaia, businessman Sergio Manetti bought Montevertine, a historic but run-down estate in Radda, a commune in Chianti Classico. A few years into the project, he brought in winemaker Giulio Gambelli as a consultant, working to perfect Montevertine's iconic Sangiovese wine, "Le Pergole Torte." Born in 1925 in between Florence and Siena, Gambelli became fascinated with Sangiovese when he was fourteen and worked in the cellar under Tancredi Biondi Santi. Early on, Biondi Santi recognized Gambelli's extraordinary ability as a taster and made him an assistant in the winery's lab. Biondi Santi later set the foundation for the Brunello di Montalcino DOCG, and Gambelli became an expert in all things Sangiovese.

Throughout his career, Gambelli opposed adding international grapes to soften Sangiovese's high acidity, beef up its body, or boost its color. There was no reason in his mind that a premium wine couldn't be made purely with Sangiovese, and that was the foundation of "Le Pergole Torte." Yet as a pure Sangiovese wine, it could not be labeled as Chianti Classico, so like Sassicaia, it was a *vino da tavola*. Until he passed away in 2012, Gambelli continued his behind-the-scenes work, reinvigorating the understanding of Tuscany's most important red grape. "Le Pergole Torte" continues to be a standout Sangiovese: sharp, with red fruits and dried flowers, and endless layers, a wine that is more than the sum of its parts. The regulations were later changed to allow 100 percent Sangiovese wine in the Classico area, and others, such as Gaiole-based Riecine, became known for pure Sangiovese Chianti Classico.

Chianti Classico producers also realized that the Sangiovese clones they had planted in the 1960s with government funding made inferior wine. In the early 2000s, the consortium of Chianti Classico began to study the best biotypes, planting different Sangiovese vines throughout the Classico area. After years of study, they narrowed down the vines that produced smaller grapes, looser bunches, and lower yields, while also adjusting their recommendations on planting—increasing the number of vines per hectare and forcing each vine to compete for water and minerals. The practice of green harvesting, removing some of the grape clusters when still green, concentrated the sugars and acids in the remaining grapes.

Yet now as the climate changes, producers are once again having to rethink their methods. Planting vines with a little more breathing room helps with ventilation and lowers the incidence of disease. Extensive green harvesting is longer necessary as warmer vintages lead to wines with higher alcohol. In a way, things are going back to the era before industrial agriculture.

Land and Wines

Separated from Emilia-Romagna by the Apennine Mountains to the north; bordering Le Marche, Umbria, and Lazio to the east and south; and touching the southern end of Liguria, Tuscany is the heart of central Italy. Nearly all the countryside is hills or mountains, and less than 10 percent is flat. Its climate is mild, though microclimates abound. Tuscany's food and wine heritage is rich in Mediterranean flavors—olives and olive oil, beans and bread, and modest portions of fish, meat, and cured pork find their way to the table. What's on the table matters, because Sangiovese—by far the dominant wine of the region—is best with food.

Sangiovese comprises about two-thirds of all grapes planted in the region, and it's essential in plenty of the region's wine zones. Chianti Classico and Chianti, Brunello, Vino Nobile, Carmignano,

Montecucco, and Morellino di Scansano all include it in their mix. Yet while Sangiovese is the lead story, there are plenty of other wines to seek out, from fresh Vermentino and Ciliegiolo along the coast to historic Vin Santo, the sherry-like amber wine once made for Mass.

Among the region's Sangiovese areas, Chianti Classico stands out for its history and climate, which the grape has adapted to over centuries. Located on the eastern side of the region, Chianti Classico is split between the province of Florence to the north and Siena to the south, covering 177,500 acres (71,800 hectares). With that broad stretch of land, it's hard to make generalizations about the wines—much of it depends on the sun exposure of the hillsides and the specific soils in the vineyards—though the consortium is working on a UGA (*unità geografiche aggiuntive*, "additional geographical unit") list, which could be added to labels to help identify where the wine comes from. It is also working with members to better understand the Classico zone's special soils, which include *alberese*, a clay-limestone mix, and *galestro*, a flaky, layered, light-colored marl. Altitudes also vary, though most vineyards are high, between 810 and 1,640 feet (250 to 500 meters) above sea level. Communes like Radda, which were once seen as too high and cool for Sangiovese, are now yielding elegant interpretations of the red wine. A descendent of sharecroppers who worked the land under the *mezzadria* system, Angela Fronti makes single-vineyard Chianti Classico from the family's separate plots in Radda and Gaiole, often harvesting in late October because of the cool climate and high altitude. Fronti's mouthwatering Chianti Classico is brimming with Sangiovese's classic sour cherry–herbal characteristics, yielding a wine that tastes satisfying in the moment but can also age elegantly.

The greater Chianti area stretches all the way to near Livorno at the coast and Arezzo to the east, though it's best in Rufina, an area directly east of Florence that was recognized for quality by Cosimo III the same year he bestowed praise on Chianti. Chianti Rufina is close to the Apennines and gets more mountain breezes than other Chianti areas. Northeast of Florence, the Carmignano DOCG was once a former vacation spot for the de' Medicis. It is one of the few areas in the region that has a long tradition of growing international grapes. There, *uva francesca* means Cabernet Sauvignon, inspired by the legend that Caterina de' Medici brought the grape variety here from France. Blending Cabernet Sauvignon or Cabernet Franc with Sangiovese has long been the tradition here, and the wines are somewhat rounder than Chianti Classico.

South of Chianti Classico is the Brunello di Montalcino zone, which has always made pure Sangiovese wines, both Brunello di Montalcino and Rosso di Montalcino, a wine made for drinking younger. Compared to Chianti, Montalcino's global success has been recent. In the 1930s there was only a handful of Brunello wines as Tancredi Biondi Santi continued the Sangiovese research started by his grandfather. The family had identified the best vines within their Il Greppo vineyard and studied how well they grafted after phylloxera. The work gave rise to 100 percent Sangiovese wine from the Brunello Biondi Santi clone, and the reputation for the wine grew after World War II. By 1980, Brunello di Montalcino became the first DOCG in Italy. It soon gained a reputation for broader, bigger Sangiovese, though much depends on the style and specific site.

Part of the success of Montalcino may have come from avoiding all the branding misfires between "Chianti" and "Chianti Classico," which have long made it hard to charge top dollar for top wines. Instead, Montalcino's challenge has been handling its explosive growth from a handful of estates to hundreds. The zone also has endured scandal: "Brunellopoli," called "Brunellogate" in America, surfaced in 2008 when some producers were suspected of adding grapes other than Sangiovese to their wine, prompting the US to block imports from the zone until the matter was sorted out. There have been other fake Brunello and Rosso di Montalcino busts over the years as well, and no one would try so hard if the wines weren't so sought-after. There is also stellar quality to be had. Laura Brunelli worked with her late husband Gianni Brunelli on an old family property called Le Chiuse di Sotto in the northeast of Montalcino. The property is 12 acres

(5 hectares), but only 5 acres (2 hectares) are for Sangiovese; the rest of the land is planted with olive trees. The result is a ruby-red wine with distinct red-fruit flavor coupled with earthy, almost minty backnotes. In the late 1970s, the husband-wife duo also founded Osteria Le Logge, which became known for elegant food and wine experiences.

East of Montalcino, the hill town of Montepulciano makes Vino Nobile di Montepulciano, and like Brunello, a *rosso*, a younger red wine. Once home to the Etruscans, Montepulciano has a history that goes back to AD 790, when a vineyard was registered to a church. The wine maintained a high reputation through the Middle Ages and after, even earning a mention in Voltaire's satire *Candide*. Montepulciano's Vino Nobile wines need to include only 70 percent Sangiovese, and the zone has been slow at reducing the amount of Cabernet or Merlot that is blended in. Between variations in soils, altitude, and grapes in the blend, the styles can vary from soft to tannic, with some carrying slightly rustic, balsamic notes. (To be clear, Vino Nobile di Montepulciano does not include the Montepulciano grape, which grows in Abruzzo, page 33.) The town also makes one of the region's most memorable Vin Santos. While the sherry-like wine can be found all over Tuscany, it reaches its deepest, sweetest flavors in Avignonesi's rare "Occhio di Pernice" Vin Santo, which is made with Sangiovese. The pressed juices of partially dried grapes are fermented in small barrels and aged for eight years before bottling.

While international grapes are losing steam in Chianti, Bordeaux varieties are here to stay on Tuscany's coast. The Maremma cuts a generous swath along the Tyrrhenian Sea starting north of the border with Lazio up to near the village of Bolgheri. While Sangiovese grows here—there's Morellino di Scansano DOCG, which requires 85 percent of the grape, and the Montecucco DOCG, which requires 90 percent—the maritime climate is better suited for Ciliegiolo. Along the Via Aurelia, the original Roman road that traces the coast to France, the soils tend to be sandy, yielding softer red wines, though prime spots, like Sassicaia's vineyards, were snatched up in the Super Tuscan boom and planted with French grapes.

Not all wines on the coast are red. The island of Elba is best known for Ansonica, the same grape called Inzolia on Sicily. Here, producer Bibi Graetz makes two wines with the grape: one aged in oak and another aged in cement. Both are floral, with stone fruits and crisp, green apple. Sharing the border with Liguria, the Colli di Luni DOC makes a saline, mineral-rich Vermentino, the kind to drink along with seafood.

And for that, you can't do much better than venturing back toward Bolgheri and stopping in Marina di Bibbona, a beach town in the Maremma. Wooden signs guide you through a campsite and coastal pine trees to La Pineta, a Michelin-starred restaurant right on the beach. On one visit, we ate fried shrimp as small as the tine of a fork, squid-ink gnocchi topped with fried baby artichokes, sea urchin, and local raw fish. In contrast with characteristic Tuscan austerity—where bread is made without salt—we feasted on the coastal abundance with glasses of briny Vermentino.

Winemaker Angela Fronti of Istine in Chianti Classico.

Tuscany Grapes

Only 10 percent of Tuscan wine is white, and most of it is either Vermentino from along the coast, Vernaccia di San Gimignano inland, or Trebbiano Toscano made under the Toscana IGT designation. Most Tuscan reds are marked by tart red fruits and savory, herbal flavors. Even the Bordeaux grapes that grow here, like Cabernet Sauvignon and Merlot, gain a similar savory quality.

White

Ansonica
(see Inzolia, Sicily chapter, page 196)

Trebbiano Toscano
This grape is one of Italy's most planted white varieties, but it has also long been overdue for a makeover. Any time a central Italian white wine is rediscovered—such as Trebbiano d'Abruzzo—the culprit behind the wine's reputation for inferior quality is this grape. In the case of Trebbiano d'Abruzzo, winemakers used Trebbiano Toscano instead of Trebbiano Abruzzese (page 40) to make the white wine until more people realized that the Abruzzese variety was superior. Even with an unfavorable reputation, Trebbiano Toscano is still one of the most common white grapes in Italy. Part of the reason is that it is easy to grow, supplying reliably high yields. And there seems to be more to the grape in certain places. The Monteraponi estate in Chianti Classico makes "Colli della Toscana Centrale," a wine that involves macerating Trebbiano Toscano on its skins for two days, then aging it for several months in oak to make a honey-colored wine with savory, lemon, and almond accents. Famed Trentino winemaker Elisabetta Foradori, who brought Teroldego (page 216) back from obscurity, started Ampeleia, a project on the Tuscan coast that works with the grape. "Ampeleia Bianco" is an orange wine made with a local biotype of Trebbiano Toscano, as well as a couple of other varieties. But the best case for Trebbiano Toscano's existence comes from the role it plays in making Vin Santo, Tuscany's classic, sherry-like meditation wine.

Verdea
(see Lombardy chapter, page 127)

Vermentino
(see Liguria chapter, page 119)

Vernaccia di San Gimignano
First, some clarification: there are different grapes in Italy named Vernaccia but it doesn't mean they are related. In modern times—with some notable exceptions—Vernaccia di San Gimignano has been relegated to simple tourist-wine status, and little else was expected of it. Yet this belies the grape's long history of being prized as one of the great wines of the region. In the Middle Ages, when the grape's reputation was established, its unique tannic skins may have helped preserve the wine, enabling it to be transported over distance. In our era of modern winemaking, the same grape makes light, crisp, refreshing wines, with citrusy notes of lemon zest, almond, sage, and thyme. Deeper versions come from Panizzi, whose wines are aged in oak, and Montenidoli, whose Vernaccia di San Gimignano sees skin contact, especially its "Tradizionale," which is a deep, savory interpretation that sheds light on why this grape was so heralded in the past.

Red

Aleatico
(see Lazio chapter, page 100)

Canaiolo
Sangiovese doesn't always show its best side on its own, which is why it's traditionally been blended with other grapes. Before winemakers started experimenting with adding Merlot and Cabernet Sauvignon to Chianti Classico, they would turn to grapes like Canaiolo. This native grape is a classic

match with Sangiovese, complementing its bright red-fruit crunch and adding softness and a subtle fennel note to draw out Sangiovese's floral side. It's rare to find the grape on its own, though along the coast, the producer Terenzuola makes "La Merla della Miniera," which is mostly Canaiolo, revealing a smooth, earthy wine that goes down easily.

Ciliegiolo

Even though Ciliegiolo historically was relegated to the role of a blending grape in Chianti, it is finally coming into its own. For those looking for a Sangiovese-like wine to serve slightly chilled, Ciliegiolo is hard to beat. According to DNA analysis, Ciliegiolo and Sangiovese are close relatives. It's unclear which came first, but the two share a common bond in crunchy red-fruit flavors underlined with wild herbs. The two grapes even look similar in the field. By Lake Bolsena in Lazio, a farmer might sell you what he thinks is Sangiovese but is actually Ciliegiolo. The difference comes down to adaptability when growing the vines. Ciliegiolo is more easygoing. Like Sangiovese, it grows well at altitude, but it also can be grown along the warm, dry coast, which is more of a challenge for Sangiovese. Antonio Camillo paved the way for showing how well Ciliegiolo performs in the Maremma, growing it in limestone bedrock with clay topsoil. There, the wines carry Ciliegiolio's signature sour-cherry flavor in a well-rounded wine. The variety is also a standout in Narni, an ancient town in southern Umbria. There, Leonardo Bussoletti has been coaxing out Ciliegiolo's cherry-herbal nuances for years.

Colorino

Colorino is not a single grape but rather a group of unrelated grapes that are used for the same reason: to give wine a deeper color. Since Sangiovese does not have as much color as a grape like Montepulciano from Abruzzo or Aglianico from Campania, Colorino grapes were useful in small doses to boost the overall hue and make the wine more attractive. The most Tuscan of the Colorinos is Colorino del Valdarno, which makes inky, blackberry-blueberry wines. Only a couple of producers vinify pure Colorino under the Toscana IGT label, making them quite rare. One worth seeking out is Montenidoli's Colorino—maybe it's no surprise that the estate that makes some of the best Vernaccia di San Gimignano wines also has found a way to work with another (often overlooked) local grape.

Sangiovese

There are a lot of synonyms for the grape: Morellino on the coast, Brunello in Montalcino, and Prugnolo Gentile in Montepulciano. Today, Sangiovese remains one of Italy's most important native grapes and one of the most misunderstood. The confusion comes from finding wines on the shelf that are near purple in color and rich in body—neither of which are characteristics of Sangiovese. In the 1990s, the wines that received the most attention were big, bold Napa Cabs and Veneto Amarone. Sangiovese didn't fit the mold, but in some cases, it was forced to be bigger than it was. Today, this direction has been reversed, and Sangiovese is being celebrated for its high acidity and signature notes of sour cherry and Mediterranean herbs. While plenty of it grows along the warmer coast, it does much better in places where the day–night temperature swings are more pronounced and the soils are poor, making the vines struggle. This is why the hills of Chianti Classico are so well suited for the grape. Even so, Sangiovese is planted all over central Italy, with varying levels of success. On the Adriatic side of the Apennines, it tends to be broader and slightly rounder. In the hills of Romagna, it's being planted on steeper hillsides instead of the plains, which has improved the quality of Romagna Sangiovese significantly. In Le Marche, it can be blended with Montepulciano, the main grape of Abruzzo for the wines of Rosso Cònero and Rosso Piceno. And in Umbria, it's key in many of the reds, including Montefalco Rosso.

Regional Foods

Beans

Bistecca alla fiorentina
Florentine steak seared and
cooked rare

Cacciucco
seafood soup from the coast

Castagnaccio
chestnut-flour cake

Cavolo nero
Tuscan kale

Cinghiale
wild boar, often braised or
turned into sausages

Lardo
cured pork lard

Olive oil

Olives

Pane toscano
Tuscan bread, which is made
without salt

Panforte
a bread made of nuts, dried
fruits, and cocoa made around
the winter holidays

Panzanella
bread salad

Pappa al pomodoro
tomato and Tuscan bread soup

Pasta
pici, hand-rolled spaghetti-
style pasta

tortelli di patate, pasta stuffed
with potato

Pecorino cheese

Ribollita
a thick soup whose name means
"reboiled"

Ricciarelli
flourless almond cookies

Recommended Producers

Chianti Classico

Badia a Coltibuono

Barone Ricasoli

Bindi Sergardi

Brancaia

Calcinaia

Castell'in Villa

Castello di Albola

Castello di Ama

Castello Volpaia

Dievole

Felsina

Fonterutoli

Fontodi

Il Palagio

Istine

Lamole di Lamole

Le Cinciole

Le Ragnaie

Monte Bernardi

Monteraponi

Montevertine

Riecine

Rocca delle Macie

San Felice

Sette Ponti

Tolaini

Val delle Corti

Montalcino

Altesino

Canalicchio di Sopra

Capanna

Casanova di Neri

Cerbaiona

Col d'Orcia

Corte Dei Venti

Fattoria dei Barbi

Gianni Brunelli

La Fortuna

Le Chiuse

Le Macioche

Poggio Antico

Poggerino

Poggio di Sotto

Romitorio

Salicutti

Salvioni

Stella di Campalto

Uccelliera

Valdicava

Montepulciano

Avignonesi

Boscarelli

Cantine Dei

Fattoria del Cerro

Figli d'Italia Leone d'Oro

Icario

La Bèrne

Maria Caterina Dei

Poliziano

Salcheto

Tenute del Cerro

Maremma, including Bolgheri

Antinori

Antonio Camillo

Argentiera

Ca' Marcanda

Duemani

Grattamacco

Isole e Olena

Le Macchiole

Ornellaia

Petra

Poggio al Tesoro

Rocca di Frassinello

Sapaio

Tenuta San Guido

Carmignano

Le Farnete/Cantagallo

Piaggia

Montecucco

ColleMassari

Parmoleto

Pianirossi

Morellino

Bruni

Le Pupille

Terenzi

Vignaioli di Morellino di Scansano

Pisa, Lucca, and Elba

Bibi Graetz

Ghizzano

Pieve Santo Stefano

Sardi

San Gimignano

Fontaleoni

Montenidoli

Palagetto

Panizzi

Teruzzi

Vermentino

San Ferdinando

Guado al Tasso

Vin Santo

Avignonesi

Capezzana

Il Borro

Torre a Cona

Umbria

At a restaurant between Spoleto and Norcia, the tagliatelle we ordered came with so many truffles, we wondered if there had been a mistake—had we planned on paying for an upgrade? But the quantity was intentional. Truffles, we learned, are valuable in Umbria but not precious. Armed with a trowel and a pocketful of dog treats, Umbrian truffle hunters walk to their favorite spots, encouraging pups to sniff around the *pianello*, the grassless ring around the base of an oak or hazel tree. From September to December, hunters go after rare white truffles. Come January, they seek out black truffles, which grow small in frozen ground. Between April and May, it's difficult to find any truffles at all, but by June, summer truffles emerge. These are larger and more aromatic than black and white varieties, though with less concentrated flavor, making them better for cooking. At the restaurant, chunks of summer truffles coated our fresh pasta strands, which we ate alongside glasses of Montefalco Rosso.

Truffles mirror Umbria's earthy personality. This is Italy's *cuore verde*, its green heart. The region's biggest celebrity is Saint Francis of Assisi, the patron saint of ecology. Umbria's Deruta ceramics are made from local clay. And its best wines are grounded in their environment. In the west, there's

Orvieto, where rivers encourage *muffa nobile*, botrytis, to form on grapes, shriveling them to make dessert wines with glycerin sweetness. In the center, Trebbiano Spoletino vines are "married" to trees. No one has quite figured out why the *viti maritate* vines yield better grapes than when vines grow alone, but the practice and research continue. And then there is all that red wine, from refreshing Ciliegiolo to tannic Sagrantino.

Shaped like an anatomic heart, Umbria borders Le Marche to the north and touches Tuscany and Lazio to the west and south. Its annual wine output is modest, about 17 million gallons (644,000 hectoliters) a year, ranking it fourteenth among Italian regions, less than Le Marche but more than Sardinia. A quarter of the region is mountainous, especially in the east along the Apennines, while most of the rest is hilly. It's a well-traveled place, easy to reach by train or car from almost all directions, its hill towns filled with Renaissance artifacts and surrounded by vines and olive trees—everything you could want from an Italian vacation. But while Umbria gets tourists, it never feels overwhelmed by them. Umbrians are more insular in personality than Tuscans or Romans, and the wines are also uniquely Umbrian: while one of the region's main grapes, Sangiovese, is grown throughout central Italy, two of Umbria's most interesting grapes, Trebbiano Spoletino and Sagrantino, aren't grown anywhere else.

Umbria also stands apart because it is so green. Long after the coastal hills in Tuscany and Lazio have dried out, the lakes, rivers, and deep underground water reserves keep Umbria lush. The Tiber River divides Umbria from north to south and is fed by the Nera River and other tributaries. Frequent rains give rise to mushrooms and truffles in forests, while farmland grows everything from beans and greens to farro and lentils. There are also regional specialties, like the tiny lentils of Castelluccio di Norcia, a mountain hamlet on the far east border of Umbria near Le Marche. Norcia, the larger town down the road from Castelluccio, is central to Umbria's culinary heritage. Butchers from Norcia have been recognized for their skills since the Middle Ages. (*Norcino* means "butcher" in Italian.) The town is even better known for guanciale, sausages, salumi, and prosciutto. All over Umbria, pork is celebrated as an essential ingredient. In the center of the region, the town of San Terenziano hosts Porchettiamo, an annual festival celebrating porchetta. Chefs and butchers from all over Italy come to roast whole pigs (or just the midsection) rolled in herbs, garlic, and fennel, cooking them slowly until the skin crisps. And all these earthy flavors are natural partners with wines like Grechetto from Todi and Orvieto, Ciliegiolo from Nari, Trebbiano Spoletino and Sagrantino from Montefalco, or Sangiovese from just about everywhere in the region.

History

Umbria is named for the ancient Umbri people, who inhabited the area before the Etruscans arrived and pushed the Umbri to the east bank of the Tiber River. Neither the Umbri nor the Etruscans could defeat the Romans, and by 272 BC, Rome had control of the territory. They constructed the Via Flaminia, a road running from Umbria to the Adriatic Sea, which became an essential route through the Apennines. After the fall of Rome, Umbria's territory was divided in messy conflicts between the Lombards, Byzantines, popes, and city-states. Umbria then became part of the dysfunctional Papal States until Italy's unification in the nineteenth century. In this way, Umbria has more in common with Le Marche, Lazio, and Romagna—other former territories of the Papal States—than it does with Tuscany, even though the two neighbors are often compared for their hill towns, olive and cypress trees, and vineyards.

Before the Romans conquered their territory, the Etruscans grew grapes up trees along the shores of Lake Trasimeno, the largest Italian lake south of the Po River, and employed sophisticated winemaking practices in the town of Orvieto. The town's bedrock is volcanic tuff, a soft stone that the Etruscans bore into, building gravity-fed wine cellars. These multilayered cellars allowed them to crush grapes on the top (ground) level, let the juices pass to a lower level where they fermented at cooler temperatures, and transfer them one more floor down to age in an even cooler environment. Centuries later, Orvieto became a vacation destination for popes and other dignitaries, and its golden, sweet wines were praised for their quality. The Church's fondness for Orvieto also helps explain why the town has such an ornate cathedral, which took four hundred years to build, and features frescoes painted by Umbrian artist Luca Signorelli. Today, it's a tourist attraction, a day trip by train from Rome.

Orvieto was famous for quality white wines until after World War II. In the second half of the twentieth century, wineries began incorporating new technology, exchanging old barrels for stainless steel vats, and even introducing a pasteurization step to stabilize the bottles for transport. (Similar changes happened in Lazio, especially in the wines of Frascati and Est! Est!! Est!!! di Montefiascone.) Though the wines were stable for shipping, they were also bland, prompting experts to question the quality of local grapes. The solution, for a time, was to plant international grapes. Tuscan Piero Antinori bought the Orvieto estate Castello della Sala and hired

Giampiero Bea's father, Paolo Bea, the family winery's namesake.

consulting enologist Renzo Cotarella, who developed "Cervaro della Sala," a Chardonnay blended with Grechetto. The wine became so popular that many believed the only way to make quality wine in the area was to blend in foreign varieties.

Across the border in northern Lazio, Sergio Mottura was an exception, dedicating much of his namesake estate to experimenting with Grechetto. (Umbria grows two Grechetto varieties; see page 241.) The estate now makes three Grechetto wines: "Poggio della Costa," "Latour a Civitella," and "Muffo," a sweet wine made from Grechetto grapes affected by botrytis.

While white wines have a longer legacy in Umbria, red wine has commanded the most attention recently, especially those made with Sagrantino grapes. In 1971, Arnaldo Caprai bought a vineyard in the town of Montefalco that grew Sagrantino and later turned it over to his son, Marco. In the 1990s, Marco went all in with Sagrantino, bringing in consultant Attilio Pagli and experimenting with rootstocks, clones, vine-training systems, and winemaking to learn how to handle the tannic grape. Caprai then evangelized Sagrantino abroad, where it gained favor for being a big, bold red in a time when big wines were favored by influential critics. Interest in Sagrantino soon developed among wine families from other regions, like the Lunellis of Ferrari in Trento, who bought land in Umbria to grow Sagrantino. Today, the Arnaldo Caprai estate is ten times the size it was in 1993, the year it released its "25 Anni," marking its twenty-fifth anniversary.

Throughout Umbria's modern wine history, international grapes have also crept into local wines. Cabernet and Merlot are the most planted non-native grapes, sometimes blended with Sagrantino to soften its sharp edges or with Sangiovese for modern, international styles. Yet the future seems to lie in native grapes like Sagrantino, Grechetto and the other local whites of Orvieto, and Trebbiano Spoletino, a grape that still grows up trees around Montefalco, just like the Etruscans would have done.

Land and Wines

With only two provinces—Terni to the southwest and Perugia covering everything else—Umbria is a small region, with under a million residents. Slightly more of the wine made here is red, and most of the red comes from Sangiovese. (Montefalco Rosso, a blend of Sangiovese with some Sagrantino, can be outstanding.) Grechetto is Umbria's mainstay white, though Trebbiano Spoletino is gaining more attention, especially among those who love wines made with Trebbiano Abruzzese grapes from Abruzzo (see page 40). As one of the few Italian regions without a coastline, Umbria has a continental climate, with cold winters and hot summers tempered by lakes and rivers. It has a broad range of soils, including sandstone, alluvial (river-based), clay, and calcareous. While volcanic soils around Lake Bolsena, a crater lake in Lazio, influence some wines from Orvieto, most of Umbria's vineyards are not volcanic.

On the west side of Umbria near the Paglia River is Orvieto, an area known for its unstable bedrock. In 1977, a landslide filled in some of Orvieto's ancient caves. By the 1990s, sinkholes swallowed buses and houses, and the government has since spent millions shoring up the cliffs. Yet it's the unique mix of soils and climate that brings character to its white grapes. The area is also one of the most ideal parts of Italy to make sweet wines from botrytized grapes. Morning fog forms in the hills and valleys near where the Tiber and Paglia Rivers and Lake Corbara connect, delivering moisture to encourage the botrytis fungus to take hold, while the afternoon sun dries the area, keeping out undesirable molds. It's here where Niccolò Barberani and his family leverage the area's microclimate to make their Orvieto dessert wine, "Calcaia."

North of Orvieto on the west side of the Paglia River, the soils are softer and sandy, while the east side has more clay. Giovanni Dubini of Palazzone has made wine here since the 1980s, proving that Orvieto bottles can age with grace. The winery's "Musco" is made without electricity: Procanico,

Verdello, and Malvasia grapes are macerated on their skins in open chestnut barrels and then fermented with native yeasts before aging in a cave. The result is a deep-golden wine, a tribute to Orvieto's past. White wines are also important in the town of Todi, a medieval hill town connected to Orvieto by a scenic road that runs through the upper Tiber Valley. The main grape is Grechetto di Todi, a thick-skinned grape known as Pignoletto in Emilia-Romagna.

Apart from Orvieto and Todi, Umbria is better known for red wines. South of Perugia, the late Giorgio Lungarotti's estate was once the only commercial winery in Torgiano, a medieval town. Today it's home to wine and olive oil museums established by Lungarotti's wife, art historian Maria Grazia Marchetti. Lungarotti's signature wine style leans on blending: "Vigna Monticchio" combines Sangiovese and Canaiolo from a single vineyard; "Rubesco" mirrors Chianti's old recipe with Sangiovese, Canaiolo, and Trebbiano added to the mix; and "Torre di Giano" combines Trebbiano and Grechetto. West of Perugia near Tuscany, Lake Trasimeno's vineyards grow a grape called Trasimeno Gamay, which is likely Garnacha (Grenache). To the south around Narni and Amelia, winemakers like Leonardo Bussoletti make lively wines with laid-back tannins with Ciliegiolo. East of Narni along the foothills of the Apennines, the Mattioli family of Collecapretta (meaning "hill of goats") grows Ciliegiolo biodynamically, making a tiny amount of rich, savory *rosato* and red wine with tangy notes of strawberries and red currants.

Then there's Sagrantino, the famous red of Montefalco, a fourteenth-century town between Narni and Perugia. The town has views for miles across the Spoleto Valley, with Trevi to the east and Assisi to the north. As one of Italy's most tannic wines, Sagrantino is not for everyone. For those looking for something gentler, the answer is Montefalco Rosso. Made of a blend of Sangiovese with 10 to 15 percent Sagrantino, it's a savory food-friendly red. Some winemakers have played around with blending Sagrantino even further, like Andrea Trulli of La Pianate. His wine "Un Paio" handles Sagrantino with a lighter hand, macerating the grapes for less time

and blending them with Merlot and Sangiovese. The result speaks of forest and earth, a blackberry-cherry blend. Another historic producer from Montefalco, Scacciadiavoli—meaning "banish the devils"—is named after an exorcism that dates to the fourteenth century and describes a possessed woman made to drink the wine to expel the devil.

Trebbiano Spoletino is the other side of Montefalco's wine image, one focused on a local white grape that was nearly lost. Giampiero Bea's family has lived in Montefalco since at least Renaissance times. The Beas have always made wine, though it wasn't sold widely until recently. An architect by training, Giampiero focuses on maintaining the identity of the place in his wines. The family keeps animals on the property, grows vegetables, and makes olive oil. His Trebbiano Spoletino grows on land where pre-phylloxera vines are trained up trees on the edge of a flat field. (In the 1990s, locals started cutting these trees down for firewood, so he rented the land to save the old vines.) The Trebbiano Spoletino vines have since proven remarkable. While older vines often produce less fruit, these vines maintain high yields. And although viticulture training teaches that high yields mean diluted grapes and inferior wines, the opposite happens with Trebbiano Spoletino. Perhaps there's something to the sturdy and deep root structure and symbiotic relationship with the tree that somehow delivers more depth and acidity to the grapes than if they grew in a more conventional way. Giampiero has tried growing Trebbiano Spoletino without trees, even building a man-made structure to simulate a tree, but nothing seems to deliver the same results. He's found that the grape takes well to skin-contact wines and makes "Arboreus," an intense amber wine.

Umbria is all about the unexpected richness of those old vines, the pasta showered with truffles, and even the handmade pottery. It's a place that looks tame and traditional at first glance, but look in the trees or dig into the ground, and you'll find plenty more under the surface.

Winemaker Giampiero Bea in his cellar.

Umbria Grapes

Umbria is best-known for Grechetto and Sagrantino, but its Ciliegiolo and Trebbiano Spoletino wines show the region's breadth in styles.

White

Grechetto Group

Even though they share a name, Umbria's popular Grechetto grapes aren't related. According to Italian wine expert Ian D'Agata, one of the differences between the two is that Grechetto di Todi has thicker skins and yields more tannic wines than Grechetto di Orvieto. But because both have been grown and blended together for so long, it's hard to tell exactly which Grechetto may be in your glass. Based in northeastern Lazio, winemaker Sergio Mottura is most associated with Grechetto from both Lazio and Umbria. The estate has been singling out Grechetto as a standalone wine for years, and its "Poggio della Costa" is among the most lauded Grechettos in Italy. Grown in volcanic soil and aged in stainless steel, it's a rich, golden wine with notes of white flowers and citrus zest.

- **Grechetto di Orvieto:** Most often blended with other white grapes, it can be hard to find pure Grechetto di Orvieto. It tends to be light in texture with simple, fresh flavors of yellow apple, pear, chamomile, and sometimes almond. It is also the key grape in the historic late-harvest wines of Orvieto; the moisture from Lake Bolsena and the Paglia and Tiber Rivers makes the area one of the best places in Italy for botrytis-affected sweet wines.

- **Grechetto di Todi (Pignoletto):** The grape most associated with the town of Todi in central Umbria, Grechetto di Todi grows in soils rich in limestone and clay (like it does in the hills around Bologna), yielding white wines

with a mineral finish. Cantina Roccafiore makes a fresh, mouthwatering 100 percent Grechetto di Todi with notes of white flowers, citrus, and apple. (For more, see Pignoletto, page 73.)

Trebbiano Spoletino

Originally from the medieval town of Spoleto, the vine has come into its own in Montefalco, where producers like Cantina Novelli, Tabarrini, and Paolo Bea have preserved pre-phylloxera vines growing up trees along the perimeter of farms. These *viti maritate* (married vines) produce a lot more grapes than a standard vine, but the yields don't hinder quality. Giampiero Bea wonders whether there's some sort of symbiotic relationship between the vine and the tree that makes both grow better. Experiments planting grafted Spoletino vines along hillsides haven't yielded the same result. The challenge is ensuring winemakers are working with actual Trebbiano Spoletino grapes. As with Abruzzo's Trebbiano Abruzzese, which for years was confused with Bombino Bianco and Trebbiano Toscano, it's likely that many growers who think they have Trebbiano Spoletino are growing something else. Golden in color, the grape can make wines with everything from crisp, citrus notes to deep, umami richness, like Paolo Bea's "Arboreus."

Other Orvieto White Grapes: Verdello, Drupeggio, and Procanico

While Grechetto (left) and Trebbiano Toscano (page 230) make up most of Orvieto wines, other grapes are also used, especially Verdello, Drupeggio, and/or one of the Malvasias. Verdello is a high-acid grape that offers bright notes of citrus and green apple to a blend. Drupeggio may be a synonym for Canaiolo Bianco, the white version of red grape Canaiolo (page 230). Procanico is likely a higher-quality biotype of Trebbiano Toscano. As a blend, Orvieto Bianco is thirst quenching, though some can be more complex, especially from producers such as Palazzone, Sergio Mottura, and Barberani.

Red

Canaiolo
(see Tuscany chapter, page 230)

Ciliegiolo
(see Tuscany chapter, page 231)

Gamay del Trasimeno

The local name for Garnacha/Grenache (and not Gamay), this grape has grown around Lake Trasimeno for decades. In the red Trasimeno DOC wines, Gamay del Trasimeno is blended with Ciliegiolo, Sangiovese, Merlot, or Cabernet Sauvignon, though some producers go all in with Gamay del Trasimeno.

The Madrevite estate makes three 100 percent Gamay del Trasimeno wines, including a fruit-forward red called "Opra," with notes of cherry, red plum, and Mediterranean herbs; a deeper, richer version called "C'osa," which comes from grapes harvested later in the year; and a *rosato* called "La Bisbetica," which is filled with notes of cherry and strawberry.

The small co-op Duca della Corgna also makes a range of wines with the grape, from juicy, herbal versions with notes of tart red cherry and raspberry to more austere renditions.

Sagrantino

Brawny, tannic, teeth-staining, "a beast." All these words could describe wines made with Sagrantino grapes. The flagship red variety of Montefalco, Sagrantino came of age in the 1990s and early '00s, when red wine was in its "go big or go home" phase. With its ample sugars, tannins, and polyphenols, Sagrantino gained a reputation as the most muscular red wine in Italy.

No one knows exactly how it came to be grown in Montefalco, but for most of its history, it was made into an entirely different wine. In Robert Camuto's book *South of Somewhere*, he explains that traditional Sagrantino wines were sweet, made from air-dried grapes, and reserved for important people such as the doctor, mayor, or priest.

In 1977, the Montefalco Sagrantino DOC was created for this sweet style. Two years later, the Adanti estate was the first to make a dry Sagrantino. (Today, sweet and dry Montelfalco Sagrantinos are DOCG wines.)

While this grape develops sugar easily, it needs a good amount of heat for its tannins to ripen. The trickiest part for winemakers is determining the right moment to harvest the grapes: when the tannins are ready but before the grapes have too much sugar. No matter what, though, these are big wines, and the best are an inky wash of black plums, blackberries, iron, and leather, all underlined by tannic grip.

Sangiovese
(see Tuscany chapter, page 231)

Trees and Trebbiano Spoletino vines grown together.

Tending Sagrantino vines at the Paolo Bea winery.

Regional Foods

Beans

Cheese
caciotta, sheep's milk cheese

goat cheese

Chocolate
Perugia is the hometown of the Perugina company, maker of Baci chocolates

Farro

Green vegetables
such as peas, nettles, fennel, and artichokes

Lentils
especially from Castelluccio di Norcia

Olive oil

Pasta
ciriole ternana, thick noodles

strascinati, flat noodles

umbricelli, long, thick noodles (though not as thick as *ciriole ternana*)

Pork
including cured products like guanciale, pancetta, and salumi

Porchetta

Tegamaccio
tomato fish soup from Trasimeno, made with eel or freshwater fish

Torta al testo d'la Maria
unleavened focaccia bread griddled on a pan and filled with sausage, cured meats, cheese, and/or herbs

Truffles

Recommended Producers

Adanti

Ajola

Alfredosa

Annesanti

Antigniano

Antonelli

Arnaldo Caprai

Barberani

Cantina Novelli

Collecapretta

Còlpetrone

Decugnano dei Barbi

Di Filippo

Fongoli

Fratelli Pardi

Goretti

I Vini di Giovanni

Leonardo Bussoletti

Le Pianate

Lungarotti

Madrevite

Milziade Antano

Moretti Omero

Napolini

Palazzone

Paolo Bea

Perticaia

Raína

Roccafiore

Romanelli

Scacciadiavoli

Sergio Mottura

Tabarrini

Valle d'Aosta

The spring of 2017 was a bad one for Valle d'Aosta winemakers. For three days, the temperature dropped well below freezing, killing new growth and affecting the entire crop of Prié Blanc. That meant no 2017 vintage for the Cave Mont Blanc de Morgex et La Salle co-op, since it only makes wine with Prié Blanc. But that wasn't the worst of it. Nicola Del Negro, winemaker at Cave Mont Blanc, had been growing Roussin de Morgex vines as an experiment. The rare grape's origin is a mystery, though it is likely part of the Prié Blanc family. With pale pink skins and piercing acidity, it's Prié wearing rose-tinted glasses. Years ago, the co-op experimented with Roussin de Morgex, but the winemaker at the time didn't think it had potential. Later, Ian D'Agata, wine writer and Italian native grape expert, insisted it was worth a second look.

D'Agata's fascination with the grape started in the 1980s when a photo of the vine in an old wine book caught his attention because of its unusually jagged leaves and pale-pink grapes. When Del Negro became Cave Mont Blanc's winemaker, D'Agata asked if he'd give Roussin de Morgex another try. Del Negro agreed, first asking co-op members to search for any rogue vines in their Prié vineyards. Of the sixty members, six found Roussin de Morgex.

Between samples from the growers and from a vineyard at the local agricultural school, Del Negro had enough for an experimental vineyard. In 2012, he made tiny batches of wine from the grapes. As a red, it left something to be desired—it was too light in color and way too acidic. But as a sparkling wine, its brightness and delicate rose color showed potential. D'Agata wrote in his 2014 book, *Native Wine Grapes of Italy*, that the wine had "fragrant aromas of wild strawberry, almond flowers, and fresh mountain herbs." The hope was that the co-op would soon offer tastes to visitors at the winery. Then the 2017 frost killed the vineyard and brought Roussin de Morgex to the brink of extinction.

Del Negro, who grew up down the road in Saint-Pierre, is no stranger to the meteorological drama that unfolds amid Europe's highest vineyards. Everything about making wine in Valle d'Aosta is extreme. The sun is intense during the day, but the nights are cold, and the weather shifts unexpectedly. Plus, the growing season is exceptionally short: snow can fall in April and the sun can reach extremes in July. Additionally, harvest starts in early fall to avoid snow. To withstand extremes, Prié vines are trained in a low pergola formation called *pergola bassa*, which keeps the plants closer to the stones of the vineyards' terraces. The stones absorb heat during the day, insulating vines from the cold at night. In most years, this keeps vineyards safe from frost damage, but the configuration demands backbreaking work to maintain and harvest grapes. Some vines are so low that workers nearly lie down to tend them. Italians call these conditions *viticoltura eroica*, heroic viticulture.

For as small and extreme as it is, Valle d'Aosta is rich in grape diversity. A mix of native, French, and Swiss varieties grow here at altitudes that range from 1,056 feet (321 meters) above sea level on the east side of the valley near the border with Piedmont all the way beyond 3,000 feet (915 meters) in the Alta Valle (High Valley), where the co-op is located. Up the road from the co-op's cellar is the ski town of Courmayeur, and past that is the great Mont Blanc ("Monte Bianco" in Italian) itself. While a visit to a Valle d'Aosta vineyard can take your breath away due to the sheer exertion required to hike up the mountain, the views are worth it, with snow-capped peaks above green hillsides that burst forth with wildflowers. The best Valle d'Aosta wines capture that environment in thirst-quenching glasses and brim with stone, grass, and flowers.

Cave Mont Blanc was not the only cellar affected by the 2017 frost. The wine output for the region, which usually amounts to only 554,761 gallons (21,000 hectoliters), was halved. Fortunately, the *valdostani* don't run from a setback. For many here, wine is a side gig to their day jobs as hiking guides, skiing instructors, dairy farmers, or gym teachers. Even Del Negro has a side hustle—making wines in Saint-Pierre with different vines, some of which are ninety years old. As for the aftermath of the frost, there is a happy ending. After a lot of careful pruning in 2018, the Prié Blanc vines are back to form, and Roussin de Morgex is getting another chance. In 2019, Del Negro replanted the experimental vineyard, and the plan is to make a special *metodo classico* wine (see Italy's Sparkling Wines, page 262) that honors the rare grape's survival.

History

The history of Valle d'Aosta is visible in the Roman walls throughout its main city, Aosta, and in the castles that once set watch over the valley. It is also echoed in the language. The House of Savoy controlled the territory before the unification of Italy, and a French-Provençal patois is still spoken among *valdostani*, a holdover from that reign.

As in Piedmont, Lombardy, and Liguria, winemaking in Valle d'Aosta predates Roman times. The Salassi, an ancient Celtic-Ligurian tribe, took up residence in the mountains, controlling the paths through the Alps. To grow vines, they built dry stone terraces along the steep mountainsides, setting up a tradition for winemaking that the Romans later took over in 25 BC, starting a colony that became present-day Aosta. Romans constructed an aqueduct that supplied Aosta with water while establishing a network of roads through the mountains.

Today, hikers can walk over the ancient Pont d'Aël, a bridge over a gorge built for the aqueduct. Some of the roads later morphed into part of the Via Francigena, the path Christian pilgrims took to get from northern Europe to Rome. After the fall of Rome, grape cultivation came under the domain of the Church, and monks continued the tradition for centuries. According to D'Agata, the Prié grape itself may have gotten its name from its use during Sunday Mass—*prier* meaning "to pray" in French. As in other parts of Europe where monks oversaw wine production, high standards endured through the Middle Ages and beyond.

After Italy's unification, Valle d'Aosta became part of Piedmont, only gaining autonomy as an independent region after World War II. Now it's one of a handful of autonomous Italian regions, which are allowed a greater degree of self-governance. (Other autonomous regions include Sicily, Sardinia, Trentino–Alto Adige, and Friuli Venezia Giulia.) Valle d'Aosta remains officially bilingual, and on wine bottles, its name is often spelled the French way, "Vallée d'Aoste." Italians from other regions feel as though they're in France when they visit Valle d'Asota while French sense they're in Italy. To the *valdostani*, though, this small corner of the Alps is uniquely their own.

In the twentieth century, Valle d'Aosta's vineyards went into decline for many of the same reasons that affected Alto Piemonte (page 139). War, bad weather, and vine disease all made it hard to continue making a living from the land, and many *valdostani* moved away to find work in bigger cities in Italy, France, or Switzerland. As vineyards were left alone, nature came in, diminishing the total area under vine in the region. Still, vintners in Valle d'Aosta have long had a hard time piecing together enough land for commercial wine production. Family plots were historically small, with five rows here and there and a neighbor's vines in between.

To make grape growing a more viable business, co-ops that focused on specific grapes and styles began to form in the 1970s and '80s. In the northwestern corner of the Aosta Valley, it was Cave Mont Blanc growing Priè; on the eastern side of the valley, it was Donnas growing Nebbiolo (called Picotendro or Picotener). In the town of Chambave, closer to the center, the co-op La Crotta di Vegneron reflects the range of grapes that grow in the center of the Aosta Valley. While it has 120 members, the co-op accounts for fewer than 100 acres (40 hectares) of land. Just like it did in the Middle Ages, the Church has had a hand in promoting quality winemaking in modern times. Joseph Vaudan, a priest, began working with local farmers in the mid-twentieth century, training them how to care for vines and make commercial wine. He became an early director of the Institut Agricole Régional, teaching a generation of winemakers the basics of cellar hygiene and quality control.

But by the end of the twentieth century, few bottles made it out of the region. Between tourists coming to ski or hike and the local population, there was barely enough to go around. A few producers did manage to reach the international market. The late Ezio Voyat drew attention to the region's wines in the 1960s with his Chambave Rouge, a jammy but toned red made with Petite Rouge grapes. Costantino

Charrère, founder of Les Crêtes, created alpine Chardonnay in a rich, lush style. The Grosjean family also began to export wines, and today, they make a range of wines with grapes including Fumin, Cornalin (a grape better known in Switzerland), and Prëmetta, the last of which is unusually light-skinned for a red grape, making pale wines that resemble *rosato*.

Many of these estates are now run by the second or third generation, ensuring that the region will continue to make great wines in small quantities for years to come.

Land and Wines

North of Piedmont and bordering Switzerland and France, Valle d'Aosta is Italy's smallest region by territory and wine production. Even without extreme weather, such as the 2017 frost, production here is limited by nature. Valle d'Aosta makes less than a third of the total production of the second-lowest-yielding region, Liguria. Framed by six of the highest peaks in the Alps, including Mont Blanc to the west and the Matterhorn to the northeast, this is true alpine terroir. To live here means to be at home in the mountains, and to make wine here requires the stamina of a mountaineer comfortable with extreme heights.

Like the Adda River, which influences the mountain wine region of Valtellina in Lombardy (page 127), the Dora Baltea River helps shape Valle d'Aosta's wines. Fed by runoff from Mont Blanc, it forms the base of a long, narrow valley that runs west to east through the region before eventually linking up to the Po. Most vineyard areas are found on the northern side, allowing for south-facing vineyards, while the southern side is less sunny and has fewer vineyards. Even with the cool alpine air, Valle d'Aosta makes more red wines than white, mainly from Petit Rouge.

Throughout the region, the soils reflect the presence of glaciers in the Alps, comprising a mix of glacial moraine, alluvial rocks, and sand. But the true difference lies in the altitude. The far west side of the region bordering Mont Blanc, known as the Alta Valle (High Valley), is the highest and has the coolest temperatures. Here, Prié Blanc grows for the Cave Mont Blanc co-op. East from there on the way to Aosta, the Enfer d'Arvier is another high-altitude growing zone of only 12 acres (5 hectares) known for red wine. The stony, south-facing vineyard gets extremely hot on sunny summer days. It is so hot, in fact, that "Enfer" means "hell" in French, a point producer Danilo Thomain emphasizes by putting cartoon devils on his labels. On the opposite end near Piedmont, in the Bassa Valle (Low Valley), the climate is warmer than the high valley. There, the Donnas co-op specializes in Nebbiolo. In the Media Valle (Middle Valley), the towns of Nus, Torrette, and Chambave are known mostly for medium-bodied reds. Among the red wine subzones, the Torrette DOC is the largest, made by blending Petite Rouge with a handful of other local grapes. While there are a few co-ops and producers that make a decent amount of wine, nearly everyone else makes tiny quantities, and nearly the only way to taste their bottles is to go to the region.

Compared with the rest of Italy, Valle d'Aosta feels like a world apart. Culturally it's always been different, more French- and Swiss-leaning than classic Italian. Due to its proximity to France and close cultural connections with France and Switzerland—from its time as part of the realm of the House of Savoy—Valle d'Aosta has success with many French grapes, from Pinot Nero, Syrah, and Gamay to Chardonnay and Pinot Grigio (called Malvoisie). But the most *valdostani* wines are the ones with grapes that don't grow anywhere else, like Prié Blanc, Prëmetta, and Fumin. Cared for with mountaineering grit, these grapes yield invigorating wines that speak to the pristine alpine countryside in which they grow.

Valle d'Aosta Grapes

Even among Italians, Valle d'Aosta wines can feel foreign, especially since many have French on their labels. Some of the grapes, too, are more French and Swiss in identity. While the white grapes are labeled as such, red wines, especially those from the Torrette DOC, are blends.

White

Moscato Bianco
(see Piedmont chapter, page 150)

Petite Arvine
This Swiss grape has been grown between Valle d'Aosta and Switzerland for centuries. Its small, compact bunches of grapes yield nervy and concentrated wines with notes of white flowers and citrus. When grown in the extreme vineyards of Valle d'Aosta, the grape gains mineral structure as well. Château Feuillet makes an intensely floral Petite Arvine with refreshing notes of grapefruit, while Elio Ottin's Petite Arvine is similarly floral with an intense color and a long, satisfying finish. With extended aging on the lees (the spent yeast cells from fermentation), the Grosjean family's Petite Arvine is structured and substantial, proof that some white wines are built to age.

Prié Blanc
The only grape grown for the Cave Mont Blanc de Morgex et La Salle co-op, Prié Blanc is an altitude-loving variety that thrives in the coldest terroir in Valle d'Aosta. It is also the grape of the Mont Blanc de Morgex et de La Salle subzone (so if you see "Blanc de Morgex et de La Salle" on a label, you know you're drinking a Prié Blanc wine). First documented in 1691 and once used to make wine for Mass, the grape is uniquely capable of surviving the cold

weather and short growing season of the Alta Valle. There, Prié Blanc yields flinty, slatelike wines, and the grape's high acidity lends itself well to sparkling styles (at which Cave Mont Blanc excels). Ermes Pavese also uses this austere, crisp grape to make still and sparkling wines. Trained close to the dry stone terraces in the *pergola bassa* method, the grapes ripen thanks to the sun and the heat reflected from the stones in some of Italy's most stunning vineyards. The vineyards are planted so high, in fact, that they can grow ungrafted—phylloxera can't survive the heights.

Red

Cornalin

Grown in the Media Valle, Cornalin is closely related to Petit Rouge, the region's most-grown red grape, and is often blended with it in Torrette DOC wines. It's one of a handful of local red grapes that the Grosjean family grows. Instead of blending it with their other grapes, they make a 100 percent Cornalin with lip-smacking red-fruit flavors and a smooth, sometimes peppery finish. La Vrille also has a ruby-hued Cornalin with notes of white flowers and blackberry jam. The red grape grows well in the mountains, reaching maturity despite shorter-than-normal growing seasons. (Note that the grape is not the same as the Swiss grape Cornalin; in Switzerland, Italian Cornalin is called "Humagne Rouge.")

Fumin

One of the oldest grapes in the region, Fumin was nearly lost for good until it began to have a renaissance at the end of the last century. For an alpine variety, the late-ripening grape is meaty, with Syrah-like weight and rustic charm. Its name conjures up smoke, which some attribute to a smoky character in the wine and others to the smoky bloom on the grapes. The French word *fumée* means "smoke"; the Italian word is *fumo*. Because of its color and body, Fumin is often used in blends for heft. Les Crêtes makes a full, velvety Fumin wine while Maurizio Fiorano of Château Feuillet makes a Fumin that is

both elegant and rustic, with pleasantly chewy tannins and bright notes of raspberry.

Petit Rouge

If you want to memorize the name of only one red grape from Valle d'Aosta, Petit Rouge is the one to know. The most-grown red grape in the region, it also goes into the main red wine, Valle d'Aosta Torrette DOC. A few enterprising winemakers make pure Petit Rouge, and nearly every bottle is a delight. (It's all Danilo Thomain grows on his hectare in the Enfer d'Arvier subzone.) There's a reason the grape is important for the region: the vigorous vine produces large, compact bunches; plus, it's resistant to cold, allowing it to grow well nearly everywhere there's vineyard land in Valle d'Aosta. In the glass, Petite Rouge yields an herbaceous, ruby-hued wine imbued with bright, alpine acidity.

Picotener (Picotendro)

(see Nebbiolo, Piedmont chapter, page 154)

Other Native Red Grapes: Mayolet, Prëmetta (Prié Rouge), Roussin de Morgex, and Vuillermin

This collection of grapes are grown in such small quantities that most of them are used in blends (especially the Valle d'Aosta Torrette DOC). Mayolet is the most common out of the four and adds hints of spice and black currant to a blend. On its own, it has an exuberant aroma and is quite light and refreshing. Prëmetta makes a wine with one of the lightest-hued reds we've ever come across—it looks almost like *rosato*—with beautiful notes of strawberry and cranberry coupled with tomato leaf aromatics. Roussin de Morgex could be the red sparkling grape answer to Prié Blanc in the de Morgex et de La Salle subzone, the coldest in Valle d'Aosta. And Vuillermin is an aromatic grape with red-fruit flavors and unexpectedly rich body. La Vrille makes a pure Vuillermin wine with notes of rose.

Regional Foods

Capriolo alla valdostana
venison stew

Cheese
Fontina Val d'Aosta, signature cows' milk cheese of the region

Toma di Gressoney, semi-firm cow's milk cheese

Costoletta alla valdostana
breaded veal chops stuffed with prosciutto and fontina

Crespelle alla valdostana
savory crepes with prosciutto

Fonduta
melted cheese (mostly fontina) made into sauce for dipping (Italy's fondue)

Mezzalune
stuffed half-moon pasta

Mocetta Valdostana
lean cured meat made from cow's legs

Polenta concia
polenta topped with fontina and butter

Seupa à la vapelenentse
soup made of Fontina, whole-grain bread, and cabbage

Tegole
wafer-thin hazelnut and almond cookies

Recommended Producers

Cave des Onze Communes

Cave Mont Blanc de Morgex et La Salle

Château Feuillet

Danilo Thomain

Donnas

Elio Ottin

Ermes Pavese

Grosjean

Institut Agricole Régional

La Vrille

Les Crêtes

Lo Triolet

Maison Anselmet

Nadir Cunéaz

Nicola Del Negro

Noussan

Veneto

Besides a few chickens strolling the grounds, no one greets you at L'Osteria senz'Oste. Down the street from the Col Vetoraz winery and overlooking the steep Cartizze vineyard, the place is true to its name: an osteria (tavern) without an *oste* (proprietor). It's a self-serve establishment: the kitchen is stocked with salumi and bread earlier in the day, and you put euros in the basket in the kitchen and take what you paid for. Feed a credit card into the vending machine outside and extract a bottle of wine. It all sounds like a lazy approach to hospitality, but the effect feels more like you're in on a secret. Instead of being stuck in a restaurant without a view, visitors can climb up the hill behind the *oste*-less osteria, spread out a modest picnic, and look down on prime vineyard real estate.

Located between the wine towns of Conegliano and Valdobbiadene but closer to the latter, Cartizze is a steep slope planted with Glera, the main grape of Prosecco. On top of the hill near the osteria, a cannon points at the sky. Every so often (so we're told), it's fired up at the clouds to break them up to prevent hail and avoid losing a valuable grape crop—whether it works or not, we can't say. Premium and Prosecco don't often go together, but Cartizze—and the entire DOCG zone surrounding it—makes

a strong case for the *spumante*'s position among Italy's most iconic wines. Cartizze grapes go into one specific Prosecco: Valdobbiadene Superiore di Cartizze DOCG. Compared to Prosecco from elsewhere, Cartizze wines are richer and rounder, with fleeting stone-fruit aromas and crisp mineral notes. Grapes from Cartizze get riper than others, leaving more residual sugar, but the high acidity balances out the sweetness in wines from quality producers, such as Col Vetoraz.

Sorting out the good stuff from the rest is not easy in the Veneto. The region is Italy's most prolific, producing roughly 20 percent of Italy's total wine output at 285.992 million gallons (10.826 million hectoliters) annually. As host city of Vinitaly, the world's largest Italian wine trade show, Verona is the heart of the Italian wine trade. Perhaps this is why Veneto producers have a knack for capitalizing on trends. Amarone, the high-octane wine made with semidried grapes, became a breakout hit in the 1990s. Today, as trends shift toward lower-alcohol wines, fresh-faced Valpolicella and Bardolino are emerging from Amarone's giant shadow. Soave, the mass-produced export white of the twentieth century, is esteemed in the Classico zone. In 2019, the *consorzio* introduced nearly three dozen UGAs (*unità geografiche aggiuntive*, "additional geographic units"), official single-vineyard designations, to promote a better understanding of historic Soave's terroir.

Meanwhile, Prosecco went through a major rebranding in 2009, changing the name of its main grape from Prosecco to Glera to make "Prosecco" a protected place of origin separate from the grape. Now anyone can grow Glera grapes, but only producers in northeastern Italy can make Prosecco. To accommodate the change, the Prosecco DOC was redrawn to include a massive amount of land, from the Veneto flatlands north of Venice to Friuli Venezia Giulia. Meanwhile, the historic Prosecco areas became DOCGs, including the hills of Asolo and between Conegliano and Valdobbiadene, the latter which became a UNESCO World Heritage site in 2019. Rebranding efforts have led to interesting experiments. In 2020, the Prosecco DOC introduced pink Prosecco made with up to 15 percent Pinot Nero.

In Prosecco—unlike in many parts of Italy—the quality pyramid holds up (see Italian Wine Quality Rankings, page 24); the best wines bear "DOCG" on the label. Still, Prosecco's biggest challenge is explaining that supermarket bubbles are one thing and that bubbles made in Prosecco's historic hills are another. In that sense, the makers of the best Prosecco, Soave, and Valpolicella—as well as the winemakers outside those silos—face the challenge of standing out amid oceans of wine (including a lot of mass-market Pinot Grigio from the Valdadige DOC, a zone shared with Trentino–Alto Adige). Another challenge is that the best-known wines of the Veneto come from grapes that most people have never heard of.

And yet, Veneto is a thrilling place to visit, not only for wine but also for sheer beauty. From the eastern shores of Lake Garda, you have the "Riviera degli Olivi," the "olive oil Riviera," where tranquil towns lining the lake's shores are destinations for summer vacations. In the north, alpine Cortina d'Ampezzo is the 2026 Winter Olympics host city. From there, it's only an hour down the mountain to Vittorio Veneto on the northern edge of the Prosecco Superiore zone. There, Cinzia Canzian of Le Vigne di Alice grows a handful of native grapes that were once more common in the area. Light, minerally, and seasoned with a dash of sweetness, Cinzia's wines are understated but sophisticated, the perfect antidote for anyone convinced all Prosecco tastes the same. That's the thing about the Veneto—for every mass-produced bottle, there's a Le Vigne di Alice alternative if you know where to look.

History

While winemaking in Veneto preceded the Romans, they're credited for the name of the region's most historic wine area, Valpolicella, which comes from the Latin *vallis polis cellae* (valley of many cellars). The Romans picked grapes in the fall, then let them dry before making wine, a process now called *appassimento*. Drying grapes yielded sweet wine, and the extra sugar helped preserve it. Over time, farmers replanted local grapes that dried better than others.

During the Middle Ages, wine production continued as monasteries grew vines for sacramental wine. In the fifteenth century, the Venetian Republic expanded from its city on the lagoon to Verona, Vincenza, and Padua, securing new territory to produce food, wine, and silk. Wealthy Venetians built villas across the countryside and began farms. The Emo family, who were among the founders of the republic, were the first to import corn to Italy. Today, the Conte Emo Capodilista estate and ancient farm, La Montecchia, is run by Giordano Emo Capodilista, a twenty-second generation Venetian. By its peak in the sixteenth century, Venice was among the richest and most diverse cities in Europe, with a large market for wine. The Arsenale, the republic's shipbuilding engine, employed fifteen hundred shipbuilders. In addition to other payments, each builder received five hundred liters of wine annually for their work. Additionally, vendors served city residents small glasses of Malvasia from stalls set in the *ombra*, the shadow of the Campanile di San Marco. The shadow was so connected to wine that *ombra* came to mean a "small glass of wine" in dialect.

Checking the wine color, clarity, and transparency
in the cellar of Graziano Prà.

The Venetian Republic stayed independent for more than a thousand years, until caving at the end of the eighteenth century to Napoleon. After Veneto became part of Napoleon's short-lived Italian kingdom, it was then taken over by the Austrians before becoming part of the Kingdown of Italy in 1866. Unlike southern Italy, which didn't initially benefit from unification, Veneto made immediate progress, driven by science-minded businessmen such as Antonio Carpenè.

Carpenè wrote extensively about the grapes and farming techniques around his home in Conegliano, the traditional area for Prosecco. He lamented the practice of mixed agriculture, which made it hard for grapes to ripen evenly, but praised hillside vineyards, which he believed grew better grapes. He also pushed for progress in agriculture through education. In 1876, aided by a royal decree from King Victor Emmanuel II, Carpenè, along with agricultural professor Angelo Vianello, founded the Conegliano School of Viticulture and Oenology. It was the first school in Italy dedicated to winemaking. (Trentino–Alto Adige's historic wine institute in San Michele all'Adige is two years older, but the region was not part of Italy until after World War I.) At the Conegliano school, there were two tiers of education: a middle school for the children of farmers, which taught practical skills for vineyard work, and a secondary school for advanced education. Similar schools soon spread across Italy in Alba, Avellino, Catania, and Cagliari. The Conegliano school also established an Italian wine club to educate the community on how to recognize good wine from bad.

Carpenè also relentlessly studied alternative ways to make sparkling wines, visiting Champagne to study the method used there. In 1868, Carpenè and Francesco Malvolti founded their winemaking firm in Conegliano, opening a winemaking plant in 1883. When the partners passed away at the beginning of the twentieth century, the winery continued under one of Carpenè's sons. The First World War destroyed the city of Conegliano, though the winery and school were soon rebuilt. In 1924, Carpenè-Malvolti was the first winery to put "Prosecco" on the label. In the 1930s, it became the first to make Prosecco using *metodo Martinotti*—tank-fermented sparkling wine (see Italy's Sparkling Wines, page 262).

In the western part of Veneto, *appassimento* continued to be used to make *recioto*, a sweet style of wine. (Recioto della Valpolicella was made with red grapes, while Recioto di Soave and Recioto di Gambellara were made with white.) Occasionally, wines would ferment dry. Over time, these wines came to be called Recioto Amarone (*amaro* means "bitter"; *amarone*, "big, bitter one"), and then, eventually, Amarone della Valpolicella. In the 1950s and '60s, producers like Bolla, Bertani, and Masi began building a market for this dry wine made from raisined grapes, but it wasn't until the 1990s—a time when wine drinkers were seeking out the biggest, richest wines they could find—that Amarone became a global wine. It continues to be the best-known red from the hills of Verona today.

Land and Wines

Molded by glaciers and rivers, Veneto has a diverse terrain. East of Verona, the hills of Valpolicella and Soave have a more temperate climate, benefiting from breezes off Lake Garda, while the southern border of the region lining the Po River is largely flat, fertile, and humid. Meanwhile, the hills around Treviso can be quite cold in the fall and winter. In Venice, the few vineyards that remain on the lagoon are prone to flooding, the wines gaining a salty note as a result. The region is mostly flat, with 29 percent comprising mountains and 15 percent hills. Taken together, there's ample room for many styles of wine.

The southern shores of Lake Garda bordering Lombardy are best known for white wine. There, the Lugana DOC grows Turbiana, the local name for the Verdicchio grape. On the eastern shores of the lake in the Bardolino zone, however, the focus shifts to reds and *rosati* made with Corvina, Rondinella, and Corvinone grapes. With the mild climate around the lake, the area's sandy, stony soils yield lighter reds imbued with red cherry flavor. Bardolino is especially known for Chiaretto, its *rosato*. Matilde Poggi of historic Chiaretto producer Le Fraghe makes a savory, refreshing *rosato* versatile enough to pair with everything from lake trout to curry. (For more examples of Italian *rosato* styles, see Cerasuolo d'Abruzzo and Italian *Rosati*, page 39.)

East of the Adige River, Bardolino gives way to Valpolicella, a series of hills and valleys north of Verona bordering the Lessini Mountains. Valpolicella can be divided into three areas: Valpolicella Classico, Valpantena, and Valpolicella Est. The Classico zone is the closest to Lake Garda, so it gets breezes from the lake and the Lessini Mountains. Its three main valleys—Fumane, Marano, and Negrar—run north to south, each with different soils ranging from volcanic to calcareous to alluvial. East of the Classico area, Valpantena is a source for marble as well as wine, and east of there, Valpolicella Est is made up of the Mezzane, Tregnago, and Illasi valleys. In the Illasi valley near the Lessinia Regional Nature Park, the Tasi winery grows vines in a former limestone quarry. The mineral-rich site was nearly turned into a dump before the local community intervened. Tasi, which had its first vintage in 2012, was created by the next generation of Fasoli Gino, a winery down the road that got its start in 1925. Almost all the red wines made in Valpolicella are blends of Corvina, along with Corvinone and Rondinella. Every estate has its own preferred mix.

With the same selection of red grapes, winemakers can create four different wines: Valpolicella, Valpolicella Ripasso, Amarone della Valpolicella, and Recioto della Valpolicella. The simplest is Valpolicella, which is vinified like other red wines. It tastes like cherries with a hint of bitter almond, with very soft tannins. When made well, it's an easy, food-friendly wine. The next two wines from Valpolicella involve drying grapes. To make Amarone, whole bunches of grapes are harvested by hand and then hung on racks or laid in crates to dry. After drying for three or four months, the grapes are vinified to make Amarone. The sweet wine Recioto della Valpolicella is made by drying

the grapes several weeks longer than Amarone. The fourth wine is Valpolicella Ripasso. The style was first made in 1967 by Sandro Boscaini of Masi Wine. After Amarone is made, its skins, seeds, and other bits remaining are still rich in flavor. Boscaini wondered what would happen if he added the bits to a vat of Valpolicella to enrich it. The experiment pushed the wine into a second fermentation, which deepened its flavor and color and raised its alcohol content. The word *ripasso* means "repassed," and it soon became popular as a bridge wine between light Valpolicella and hearty Amarone. In the Classico area, the Bussola estate makes "Ca' del Laito," a Valpolicella Ripasso sourced from vineyards in the Negrar area. It has a rich, Amarone-like nose but a dry, food-friendly finish, a good bottle to pair with rich stews.

Just east of the Valpolicella area, the Soave zone is best known for Garganega, though Trebbiano di Soave (another local word for Verdicchio) often adds a dash of brightness to the wines. The Classico zone between the towns of Soave and Monteforte d'Alpone produces the best Soave wines. In general, the hills closest to Soave are limestone-rich, while the sites closer to Monteforte d'Alpone are known for volcanic soils. Imbued with lemon and almond, great Soave tastes full, soft, and light all at the same time. In the hands of producers like Pieropan or Prà, the wines can age for years. In the 1970s, Graziano Prà, who came from a family that grew grapes, attended the enology school in Conegliano to learn how to make wine. When he started out, Soave's reputation for quality was anything but stellar—the zone's borders had been expanded far from the classic production area to the flat, warm plains, and the wines tasted like watered-down versions of the original. Yet the entire range of Prà's Garganega wines—from "Otto," a bright, citrusy everyday Soave, to "Monte Grande," a deep, single-vineyard wine with notes of waxy lemon and almond—shows the depth that can be explored in Soave Classico.

Compared to the western side of Veneto, the eastern hills outside Treviso can be wet and rainy, but the cooler climate and well-draining soils

Graziano Prà and his border collie, Lapo.

suit production of sparkling wine just fine. In the UNESCO-recognized hills of Conegliano and Valdobbiadene, it's remarkable how dry the hillsides feel, even after drenching rains bring floods to Venice. The Prosecco Superiore DOCG area also includes *rive*, specific vineyards between Conegliano and Valdobbiadene that can be mentioned on the label. At the top of the quality pyramid of these single-vineyard designations is Cartizze. In general, vineyards closer to Conegliano make stronger wines because they have more clay in their soils, while the vineyards closer to Valdobbiadene are finer, with more white sandstone and marl, producing more aromatic, lighter wines, though each site has its own variations. The drive between both towns is one of Italy's prettiest wine roads, with snow-capped mountains in the distance. On a clear day, you can see the Venetian lagoon. Down from the hills, Prosecco production becomes more utilitarian, with large stretches of Glera vines growing in the flatlands to supply the world with affordable bubbles.

Away from the western areas around Verona and the eastern hills of Treviso, there is plenty of other wines to discover. Some of the most interesting come from the Colli Euganei, volcanic hills best known for Moscato Giallo made in dry, sparkling, and *passito* styles, as well as red wines made with Merlot (which has grown here for centuries) and Raboso, a lesser-known red. Manzoni Bianco, an aromatic white crossing made by a late professor at the school in Conegliano, also comes into its own in the vineyards in central Veneto. Then there's Durella, a grape made into bubbles next to the Lessini Mountains, and a good alternative sparkler for anyone venturing away from Prosecco. In a region saturated in wine production, it can be hard to know where to start. So, head to Venice, stop for an *ombra*—or an Aperol spritz (Prosecco with Aperol) and go from there.

Life is a bubble, or so says Cinzia Canzian of Le Vigne di Alice in Vittorio Veneto, one of our favorite Prosecco makers. In a way, it's true: *spumante* (sparkling wine) is part of life in Italy, a simple way to start a meal or extend *aperitivo* hour.

There are three main ways to make sparkling wine. The first two methods involve two fermentations: one to make the base wine and a second to create the bubbles. The third method ferments only once, but it finishes fermenting in the bottle.

Metodo Classico

Based on the same method used in Champagne, this sparkling wine category (also called classic method and traditional method) is among the most prestigious sparkling wine styles in the world. True to the method's country of origin, the words used to describe the many steps and styles are French or an Italianized version of a French term. A *metodo classico* sparkling wine starts first with a base wine. Grapes are pressed gently so the skins and seeds don't impart tannins or color. Base wines are low in alcohol and high in acidity. They are also often blended with other base wines, creating what's known as a cuvée. Base wines are almost always white, though rosé sparkling wines get their color when winemakers blend in a little red wine into the cuvée. To get their bubbles, the base wine is bottled with a splash of wine mixed with yeast and sugar, capped, and is left to ferment again. When the second fermentation is done, bubbles are trapped in the bottle along with lees (dead yeast cells). To remove the lees, bottles are gradually tilted and turned (by hand or by a machine called a gyropalette) until they are nearly upside down so the yeast settles in the neck of the bottle. The necks are then frozen so the yeast can be extracted in one chunk (a process called disgorgement). Next, a tiny amount of sugar and wine is added (*dosage* in French and *dosaggio* in Italian) and the bottle is stoppered with a cork.

Within that method, there are countless variations. Some *metodo classic* wines are held on their lees for months or years before disgorgement because the extra time imparts notes of toasted bread or nuts and helps preserve the wine. Named after the winery's founder, Trento-based Ferrari's "Giulio Ferrari Riserva del Fondatore" ages for about a decade before disgorgement, for instance. The amount of sugar used for the *dosaggio* also varies, and some wines do without the sugar altogether (look for *dosaggio zero*, *pas dosè*, or *brut nature*).

There are great *metodo classico* wines in nearly every region, but the areas most associated with the style are Franciacorta (page 125, in Lombardy), Trento (page 210, in Trentino), Alta Langa (page 146 in Piedmont), and Oltrepò Pavese (page 126, in Lombardy). Most of these wines are made with traditional French Champagne grapes Chardonnay and Pinot Nero (Pinot Noir), though they occasionally contain Pinot Bianco and (very occasionally) Pinot Meunier. Outside these areas, *metodo classico* wines are made with native Italian grapes, and some, like Sicily's Nerello Mascalese and Campania's Fiano, have become favorites of ours. Conegliano Valdobbiadene Prosecco Superiore DOCG wines can also be made using *metodo classico*, though the larger Prosecco DOC cannot.

Metodo Martinotti

This method—also called Charmat method, tank method, and Charmat-Martinotti method—is how most Prosecco, Lambrusco, Asti Spumante, Brachetto d'Acqui, and many other popular sparkling Italian wines are made. The technique evolved from the efforts of two people: Federico Martinotti, director of the Regia Stazione Enologica in Asti, who invented a new device and method for making sparkling wine in 1895, and French engineer Eugène Charmat, who patented the process. In the 1930s, the Carpenè-Malvolti winery was the first to use it to make Prosecco. At its best, the *metodo Martinotti* method captures the fresh, bright aroma and acidity of delicate grapes.

Like *metodo classico,* a *metodo Martinotti* sparkling wine starts with a base wine. This wine is stored at about 39°F (4°C) until it's time for the second fermentation. It's then put in a temperature-controlled pressure tank called an autoclave and heated to 59°F (15°C). Yeast and sugar are added to the wine, starting a second fermentation that becomes trapped in the tank. The wine is then filtered, sweetened according to the desired style, and bottled. *Metodo Martinotti* sparkling wines are meant to be fresh. Wineries keep base wines in tanks until they need to fulfill orders for accounts. It's common to forgo a vintage on the label because a winery may switch midyear into the newer vintage, and some producers blend past vintages with newer vintages to maintain a consistent style. The longer the second fermentation in the tank, the more sophisticated the bubble, and premium Prosecco often has a fine, creamy texture.

Occasionally, a wine will go from start to finish in a pressure tank, needing only one fermentation. Its bubbles are trapped in the wine when the winemaker seals the tank partway through fermentation. Before bottling, the wine is filtered to remove any remaining yeast. This method is key to making gently bubbly, sweet Moscato d'Asti.

Metodo Ancestrale/Frizzante

Inspired by the oldest way of making sparkling wine, this method is all about capturing bubbles in the bottle in the simplest way possible. A base wine begins its fermentation like any other wine, but before it finishes, it is transferred into bottles and capped. The bubbles in the wine simply come from the wine finishing its fermentation.

Metodo ancestrale wines have plenty of fans in the low-intervention wine world. These bottles are most associated with French pét-nat (*pétillant naturel,* French for "naturally sparkling," yet Italy also has a long tradition of making wines this way. Most of them are simply called *frizzante.* Many artisan Lambrusco and Prosecco wines are made with this method. Among Prosecco producers, look for wines called *col fondo* or *sui lieviti,* both of which mean with sediment or with lees.

Some wines inspired by the ancestral method do have a second fermentation in the bottle. For instance, Cinzia Canzian's "A Fondo" *frizzante* is inspired by classic *col fondo* wines, but with a twist: The base wine is fermented as usual, then it's bottled with unfermented grape juice saved from the harvest to ferment again. The result is a gently yeasty, savory interpretation of Prosecco.

Sparkling Wine Styles

Effervescence

Measured in bars, atmospheric pressure is the force of CO_2 inside the bottle. The higher the number, the brisker the bubble.

- **Spumante:** between 3 and 6 bars. The variation comes down to style preference. Franciacorta wines can have 6 bars, except for Satèn, a white sparkling wine whose name means "silk," which has a maximum of 5 bars to ensure its bubbles are delicate and creamy.

- **Frizzante (semi-sparkling):** a maximum of 2.5 bars. *Col fondo* Prosecco and other *metodo ancestrale* wines fit this category.

continued

Sugar levels

Some wines benefit from a little sweetness to round out the flavors, though wine trends are shifting to drier (less sweet) wines. These categories reflect the *dosaggio* added prior to bottling, which determines its level of residual sugar. Depending on the regulations within a wine area, certain categories of sweetness may be off-limits.

- **Brut nature:** 0 to 3 grams of residual sugar per liter. This is a growing category among *metodo classico* wines, especially from warmer areas where grapes get riper.

- **Extra brut:** 0 to 6 grams of residual sugar per liter: A small but growing percentage of Prosecco Superiore is made this way.

- **Brut:** 0 to 12 grams of residual sugar per liter. Franciacorta's Satèn can be made only as a *brut* wine.

- **Extra dry:** 12 to 17 grams of residual sugar per liter. For Prosecco, this is the most common style. In the best cases, the sweetness is subtle.

- **Dry/Sec:** 17 to 32 grams of residual sugar per liter. This style is on the decline as people turn to drier sparkling wines, though it remains the traditional style for Prosecco from Cartizze.

- **Demi-sec:** 32 to 50 grams of residual sugar per liter. A noticeably sweeter wine for desserts. The European community also has a *doux* category for even sweeter wines, but these are not common in Italy.

Veneto Grapes

While the Veneto makes many of Italy's most familiar wines, the grapes that go into Prosecco, Soave, Amarone, and Valpolicella aren't nearly as well known. Most of the wines made here are white, and red wines are typically blends.

White

Durella

Durella's name stems from *dura*, meaning "hard," because the grape has thick, leathery skins, though the wines it produces are bright and lean. Once ignored, Durella has made a comeback among those looking for lower-alcohol and lighter styles of wines. The grape comes from the Lessini Durello DOC, a volcanic area just east of the Lessini Mountains regional park. (To clarify, the grape is Durella; the name of the wine zone is "Lessini Durello.") Bright in acidity with notes of fresh-squeezed lemon, the grape lends itself well to sparkling wines made via *metodo Martinotti* or *metodo classico* (see Italy's Sparkling Wines, page 262). Close to the regional park, the Fongaro estate was the original champion of Durella, making a range of *metodo classico* Durella wines, while Dama del Rovere, a producer in Soave Classico, makes a *metodo classico* version with apple-like nuances, perfect to pour during fall.

Garganega

Best known as the leading variety in Soave wines, Garganega is one of the Veneto's oldest grapes, giving rise to other natives, including the ubiquitous Trebbiano Toscano. It has many biotypes, including Grecanico Dorato from Sicily. Grown in the traditional pergola system, Garganega is a productive variety. This hurt its reputation in the twentieth century, when it was planted in warm, flat areas making low-cost Soave. But a few winemakers, such as Pieropan and Prà, knew the grape was capable of much more. This is especially the case when Garganega grows in the Classico zone between the towns of Monteforte d'Alpone and Soave. Single-vineyard wines from Monteforte d'Alpone volcanic soils, such as Prà's Soave Classico "Staforte," are richer and riper, with spicy notes and a dash of salt. Vineyards closer to Soave have more limestone, making aromatic, mineral wines. The best Garganega wines are full and light at the same time, with white flowers and bitter almond, herbal, apple, and citrus notes. In the right hands, Garganega creates some of Italy's best, most age-worthy whites, such as Pieropan's "La Rocca," which can age for more than a decade. There is also the sweet Recioto di Soave style, in which the grapes are partially dried before being pressed. In Sicily, Grecanico Dorato grows all over, but mostly in the provinces of Agrigento and Trapani, where it makes bright, balanced, food-friendly whites.

Manzoni Bianco

The Perenzin dairy outside Conegliano makes superlative Montasio, an alpine cows' milk cheese, which is a near-perfect pairing with Manzoni Bianco. A cross between Riesling and either Pinot Bianco or Chardonnay, Manzoni Bianco is the sort of wine that has both acidity and roundness, which complements the creamy, tangy notes of the cheese. Starting in the 1920s, Professor Luigi Manzoni of the viticulture and enology school in Conegliano developed a line of crossings in the school's experimental vineyard. While the vineyard was ripped out after he retired, several samples survived. (The school has since cemented his legacy in a small museum dedicated to his research.) Among the crossings the professor created, Manzoni Bianco is the best so far. Its full name is "Incrocio Manzoni 6.0.13"—*incrocio* means "crossing," "Manzoni" is for the creator, and the number is for its location in the vineyard—and it sometimes appears this way on the label. The wines are round, with a pleasantly floral nose. In Colli Euganei, Reassi makes a refreshing Manzoni Bianco called "Terre D'Argilla," while under the Vigneti delle Dolomiti IGT, Foradori's "Fontanasanta" Manzoni Bianco is aged in acacia wood and shows a more savory side of the variety.

Moscato Giallo

A branch of the broader Moscato Bianco (page 150) family, Moscato Giallo also grows in Friuli Venezia Giulia and Trentino–Alto Adige (where it also goes by the name Goldmuskateller). It's a hardy, early ripening grape that grows best in vineyards with limestone or volcanic soils. Like all Moscato types, its wines are aromatic with spicy, floral, and (sometimes) intense aromas. Redolent of orange blossom and peach yogurt, Conte Emo Capodilista La Montecchia's Colli Euganei Fior d'Arancio DOCG *spumante* from the hills outside Padua is a refreshing aperitivo or after-dinner palate cleanser. The estate also makes a collection of *passiti* with Moscato Giallo, including one aged in amphora (a terracotta vessel).

Prosecco Grapes

The original blend and formula for Prosecco included a third each of the grapes Glera, Bianchetta Trevigiana, and Verdiso. Somewhere along the way, Glera was singled out, and today Prosecco requires 85 percent Glera at minimum, with up to 15 percent made up of other local grapes.

- **Bianchetta Trevigiana:** Originally from the city of Treviso, Bianchetta Trevigiana is a minor Prosecco grape these days, though it once had a nobler past as a still wine. With thick skins and tight grape bunches, it can be susceptible to rot. It imparts acidity to Prosecco blends.

- **Glera:** In 2009, the name of this grape was changed from "Prosecco" to "Glera." The change came to protect territory and style. Much like Champagne can come only from the region of Champagne, Prosecco can come only from a (large) swath of land in northeastern Italy. To prevent "Prosecco" from being grown and made in other parts of the world, officials changed the name of the grape. Prior to 2009, the grape was named after the town of Prosecco near Trieste, where it's believed to be from. There is more than one Glera grape, but the main one, Glera Tondo, dominates planting. While it grows all over the flatlands stretching from eastern Veneto to Friuli, Glera reaches its highest levels of quality in the hills between Conegliano and Valdobbiadene as well as in Asolo. Planted in well-draining, light soils, the grape develops refined aromas and flavors of white peach and pear, with enough acidity to offset sweetness. (The traditional style is Extra Dry, which has a bit more residual sugar than Brut.) Glera's delicate flavors are best shown off as a *metodo Martinotti* sparkler, which preserves freshness, and these are wines designed to drink when young. Some try putting Glera through *metodo classico* production, but the delicate pear flavors are often lost. A more classic way to experience bottle-fermented Glera is with *col fondo* Prosecco (see Italy's Sparkling Wines, page 262).

- **Perera:** A historic grape in the Prosecco area, Perera adds a dash of acidity to the mix. The grape is sensitive to disease, so it's fallen out of favor. The Marchiori family, who make Prosecco Superiore with five native Prosecco grapes, uses a splash of Perera to add aroma and depth.

- **Verdiso:** This green-colored grape is a blending partner in Prosecco, though Cinzia Canzian of Le Vigne di Alice gives the grape more attention in "Tajad," a dry, lean *frizzante* made with 40 percent Verdiso. It's blended with Glera and a local grape called Boschera that grows only around Canzian's estate in Vittorio Veneto.

Trebbiano di Soave

(see Verdicchio, Le Marche chapter, page 110)

Red

Marzemino

(see Trentino–Alto Adige chapter, page 214)

Raboso

In truth, there are two Raboso grapes—Raboso Piave and Raboso Veronese—but the grapes are similar enough to describe together. Giordano Emo Capodilista of Conte Emo Capodilista La Montecchia near Padua told us that "Raboso" means "the angry one." The thick-skinned grapes are high in acidity, and in the old days the wines tasted harsh. Over time, winemakers learned that harvesting grapes late and partially drying the bunches helped smooth out the wine's temper. Expect modern Raboso wines to carry flavors of red cherries and strawberry jam balanced by a bitter edge, just the kind of wine to drink with game meats. Conte Emo Capodilista La Montecchia's full-bodied "Forzatè," a Raboso IGT Veneto wine (with both Piave and Veronese varieties), comes from grapes harvested in November and dried briefly before being vinified. Meanwhile, Prosecco producer Col de' Salici makes "Rosé de' Salici," a dry aperitivo sparkler made from a blend of Glera and Raboso Piave grapes.

Valpolicella/Bardolino Grapes

From the eastern shores of Lake Garda to the city of Vincenza, red wines are typically a blend of native red grapes. This includes (in ascending order of intensity) Bardolino's Chiaretto and red wine, Valpolicella, Valpolicella Ripasso, Amarone, and Valpolicella Recioto. Except for the Molinara grape, these are all *uve uccelli*, grapes named after birds.

- **Corvina:** The first of the bird grapes (the name means "little raven"), Corvina is temperamental to grow but essential in most of the red wines from western Veneto. Corvina vines produce a lot of grapes, but they are sensitive to heat and humidity. Training the vines in a pergola system helps by keeping the grapes away from ground moisture and allowing for more air circulation. Too much sun and Corvina grapes become spotted from sun damage, but a pergola's canopy of leaves protects bunches. Winemakers put up with the grape's Goldilocks personality because of what it delivers: cherry intensity, the signature flavor of all Bardolino and Valpolicella wines. Corvina's thick skins and loose bunches are also ideal for drying. The grape is low in tannins and average in acidity, delivering subtle notes of black pepper and other spices to wines in addition to cherry. It makes up most of the wine blends of western Veneto. For lighter reds, like Bardolino or Valpolicella (without the Ripasso treatment), Corvina-dominant blends are great served slightly chilled. Tenuta Sant'Antonio di Famiglia Castagnedi makes a pure Corvina wine that offers a more savory, spiced side of the grape, pairing soft tannins with juicy red fruit.

- **Corvinone:** "Corvinone" means "big raven," though it is not related to Corvina. This "bird grape" is larger and more tannic. In the government's wine-zone regulations, it can be used in place of Corvina, though this isn't common. Instead, it's been planted with it because Corvinone helps boost Corvina blends' tannins. It also carries a red cherry flavor, but it is sometimes more green in flavor.

- **Molinara:** Molinara's name comes from its appearance. In the vineyard, the grapes look like they've been dusted with flour. (*Mulino* is "mill" in Italian.) The grape produces wines that are light in color and slightly savory, with delicate floral aromas. Because it produces light wines, it fell out of favor in the 1990s, when the wine market couldn't get enough of big, muscular Amarone, though it did find new life in *rosati* production. In the center of the Valpolicella Classico area, producer Le Salette makes a pure Molinara *rosato*, a fresh, food-friendly wine. In Marano, the Santa Maria Valverde estate uses only 15 percent each Corvina and Corvinone but up to

30 percent Molinara and Rondinella in its Amarone.

- **Oseleta:** The name of this late-ripening grape means "little bird"; its black grapes come in tiny bunches that fit in the palm of a hand. Making wine Oseleta is tough. The grapes are small, the seeds are large, and the small amount of juice yielded is fiercely tannic. The Masi estate rediscovered the grape in the 1980s and started making wine with it in the 1990s. In 2010, Oseleta was accepted as an official Valpolicella grape. Its purpose in a blend is to provide tannic structure, though a little goes a long way. Masi's "Toar" includes 10 percent Oseleta with Corvina and Rondinella, while Tasi blends a modest 2 percent into its Valpolicella and Amarone.

- **Rondinella:** Named after another bird, the swallow, Rondinella has inky, blue-black grapes and thick skins. It accumulates sugar easily, making it ideal for Recioto della Valpolicella blends. After phylloxera, the variety grafted well to American rootstocks, and it holds up better than others in cold and drought, making it hardy enough to weather climate-change swings. It's rare to find pure Rondinella wine, but the variety routinely finds its way into western Veneto's most venerated wines, such as those of Quintarelli. Tommasso Bussola uses 10 percent Rondinella in his Valpolicella and Amarone wines, but for Recioto della Valpolicella, he ups it to 30 percent for the sweetness.

Regional Foods

Artichokes

Baccalà
salt cod

Cheese
Asiago, tangy aged cows' milk cheese

Montasio, aged cow's milk cheese made according to its own consortium

Monte Veronese, ancient cows' milk cheese made with skim milk

Cicchetti
small plates, such as crostini, served with wine

Esse
s-shaped butter cookies

Pasta
bigoli with duck ragù

pasta e fagioli, a soup of pasta and beans

spaghetti al nero di seppie, spaghetti in squid ink

tagliolini au gratin, baked pasta with eggs, Parmigiano-Reggiano, and ham

Polenta

Radicchio

Risi e bisi
rice and peas

Risotto

Sarde in saor
sardines seasoned with sweet-and-sour onions

Scallops, shrimp, octopus, and other fresh seafood

Tiramisu

White asparagus

Recommended Producers

Bardolino and Lugana

Albino Piona

Giovanna Tantini

Il Pignetto

La Sansonina

Le Fraghe

Lenotti

Zeni 1870

Colli Euganei and Elsewhere

Conte Emo Capodilista La Montecchia

Loredan Gasparini

Maculan

Montegrande

Vignalta

Ottella

Prosecco Superiore

Adami

Al Canevon

Andreola

Bellenda

Biancavigna

Bisol

Borgoluce

Bortolotti

Bortolomiol

Carpenè-Malvolti

Col Vetoraz

Drusian

Gemin

Guia

Il Colle

La Tordera

Le Vigne di Alice

Marchiori

Nino Franco

Ruggeri

Silvano Follador

Sommariva

Sorelle Bronca

Villa Sandi

Soave

Gini

I Stefanini

La Cappuccina

Monte Tondo

Pieropan

Prà

Suavia

Tamellini

T.E.S.S.A.R.I

Vicentini Agostino

Valpolicella/Amarone

Anselmi

Allegrini

Bertani

Boscaini

Brigaldara

Bussola

Ca' La Bionda

Ca' Rugate

Cavalchina

Cecilia Beretta

Corte Rugolin

Fasoli Gino

Fumanelli

I Campi

Le Salette

Masi

Monte dall'Ora

Mosconi Bertani

Quintarelli

Secondo Marco

Speri

Stefano Accordini

Tasi

Tedeschi

Tenuta Sant'Antonio Famiglia Castagnedi

Villa Spinosa

Viviani

Resources

Glossary

abboccato: Semisweet. Often used to describe the traditional wines of Orvieto and Frascati.

agriturismo: Traditionally a farm stay, though now it's mostly like staying in an inn or bed-and-breakfast on a farm or at a winery. Countless wineries run them, and they are some of the best places to stay while traveling through the Italian countryside.

alberello: Literally "little tree." A reference to when vines are trained to stand alone without supports, a style usually associated with southern Italy. Also called "bush-trained," since the vines resemble free-standing bushes.

amabile: Semisweet. May be sweeter than wines described as *abboccato*.

amaro: Bitter.

ampelography: The science of identifying and classifying grape varieties based on how they look (from the shape of the leaves to the size and shape of the grape bunches, etc.). An ampelographer is a specialist in grape varieties. For example, although the grapes Pigato and Vermentino are genetically identical, an ampelographer will note how the grapes look and grow differently in similar vineyards.

ampelology: The study of vines that builds on ampelography, describing and identifying grape varieties, while also adding molecular biology and DNA profiling to the analysis. These DNA markers can help show the lineage of a grape's family tree, though they are not always perfect. Some grapes are genetically identical but look and act different in person.

amphora: Terracotta vessel with a narrow opening at the top and a pointed base. Ancient amphorae (plural) were used to transport wine by ship, though today the vessel is most associated with low-intervention winemaking. Sometimes an amphora is stored in the ground with only the top visible.

annata: Vintage (year) a wine was made.

appassimento: The step of drying grapes after harvest before turning them into wine. The technique is most associated with Amarone, but it is also common with dessert wines. Grapes can be dried in the sun, on straw mats in well-ventilated rooms, or in temperature-controlled driers.

autostrada/autostrade: Highway(s).

azienda agricola: Farm; sometimes used at the beginning of a winery name.

barrique: Small 225-liter barrel made of French oak; often referenced in modern or international styles of wine.

bianco: White; "vino bianco" is white wine.

bicchiere/bicchieri: Glass(es). The *Gambero Rosso* Italian wine guide gives out its Tre Bicchieri (Three Glasses) awards for the best wines in its annual tastings.

biotypes: Slightly different versions of the same grape variety.

Botrytis cinerea: see *muffa nobile*.

botte/botti: Large barrel(s) made of oak or chestnut wood. Though capacity varies, it is larger than a barrique and used when winemakers want wines to age in a vessel that breathes gently but contributes little or no flavors and tannins from the wood itself. Old botti are often described as "neutral oak."

bottiglia/bottiglie: Bottle(s).

cantina/cantine: Cellar(s); often used at the beginning of a winery name.

cerasuolo: The word means "cherry" in Italian, and it refers to two different wines: Cerasuolo d'Abruzzo, a *rosato* (rosé) made with Montepulciano grapes in Abruzzo, and Cerasuolo di Vittoria, a red wine made with Frappato and Nero d'Avola grapes in Sicily.

Charmat method: see "metodo Martinotti."

Chiaretto: A *rosato* wine made around Lake Garda in Lombardy and the Veneto.

classico: The historic and/or original area of production for a wine. For example, Chianti Classico in Tuscany or Soave Classico in the Veneto.

clone: A vine started from the cuttings of another vine and grafted onto rootstock.

colle/colli: Hill(s). For example, "Colli Piacentini" are the hills of Piacenza.

consorzio: A consortium of producers from a specific area who work together to learn about and promote an area's wines.

contadino: Farmer.

"contiene __mg/l di solfiti totali": "means that a wine contains this amount of sulfites." This is an optional note that some labels include to show a low sulfite quantity.

contrada/contrade: Area(s) that loosely translates to "neighborhood(s)," but is used to signify specific vineyards. The term is common in Sicily.

cordon: The main branch from a grapevine.

crossing: Creating a new grape variety by crossing two existing *Vitis vinifera* grapes. (See Manzoni Bianco, page 265.)

cru: French word for "single vineyard." A *cru* wine is made with grapes from one vineyard.

cuvée: French word for a wine blended from other wines; common in sparkling wine production.

DOC/denominazione di origine controllata: Denomination of controlled origin. A government-created quality designation for Italian wines, started in 1963. Wines with DOC labels have to meet government standards for a wine created in a specific place with specific grapes.

DOCG/denominazione di origine controllata e garantita: Denomination of controlled and guaranteed origin. DOCG wines fall under DOP in the EU's wine-quality pyramid (see *DOP*).

dolce: Sweet.

DOP/denominazione d'origine protetta: Protected designation of origin (PDO). The European Union's way of identifying that a product originated in a specific place and is often made in a specific way. In this case, the classification is more specific than IGP. DOC and DOCG wines are part of the DOP category.

dosaggio: The Italianized word for *dosage*, the French term describing the addition of a mix of wine and sugar to *metodo classico* (classic method) sparkling wine before adding the cork. The amount added determines the level of sweetness, though some wines boast *dosaggio zero* on their label to indicate the wine is dry.

enoteca: Wine bar.

fattoria: Farm or winery; often used at the beginning of a winery name.

fiasco: A straw-covered, bulbous bottle used in Chianti production.

frizzante: Lightly sparkling.

grappa: Alcohol distilled from grape pomace (the skins, seeds, stems, and other plant material left over from the winemaking process).

green harvesting: Removing some unripe grape bunches partway through the growing season to allow the remaining grapes to ripen more quickly and evenly, with a higher concentration of sugars. It's associated with higher-quality red wines, though the practice is not essential everywhere and is being phased out in some places.

guyot: A vine-training system developed in France in the nineteenth century by French agronomist Dr. Jules Guyot to limit vine growth. It is one of the most popular vine-training systems in the world and can be done in one of two ways: with one main branch (cordon) running parallel to the ground or with two branches running in opposite directions. In many areas, Guyot replaced older pergola systems.

hectare: A unit of land in Europe that equals about 2.47 acres.

hybrid: When two vines of different species are merged into one new vine to make a more resistant vine. For instance, a European *Vitis vinifera* vine could be crossed with an American *Vitis rupestris* vine and be tolerant of phylloxera. Hybrids are not the same as European vines grafted onto American vine rootstock.

IGP/indicazione geografica protetta: Protected geographical identification. The European Union's way of identifying that a product originated in a specific place.

IGT/indicazione geografica tipica: Typical of the geographical growing area. An Italian government designation that indicates a broader area with fewer government requirements to meet compared with wines that carry a DOC or DOCG designation.

lees: The name for the spent yeast cells remaining after fermentation.

liquoroso: Fortified wine.

low-intervention wines: Also called natural wines, these are wines made on a small scale as gently as possible. The grapes come from biodynamic or organic vineyards, and the winemaker uses low-tech processes in the cellar, relying on naturally occurring yeasts in the air and on the grapes to start fermentation rather than commercial yeasts. The wines are not filtered and include no additives. Minimal sulfur is used, though some wines do not include sulfur. (Italian labels may say *senza solfiti* to indicate no sulfur is added.) It's important to clarify that "natural wine" is not a wine style or taste preference, it's a wine ideal.

maceration: The step in the winemaking process when grape skins are left in contact with the juice to impart color and other characteristics. Since white wines change color quickly, they have limited contact with the skins, thus little to no maceration time, while red wines are often macerated for a few weeks. Orange wines are white wines that have longer contact with the skins than a typical white wine (see *vino macerato*).

malolactic fermentation: Also called "malo," it's a process in which tart malic acid (the kind you taste in green apples) is converted into lactic acid, forming a smoother, richer wine. It can occur naturally, though winemakers can encourage malolactic fermentation with heat or other techniques. Some also try to prevent malolactic fermentation so a wine retains bright acidity.

masseria: A farm or large estate in southern Italy, especially Puglia.

metodo ancestrale: see *rifermentato in bottiglia*.

metodo classico/metodo tradizionale: The classic way of making sparkling wines in Champagne in which the base wine is put through a second fermentation in the bottle. Before the wine is stoppered with a cork, the spent yeast cells are extracted from the bottle. (This used to be called "Champagne method," but the word "Champagne" can be used only for wines made within the Champagne region in France.)

metodo Martinotti: Also called tank method, Charmat method, and Charmat-Martinotti method, it's a way of making sparkling wine in which a base wine is put through a second fermentation in a pressurized tank. It is most associated with Prosecco but is used throughout the world to make sparkling wines. It requires less labor than metodo classico (see previous entry), and the wines are more affordable as a result.

MGA/menzioni geografiche aggiuntive: Additional geographic mentions. The specific vineyards delineated in Barolo and Barbaresco.

millesimato: Sparkling wine made from a specific vintage; often used in Franciacorta.

muffa nobile: Italian term for *Botrytis cinerea*, a fungus that forms on grapes and causes them to shrivel up. It is also called noble rot. Under specific circumstances, it's desirable and crucial for the production of late-harvest dessert wines, such as those from Orvieto on the Lazio-Umbrian border.

novello: A "new" wine, referring to a light, simple wine made to drink young, like Beaujolais nouveau. These wines are made with carbonic maceration, a process in which grapes are kept whole to ferment in a tank without oxygen.

orange wine: When white grapes are made like red wines, allowing the grape juices to macerate with the grape skins. This longer skin contact gives the wine its "orange" color. These wines are also called macerated wines and skin-contact wines. In Italian, they are sometimes called *vini macerate* (see page 280).

osteria: Traditionally an inn or tavern that served wine; today they are more like casual restaurants with short menus.

palmento: Ancient structure used to make wine in Sicily, especially on Mount Etna. Powered by gravity, it had a vat for crushing grapes and another for fermenting juices. Today, some Sicilian *palmenti* have been restored.

passito: Sweet wine made from grapes dried after harvest, either on mats in temperature-controlled rooms, in drafty rooms, or in the sun. The raisined grapes have more concentrated sugars, giving the wines a rich sweetness and viscosity.

pergola: A vine-training method that encourages vines to grow overhead with a high canopy of leaves. The leaves provide shade from strong summer sun and protection from rain, which is especially important in extreme alpine areas such as Trentino–Alto Adige and Valle d'Aosta. Pergolas are also common in central Italy, especially Abruzzo. Once believed to be an inferior way to grow grapes (because the leaves shaded the grapes, sometimes keeping them from ripening), the training technique is making a comeback due to climate change.

physiological ripeness: The point at which the skins, seeds, and tannins of the grape have matured. Winemakers used to measure grape sugars to assess when it was time to harvest, but as climates change, hot summers can mean grapes accumulate sugar quickly before the rest of the grape is mature. Physiological ripeness is also often called "phenolic ripeness."

phylloxera: An insect from North America that destroys the roots of European grapevines. Upon its arrival in Europe in the late nineteenth century, it caused the largest loss of grape biodiversity in modern history. Today, European vines (from the species *Vitis vinifera*) are grafted onto American rootstock (from a different *Vitis* species), since American vines tolerate phylloxera. The exception is in vineyards with sandy soils or set at high altitudes. In these instances, vines can sometimes grow on their original rootstock without damage from the pest. (These are called "ungrafted" vines.)

recioto: A *passito*-style dessert wine from northeastern Italy most associated with Veneto. The most common are Recioto di Soave and Recioto di Gambellara (made with the white grape Garganega) and Recioto della Valpolicella (made with Corvina and other red grapes used in the Valpolicella area).

rifermentato in bottiglia: Refermented in bottle. A way to trap bubbles in a bottle when making sparkling wine. It is also called *metodo ancestrale* and is common in Emilia-Romagna. This is different from *metodo Martinotti*, which is when the second fermentation happens in a pressurized tank.

ripasso: Adding the pressed grape skins left from making Amarone to Valpolicella wine, refermenting it, and making it sweeter and sometimes slightly sparkling.

riserva: A wine that undergoes an extended aging period as determined by the DOP guidelines. For white wines, it can be a year; for red wines, it can be several years.

ronc/ronchi: A term in Friuli Venezia Giulia for hillside vineyard(s).

rootstock: The base of a vine, including its roots. In the early twentieth century, nurseries began grafting European vines to American rootstock because American vines were resilient to phylloxera.

rosato/rosati: Rosé wine(s). Some of the best-known *rosati* include Cerasuolo d'Abruzzo from Abruzzo and Chiaretto from Lake Garda. Puglia, Calabria, and Sicily also are know for *rosati*.

rosso: Red; *vino rosso* is a red wine.

secco: Dry.

senza solfiti: Without sulfites. American wine labels will still say "contains sulfites," even if no sulfites have been added, since they occur naturally during the winemaking process.

sfursat/sforzato: The method used in Valtellina of partially drying grapes before making wine.

sirocco: Hot winds originating in the Sahara Desert that blow north, especially affecting Sicily and Puglia.

spontaneous fermentation: When a wine begins to ferment with the help of naturally occurring yeasts on the grapes and in the winery. Wines made with spontaneous fermentation do not have commercial yeasts.

spumante: Sparkling wine.

stuck fermentation: When a wine stops fermenting midway through the winemaking process. The wine could have become too cold or too hot. High alcohol levels can also cause fermentation to stop because alcohol kills yeast. High-alcohol wines, like Amarone, need to be fermented with yeasts that can withstand higher levels of alcohol.

superiore: DOP wines produced with more stringent rules than the same DOP wine without the "superior" designation. These rules may pertain to lower grape yields and higher alcohol content, attributes that were once more valuable before climate change made it easier for grapes to achieve high sugar content.

tannins: The component in wine that gives it mouth-drying astringency and helps preserve it. It can come from grape skins, seeds, and stems.

tendone: A system of training vines in a high trellis; it supported high yields and was once popular in central and southern Italy.

tenuta: Farm.

terroir: French term (sometimes *territorio* in Italian) that describes the subtle interaction between natural factors and humans that defines a wine area. Wine writer Matt Kramer is credited for describing terroir as "somewhereness."

tufa: A limestone soil of sedimentary origins (see Rock Types: Sedimentary, Igneous, and Metamorphic, page 16).

tufo: Volcanic tuff, a type of soil originating from volcanoes. It can be fine or rocky depending on how it formed and cooled (see Rock Types: Sedimentary, Igneous, and Metamorphic, page 16).

UGA/unità geografiche aggiuntive: Additional geographical unit. Similar to the MGAs of Barolo and Barbaresco, these units indicate specific vineyard areas in zones such as Soave Classico.

uva: Grape.

vecchio: Old; sometimes used to describe old vines.

vendemmia: Grape harvest. On a bottle, it usually is followed by the year of harvest. *Vendemmia tardiva* means "late harvest" and often signifies a sweet wine.

vigna: Vineyard.

vino da taglio: Cutting wine, otherwise known as bulk wine made to be blended with wine from elsewhere.

vino da tavola: Table wine.

vino perpetuo: A wine made by adding new wine to older vintages, allowing the same wine to continue through many years. High alcohol levels are important to preserve the wine from spoilage. This method is traditional in the wines of Oristano in Sardinia and in the unfortified wines of Marsala in Sicily.

vino vivo: Wine that's alive; often used in conjunction with low-intervention (natural) wines (see page 277).

vino macerato/vini macerati: White wine(s) made like red wines, with extended contact with the grape skins. A wine made like this is also called "orange wine" because it can take on an orange hue (see page 278).

Vitis vinifera: The European vine species to which nearly all wine grapes belong. *Vitis vinifera* vines are vulnerable to diseases that do not affect American vines. To keep vineyards free of the vine pest phylloxera, most *Vitis vinifera* vines are grafted onto American vine rootstock (such as *Vitis rupestris*).

vivace: Lightly fizzy/sparkling.

Recommended Reading

Barolo and Barbaresco: The King and Queen of Italian Wine by Kerin O'Keefe (University of California Press, 2014)

Chianti Classico: The Search for Tuscany's Noblest Wine by Bill Nesto and Frances Di Savino (University of California Press, 2016)

Friuli Food and Wine: Frasca Cooking from Northern Italy's Mountains, Vineyards, and Seaside by Bobby Stuckey and Lachlan Mackinnon-Patterson with Meredith Erickson (Ten Speed Press, 2020)

Italy's Native Wine Grape Terroirs by Ian D'Agata (University of California Press, 2019)

Native Wine Grapes of Italy by Ian D'Agata (University of California Press, 2014)

The New Wines of Mount Etna by Benjamin North Spencer (Gemelli Press, 2020)

South of Somewhere: Wine, Food, and the Soul of the Italian South by Robert Camuto (University of Nebraska Press, 2021)

Vino: The Essential Guide to Real Italian Wine by Joe Campanale with Joshua David Stein (Clarkson Potter, 2022)

Vino Italiano: The Regional Wines of Italy by Joseph Bastianich and David Lynch (Clarkson Potter, 2002)

The Wine Atlas of Italy by Burton Anderson (Simon & Schuster, 1990)

The World of Sicilian Wine by Bill Nesto and Frances Di Savino (University of California Press, 2013)

Digital and Audio Resources

DOP IGP

dopigp.politicheagricole.it/en/web/guest/home

The Italian Ministry of Agriculture, Food and Forestry Policies offers descriptions of all DOP/IGP wines for each region. There are also descriptions of all regional foods that have DOP status.

Federdoc

federdoc.com/en/production-areas/

The national consortia that protects Italian wine designations has wine-zone maps for each region.

Italian Wine Central

italianwinecentral.com

A robust resource for all regions, grapes, and growing areas in Italy; it stays up to date with the listings on the Italian Ministry of Agriculture's site and conveys the information in a straightforward way.

I'll Drink to That!

illdrinktothatpod.com

Levi Dalton's podcast offers in-depth interviews with winemakers around the world, including many of Italy's most famous names.

Jancis Robinson

jancisrobinson.com

A website filled with articles, tasting notes, and grape descriptions from around the world, including Italy.

Wine for Normal People

winefornormalpeople.com

Elizabeth Schneider's wide-ranging podcast includes breakdowns of Italian wines and regions, including describing specific DOC/G wine areas.

Selected Bibliography

In addition to the previous resources listed on page 282.

Anderson, Burton. *Burton Anderson's Best Italian Wines*. London: Little, Brown, 2001.

———. *Vino: The Wines & Winemakers of Italy*. Boston: Little, Brown, 1980.

Belfrage, Nicolas. *Barolo to Valpolicella: The Wines of Northern Italy*. London: Faber and Faber, 1999.

———. *Brunello to Zibibbo: The Wines of Tuscany, Central and Southern Italy*. London: Mitchell Beazley, 2003.

Brostrom, Jack, and Geralyn Brostrom. *Into Italian Wine*. 6th ed. Annapolis: Italian Wine Central, 2021.

Clark, Letitia. *Bitter Honey: Recipes and Stories from the Island of Sardinia*. London: Hardie Grant, 2020.

Costantino, Rosetta, with Janet Fletcher. *My Calabria: Rustic Family Cooking from Italy's Undiscovered South*. New York: W. W. Norton, 2010.

De Leo, Carolina, and Giovanni Favero. *Ca' Foscari and Carpenè Malvolti: The Risorgimento in the Economy of the Veneto in the Nineteenth Century*. Venice: Edizioni Ca' Foscari, 2019.

Douglas, Norman. *Old Calabria*. New York: Cosimo, Inc., 2007.

Duggan, Christopher. *A Concise History of Italy*. Cambridge University Press, 2014.

Erickson, Meredith. *Alpine Cooking: Recipes and Stories from Europe's Grand Mountaintops*. New York: Ten Speed Press, 2019.

Evans, Laurel. *Liguria: The Cookbook: Recipes from the Italian Riviera*. New York: Rizzoli, 2021.

Fanet, Jacques. *Great Wine Terroirs*. Berkeley and Los Angeles: University of California Press, 2004.

Filiputti, Walter, ed. *The Modern History of Italian Wine*. Milan: Skira Editore, 2016.

Gariglio, Giancarlo, and Fabio Giavedoni. *Slow Wine Guide 2017: A Year in the Life of Italy's Vineyards and Wines*. Trebaseleghe, Italy: Grafica Veneta S.p.a., 2016.

Gill, Kristina, and Katie Parla. *Tasting Rome: Fresh Flavors and Forgotten Recipes from an Ancient City*. New York: Clarkson Potter, 2016.

Gilmore, David. *The Pursuit of Italy: A History of a Land, Its Regions, and Their Peoples*. New York: Farrar, Straus and Giroux, 2011.

Grizzuti Harrison, Barbara. *Italian Days*. New York: Atlantic Monthly Press, 1989.

Hazan, Victor. *Italian Wine.* New York: Knopf, 1982.

Johnson, Hugh, and Jancis Robinson. *The World Atlas of Wine*. 8th edition. London: Mitchell Beazley, 2019.

Leeuwen, Cornelis, and Laure de Rességuier. "Major Soil-Related Factors in Terroir Expression and Vineyard Siting." *Elements* 14 (June 2018): 159–165.

Little, Ben. *Pignolo: Cultivating the Invisible*. Friuli Venezia Giulia: TheNativeGrapes.com, 2021.

Maltman, Alex. *Vineyards, Rocks, and Soils: The Wine Lover's Guide to Geology*. New York: Oxford University Press, 2018.

McGovern, Patrick E. *Ancient Wine: The Search for the Origins of Viticulture*. Princeton: Princeton University Press, 2003.

Meinert, Lawrence D. "The Science of Terroir." *Elements* 14 (June 2018): 153–159.

Minchilli, Elizabeth. *Eating My Way Through Italy: Heading Off the Main Roads to Discover the Hidden Treasures of the Italian Table.* New York: St. Martin's Griffin, 2018.

Muller, Melissa. *Sicily: The Cookbook: Recipes Rooted in Traditions*. New York: Rizzoli, 2017.

Parr, Rajat, and Jordan Mackay. *The Sommelier's Atlas of Taste: A Field Guide to the Great Wines of Europe*. New York: Ten Speed Press, 2018.

Robinson, Jancis, Julia Harding, and José Vouillamoz. *Wine Grapes*. New York: HarperCollins, 2012.

Scienza, Attilio, and Serena Imazio. *Sangiovese, Lambrusco, and Other Vine Stories*. Verona, Italy: Positive Press, 2019.

Sussman, Zachary. *The Essential Wine Book: A Modern Guide to The Changing World of Wine*. New York: Ten Speed Press, 2020.

———. *Sparkling Wine for Modern Times: A Drinker's Guide to the Freewheeling World of Bubbles*. New York: Ten Speed Press, 2021.

Wright, Clifford A. *A Mediterranean Feast: The Story of the Birth of the Celebrated Cuisines of the Mediterranean, from the Merchants of Venice to the Barbary Corsairs*. New York: William Morrow, 1999.

About the Authors and Contributors

Shelley Lindgren is the wine director and owner of San Francisco's beloved Italian restaurant A16. She has received the James Beard Award for Outstanding Wine Program and has been knighted by the Italian government, receiving the prestigious Cavaliere dell'Ordine Della Stella Italia (Dott.ssa) distinction for her professional dedication to Italian wine. Shelley's work has been featured in the *Wall Street Journal*, *Food & Wine*, *Punch*, the *San Francisco Chronicle*, and many other publications. She served on the board of La Cocina, the Guild of Sommeliers, and Slide Ranch and is a member of Les Dames d'Escoffier. She lives in San Francisco with her husband, two sons, and a border collie.

Kate Leahy is an author and coauthor of more than a dozen books, including *Wine Style*, *Lavash*, *La Buvette,* and *Burma Superstar*. Her work has been featured in *Food & Wine*, *Bon Appétit*, and *Smithsonian*. A former line cook turned writer, she lives in San Francisco with her partner and their corgi.

Shelley and Kate's first book together, *A16 Food + Wine,* was IACP's Cookbook of the Year in 2009. They are also coauthors of *SPQR: Modern Italian Food and Wine.* This is their third book together, a culmination of two decades of traveling and tasting Italian wine.

Valentin Hennequin is a photographer born in France who grew up on a small fishermen island off the Atlantic coast. After a few years as an art director in London, he now divides his time between Paris and Milan, shooting for publications like *Vogue*, *GQ*, and *Apartamento*, among others.

Flóra Lénárt is a part-time illustrator of simple yet playful pieces. Her work revolves around feminine themes and aspects of everyday life. She lives in Budapest with her husband and has some experience in harvesting grapes with the family.

Acknowledgments

When we signed the contract to write this book in March of 2019, we could never have anticipated how much the world would change a year later. We are profoundly grateful for all the people who hosted us, answered our emails, helped refine our words, and trusted that (eventually) we would reach the finish line. *Chin-chin!* We couldn't have done it without you.

To our Ten Speed team, who stuck with us in thick and thin and made this book so beautiful: Claire Yee, Annie Marino, Emma Campion, Mark McCauslin, Heather Rodino, Mari Gill, Faith Hague, Jane Chinn, David Hawk, Stephanie Davis, Kelly Snowden, Emma Rudolph, Lorena Jones, Hannah Rahill, Aaron Wehner.

To photographer Valentin Hennequin and Nico Sciackitano, for capturing beautiful, cinematic images of Italy despite endless lockdown challenges and other snafus.

To illustrator Flóra Lénárt, for lending whimsy to the book.

To agent Amy Collins, who worked with us on this idea for six years to make this book happen.

To all the winemakers, wineries, and importers who hosted us or otherwise took time to help with the book: Alberto Taddei, Alfredo Falvo, Angela Fronti, The Antinori family, Arianna Occhipinti, The Benanti family, Brittany Carlisi, Bruno DeConciliis, Cantina Terlano, Ciro Biondi, Christophe Künzli, Cristiana Tiberio, Cinzia Canzian, Clelia Romano, Cosimo Taurino, Cristian Valbruzzoli, Damiano Ciolli, DiMeo family of La Sibilla, Dino Briglio, Dino Capriotti, Emiliano Falsini, Fasoli Gino and Tenuta Le Cave teams, Florian Gojer, Gaetano Bove, Giampiero Bea, Giovanni Ascione, Giuseppe Russo, Graziano Prà and Diego Corradi, Isabella Pelizzatti Perego, I Favati, J. Hofstätter, La Stoppa, Lunelli family of Ferrari, Mario Andrion and Castello di Verduno, Mario Zanusso, Massimiliano Franci, Massimo and Talita Alois, Natalino Del Prete, Nicola Del Negro, Oliver McCrum, Michele Boscia, and team, Paola and Piera Rinaldi, Paolo Librandi, Pasquale Cenatiempo, Piccin Family, Sabino Loffredo, Salvo and Andrea Foti, Salvatore Molettieri, Sebastiano Capponi, Sergio Germano, Vito Palama, Vittorio Marzotto.

To Ian D'Agata, for answering our questions, making introductions, and writing such important books on Italian wine.

To the A16 Famiglia: the coworkers past and present, our customers who have been with us for more than two decades, and our Italian community in San Francisco and Italy.

To our own *famiglie*:

Greg, Phineas, and Asher Lindgren.

Patrick Kim, and Kathy and Tom Leahy.

Grape Index

M

Maceratino Bianco, 109–10
Magliocco (Magliocco Dolce/
   Magliocco Tondo), 54
Magliocco Canino, 54
Malvasia group, 98
   Malvasia Bianca di Basilicata, 46
   Malvasia Bianca di Candia, 98
   Malvasia di Candia Aromatica,
      72–73, 124
   Malvasia di Casorzo, 154
   Malvasia di Lipari, 196
   Malvasia di Schierano, 154
   Malvasia Istriana, 86
   Malvasia Puntinata (Malvasia
      del Lazio), 100
Malvasia Nera family
   Malvasia Nera di Brindisi, 168
   Malvasia Nera di Lecce, 168
Mantonico Bianco, 53
Manzoni Bianco, 265
Marzemino, 214
Massaretta, 119
Mataòssu, 118
Mayolet, 252
Minutolo, 167
Monica, 180
Montepulciano, 33, 39, 40
Morellino, 231
Moscato Bianco, 150
Moscato Canelli, 145
Moscato di Alessandria, 196–97
Moscato di Scanzo, 130
Moscato di Terracina, 100
Moscato Giallo, 266
Moscato Reale, 150, 165
Mostosa, 73
Müller-Thurgau, 211, 213

N

Nascetta, 150
Nasco, 179
Nebbiolo, 129, 139, 140, 154–55
Nebbiolo Rosé, 155
Negroamaro, 162, 168
Nerello Cappuccio, 197
Nerello Mascalese, 198
Nero Buono, 102
Nero d'Avola, 197–98
Nero di Troia, 170
Nosiola, 213
Nuragus, 178

O

Ormeasco, 119, 153
Ortrugo, 73

P

Pagadebit, 73, 167
Pallagrello Bianco, 3, 63
Pallagrello Nero, 64
Pampanuto, 167
Passerina, 109
Pecorello Bianco, 53
Pecorino, 37, 40, 108
Pelaverga group, 155
   Pelaverga Grosso, 155
   Pelaverga Piccolo, 155
Pepella, 61–62
Perera, 266
Perricone, 198
Petite Arvine, 250
Petit Rouge, 252
Picolit, 86
Picotener (Picotendro), 154
Piedirosso, 64
Pigato, 118
Pignatello, 198
Pignoletto, 73, 241
Pignolo, 88
Pinot Bianco (Pinot Blanc), 213

Pinot Grigio, 86
Pinot Nero (Pinot Noir,
   Blauburgunder), 214
Pollera Nera, 119
Prëmetta, 252
Prié Blanc, 12, 247–48, 250, 252
Prié Rouge, 252
Primitivo, 164, 168, 170
Procanico, 241
Prugnolo Gentile, 231

R

Refosco group, 88–89
   Refosco dal Peduncolo Rosso, 88
   Refosco di Faedis (Refosco
      Nostrano), 89
   Refosco d'Istria, 89
Ribolla Gialla, 86–87
Ribolla Nera, 89
Ribona, 109–10
Ripoli, 61–62
Rossese, 119–20
Roussin de Morgex, 247, 248, 252
Ruchè, 155

S

Sagrantino, 238, 239, 242
Sangiovese, 72, 225, 227, 231
Sauvignon Blanc, 87
Schiava (Vernatsch) group,
   214, 216
   Schiava Gentile, 214
   Schiava Grigia, 214
   Schiava Grossa, 214
Schioppettino, 89
Semidano, 179
Silvaner. *See* Sylvaner
Spanna, 154
Spergola, 73
Susumaniello, 170
Sylvaner, 213

General Index

Library of Congress Cataloging-in-Publication
Data is on file with the publisher.

Hardcover ISBN: 9781984857620
eBook ISBN: 9781984857637

Printed in China

Acquiring editor: Lorena Jones | Project editor:
Claire Yee | Production editor: Mark McCauslin
Designer: Annie Marino | Art director: Emma
Campion | Production designers: Mari Gill and
Faith Hague | Production manager: Jane Chinn
Copyeditor: Heather Rodino | Proofreaders: Robin
Slutzky, Jacob Sammon, and Lydia O'Brien
Indexer: Ken DellaPenta | Publicist: David Hawk
Marketer: Stephanie Davis
10 9 8 7 6 5 4 3 2 1

First Edition